Principles of Environmental Economics

Second edition

'The second edition builds on the strengths of the first. It is well written, well organized, and provides a broad survey of environmental economics from a range of perspectives.'

Jo Crotty, Aston Business School, UK

'This is a well researched and comprehensive text that offers an alternative and refreshing perspective on environmental economics.'

J. Bussel, University of Teesside, UK

'This is a logically organized, well written text. Its distinguishing element is its explicit consideration of ecology, ecological economics, and sustainable development.'

Douglas E. Booth, Marquette University, Wisconsin, USA

Can economic growth be environmentally sustainable? This crucial question goes right to the heart of environmental economics and is a matter of increasing concern globally.

The first edition of this popular textbook was the first introductory textbook in environmental economics that truly attempted to integrate economics with not only the environment but also ecology. This new version builds and improves upon the popular formula with new material, new examples, new pedagogical features and new questions for discussion.

With international case studies and examples, this book will prove an excellent choice for introducing both students and other academics to the world of environmental economics.

Ahmed M. Hussen is Professor of Economics, Kalamazoo College, Michigan, USA.

Books are to be returned on or before
the last date below.

Principles of Environmental Economics

Ahmed M. Hussen

LONDON AND NEW YORK

First edition published 2000 by Routledge
2 Park Square, Milton Park, Abingdon, Oxon, OX14 4RN

Second edition published 2004

Simultaneously published in the USA and Canada
by Routledge
270 Madison Ave, New York, NY 10016

Reprinted 2005

Routledge is an imprint of the Taylor & Francis Group

© 2000, 2004 Ahmed M. Hussen

Typeset in Times by Steven Gardiner Ltd, Cambridge
Printed and bound in Great Britain by TJ International, Padstow, Cornwall

British Library Cataloguing in Publication Data
A catalogue record for this book is available from the British Library

Library of Congress Cataloging in Publication Data
A catalog record for this book has been requested

ISBN 0-415-27559-8 (hbk)
ISBN 0-415-27560-1 (pbk)

Summary contents

Contents

Figures

Tables

Case studies

Exhibits

Preface

The primary objective of this book is to present the economic and ecological principles essential for a clear understanding of complex contemporary environmental issues and policy considerations. Several books have been written on this subject in recent years. One may ask, then, what exactly differentiates this one from the others?

Level

This book is written for an introductory-level course in environmental economics. It is primarily designed for college sophomores and juniors who want to study environmental concerns with an *interdisciplinary* focus. The academic majors of these students could be in any field of study, but the book would be especially appropriate for students with majors in economics, political science, environmental studies, or biological sciences.

The claim that environmental and resource economics should be studied within an interdisciplinary context is taken very seriously. Such a context requires students to have, in addition to microeconomics, a good understanding of the basic principles of the natural and physical sciences that govern the natural world. This book addresses this concern by devoting a chapter to ecology. This is done not only to make certain relevant ecological principles understandable to non-science students, but also to present clearly the disciplinary tie between economics and ecology, especially in addressing pressing environmental issues. This chapter assumes no prior knowledge of ecology. Instead, it discusses thoroughly and systematically ecological concepts that are considered highly relevant to the study of environmental economics, such as ecosystem, ecosystem structure, material recycling, the law of matter and energy, entropy, and ecological succession. These are concepts especially pertinent to the understanding of the nature of the interrelationships between the human economy and the natural environment, and the extent to which biophysical limits could hinder or even cease future human technological and economic progress. These ecological concepts should also contribute to better understanding of recent concerns with global environmental issues such as loss of biodiversity and climate change.

This book requires no more than a semester course in microeconomics. Thus, unlike many other textbooks in this field, it does not demand knowledge of intermediate microeconomics, either implicitly or explicitly. Furthermore, an Appendix (Appendix A) at the end of the book provides an account of fundamental economic concepts specifically relevant to environmental economics. In this Appendix, economic concepts such as demand and supply analysis, willingness to pay, consumers' and producers' surplus, rent, Pareto optimality, and alternative economic measures of scarcity are thoroughly and systematically explained. The material in this Appendix is referred to throughout the text, and could also serve as a good review for economics students and a valuable foundation for students with a major in fields other than economics.

This book is primarily a theoretical exposé of environmental and resource economics. The emphasis is on a systematic development of theoretical principles and conceptual frameworks essential for a clear understanding and analysis of environmental and resource issues. To catch students' imagination and attention, as well as to reinforce understandings of basic theoretical principles, case studies and 'exhibits' are incorporated into most of the chapters. These are taken from newspaper clippings, brief magazine articles, articles and summaries of empirical studies from professional journals, and excerpts from publications by government and private research institutions.

Orientation

Unlike other textbooks in this area, *this book is written in the belief that a course in environmental economics cannot be treated as just another course in applied economics.* It must include both economic and ecological perspectives and, in so doing, must seek a broader context within which environmental and natural resource issues can be understood and evaluated. In this regard, the book does *not* approach environmental and natural resource problems from only or even predominantly a standard economic perspective.

From my experience of two decades of teaching courses in environmental and resource economics, I have come to realize that it is extremely difficult for students to understand and appreciate the subtle differences between the economic and ecological perspectives until they are made aware of the 'axiomatic' foundations (the conceptual starting point of analysis) of each one of these perspectives. With this in mind, this book starts (Chapter 1) with a careful examination of the pre-analytic or axiomatic assumptions and theories at the fundamental level that pertain to the standard economic perspective of environmental resources and their scarcity, and the role these resources play in the economic process. This is immediately followed (Chapter 2) by a thorough and systematic discussion of the axiomatic assumptions and theoretical principles particularly relevant to understanding the ecological perspectives concerning the natural environment and its relationship with the human economy. Thus, the clear delineation of the 'anthropocentric' and 'biocentric' views of natural resources and their scarcity is a unique feature of this book.

Most textbooks on environmental and resource economics are neoclassical in their orientation. For this reason their emphasis is mainly on intertemporal *optimal allocation* among alternative uses of the *total* resource flow, including the services of the natural environment. In this regard the overriding concern is *efficiency*. This book does not disregard the importance of this approach, but it does add to it another important dimension – the concern with achieving the *optimal scale* of total resource flow relative to the natural environment. The key issue here is to keep the *economic scale* within certain ecological boundaries, and this requires the recognition of *biophysical limits*. Several chapters are assigned to discuss alternative views on biophysical limits to economic growth and the economics of sustainable development. This is one of the most significant and unique features of this book.

Organization

The book consists of fourteen chapters, which are grouped into five parts, as shown in the diagram below. In this diagram, the four boxes represent the major organizational themes of the book. As indicated by the direction of the arrows, these four themes or major groupings are related in both specific and general terms. The exact nature of these relationships will become evident from the discussions that follow.

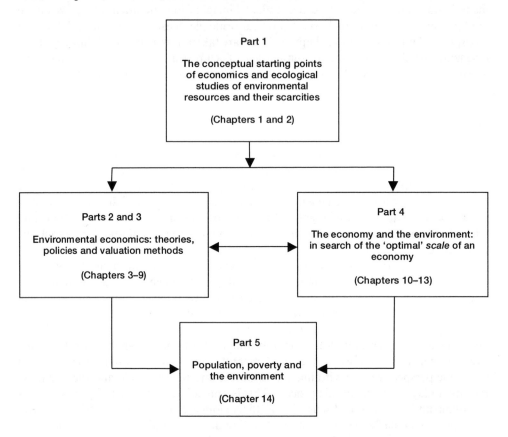

Fundamental economic and ecological concepts and perspectives

The two chapters of Part 1 constitute what I consider to be the conceptual starting point of economic and ecological analyses of environmental resources and their scarcity. Chapter 1 deals with the 'axiomatic' assumptions that are fundamental to understanding the standard economic perception of environmental resources and their role in the economic process. An early explanation of these assumptions, even if it does not serve to correct logical errors, helps clarify the position neoclassical economists tend to take on environmental issues in general.

Chapter 2 is intended to provide students with basic concepts and principles of ecology, thereby encouraging economics students to venture beyond the realm of their discipline. The position taken here is that no serious student of environmental and resource economics can afford to be ignorant of the important lessons of ecology.

However, it should be understood that the inquiry into this subject matter is quite focused and limited. The primary intent is to familiarize students with carefully selected ecological concepts and principles so that they will acquire by the end, if not an appreciation, then a clear understanding of ecologists' perspective on the natural world and its relationship with the human economy. This is also a chapter of vital importance to understanding the arguments for the existence of biophysical limits, in general.

The economics of environmental management

The unifying feature of Part 2 and Part 3 (which consist of Chapters 3–9) is that they deal with environmental economic issues from a predominantly neoclassical economics perspective. The emphasis in these chapters is on 'getting the prices right'. That is, environmental resources are optimally allocated provided market prices reflect their 'true' scarcity values. The material covered in Part 2 and Part 3 represent *core* theoretical and policy concepts that are absolutely essential in understanding the contributions of economics to the field of environmental studies.

Chapter 3 develops fundamental theories to understand the relationship between economic activity and the natural absorptive capacity of the environment. This is followed by a thorough investigation of the root causes and consequences of environmental externalities. In this chapter the condition for the optimal trade-off between environmental quality and economic goods and services is derived, which is then followed by an extended discussion of both the micro and macroeconomic effects of environmental regulation. The unique feature of this chapter is the effort taken to demonstrate clearly and effectively how the basic concepts of economics and ecology studied in Part 1 (Chapters 1 and 2) can be used to help understand what it means (in terms of costs and benefits) to aspire to a higher level of environmental quality.

Chapter 4 develops theoretical models that can be used as a policy guide to control environmental pollution. In Chapters 5 and 6, a number of pollution control policy instruments are thoroughly discussed and analyzed. The scientific, economic and public policy aspects of environmental pollution that have global dimensions are discussed in Chapter 7. Chapter 8 examines alternative economic approaches to measuring the value of environmental services. Chapter 9 deals with economic valuation of environmental *projects* using a cost–benefit analysis framework. Several other alternative resources valuation methods are also considered, such as the precautionary principle, cost-effectiveness, environmental impact analysis, risk assessment and management, and environmental ethics and justice.

An important point to emphasize here is that even though the seven chapters in Part 2 and Part 3 are predominantly neoclassical in their orientation, this should not suggest the total abandonment of the ecological theme that is central to this text. *As much as possible, the major conclusions drawn from each chapter are subjected to critical appraisal on the basis of their conformity or lack thereof to relevant ecological principles.* Finally, it is important to point out that Parts 2 and 3 involve rigorous applications of economic tools and analysis.

Biophysical limits to economic growth

The four chapters in Part 4 are unique in their organization and contain some topics that are rarely discussed in standard textbooks on environmental economics. The major concern here is the *scale* of the economy relative to the natural environment. What this Part in effect attempts to do is to trace the historical development of the ideas pertaining to limits to economic growth.

Chapters 10, 11 and 12 discuss limits to economic growth from three distinctive perspectives: Malthusian, neoclassical and ecological economics, respectively. Chapter 13 deals with the economics of sustainable development. The key questions that these four chapters address are:

1 Can we expect unlimited economic growth in a world endowed with finite environmental resources?
2 If ecological limits are important factors in determining future trends of economic growth, what steps or precautions should be taken in order to avoid transgressing these natural limits?

Population, economic development and environmental degradation

Part 5, which is composed of a single chapter, Chapter 14, analyzes the contemporary population, resources and environmental problems of developing nations. The main focuses are on poverty and environmental degradation. This is a very important topic and entails a concern for environmental sustainability that requires immediate attention. In this regard, the solution to rapid and continued environmental degradation requires not only an economic and ecological understanding of the problem(s) under consideration, but also of the social, cultural and political circumstances of the relevant stakeholders – the people from the developing countries. This book makes a concerted effort to discuss and, at some length, analyze the significance of several social, cultural and political factors identified as crucial to the on-going search to find lasting solution(s) to the environmental woes in developing countries.

About the second edition

In this second edition, there are a number of broad changes from the first edition:

1 The new edition has a narrower scope; it deals exclusively with subject matters that are covered in environmental economics. For this reason the two chapters dealing with the economics of renewable and non-renewable resources (topics covered in resource economics) have been omitted. This is done, in large part, to allow expanded coverage of several topics in environmental economics without exceeding the limits on the size of the book. The new edition contains plenty of topics for a one-semester course.
2 The organization of the book has been altered significantly. The new edition contains *fourteen* chapters, which are grouped into *four* major parts. The first edition had *eighteen* chapters and they were grouped into *eight* parts. The organization of the new edition is less intricate and, in some respects, more conventional.
3 The primary focus of the book remains unchanged – environmental economics with an interdisciplinary focus. In the new edition, considerable efforts were made (in terms of changes in emphasis and inclusion of new material) to make the interdisciplinary focus of the book even more pronounced.

Specific changes and additions

1   Revisions have been made to *all* chapters but not to the same extent. Two chapters have essentially been rewritten (Chapters 1 and 18). These chapters appear as Chapters 1 and 14, respectively, in the new edition.

2   In *four* of the chapters (Chapters 6, 7, 14, and 15 in the first edition), the revisions have been, if not total, then quite considerable. These chapters appear as Chapters 10, 11, 8, and 9, respectively, in the new edition. In these chapters, among others, a number of new concepts have been added.

3   The modifications made to the rest of the chapters (Chapters 4, 5, 8, 9, 10, 11, and 12, in the first edition, or Chapters 2, 3, 12, 13, 4, 5, and 6 respectively, in the new edition), although modest by comparison, add significantly to the clarity and inter-connectedness of the material covered throughout the text. For example, the changes to Chapter 4 (Chapter 2 in the new edition) not only make the material in this chapter easier to read but also contribute to the clarification and amplification of the important links between the basic principles covered in Chapters 1 and 2 – the anthropocentric versus bio centric views of environmental resources and their scarcity. Similar claims can be made for several other related chapters of the book.

4   The descriptions of the figures in the entire book are expanded. This is done purely to make it easier for students to grasp the main ideas about major concepts in the text by looking at the figures and their descriptions.

5   For reasons discussed earlier, Chapters 16 and 17 of the first edition have been omitted. However, some concepts from these two chapters are used in some of the chapters of the new edition.

6   The new edition incorporates two appendices:

   Appendix A: This appendix contains a somewhat condensed version of the basic microeconomic concepts that were included in Chapters 2 and 3 of the first edition. It provides a theoretical understanding of why mainstream economists have such deeply felt convictions about the power of the market as a means of allocating scarce resources in an orderly and effective manner.

   Appendix B: This appendix contains a carefully selected list of website addresses that are considered to be helpful to students with interest in the environment and resource management and policy, in general. Included also are brief descriptions of each website's officially stated objective(s) and the primary organization(s) providing the contents of the site.

Acknowledgements

I would like to thank several individuals for their specific and significant contributions to this text. These people include the following: Marvin Soroos for updating the materials in Chapter 7 (the chapter on global environmental pollution); Paul Olexia for his continued friendship and his many concrete and invaluable contributions to the materials covered in Chapter 2 (the chapter on ecology); Charles Stull for his valuable and substantive comments on Chapter 1 – a chapter I had a hard time to construct; and Tim Moffitt for editing the first draft of Section 13.7 of Chapter 13, on the case of the Interface company.

As was the case in the first edition, the new edition uses numerous quoted remarks, exhibits and case studies. These items are not included for mere appearance or style; they significantly contribute to the effectiveness of the book in conveying certain important ideas. Obviously, my debt to those whose work I have quoted and summarized is immeasurable. However, I have the sole responsibility for the interpretation placed on these works.

I would like to thank my editor, Robert Langham, and his associate, Terry Clague, for their patience, encouragement, understanding, and above all for their tremendous and persistent efforts to provide me with positive feedback on all of my endeavors to prepare the second edition.

I would also like to express my sincere appreciation of the valuable comments I received from two anonymous reviewers in two different stages of my efforts to write the second edition. Not only has the book benefited from their specific suggestions and comments, but it was also personally gratifying to realize that there are people within my own profession who both appreciate and take my work seriously.

I am grateful to five of my students: Dia Vinyard '03 and Alexis Grieco '03, for help in the final preparation of the typescript; Tara McClure '00 and Jennifer Samuilow '01 for providing me with valuable background information on the company Interface; and and Sarah Rockwell '01 for her contribution to the preparation of Exhibit 8.1.

Finally, I would like to dedicate this book to all those people who have had significant influences on my life. Most notable among them: my parents Rukiya and Mohammed Hussen; Christine and Philip Roach; Frances and Jim Dimick; and my mentor and teacher Professor William G. Brown.

Introduction

Overview of environmental and resource economics as a subdiscipline in economics

Labor is the father and nature is the mother of wealth.

(Petty 1899: 2: 377)

The concept of natural resources

The study of natural resources, the subject matter of this book, involves theories and concepts that seem to be continually evolving with the passage of time and with our improved understanding of the natural circumstances that govern these resources. For example, the preclassical or Physiocratic school (1756–78) and classical economists (1776–1890) typically used land as a generic term to describe natural resources. To these economists, land or natural resources represented one of the three major categories of basic resources essential to the production of goods and services – the other two being labor and capital.

This three-way classification of basic resources or factors of production seems to persist, although our understanding of natural resources and their roles in the economic process has changed markedly. Advances in the natural and physical sciences have increased our knowledge of the laws that govern the natural world. Furthermore, as the human economy continues to expand, its impacts on the natural world have become sizeable and potentially detrimental. Inevitably, our conception of natural resources tends to be influenced by our current understanding of the human economy and its interrelationship with the natural world.

Broadly defined, natural resources include all the 'original' elements that comprise the Earth's natural endowments or life-support systems: air, water, the Earth's crust, and radiation from the Sun. Some representative examples of natural resources are arable land, wilderness areas, mineral fuels and nonfuel minerals, watersheds, and the ability of the natural environment to degrade waste and absorb ultraviolet light from the Sun.

Natural resources are generally grouped into two major categories: renewable and nonrenewable natural resources. Renewable resources are those resources that are capable of regenerating themselves within a relatively short period, provided the environment in which they are nurtured is not unduly disturbed. Examples include plants, fish, forests, soil, solar radiation, wind, tides, and so on. These renewable resources can be further classified into two distinct groups: biological resources and flow resources.

Biological resources consist of the various species of plants and animals. They have one distinctive feature that is important for consideration here. While these resources are capable of self-regeneration, they can be irreparably damaged if they are exploited beyond a certain critical threshold. Hence, their use should be limited to a certain critical threshold. As will be explained later, natural biological processes govern both the regenerative capacities of these resources and the critical zone. Examples of this type of resource are fisheries, forests, livestock, and all forms of plants.

Flow resources include solar radiation, wind, tides, and water streams. Continuous renewal of these resources is largely dictated by atmospheric and hydraulic circulation, along with the flow of solar radiation. Although these resources can be harnessed for specific uses (such as energy from solar radiation or waterfalls), the rate at which the flows of these potential resources are regulated is largely governed by nature. This does not, however, mean that humans are totally incapable of either augmenting or decreasing the amount of flow of these resources. A good illustration of this would be the effect greenhouse gas emissions (in particular carbon dioxide) have on global warming.

Nonrenewable resources are resources that either exist in fixed supply or are renewable only on a geological timescale, whose regenerative capacity can be assumed to be zero for all practical human purposes. Examples of these resources include metallic minerals like iron, aluminum, copper, and uranium; and nonmetallic minerals like fossil fuels, clay, sand, salt, and phosphates.

Nonrenewable resources can be classified into two broad categories. The first group includes those resources that are recyclable, such as metallic minerals. The second consists of nonrecyclable resources, such as fossil fuels.

As indicated by the title of this introduction, mainly for pedagogical purposes the study of natural resources is subdivided into two major subfields: environmental economics and resource economics. The difference between these two subfields is primarily a matter of focus. In environmental economics the primary focus is how to use or manage the natural environment (air, water, landmass) as a valuable resource for the disposal of waste. It should be pointed out that this subject, the environment, is the primary focus of this book. In natural resource economics the emphasis is on the intertemporal allocation of extractive nonrenewable resources (such as petroleum, iron ore, potash, etc.) and the harvest of renewable resources (such as fish, forest products, and other plant and animal species). Of course, as would be expected, there are considerable overlaps in both the methodologies and the core subject matter addressed in these two subfields.

Environmental economics: scope and nature

As a subdiscipline of economics, environmental economics originated in the 1960s – the early years of the so-called environmental movement. However, despite its brief history, over the past three decades it has become one of the fastest-growing fields of study in economics. The growing popularity of this field of inquiry parallels the increasing awareness of the interconnectedness between the economy and the environment – more specifically, the increasing recognition of the significant roles that nature plays in the economic process as well as in the formation of economic value.

The nature and scope of the issues addressed in environmental economics are quite varied and all-encompassing. Below is a list of some of the major topics addressed in this field of study. The list is also representative of the issues addressed in this book.

- The causes of environmental degradation
- The need to re-establish the disciplinary ties between ecology and economics
- The difficulties associated with assigning ownership rights to environmental resources
- The trade-off between environmental degradation and economic goods and services
- The ineffectiveness of the market, if left alone, in allocating environmental resources
- Assessing the monetary value of environmental damage
- Public policy instruments that can be used to slow, halt and reverse the deterioration of environmental resources and/or the overexploitation of renewable and nonrenewable resources
- The macroeconomic effects of environmental regulations and other resource conservation policies
- The extent to which technology can be used as a means of ameliorating environmental degradation or resource scarcity, in general – that is, limits to technology
- Environmental problems that transcend national boundaries, and thus require international cooperation for their resolution
- The limits to economic growth
- The extent to which past experience can be used to predict future events that are characterized by considerable economic, technological and ecological uncertainties
- Ethical and moral imperatives for environmental resource conservation – concern for the welfare of future generations
- The interrelationships among population, poverty and environmental degradation in the developing countries of the world
- The necessity and viability of sustainable development.

This list by no means exhausts the issues that can be addressed in environmental economics. However, the issues in the list do provide important clues to some of the fundamental ways in which the study of environmental economics is different from other subdisciplines in economics.

First, the ultimate limits to environmental resource availability are imposed by nature. That is, their origin, interactions and reproductive capacity are largely governed by nature.

Second, most of these resources have no readily available markets: for example, clean air, ozone, the genetic pool of a species, etc.

Third, no serious study of environmental economics can be entirely descriptive. Normative issues such as intergenerational fairness and the distribution of resources between the poor and rich nations are very important.

Fourth, uncertainties are unavoidable considerations in any serious study of environmental and natural resource issues. These uncertainties may take several forms, such as prices, irreversible environmental damage, or unexpected and sudden species extinction.

Such is the nature of the subject matter that we are about to begin exploring in this book.

References

Howe, C. W. (1979) *Natural Resource Economics*, New York: John Wiley.
Petty, W. (1899) *The Economic Writings of Sir William Petty*, ed. C. H. Hull, Cambridge.

Part 1

Fundamental assumptions, concepts, and theories of economics and ecology essential for understanding the links between the natural environment and the human economy

Over the years, there has been a pronounced divergence between the standard view of economists and that of ecologists concerning humans' ability to coexist with the natural world. Without a doubt, one of the most important reasons for this development can be attributed to the difference in the core assumptions the standard practitioners of these two disciplines hold concerning the relationships between the economic and the natural world. Part 1 of this book, which consists of two chapters, Chapters 1 and 2, examines the economic and the ecological perspectives on environmental resources and their implications for the economic and the natural world.

Chapter 1 examines what could be called the mainstream economists' 'preanalytic' vision of the economy and its relationship with the natural world. What can be observed from the discussion in this chapter is the treatment of the natural environment as one of the many 'fungible' assets that can be used to satisfy human needs. In this regard, the emphasis is on the general problems of resource scarcity. This being the case, the roles of consumers' preferences, efficiency, markets, and technology are stressed.

Chapter 2 is intended to provide the assumptions vital to understanding the ecological perspective on natural resources – elements crucial to the sustenance of human economy. More specifically, in this chapter economics students are asked to venture beyond the realm of their discipline to study some basic concepts and principles of ecology. The inquiry into this subject matter is quite focused and limited in scope. The primary objective is to familiarize students with carefully selected ecological concepts and principles so that they will have, by the end of the chapter, if not an appreciation, then at least a clear understanding of ecologists' perspectives on the natural world and its relationship with the human economy.

The material covered in Part 1 is an extremely important prerequisite for a thorough and comprehensive understanding of the seemingly perennial debate between economists and ecologists on the 'limits to economic growth' – a subject discussed in

Part 4. Furthermore, the ecological concepts and principles covered in Chapter 2 add a good deal of insight into the analyses and discussions of what may be considered the standard economic approaches to environmental economics – the seven chapters covered in Part 2.

1 The natural environment and the human economy

The neoclassical economics perspective

1.1 Introduction

It is safe to say that mainstream economists have a peculiar conception of the natural environment, including how it should be utilized and managed. The primary aim of this chapter is to expose the axiomatic assumptions and, at the fundamental level, the analytical principles that are the cornerstones for the understanding of the standard mainstream economists' conception of the natural environment and its interactions with the human economy. This is a crucial issue to address early on because it helps to identify clearly the ideological basis of neoclassical economics, the dominant approach to economic analysis since about the 1870s, as it is applied to the management of the natural environment.

How do neoclassical economists perceive the role the 'natural' environment plays on the human economy? For our purpose here, the natural environment could be defined as the physical, chemical and biological surroundings that humans and other living species depend on as a life support. As shown in Figure 1.1, in specific terms the economy is assumed to *depend* on the natural environment for three distinctive purposes: (a) the extraction of nonrenewable resources (such as iron ore, fossil fuels, etc.) and the harvest of renewable resources (such as fish of various species, agricultural products, forest products, etc.) to be used as *factors of production*; (b) the disposal and assimilation of wastes; and (c) the consumption of environmental amenities (such as bird watching, canoeing, hiking national park trails, observing a morning sunrise or an evening sunset, etc.). Thus, broadly viewed, the economy is assumed to be completely dependent on the natural environment for raw materials, the disposal of waste materials and amenities.

Furthermore, since the Earth is 'finite' there exists a *theoretical* upper limit for resource extraction and harvest and the disposal of waste into the natural environment. The qualities of environmental amenities and the maintenance of life support systems (such as climate regulation and genetic diversity) are also affected adversely in direct proportion to the amount of resource extractions and/or harvesting and the disposal or discharge of waste into the natural environment. Thus, as with any other branch of economics, fundamental to the study of environmental economics is the problem of *scarcity* – the trade-off between economic *goods* and the preservation of environmental *quality*. There are some *fundamental* assumptions that the standard economics approach uses in addressing this subject matter; these are outlined below.

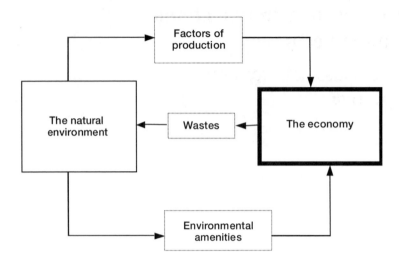

Figure 1.1 A schematic view of how the human economy depends on the natural environment for factors of production, disposal of waste and consumption of amenities.

- Environmental (natural) resources are 'essential' factors of production. A certain
  minimum amount of natural resources is needed to produce goods and services.
- Environmental resources are of economic concern to the extent that they are *scarce*.
- The economic value of natural resources (including the services of the natural
  ecosystems) is determined by *consumers' preferences*, and these preferences are best
  expressed by a freely operating private *market system*.
- *Market price* can be used as a measure (indicator) of resource scarcity, including the
  environment.
- In both the production and consumption sectors of an economy, a specific natural
  resource can always be replaced (partially or fully) by the use of other resources that
  are either man-made (manufactured) or natural.
- Technological advances continually augment the scarcity of natural resources.
- Nothing is lost in treating the human economy in isolation from the natural
  ecosystems – the physical, chemical and biological surroundings that humans and
  other living species depend on as a life support. That is, the natural ecosystem is
  treated as being outside the human economy and exogenously determined. Note
  that to indicate this, in Figure 1.1 the human economy and the natural environment
  are drawn as two distinctly separate entities. The full extent of the implications of
  this worldview will be discussed in Chapter 2.

Clearly, from the above discussions it should be evident that, at the fundamental level,
central to the neoclassical economics worldview with respect to the natural environment
and its role in the economic process are the following *four* key issues: (i) the market as
a provider of information about resource scarcity; (ii) resource (factor) substitution;
(iii) scarcity augmenting technological advance; and (iv) the nature of the relationships
between the human economy and the natural environment. The rest of this chapter will
address these four issues one at a time.

1.2 The market as a provider of information on resource scarcity

From the perspective of neoclassical economics, the market system is considered to be the preferred institution for allocating scarce resources. Under certain assumed conditions (see Exhibit 1.1) the market system guided by the free expression of individual consumer and producer choices would lead to the maximization of the well-being of the society as a whole – the so-called Invisible Hand theorem. The market system accomplishes this wonderful feat using prices as a means of gauging resource scarcity. In this section, an attempt will be made to outline the various essential roles of market-generated prices in an ideal market setting, especially as a measure of natural resource scarcity.

1.2.1 Price as an indicator of absolute scarcity

Under normal conditions, we do not pay for the oxygen we inhale from the atmosphere. On the other hand, although less essential than oxygen for our survival, we would not expect to get a membership to a local golf club at zero prices. Why is this so? The answer for this question is rather straightforward and is explained using Figures 1.2 and 1.3. In Figure 1.2, the prevailing market equilibrium (or market clearing) price, P_e, is *positive*. Hence, a unit of this service, membership at a golf club, can be obtained only if one is willing and able to pay the prevailing market price. In other words, this service can be obtained only at a cost (is not free). On the other hand, in Figure 1.3, supply exceeds demand everywhere. Under this condition, the price for this resource will be *zero*, hence, a *free good*. This clearly explains why our normal use of oxygen from the atmosphere is obtained at zero prices. *Thus, economists formally define a scarce resource as any resource that commands a positive price.* In this regard, market price is supposed to measure the *absolute* (as opposed to relative) scarcity of a resource.

1.2.2 Price as an indicator of relative scarcity or opportunity cost

As discussed above, the notion of absolute scarcity implies that a resource is scarce if its price is *positive*, but nothing else. What may be a more interesting and meaningful measure of scarcity in resource management is the notion of relative cost or scarcity. In this regard, the standard economic theory contends that, under certain ideal market assumptions (see Exhibit 1.1), *relative scarcity* could be effectively measured by a *ratio* of two market-clearing prices. Suppose we have two resources, gold and crude oil. Let X and Y represent gold and crude oil, respectively. Then, P_x/P_y (the ratio of the market prices of gold to crude oil) would be a measure of relative scarcity. To be more specific, suppose, the price for gold is \$300 per ounce and price of crude oil is \$25 per barrel. In this instance, the relative price would have a numerical value of 12. In what sense does this number measure relative scarcity?

Obviously, this number suggests that gold is relatively more scarce (or costly) than crude oil. More specifically, under ideal market conditions, the above numerical value suggests that the value or the cost of the resources (labor, capital, raw materials, etc.) used to extract and bring about an ounce of gold to the market is 12 times more than a barrel of crude oil. Hence, this provides the justification for why the market price of an ounce of gold should be 12 times that of a barrel of crude oil.

Exhibit 1.1   The perfect market structure and its corollary, the Invisible Hand theorem

This exhibit is written to specify clearly the conditions under which Adam Smith's notion that individuals working in their self-interest will promote the welfare of the whole of society holds good – the so-called Invisible Hand theorem.

In an idealized capitalist market economy, consumers' (the final users of goods and services) well-being is a paramount consideration. What this means is that the effectiveness of an economy is judged by how well it satisfies the material needs of its citizens – the consumers. Therefore, given that resources are scarce, an effective economy is one that is capable of producing the maximum output from a given set of basic resources (labor, capital and natural resources). Furthermore, outputs are produced in response to consumers' preferences. Of course, the implication of this is that scarce resources must be utilized (produced and consumed) efficiently. Thus, an important working principle of a market economy is that efficiency is the primary criterion, if not the sole criterion, to be used as a measure of institutional performance.

The question then is, what conditions must a market system satisfy in order to be considered an efficient institution for allocating resources? In other words, what are the conditions consistent with the ideal or perfect form for a market structure? According to prevailing economic thought, a market has to satisfy the following broad conditions in order to be regarded as an efficient institutional mechanism for allocating resources:

1 *Freedom of choice based on self-interest*: Buyers and sellers are well informed and act in their own self-interest. It is further stipulated that these actors in the market are provided with an environment conducive to free expression of their choices – choice being inevitable because of resource scarcity.
2 *Perfect information*: Economic agents are assumed to be provided with full infor-

mation regarding any market transactions. They are also assumed to have perfect foresight about future economic events.
3 *Competition*: For each item subjected to market transaction, the number of buyers and sellers is large. Thus, no one buyer or seller can single-handedly influence the terms of trade. In modern economic jargon, this means that both buyers and sellers are price-takers. This is assumed to be the case in both the product and the factor markets.
4 *Mobility of resources*: In a dynamic economy, change is the norm. Significant shifts in economic conditions could result from a combination of several factors, such as changes in consumer preference, income, resource availability, and technology. To accommodate changes of this nature in a timely fashion, resources must be readily transferable from one sector of the economy to another. This is possible only when barriers to entry and exit in an industry are absent (or minimal).
5 *Ownership rights*: All goods and services, as well as factors of production, have clearly defined ownership rights, i.e. property rights are protected by binding social rules and regulations.

When the above *five* conditions are met, an economy is said to be operating in a world of perfectly competitive markets. In such a setting, Adam Smith (the father of modern economics) declared over two centuries ago, the market system through its Invisible Hand will guide each individual to do not only what is in her or his own self-interest, but also that which is for the 'good' of society at large. A profound statement indeed, which clearly presents the most appealing features of the market economy in its ideal form. (Refer to Appendix A for an elaborated derivation of this theorem and its implications.)

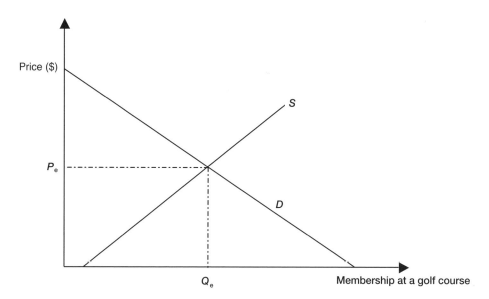

Figure 1.2 Demand and supply and market clearing (equilibrium) price, P_e, for a local golf club membership. The service of a local golf club is scarce because at zero price, quantity demanded far exceeds quantity supplied – creating a shortage.

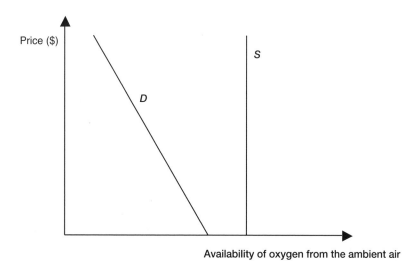

Figure 1.3 Demand and supply of oxygen. Oxygen is treated as a free good because at zero price quantity supply exceeds quantity demanded – a surplus.

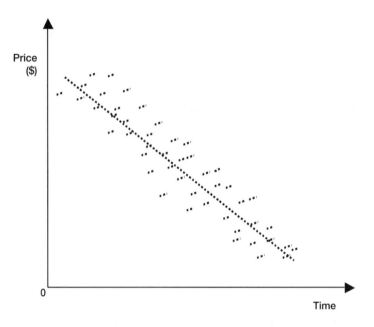

Figure 1.4 Long-run price trend of a hypothetical natural resource. A declining price trend over time indicates increasing abundance of the resource under consideration.

Furthermore, if the economy under consideration were at full employment, it would be possible to interpret the above numerical value (i.e. 12) as a measure of an *opportunity cost*. That is, it would indicate the number of barrels of crude oil that have to be foregone if society decides to shift its resources (labor, capital, etc.) to extract one more ounce of gold.

1.2.3 *Price as a signal of emerging resource scarcity*

The key issue here is the extent to which price trends over a long period of time (such as 20–100 years) can be used as an indicator of emerging resource scarcity or abundance. For example, a falling price trend of a *hypothetical* natural resource depicted in Figure 1.4 would suggest increasing abundance or decreasing resource scarcity over time. The reverse will be true if an increasing price trend is observed.

Accordingly, if the vertical axis of Figure 1.4 represents a relative price (e.g. the price ratio of Coca Cola and water), a falling price trend would imply Coca Cola is getting less scarce or more abundant relative to water. It is important to note, however, that *such a claim can be justified only if we accept that market prices indicate the 'true' scarcity values of the resources under consideration*. The conditions that are necessary for this to happen are discussed in Appendix A (Section A.5).

Thus, at least in principle, in managing environmental resources, market prices not only could provide valuable information on opportunity costs but also could serve to detect emerging resource scarcity. The extent to which these claims are valid, in particular as they applied to environmental resources, will be explored in Chapter 3.

The second fundamental principle that influences and shapes the mainstream economics approach to environmental and natural resource management is technology – the role it plays in the amelioration of natural resource scarcity. A formal discussion of the general characteristics of scarcity-augmenting (resource saving) technological advances is the subject of the next section.

1.3 Factor substitution possibilities, technological changes and resource scarcity

In this section, an attempt will be made to examine how factor substitution possibilities and technological change alleviate resource scarcity, with an emphasis on natural resources – a very important subject matter in environmental and resource economics.

Factor substitution suggests that basic resources are used in combinations. Furthermore, resources are generally considered to be *fungible*. That is, one kind of resource (such as a machine) can be freely replaced by another (such as a labor) in the production process. Or, one type of energy resource (such as petroleum) can be replaced by another form of energy (such as natural gas). For example, in Case Study 1.1 below, it is shown that water purification for the city of New York can be attained by investing either in the preservation of a 'natural' kind of capital (a forest watershed) or by building a filtration plant – a 'manufactured' kind of capital. In other words, manufactured capital can be replaced by natural capital.

1.3.1 Factor substitution and its implications for resource scarcity

An economy is constantly engaged in the production of goods and services (oranges, hand calculators, restaurant foods, national parks, etc.) using the available labor, capital and other basic resources available at its disposal. The existing state of technology determines how inputs (labor, capital and natural resources) are combined to produce goods and services. Economists use production functions to describe this relation mathematically. The important assumption here is the *substitutability* of different factors of production. Input substitutability may be divided into three different categories:

Constant factor substitution possibilities: In this situation inputs can be substituted at a *constant* rate (for example, one unit of manufactured capital for two units of natural capital) implying that the *opportunity costs* of the two factors of production is constant. Under this circumstance, at least conceptually, the use of an input (such as natural capital) can be reduced to zero without *raising* the opportunity cost (in terms of other inputs sacrificed, such as manufactured capital). The implication of this is that increase in the scarcity of natural capital will *not* be accomplished by increased opportunity cost – a rather optimistic scenario for the impact of increasing natural resource scarcity. Although conceptually interesting, however, this case is obviously rather unrealistic.

Diminishing factor substitution possibilities: A more realistic case may be when natural capital can still be substituted by other factors of production but *not* at a constant rate. One possibility is a situation where each incremental reduction in natural capital requires a progressively increasing amount of manufactured capital in order to produce a given level of desired output (such as the production of clean water in Case Study 1.1). In this regard, the opportunity cost of using natural capital, in terms of other inputs sacrificed, increases *at an increasing rate as natural capital becomes scarce*.

Case Study 1.1   Economic returns from the biosphere

Garciela Chichilnisky and Geoffrey Heal

. . . The environment's services are, without a doubt, valuable. The air we breathe, the water we drink and the food we eat are all available only because of services provided by the environment. How can we transform these values into income while conserving resources?

We have to 'securitize' (sell shares in the return from) 'natural capital' and environmental goods and services, and enroll market forces in their conservation. This means assigning to corporations – possibly by public–private corporate partnerships – the obligation to manage and conserve natural capital in exchange for the right to the benefits from selling the services provided.

In 1996, New York City invested between $1 billion and $1.5 billion in natural capital, in the expectation of producing cost savings of $6 billion–$8 billion over ten years, giving an internal rate of return of 90–170 per cent in a payback period of four to seven years. This return is an order of magnitude higher than is usually available, particularly on relatively risk-free investments. How did this come about?

New York's water comes from a watershed in the Catskill Mountains. Until recently, water purification processes by root systems and soil micro-organisms, together with filtration and sedimentation during its flow through the soil, were sufficient to cleanse the water to the standards required by the US Environmental Protection Agency (EPA). But sewage fertilizer and pesticides in the soil reduced the efficacy of this process to the point where New York's water no longer met EPA standards. The city was faced with the choice of restoring the integrity of the Catskill ecosystems or of building a filtration plant at a capital cost of $6 billion–$8 billion, plus running costs of the order of $300 million annually. In other words, New York had to invest in natural capital or in physical capital. Which was more attractive?

Investing in natural capital in this case meant buying land in and around the watershed so that its use could be restricted, and subsidizing the construction of better sewage treatment plants. The total cost of restoring the watershed is expected to be $1 billion–$1.5 billion. . . .

To address its water problem New York City has floated an 'environmental bond issue', and will use the proceeds to restore the functioning of the watershed ecosystems responsible for water purification. The cost of the bond issue will be met by the savings produced: avoidance of a capital investment of $6 billion–$8 billion, plus the $300 million annual running costs of the plant. The money that would otherwise have paid for these costs will pay the interest on the bonds. New York City could have 'securitized' these savings by opening a 'watershed saving account' into which it paid a fraction of the costs avoided by not having to build and run a filtration plant. This account would then pay investors for the use of their capital.

Source: *Nature* Vol. 391, February 12, 1998, pp. 629–30. Reprinted by permission.

This implies that depletion of natural capital will be encountered with steady increases in resource procurement for the purpose of producing goods and services. According to standard microeconomic theory, this situation is viewed as being the most plausible scenario.

No factor substitution possibilities: A more extreme case is when factor substitution possibilities are totally absent. In this situation, natural capital and other factors of production are used in a predetermined *fixed proportion* to produce a given level of output. For example, to produce a certain level of output, a fixed amount of natural capital may be needed regardless of the level of the other inputs being utilized. Therefore, one important implication of this situation is that to produce a given level of output *a certain minimum of natural capital input is needed*.

From the discussion thus far, we can generalize that the concern about the availability of natural resources very much depends on the assumption one makes about the nature of the *rate* of substitution possibilities between natural resources and other factors of production. If a natural resource is viewed as being perfectly substitutable by other factors of production, then, its availability should be of little or no concern. On the other hand, if the substitution possibility between a natural resource and other factors of production is zero, then a certain critical minimum of this resource would be needed to produce a given level of output. In this case, availability of natural resources would be a major concern since a decline of natural resources below this minimum entails an automatic lowering of living standards or output.

As stated earlier, the case that is most realistic in depicting the nature of the substitution possibilities between a natural resource and other factors of production is when natural resources can always be substituted by other factors of production, *but it would be at an increasing opportunity cost*. That is, successive reduction in natural resources requires an incrementally larger increase in other factors in order to maintain the production of a constant level of output. *It is in this sense, therefore, that the scarcity (availability) of natural resources would become a concern.*

1.3.2 Changes in production technology and its implications for resource conservation

In the above discussion of substitution possibilities, production technology was assumed to remain constant. In other words, factor substitution possibilities were discussed assuming no change in the current techniques (or state of the art) of production. However, in a dynamic economy, technological advance that entails a fundamental change in production techniques is a normal experience. If this is the case, it would be instructive to address three related questions: (1) In what specific ways does a change in production technique affect the use of factors of production? (2) Are all factors of production equally affected by a change in production techniques? (3) What exactly are the broader implications of changes in production technology for the issue of natural resource adequacy (scarcity)?

In production analysis, technological advance is defined as the ability to produce a given amount of output by using less of *all* inputs. For example, in Case Study 1.1 the same amount of water can be produced by using *less* of both factors of production. Viewed this way, technological advance in production techniques entails resource *conservation*.

Technological changes are seldom *unbiased*. In other words, technological advance in production technology often enhances the productivity of one input in a disproportionate manner. For instance, the technological change could be capital biased if the advance in technological change enhances the productivity of manufactured capital more than natural capital. Similarly, a natural capital biased technological change would tend to enhance the productivity of inputs in this category more than manufactured capital.

From the above discussions, two points should be evident: first, technological advance implies the possibility of producing a given level of output with less of inputs – a conservation of resources. Second, the amount of resource conservation (saving) in each category of inputs used in the production process would largely depend on the impact that technological advance has on the *relative productivity* of each of the inputs under consideration. Rarely does technological advance equally enhance the productivity of all inputs; hence, a bias is unavoidable in technological advances.

To summarize the discussion in this section, the *scarcity* (availability) of natural resources cannot be adequately addressed without careful consideration of technological factors such as factor substitution possibilities and technical advances in production (Solow 1991). According to the standard economic paradigm, as will be evident from the discussion in Chapter 11, consideration of this issue is central to any attempt to assess the impact of natural resource scarcity on future standards of living.

1.4 The human economy and the natural world: the neoclassical worldview

The third and final issue that needs to be considered is how, at the fundamental level, the proponents of the neoclassical school of economics perceive the interrelationships (interconnectedness) between the human economy and the natural world. To what extent and in what specific ways is the human economy dependent on the natural environment? Is there evidence of inconsistencies in the ways the human economy is designed to function and the laws of nature? If so, would it matter? These are the kind of issues addressed in the last section of the chapter.

In this section of the chapter, a very broad view of the human economy is presented with three objectives in mind: (1) to provide a schematic view of the basic institutional components of a market-oriented economy; (2) to show how the flows of materials (inputs and outputs) circulate within a 'self-contained' human economic process; and (3) to note the implied relationships (if any) between the human economy and the natural world.

As a working definition, an *economy* can be viewed as a rather complex institutional mechanism designed to facilitate the production, consumption and exchange of goods and services, given resource scarcity and technology, the preferences of households, and the legal system for resource ownership rights (Randall 1987). All economies are alike in the sense that they are devised to help facilitate the production, consumption and exchange of goods and services, and they are constrained by resource scarcity and technology. On the other hand, economies differ in the degree of empowerment given to households and firms in their ability to make economic choices, and the legal view of property ownership rights. For example, in a capitalistic and market-oriented economy, freedom of choice and private ownership of property are strongly entrenched

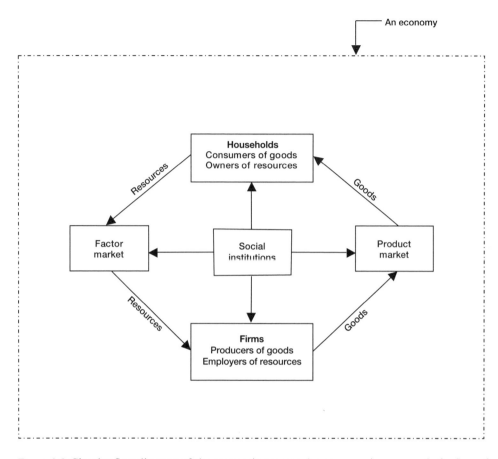

Figure 1.5 Circular flow diagram of the economic process. An economy is composed of a flow of
   commodities (in the form of basic resources, goods and services); *social institutions*
   (primarily markets and legal tenders); and *people* (broadly identified as households
   and firms).

institutional principles. In contrast, in a centrally planned economy, the production and
distribution of goods are dictated by bureaucratic choices, with resource ownership
retained by the state.

   In this section, using a circular flow diagram (an approach familiar to all who have
taken a course in introductory economics), an attempt will be made to present a
schematic view of the basic institutional components of a market economy. The
circular flow diagram in Figure 1.5 is designed to show that the operation of a market-
oriented economy is composed of the following elements:

1   *Economic entities* (households and firms). Households are the final users of goods
    and services, and the owners of resources. In a market economy, given resource
    scarcity, the primary goal is to find effective ways to address the material

needs of consumers (households). At least in principle, *consumers' well-being (the maximization of consumers' utility) is the primary goal of a market-oriented economy*. While households are final users of goods and services, firms enter the economic process as transformers of basic resources (labor, capital and natural resources) into goods and services, and this is done in response to consumers' preferences (demand).

2   *Commodities* are flows of resources both as factors of production and final goods and services. In broad terms, these resources are recognized as being directly or indirectly capable of satisfying human wants and are found in limited quantities and/or qualities – i.e. they are scarce.

3   *Markets* represent an institutional arena in which exchanges (buying and selling) of final goods and services and factors of production (labor, capital and natural resources) take place. Traditionally, economists group markets into two broad categories: product markets and factor markets. The *product market* is where the exchange of *final* goods and services occurs. In this market, demand and supply provide information about households and firms, respectively. The *factor market* refers exclusively to the buying and selling of basic resources, such as labor, capital and natural resources. In this sub-market, demand imparts market information about firms and supply provides information about households. That is, households are the suppliers of labor, capital and natural resources, while firms are the buyers, who, in turn, use these items to produce final goods and services for the product market. Clearly then, the role played by households and firms in the factor market is the reverse of their role in the product market.

   In both the product and factor markets, information about resource scarcity is transmitted through prices. As discussed earlier, these prices are formed through the interactions of market demand and supply; and, under certain conditions, market prices can be used as reliable indicators of both present and future resource scarcities.

4   *Non-market public and private institutions*. A market does not function in a vacuum; for a market to operate efficiently, *ownership rights* need to be clearly defined and enforced. This requires the establishment of public agencies designed to articulate and enforce the rules and regulations by which ownership rights are attained, relinquished (transferred) and enforced (more on this in Chapter 3). In addition, *competition* in the market place is fostered through public intervention in some instances. The public and private entities (social institutions) that legislate the rules for assigning resource ownership rights and regulate the degree of competition in the market place are represented by the box at the center of Figure 1.5. It can be seen that what flows from this box to households, firms, and markets are not physical goods but information services. In general, the main function of these flows of information is to ensure that economic agents (households and firms) are playing by some socially predetermined rules of the game. In this regard, *ideally*, social institutions may be conceived as a conductor of a symphony orchestra or a traffic director in a busy intersection.

Viewed this way, social institutions have important economic functions. However, they should not be assumed to be either perfect or costless (North 1995). When they are not functioning well, the information communicated through them could distort market signals (prices) and in so doing, significantly affect the allocation of scarce resources. This will become evident in Chapter 3, which deals specifically with environmental resources.

Several lessons can be drawn from the above depiction of the human economy.

- First, the human economy is composed of *three* entities: people, social institutions and commodities.
- Second, since the value of resources is assumed to emanate exclusively from their usefulness to human, the economic notion of a resource is strictly *anthropocentric*. What this implies is that basic resources (such as, the various services provided by the natural environment) have no *intrinsic* value. Something is of intrinsic value if it has value in its own right, or for its own sake (Attfield 1998). For example, in Case Study 1.1, the worth of a watershed service (water purification by root systems and soil micro-organisms) is identified solely by its *commercial* value. The fact that the watershed under consideration may have other, non-economic, value is not considered. These other services include flood control, air purification, generation of fertile soil, and production of a range of goods from timber to mushrooms, as well as sites for recreation, inspiration, education, and scientific inquiry.
- Third, in the production sector, what is being continually created is *value*. Trees are cut and used to make chairs only if the monetary value of the chairs exceeds the monetary value of the wood used to make the chairs. Similarly, in the consumption sector, what is continuously being created is an influx of *utility* from the final use (consumption) of goods and services. Therefore, in the human economic system matter and energy from the natural environment are continuously transformed to create an immaterial (psychic) flow of value and utility. As will become evident in Chapter 2, this observation is quite inconsistent with a purely ecological worldview of the transformation of matter and energy, and the ultimate implications of this natural process.
- Fourth, in the above simple model, no explicit consideration is given to the extent to which the flow of material (commodities) in the human economy is dependent on natural ecosystems. The fact that the economic process continually depends on the natural world for both the generation of raw material 'inputs' and absorption of waste 'outputs' (see Figure 1.1) is simply *taken for granted*. More specifically, natural ecosystems are viewed simply as a 'gift of nature' ready to be exploited by humans and in strict accordance to the laws of demand and supply. Or, as O' Neill and Kahn (2000: 333) put it, the environment is viewed as 'the constant and stable background for economic activity'.

It is appropriate to end the discussion in this section with a quote from Nicholas Georgescu-Roegen – one of the most ardent critics of neoclassical economists:

A curious event in the history of economic thought is that, years after the mechanistic dogma has lost its supremacy in physics and its grip on the philosophical world, the founders of the neoclassical school set out to erect an economic science after the pattern of mechanics – in the words of Jevons, as *'the mechanics of utility and self-interest'*. . . . A glaring proof is the standard textbook representation of the economic process by a circular diagram [such as Figure 1.5], a pendulum movement between production and consumption within a completely closed system. . . . *The patent fact that between the economic process and the material environment there exists a continuous mutual influence which is history making carries no weight with the standard economist.* (p. 75)

A basic understanding of ecological principles is needed in order to fully understand and appreciate the above criticism by Georgescu-Roegen, and the next chapter, Chapter 2, is devoted to this end.

1.5 Chapter summary

The primary objective of this chapter has been to present the neoclassical or standard economics worldview of the natural environment and its role in the economic system at the fundamental level. This involved presenting the key axiomatic assumptions and theoretical explanations that have been considered critical in the construction of the basic foundation for standard environmental and resource economics. With this in mind, these are the key issues addressed in this chapter:

- The natural environment is viewed as having three distinctive functions. It is the source of basic raw materials for the human economy. It functions as a repository and eventually a decomposer of the waste materials emanating from the production and consumption sectors of the human economy. Finally, the natural environment provides humans with valuable amenities and ecological services.
- Environmental resources are regarded as of economic concern to the extent that they are considered *scarce* – demand exceeds supply at zero prices.
- The *economic value* of scarce environmental resources is ultimately determined by consumers' preferences. Furthermore, consumers' preferences are best expressed by a market economy, and as such, the market system is the preferred institution for allocating scarce resources, including the natural environment (more on this in Chapter 3).
- Given that economic value is determined solely by human preferences, the neoclassical worldview of environmental resources is strictly *anthropocentric*; i.e. environmental resources have no *intrinsic* value, as such.
- Environmental (natural) resources are *essential* factors of production. An economy cannot produce goods and services without the use of certain minimum amounts of natural resources. However, to the extent that resources are *fungible*, i.e. one kind of resource (such as natural capital) can be freely replaced or substituted by another (such as manufactured capital) in the production process, natural resources need not be seen as the sole or even primary factor in determining an economy's production capacity.
- Scarcity of resources (including environmental/natural resources) is continually augmented through technological advances.
- According to the neoclassical worldview, the human economy, as depicted in Figure 1.5, is composed of people, flows of commodities (or flows of matter–energy at the fundamental level) and human institutions. The primary focus of the human economic system is not so much on the conversion of matter–energy that are found in nature to goods and services (i.e. the production process) but the generation of utility – an immaterial flux of satisfaction to humans. In this worldview, it appears that the link between the flow of matter–energy in the economic system and the natural environment is very much ignored. The next chapter deals with the

implications of this important oversight or omission for both the human economy and natural ecological systems.

Review and discussion questions

1 Carefully review the following economic concepts and make sure you have a clear understanding of them:
Neoclassical economics, absolute scarcity, relative scarcity, natural capital, manufactured capital, factors substitution, technical advance, an economy, households, a firm, product and factor markets, environmental amenities, and intrinsic value.

2 Identify the *three* distinctive contributions of the natural environment to the human economy.

3 State whether the following are *true* or *false* and explain why:

- Environmental resources should be of economic concern only if they are scarce.
- Factor substitution possibilities render the problem of resource scarcity to be manageable, but not necessarily irrelevant.

4 'Resources are culturally determined, a product of social choice, technology and the workings of the economic system' (Rees 1985: 35). Do you agree or disagree with this assertion? Why?

5 'Against the anthropocentric tendencies of most value theory, intrinsic values do exist apart from man's knowledge of them' (Cobb 1993: 214). Comment.

6 To view the human economy in isolation from the natural ecosystems is not only absurd but also very dangerous. Comment.

References

Attfield, R. (1998) 'Existence Value and Intrinsic Value', *Ecological Economics* 24.

Cobb, J. (1993) 'Ecology, Ethics, and Theology', in H. E. Daly and K. N. Townsend (ed.) *Valuing the Earth: Economics, Ecology, Ethics*, Cambridge, Mass.: MIT Press.

Georgescu-Roegen, N. (1993) 'The Entropy Law and the Economic Problem,' in H. E. Daly and K. N. Townsend (ed.) *Valuing the Earth: Economics, Ecology, Ethics*, Cambridge, Mass.: MIT Press.

North, D. C. (1995) 'The New Institutional Economics and Third World Development', in J. Herris *et al.* (ed.) *The New Institutional Economics and Third World Development*, London: Routledge.

O'Neill, V. R. and Kahn, J. (2000) 'Homo economus as a Keystone Species', *BioScience* 50, 4: 333–7.

Randall, A. (1987) *Resource Economics: An Economic Approach to Natural Resource and Environmental Policy*, 2nd edn, New York: John Wiley and Sons.

Rees, J. (1985) *Natural Resources: Allocation, Economics and Policy*, London and New York: Methuen.

Solow, R. M. (1991) 'Sustainability: An Economist's Perspective', in R. Dorfman and N. Dorfman (eds) *Economics of the Environment: Selected Readings*, 3rd edn, New York: W. W. Norton.

2   The natural environment and the human economy

An ecological perspective

2.1 Introduction

Consistent with the discussion in Chapter 1, environmental resources, in broad terms, include all the living and non-living endowments of the Earth, and for that matter, the entirety of the *biosphere*. The primary objective of this chapter is to establish a clear understanding of the *basic principles* governing the nature, structure and function of the biosphere (hence, environmental resources) and the functional *linkages* (relationships) between the biosphere and the human economy.

From a *purely* ecological perspective, these basic principles and linkages are identified as follows:

- Environmental resources of the biosphere are *finite*. Hence, environmental resources are scarce in *absolute* terms.
- In nature, everything is related to everything else. Moreover, survival of the biosphere requires recognition of the *mutual interdependencies* among all the elements that constitute the biosphere.
- At a functional level and from a *purely* physical viewpoint, the biosphere is characterized by *a continuous transformation of matter and energy*. Furthermore, the transformation of matter and energy are governed by some immutable *natural laws*.
- *Material recycling* is essential for the growth and revitalization of all the subsystems of the biosphere, including the human economy.
- Nothing remains *constant* in nature. Furthermore, changes in ecosystems do not appear to occur in an absolutely *linear* and predictable manner. However, measured on a *geological time scale*, the natural tendency of an ecological community (species of plants, animals and micro-organisms living together) is to progress from simple and unstable relationships (pioneer stage) to a more stable, resilient, diverse, and complex community.
- The human economy is a *subsystem* of the biosphere and it would be dangerously misleading to view natural resources as just factors of production lying outside the confines of the larger system.
- The natural tendency of human technology is towards the *simplification* of the natural systems, eventually leading toward less stable, less resilient and less diverse ecological communities.

Figure 2.1 attempts to portray a worldview that is consistent with these principles, and more specifically the ecological (biocentric) perspective of the relationship between the

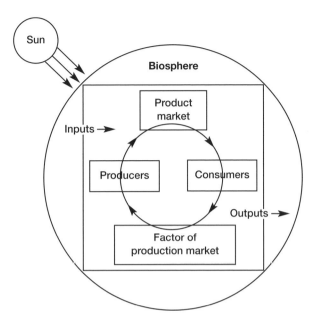

Figure 2.1 Ecologically enlightened economic view. The biosphere is continuously energized
by solar power. The human economy (comprising the activities in the inner circle)
depends on *inputs* (throughput) and *outputs* (disposal of waste) to the biosphere.
The biosphere is *finite*, as indicated by the outer circle.

biosphere and the human economy. This perspective is biocentric in the sense that it
does not explicitly recognize the main output of the economic system – non-material
flows of utility (enjoyment). It describes nature and the interactions that occur in nature
between living and non-living matter in *purely* physical (energy and matter) terms.

These features are clearly evident in the following specific aspects of Figure 2.1. First,
a clearly demarcated circle, perhaps symbolizing the Earth and its finiteness, represents
the biosphere.

Second, by locating it inside the circle, the human economy is perceived as a subsystem of the biosphere. The box inside the circle indicates that the growth of the
economic subsystem is 'bounded' by a non-growing and finite ecological sphere.

Third, Figure 2.1 suggests that the human economy is dependent on the biosphere
for its continuous withdrawal (extraction and harvest) of material *inputs* and as a
repository for its *waste* (outputs) – degraded matter and energy that are the eventual
byproducts of the economic process.

Fourth, the biosphere (and hence the human economy) requires a continuous flow of
external energy – from the Sun.

Fifth, while both the human economy and the biosphere are regarded as an 'open
system' with regard to energy (i.e. both systems require an external source of energy),
the biosphere taken in its entirety is regarded as a 'closed system' with respect to
matter. Note that this is in stark contrast to the way the human economy is depicted in
Figure 1.5 – the circular-flow diagram discussed in the last section of Chapter 1. That

diagram actually treats the human economy as an 'open system' with regard to both energy and matter. That is, the human economy is continuously dependent on external (outside) sources for inputs of energy and matter and on external repositories for its outputs.

The upshot is clear. A worldview as represented in Figure 2.1 appears to incorporate the principle that the human economy is completely and unambiguously dependent on natural ecological systems for its material needs. Furthermore, the human economy (as a subsystem) cannot outgrow the biosphere. The implication of this is that, as mentioned earlier, the growth of the economic subsystem is 'bounded' by a non-growing and finite ecological sphere. A comprehensive and systematic understanding of the extent to which nature acts as both a *source* of and a *limiting factor* on the basic material requirements for the human economy demands some level of understanding of ecology – which is the subject of the remainder of this chapter.

What is ecology? Ecology is a branch of science that systematically studies the relationships between living organisms and the physical and chemical environment in which they live. Ecology as a scientific discipline is highly evolved; it has gone through various developmental stages extending over more than a century. In this chapter, no attempt is made to explore the subject matter of ecology in its entirety. To some extent, the coverage of ecological principles in this chapter may be considered-broad brush.

While acknowledging this, I should point out that the breadth and depth of the coverage of ecological principles depends on the intended purpose for discussing these principles. In this chapter, the main aim is to offer a preliminary exploration of ecology principally directed at addressing these specific objectives:

- To provide a broader and deeper understanding of the natural processes by which natural resources are created and maintained
- To understand some of the natural laws that impose limitations on the interaction of organisms (including humans) with their living and nonliving environment
- To show specific ways in which human interaction with nature has been incompatible with the proper functioning of ecosystems
- To identify some of the important links between ecology and economics, two disciplines that are essential for a holistic view of natural resource problems and issues.

It was in recognition of these points that David Pearce, an eminent environmental and resource economist, made the assertion that 'No serious student of environmental economics can afford to ignore the subject matter of "ecology", the widely embracing science which looks at the interrelationship between living species and their habitats' (1978: 31).

2.2 Ecosystem structure

The hierarchical organization of biological systems that is often used as a starting point for ecological study is the *ecosystem*. An ecosystem includes living organisms in a specified physical environment, the multitude of interactions among the organisms, and the nonbiological factors in the physical environment that limit their growth and reproduction, such as air, water, minerals, and temperature. Viewed this way, an

Figure 2.2 The Ive Road Fen Preserve. Fens are wetland ecosystems that receive water from underground alkaline springs rather than from precipitation. The Ives Road Fen Preserve is one of the largest and least disturbed fen wetlands in Michigan, USA. This preserve provides ideal habitat for many rare plants and animals. The plants include the carnivorous sundew and pitcher plant, as well as the showy coneflower, prairie dropseed grass, prairie Indian-plaintain, hairy-fruited sedge, beak grass and prairie rose. Spectacular sycamore and silver maple trees spread over the floodplain. In terms of animals, the fen provides habitats for the tree frog, and a chorus of migratory and breeding birds such as the yellow-breasted chat, blue-winged warbler and alder flycatcher.

ecosystem is in practice the 'house of life' (Miller 1991). The definition of boundaries and the spatial scale of an ecosystem can vary: an ecosystem can be as small as a pond or as big as the entire Earth. We can, therefore, refer to the ecosystem of a pond or the ecosystem of the Earth in its entirety. What is important in each case is the definition of boundaries across which inputs and outputs of energy and matter can be measured (Boulding 1993).

Generally, an ecosystem is composed of four components: the atmosphere (air), the hydrosphere (water), the lithosphere (soil and rock), and the biosphere (life). The first three comprise the *abiotic* or nonliving components of the ecosystem, whereas the biosphere is its *biotic* or living component. It is important to recognize that the living and nonliving components of an ecosystem interact with each another. The dynamic interaction of these components is critical to the survival and functioning of the ecosystem, just as breathing and eating are essential to the survival of animals. Further-more, these components are capable of co-existing so that the ecosystem itself is in a sense alive (Schneider 1990; Miller 1991). For example, soil is a living system that develops as a result of interactions between plant, animal and microbial communities (living components), and parent rock material (abiotic components). Abiotic factors such as temperature and moisture influence the process of soil development.

In an ecosystem, the abiotic components serve several functions. First, the abiotic components are used as a habitat (space), and an immediate source of water and oxygen for organisms. Second, they act as a reservoir of the six most important elements for life: carbon (C), hydrogen (H), oxygen (O), nitrogen (N), sulfur (S), and phosphorus (P). These elements constitute 95 per cent of all living organisms. Furthermore, the Earth contains only a fixed amount of these elements. Thus, continual functioning of an ecosystem requires that these elements be recycled since they are critical to the overall welfare of the ecosystem.

The biotic (living) component of the ecosystem consists of three distinct groups of organisms: producers, consumers and decomposers. The *producers* are those organisms capable of photosynthesis: the production of organic material solely from solar energy, carbon dioxide and water. This organic material serves as a source of both energy and mineral nutrients, which are required by all living organisms. Examples include terrestrial plants and aquatic plants, such as phytoplankton. The *consumers* are organisms whose very survival depends on the organic materials manufactured by the producers. The consumers comprise animals of all sizes, ranging from large predators to small parasites such as mosquitoes. The nature of the consumers' dependence on the producers may take different forms. Some consumers (herbivores such as rabbits) are directly dependent on primary producers for energy. Others (carnivores such as lions) are indirectly dependent on primary producers. The last group of living organisms is the *decomposers*. These include micro-organisms such as fungi, yeast, bacteria, etc., as well as a diversity of worms, insects and many other small animals that rely on dead organisms for their survival. In their efforts to survive and obtain energy, they decompose material released by producers and consumers to their original elements (C, O, H, N, S, P). This, as we shall see shortly, is what keeps material cycling within an ecosystem.

Basic lesson: In a natural ecosystem, living and nonliving matter have *reciprocal* relationships. For that matter as will be further explained in the next section, the survival and 'proper' functioning of an ecosystem entails mutual interactions (interdependence) among organisms and between them and the abiotic environment.

2.3 Ecosystem function

As stated above, an ecosystem itself can be viewed as a living organism. Where does life start and end in this system? What sets off, controls and regulates the movements and transformations of material in this system? How are the various components of an ecosystem interrelated? Is a natural ecosystem self-regulated? If so, how? In this section an attempt will be made to answer these and other related questions, in an effort to identify clearly the general principles that govern the functioning of a natural ecosystem.

In the previous section, the structural organization (i.e. how the components and the relationships of biotic and abiotic elements of an ecosystem are organized and defined) of an ecosystem was outlined. However, for any movements or transformations of energy and matter to occur in an ecosystem, an external source of energy is needed. For our planet, the primary source of this energy is solar radiation: the energy from the *Sun*. Solar energy, then, fuels the flow of energy and matter in an ecosystem.

It is through the interactions of the hydrosphere, the atmosphere and the lithosphere, activated and facilitated by solar energy, that atmospheric and water circulation (such as wind, tide, cloud, water currents, and precipitation) occur. In turn, it is the impact of this atmospheric and water circulation over a long period of time that causes (a) the removal and the reshaping of parts of the Earth's crust (such as by erosion and sedimentation), and (b) the flows and formation of the reservoirs of water (streams, rivers, waterfalls, and lakes). Essentially, as will be further elaborated later, these are the types of natural and perpetual cyclical process that create what we identify as natural resources (such as water supplies, fossil fuels and fertile soil, and the aesthetic values of the natural environment).

The biotic component of an ecosystem relies on the ability of producers (terrestrial and aquatic plants) to convert solar energy directly into chemical or stored energy in the form of organic matter. As discussed above, this transformation of one form of energy into another is accomplished through the process of *photosynthesis*. Essentially, it involves synthesis of complex organic compounds from basic elements (C, O, H, N, etc. obtained from soil or water), fueled by solar radiation. From this, it should be evident that the abiotic components of an ecosystem are linked to the photosynthetic process the production of an energy base to support life. Also, through this process the flow of materials becomes linked to the flow of energy (more on this later).

It is important to recognize that the producers are indispensable to the biotic component of the ecosystem. Without these organisms, it would be impossible to create the organic matter (such as plant tissue) that is essential for the growth and reproduction of other organisms (consumers and decomposers). While the nature of the dependency between the producers and other forms of organisms may appear to be linear at this fundamental level (the flow of the material is from producers to consumers and decomposers), the functioning of the ecosystem as a whole is characterized by a network of mutual interdependencies among many species of organisms at each level – a food web (Miller 1991). As shown in Figure 2.3, the consumers depend on the producers for energy, various nutrients and oxygen. The oxygen is a by-product of photosynthesis. The producers, in turn, depend on consumers and decomposers for carbon dioxide (CO_2) and on decomposers and abiotic processes for mineral elements (P, S, etc.). All members of the biotic component, through respiration, release CO_2. Finally, in the process of consuming the dead plants and animals, the decomposers convert organic compounds to inorganic minerals, which plants can use. Thus, in a natural ecosystem, survival and 'proper' ecosystem functioning require mutual inter-actions (interdependence) among organisms and between them and the abiotic environment (Miller 1991).

Basic lessons: At a fundamental level and from a *purely* physical viewpoint, a functioning natural ecosystem is characterized by a constant transformation of matter and energy. It is through this process of transformation that: (a) the substances that we often identify as natural resources (air, water, food, minerals, valleys, mountains, forests, lakes, watersheds, waterfalls, wilderness, etc.) have developed from a multitude of complex interactions among living and nonliving organisms that are powered by the energy of the Sun over a period of time measured on a geological timescale; and (b) biological organisms have evolved and been sustained. Furthermore, as will be discussed in the next two subsections, the two prerequisites for sustaining the efficient functioning of an ecosystem are materials recycling and a source of continuous flows of energy from an external source.

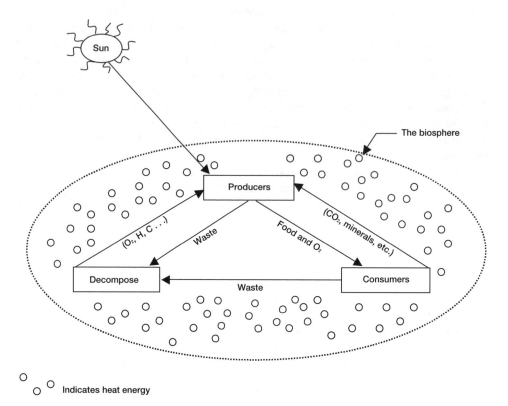

Figure 2.3 The basic life cycle. The biotic component of an ecosystem is composed of three major
groups of organisms: the producers, the consumers and the decomposers. As indicated
by the direction of the arrows, functionally these three groups of organisms are
mutually interdependent. The ability of the producers to convert solar energy to
chemical or stored energy is what starts the biological cycles, and the sustainability of
these cycles, among others, depends on the presence of continuous flows of energy
from an external source (the Sun).

2.3.1 Materials recycling

As is evident from the earlier discussion (see also Figure 2.3), the natural recycling
process starts with the formation of plant tissue through the processes of photosynthesis
and biosynthesis. At this early stage, some oxygen is released into the environment.
Virtually all of the free molecular oxygen (O_2) in the atmosphere and in the oceans has
originated from the process of photosynthesis. In many ecosystems, the second major
stage of the recycling process occurs when animals, in their effort to metabolize the
stored energy in plant tissues, release CO_2 and organic wastes. Major recycling
(decomposition), however, is done by micro-organisms. The micro-organisms ultimately
break down dead organic matter into its simpler (inorganic) components. This stage in
the recycling process is particularly important because the amount of mineral elements
in an ecosystem (especially N and P) is finite, and can be limiting to the growth and
reproduction of organisms.

However, decomposition may not always be complete. The oxidation process involved in decomposition depends on the availability of oxygen and the energy present in a given environment. For example, oxidation takes place at a much faster pace in a tropical forest than at the bottom of a lake or in a desert. Thus, in nature, material recycling is not 100 per cent efficient, and some amounts of organic matter may remain only partially decomposed. This incompletely decomposed organic matter, accumulated and aged over long periods of time, will develop peat, coal and petroleum – that is, fossil fuels. Such matter forms the basis of the energy resources so crucial to the modern human economy. It also constitutes a large reserve of carbon that is rapidly released when fossil fuels are burned thereby contributing to global warming by releasing CO_2 to the atmosphere at an unprecedented rate.

Recycling of materials is not limited to the biological and material cycles in an ecosystem as discussed above. The well-known atmospheric cycles (such as those of C, N and S) contribute to the circulation of these elements within the various components of an ecosystem. Furthermore, it is through atmospheric cycles that the concentration of these elements in a given environmental medium is maintained or regulated. For example, the atmosphere is composed of approximately 20 per cent O_2, 78 per cent N_2, 0.9 per cent argon (Ar) (which is not significant biologically), and 0.03 per cent CO_2 (but this amount has been increasing over the past 200 years).

It is very important to note, when the concern is the functioning of an ecosystem, that these atmospheric cycles cannot be viewed in isolation from other cycles (i.e. geologic and biological cycles). For example, there is a large reserve of N_2 in the atmosphere, and only a small number of micro-organisms are responsible for converting atmospheric N_2 to a form that plants can use, through a process called *nitrogen fixation*, whereas there is no large reserve of N in rocks. Thus, nitrogen fixation is the critical process of converting what is for plants unavailable gaseous nitrogen (N_2) from the atmosphere to available (inorganic) nitrogen (N) for plants. Furthermore, physical and chemical processes associated with volcanic activity and the combustion of fossil fuels can also increase the availability of useful nitrogen to ecosystems.

In addition to the atmospheric cycles, geological processes also contribute to the constant recycling of materials in ecosystems. For example, it is through erosion and water movement that nitrates, sulfates and phosphates in the soil, rocks and sediments can be freed and re-introduced to the roots of plants. This process is particularly important for the recycling of phosphates, as there is a large reserve of phosphorus (P) in rocks and virtually none in the atmosphere. Thus, the process of converting available (inorganic) phosphorus in rock to available phosphates for plants is primarily a physical and chemical process (erosion).

Therefore, from this discussion, it is apparent that the recycling process of an ecosystem is all-encompassing and demands the interaction of every facet of the ecosystem. Strictly speaking, then, the decomposition and recirculation of materials in an ecosystem is facilitated by these *biogeochemical* cycles, i.e. the nitrogen cycle, phosphorus cycle, carbon cycle, etc. (Miller 1991; Pearce 1978).

Basic lessons: Material recycling is essential for the growth and revitalization of all the components of the ecosphere (Miller 1991). In every natural ecosystem, what is a by-product (waste) for one organism is a resource for another. In this sense there is no such thing in nature as waste. Furthermore, in nature materials are continuously circulating through the biosphere via a combination of atmospheric, geologic, biologic, and hydrologic cycles. These cycles are essential for maintaining the long-run equilibrium of the elements in the atmosphere, hydrosphere and lithosphere.

2.3.2 Energy and thermodynamics: why ecosystems need continuous flows of energy from an external source

In the discussion so far, we have briefly examined the crucial role energy plays in the functioning of natural ecosystems. The availability of chemical energy in the form of organic molecules supports all forms of living organisms, and the maintenance of the circulation of matter within ecosystems – which is essential for their revitalization – requires a continuous flow of energy from an external source or sources. For our planet, this external source of energy has primarily been the radiation from the Sun.

Why is it that natural ecosystems need to have a continuous flow of energy from an external source? An adequate answer to this question requires a discussion of the laws governing the transformation of matter and energy.

As a working definition, *matter* may be identified as anything that occupies space and has mass; while *energy* may be viewed as something that lacks mass but has the capacity to move and/or transform an object(s) – the capacity to do work.

A living ecosystem is characterized by a continuous transformation of matter and energy. A number of laws of physics govern the flow and transformation of matter and energy. Of these, there are two that are especially relevant to our understanding of the functioning of natural ecosystems. These two laws (the first two laws of thermo-dynamics) deal with energy, and their respective implications will now be discussed.

The first law of thermodynamics refers to the principle of conservation of energy. This law states that matter and energy can neither be created nor destroyed, only transformed. The ecological implication of this law is rather straightforward. It clearly suggests that in a natural ecosystem we can never really throw matter away, or that 'everything must go somewhere'. The same principle holds for energy. This is clearly apparent in Figure 2.3, which shows how energy is released on each ecological pathway. However, the first law dictates that the energy lost in one process must equal the energy gained by the surrounding environment. Therefore, in terms of quantity, the total energy is always constant. This is why, at times, the first law is referred to as the law of conservation of energy.

The second law of thermodynamics deals with energy transformations and with the concepts of energy *quality* (useful versus useless energy). Energy can exist in a number of different 'states'. For example, light is a form of energy, as are various types of fossil fuels, wind, nuclear power sources (fuels), gunpowder, and electricity, among others. Energy from fossil fuels can be converted to heat energy to boil water and produce steam that can turn a turbine to produce electricity, which in turn can be converted to incandescent energy to make a lightbulb work or rotary motion to run an electric motor. We may consider each of these forms of energy to be useful since they can be used to do work (turn a turbine, move an automobile) or provide light by which to see. The second law of thermodynamics states that each time useful energy is converted or transformed from one state (or form) to another, there always is less *useful* energy available in the second state than there was in the first state. Therefore, in accordance with the first law of thermodynamics (which deals with energy conversion), the second law says that in every energy conversion some useful energy is converted to useless (heat) energy (Georgescu-Roegen 1993; Miller 1991). In the case of an incandescent light bulb, electrical energy is converted to useful light energy as well as some useless heat, which you can detect by touching a lightbulb that has been turned on for a few minutes. For incandescent light only approximately 5 per cent of the electrical energy becomes light and 95 per cent becomes heat – a 5 per cent energy efficiency. Similarly, the energy of fossil fuel used to do the work of moving an automobile generates a substantial amount of useless heat that must be dissipated through the cooling system (i.e. the radiator and water pump), or it will ruin the motor. Therefore, in any transformation of energy, in terms of energy quality (useful energy) there is an apparent loss of available energy. This phenomenon is often referred to as the principle of energy degradation or *entropy*, and it is universally applicable (Georgescu-Roegen 1993).

As a whole, the significant implications of the second law are the following:

- Energy varies in its quality or ability to do work.
- In all conversion of energy to work, there will always be a certain waste or loss of energy quality. Thus, we shall never be able to devise a 'perfect' energy conversion system, or perpetual motion machine. Furthermore, useful energy cannot be recycled. Hence, there are limits to energy conservation through technological means (see Exhibit 2.1).
- Since energy moves unidirectionally, from high to low temperature (or from a concentrated to a dispersed condition), it follows that a highly concentrated source of energy (such as the energy available in a piece of coal or wood) can never be re-used. We can never recycle useful energy. *This clearly explains, then, why natural ecosystems require continual energy flows from an external source.*

Basic lessons: The biosphere cannot escape the fundamental laws that describe and dictate the behavior of matter and energy. According to the first law of thermodynamics, the biosphere is composed of a constant amount of matter. In this sense, what typifies the activity of nature is not the creation but the transformation of matter. No activity in the biosphere creates matter (Georgescu-Roegen 1993). The first law clearly instructs us that natural resources are finite (Boulding 1993; Georgescu-Roegen 1993). Furthermore, it informs us that in the process of transformation of matter, we cannot get rid of anything. An important implication of this is that waste (pollution) is an inevitable by-product of any transformation of matter–energy (including, of course, the human economy). Waste (especially in the form of heat energy) is ultimately dispersed into the atmosphere and from there into space unless it is prevented from exiting, such as by atmospheric CO_2, moisture or other compounds.

The biosphere also operates within another restriction stemming from the second law. For any activities (i.e. transformation of matter) to occur in the biosphere, a continuous flow of energy from an external source is required. As discussed earlier, this is because the second law states that useful energy cannot be recycled. Furthermore, the fact that useful energy cannot be recycled raises an important issue about the use of terrestrial energy resources such as fossil fuels. These terrestrial resources are not only finite, but also nonrecyclable. As will be shown in Chapters 12 and 13, these requirements and limitations are *core concepts* essential to the understanding of ecological economics and the arguments for sustainable economic development.

This completes the discussion of ecosystem functions and structures relevant for the purpose of this book. The next section covers the factors leading to the dynamic changes (growth and decay) that occur in species composition of an ecosystem over a

Exhibit 2.1   Perpetual motion, a sort of 'original sin' in science

Garrett Hardin

Perpetual motion is an anti-Epicurean notion. Derek Price argues that it was probable, though not certain, that the pursuit of perpetual motion did not become a 'growth industry' until after AD 1088, when 'some medieval traveler . . . made a visit to the circle of Su Sung' in China. At this place there was exhibited a marvelous water clock that seemed to run forever without any motive force being required to replenish the elevated water supply. 'How was the traveler to know that each night there came a band of men to turn the pump handles and force the tons of water from the bottom sump to the upper reservoir, thus winding the clock for another day of apparently powerless activity?'

Such may have been the historical origin of what Price calls 'chimera of perpetual motion machines . . . one of the most severe mechanical delusions of mankind'. The delusion was not put to rest until the late nineteenth century when explicit statements of the conservation of matter and energy were advanced by physicists and accepted by scientists in general. It should be noted that a comparable advance was made in biology at about the same time when Pasteur (and others) demolished the supposed evidence for the spontaneous generation of living organisms. Modern public health theory is based on, and committed to, the belief that Epicurus was right: there is indeed a 'need of seeds', for disease germs to appear in this world of ours.

The 'conviction of the mind' that limits are real, now firmly established in the natural sciences, has still to be made an integral part of orthodox economics. As late as 1981 George Gilder, in his best-seller *Wealth and Poverty*, said that 'The United States must overcome the materialistic fallacy: the illusion that resources and capital are essentially things which can run out, rather than products of the human will and imagination which in freedom are inexhaustible.' Translation: 'Wishing will make it so'.

Six years later at a small closed conference two economists told the environmentalists what was wrong with their Epicurean position. Said one: 'The notion that there are limits that can't be taken care of by capital has to be rejected'. (Does that mean that capital is unlimited?) Said another: 'I think the burden of proof is on your side to show that there are limits and where the limits are'. Shifting the burden of proof is tactically shrewd: but would economists agree that the burden of proof must be placed on the axiom 'There's no such thing as a free lunch'?

Fortunately for the future progress of economics the wind is shifting. The standard ('neoclassical') system of economics assumes perpetual growth in a world of no limits. 'Thus', said economist Allen Kneese in 1988, 'the neoclassical system is, in effect, a perpetual motion machine'. The conclusion that follows from this was explicitly laid out by Underwood and King: 'The fact that there are no known exceptions to the laws of thermodynamics should be incorporated into the axiomatic foundation of economics'. But it will no doubt be some time before economics is completely purged of the covert perpetual motion machines that have afflicted it from the time of Malthus to the present.

Source: *Living within Limits: Ecology, Economics, and Population Taboos* (1993: 44–5). Copyright © 1993 by Oxford University Press, Inc. Used by permission.

long period of time. This is an important topic to discuss because changes in species composition can be significantly affected by large-scale human interference with natural ecosystems.

2.4 Ecological succession

Ecological succession involves natural changes in the species composition (types of plants, animals and micro-organisms) that occupy a given area over a period of time, as well as changes that occur in ecosystem dynamics, such as energy flows and nutrient cycling, discussed above. In a given area, with a specific climate and soil type, the stages of succession (typically recognized by the changes in species composition) are somewhat predictable.

The developmental stages of any ecosystem tend to follow a general pattern. At the pioneer (or primary) stage, an ecosystem is populated by only a few different species (mostly weeds) and is characterized by uncomplicated interrelationships. This stage tends to be unstable and, as such, highly vulnerable to environmental stress. Barring severe environmental disturbances, however, the system gradually changes in species composition and ecosystem dynamics, until it reaches what is known as the 'climax' stage. At this stage, the ecosystem is stable and supports a large number of organisms with complex and diverse interrelationships. In other words, a mature ecological system is characterized by diversity, while the dynamic processes of energy flows and nutrient cycling continue. This built-in diversity is what makes the ecosystem in this mature stage quite resilient to changes in the physical environment (Holling 1997). However, it should be pointed out that there is controversy over the claim that ecological succession will eventually reach a steady-state stage that will persist indefinitely. The counter argument is that nature is never constant, and all ecosystems undergo continual change, such as from severe storms, floods or fire (Botkin and Keller 2003). Nevertheless, healthy and reasonably mature ecosystems tend to endure over relatively long time periods and are at least somewhat, if not completely, self-sustaining over several hundred years.

A good example of succession is abandoned farmland in the eastern United States. The first year after a cultivated field (such as corn) is abandoned, it tends to be populated by a few aggressive weedy plants that are sparsely distributed, exposing much of the soil to precipitation and intense heating (and evaporation) by the Sun during the day and maximum cooling at night. The rather small number of plants permits potential removal of soil nutrients through the physical processes of erosion and/or the chemical process of leaching. If left alone for a few years, this field is likely to become a dense meadow populated by a diversity of grasses, Queen Anne's lace and/or goldenrod. Still later, woody species (shrubs) such as blackberries or sumac begin to appear. These shrubby species typically grow taller than the herbaceous weeds of the meadow and may provide more shade than some meadow species can tolerate. At the same time, these woody shrubby species do not 'die back' to their roots each year; consequently, more of the mineral nutrients in the ecosystem remain in 'standing biomass' (organic material) rather than being returned to the soil through dead biomass.

After a few more years, deciduous tree species can be seen emerging above some of the shrubby species and patches of open meadow. As these grow above the shrubs, they typically produce more shade than the shrubs can tolerate and the shrubs will eventually die. The larger woody stems of tree species also result in more nutrients within the ecosystem being stored in standing biomass, with less in the soil, where it may be susceptible to loss by physical or chemical processes.

In this example, at least four different successional stages have been described: (a) an abandoned 'weedy' field (pioneer stage); (b) a meadow or 'old field' stage with abundant grasses and other herbs; (c) a shrubby community; and (d) a forest. Over time, the species composition of the forest is likely to change as well. But ultimately a forest type will develop where little change will be evident over long periods of time (centuries), barring major human influence or substantial climate change (possibly associated with glaciation or global warming). Such a community type is often referred to as the climax community.

An area that is covered by a given type of 'climax' community is often referred to as a *biome*. Much of the eastern United States is made up of the 'Eastern deciduous forest biome', whether it be the ancient forests of parts of the Appalachian Mountains that have never been cut or the cities of New York or Detroit which, if abandoned, eventually would most likely become deciduous forests. Other North American biomes include the 'prairies' of the Midwest, the 'conifer forests' of the Rocky Mountains and the deserts of the Southwest, among others.

The important lesson of succession is that an ecosystem is continually undergoing changes and the transitional time between successional changes may be considerable. The question is, then, how does the ecosystem maintain its equilibrium during this transitional period? In other words, once an ecosystem has achieved a certain developmental stage (in particular, the climax stage), how does it maintain its balance?

In the context of an ecological system, *equilibrium* refers to the apparent lack of visible changes in the biotic components of the system in spite of the many important interactions that continue to occur. As discussed above, ecological interrelationships are clear manifestations of the biological interdependencies among organisms. Depending on the stage of the ecological development of the given ecosystem, the biological interdependencies could be simple and represented by a food chain, or complex and characterized by a food web. To offer a simple example, suppose that due to a random natural event, the population of a certain organism (such as rabbits) starts to multiply at an above-normal rate. The immediate effect of this is an increase in the population of rabbits, which thereby creates a disturbance in the system. However, the disproportionate growth in the population of rabbits will eventually be suppressed by the limitation of food or an increase in the number of their predators as more of their prey become available. In general, then, in the biosphere equilibrium is attained through the reciprocal needs for food and other materials among organisms. In addition, as mentioned in the above discussion, in healthy ecosystems, elements and processes in the atmosphere, hydrosphere and lithosphere are maintained in long-run equilibrium states through various well-known material cycles; hence they are in dynamic equilibrium. However, as will be discussed shortly, human activities can disrupt these natural processes significantly.

In this subsection, so far we have covered some key ecological concepts such as succession, diversity, stability, resilience and equilibrium. These are interrelated concepts of major significance in understanding the limits or in defining the boundaries

of human co-existence with nature. Thus, it would be instructive to have a clearer understanding of each one of these concepts and how they are related to each other. This
will also help us discover and understand the nature of some important controversial
ecological issues such as *biodiversity*.

Earlier, succession was defined as the changes that occur naturally in the species
composition of an ecosystem over time. Generally, the time span is measured in terms
of tens or hundreds of years. It was also postulated that succession would eventually
lead to a 'climax' community. This last stage of succession is characterized by diversity:
complex and wide-ranging interrelationships among multitudes of species. Accordingly,
at the climax stage both the interrelationships and the number of species are near
maximum. Furthermore, increasing diversity was considered an important factor in
ecological stability, especially in the climax stage. The intuitive explanation for this is
that the more an ecosystem is characterized by wide-ranging interrelationships among
a large number of species, the lesser the effect of loss of a single species on the overall
structure and functioning of that ecosystem (Holling 1997).

Stability, as defined here, refers to the ability of a natural ecosystem to return to its
original condition after a change or disturbance. A system in dynamic equilibrium
inherently tends to be more stable than one in disequilibrium. The *resilience* of a system
refers to the rate at which a perturbed system will return to its original state (Holling
1997). The conventional wisdom seems to be that as succession proceeds there tends to
be an increase in stability, resilience, diversity, and complexity.

However, the seeds of many ecological controversies sprout from the lack of
general agreement about these generalizations (Holling 1997). These controversies are
fueled by different conclusions drawn from manipulated experiments versus natural
field studies. The differences are exacerbated further by the argument that the more
interconnected the components of the system are, the less stable the system is likely
to be. There can be major impacts on closely connected species, initiating a 'ripple
effect' through the system. Another case that can be made is that diversity does not
always lead to stability. Some of the more resilient ecosystems – the Arctic tundra,
for instance – are actually very simple. Suffice it to say that considerably more
research is necessary before these controversies can be resolved. An important
consideration in this discussion is that not only do we not understand clearly
how these factors are related, but also that we have relatively little knowledge of the
kinds or magnitudes of environmental changes that might lead to major ecosystem
disruptions (Holling 1997). This important point is particularly salient with regard to
actual and potential anthropogenic perturbations such as deforestation and global
warming. Our inability to predict what changes might occur as a result of such
human activities is cause of major concern. This concern is compounded when the
scientific uncertainty over the long-term effects of certain environmental problems
such as global warming is used to justify inaction.

Basic lessons: The various components of the biosphere (the ecosystems) go through
'developmental' stages leading to a mature ecosystem that supports a large diversity of
species with a web of interrelationships. These diverse interrelationships in turn make
the ecosystem quite resilient to changes in the physical environment. Thus, according
to the conventional wisdom, in nature it is through a diversity of relationships that
a particular ecosystem maintains stability. Included in these is diversity of producers,
consumers and decomposers.

2.5 Ecology and its implications for the human economy

So far, we have identified specific basic lessons that can be drawn from a focused study of some key sub-topics in ecology. In this section, an attempt will be made to discuss the broad implications that ecology may have for the functioning of the human economy. More specifically, the task is to show: (a) how the human economy is related (or interrelated) to the natural world when viewed from an ecological perspective; and (b) the fallacy of viewing natural resources simply as factors of production and with an infinite number of substitution possibilities. Another important point discussed in this section is the specific roles humans have played in modifying nature to their advantages, and the possible ramifications of these actions.

1   *The human economy is a subsystem of the biosphere.* Why is it so? A basic principle of ecology informs us that in a natural ecosystem everything is related to everything else. Hence, survival of the biosphere requires recognition of the mutual inter-dependencies among all the elements that constitute the biosphere. Strictly from an ecological viewpoint, then, the human economy cannot be viewed in isolation from natural ecosystem or the biosphere, as depicted in the circular diagram Figure 1.1 in Chapter 1 (Georgescu-Roegen 1993). Instead, the economy is a subsystem of the natural environment, which is both a source of its raw material inputs and as a 'sink' for its waste (output) as shown in Figure 2.1. As will be further explored in Chapters 12 and 13, this vision of the human economy as a subsystem of the biosphere has very profound implications – especially for the issue of 'optimal' scale, the size of human economy relative to the natural ecosystem.

2   *Natural resources cannot be viewed merely as factors of production.* As discussed before, from an ecological perspective the term natural resource refers to all of the elements that constitute the biosphere. In other words, natural resources include all the 'original' elements that comprise the Earth's natural endowments and life-support systems: the lithosphere, the hydrosphere and the atmosphere, together with radiation from the Sun. Furthermore, even from a purely anthropocentric perspective, some of the services provided by natural ecosystems include the items in Exhibit 2.2. An important implication of this is that it would be wrong to conceive of natural resources just as factors of production that can be directly used in the production and consumption processes of the human economy (see Chapter 1). This will be an important issue in Chapter 8, where valuation of environmental resources is the primary focus.

3   Ever since humankind acquired technology in the form of fire and stone tools, the pace of its dominance and exploitation of nature has been dramatic. In general, the consequences of continuous and rapid harvesting and mining of natural resources by humans have been twofold:

  • *Simplification of ecosystems.* As a whole, human actions can be looked at as efforts to simplify the biological relationships within ecosystems, to their own advantage (Miller 1991). By clearing land and planting crops or orchards, a complex and mixed flora of wild plants, which once extended over a wide area, is now replaced by a single kind of plant – monoculture (see Exhibit 2.3). To increase yield, fertilizers are applied to the soils, disrupting natural nutrient cycles. Competition from other organisms (insects, weeds and disease pests)

Exhibit 2.2 Nature's ecosystem services

- Raw materials production:
  food, fisheries, timber and building materials, nontimber forest products, fodder, genetic resources, medicines, dyes
- Pollination
- Biological control of pests and diseases
- Habitat and refuge
- Water supply and regulation
- Waste recycling and pollution control

- Nutrient cycling
- Soil building and maintenance
- Disturbance regulation
- Climate regulation
- Atmospheric regulation
- Recreation, cultural, educational/scientific

Source: Worldwatch Institute, *State of the World 1997*, p. 96. Copyright © 1997. Reprinted by permission.

is reduced or eliminated through biochemical poisoning, such as insecticides, herbicides and fungicides. The ultimate effect of all this is loss of biodiversity, which as Dasgupta *et al.* (2000: 343) pointed out, have the following sobering economic implications:

> To rely on substitutability among natural resources in commodity production to minimize the utilitarian importance of biodiversity, as is frequently done . . . is scientifically flawed. First, without biodiversity, substitutability is lost entirely. And more fundamentally, certain species and groups of species play unique roles in the functioning of ecosystems and thus have no substitutes. Preservation of biodiversity is hence important, both to provide unique services and to provide insurance against the loss of similarly functioning species.

- *Creation of industrial pollution (waste)*. No organism can function without creating waste. In a natural ecosystem, the normal amount of waste created by organisms poses no problem because, as noted earlier, one organism's waste is another's food. In this sense, in a well-functioning ecosystem there is no such thing as waste. In general, in their natural settings ecosystems are self-repairing, self-maintaining and self-regulating (Miller 1991). One could therefore infer from this that ecosystems are well prepared to handle major environmental stress caused by humankind. Why, then, are human-generated wastes a problem for ecosystems?

  Two explanations can be offered for this. First, as humankind has asserted its dominance by the rapid increase of its population, the amount of waste created by humans has increased at an alarming rate. The impacts of these increased volumes of waste have been intensified by continued human efforts to simplify the natural ecosystem, which have the undesirable effect of reducing the number of decomposers. Furthermore, beyond certain thresholds, increased waste could cause the total collapse of or irreversible damage to an ecosystem. Second, with advances in technology, humanity started to introduce wastes that were new to natural ecosystems (Commoner 1974). These human-made wastes, such as synthetic chemicals (e.g. plastics) and large doses of radiation – for

Exhibit 2.3   The Irish potato famine

Catharine Japikes

More than a million Irish people – about one in every nine – died in the Great Potato Famine of the 1840s. To the Irish, famine of this magnitude was unprecedented and unimaginable. . . .

When the famine hit in 1845, the Irish had grown potatoes for over 200 years – since the South American plant had first arrived in Ireland. During this time, the lower classes had become increasingly dependent on them. Potatoes provided good nutrition, so diseases like scurvy and pellagra were uncommon. They were easy to grow, requiring a minimum of labor, training and technology – a spade was the only tool needed. Storage was simple; the tubers were kept in pits in the ground and dug up as needed. Also, potatoes produce more calories per acre than any other crop that would grow in northern Europe.

To increase their harvest, farmers came to rely heavily on one variety, the lumper. While the lumper was among the worst-tasting types, it was remarkably fertile, with a higher per-acre yield than other varieties. Economist Cormac O Grada estimates that on the eve of the famine, the lumper and one other variety, the cup, accounted for most of the potato crop. For about three million people, potatoes were the only significant source of food, rarely supplemented by anything else.

It was this reliance on one crop – and especially one variety of one crop – that made the Irish vulnerable to famine. As we now know, genetic variation helps protect against the devastation of an entire crop by pests, disease or climate conditions. Nothing shows this more poignantly than Ireland's agricultural history.

In 1845, the fungus *Phytophthora infestans* arrived accidentally from North America. A slight climate variation brought the warm, wet weather in which the blight thrived. Much of the potato crop rotted in the fields. Because potatoes could not be stored longer than 12 months, there was no surplus to fall back on. All those who relied on potatoes had to find something else to eat.

The blight did not destroy all of the crop; one way or another, most people made it through winter. The next spring, farmers planted those tubers that remained. The potatoes seemed sound, but some harbored dormant strains of the fungus. When it rained, the blight began again. Within weeks the entire crop failed.

Although the potatoes were ruined completely, plenty of food grew in Ireland that year. Most of it, however, was intended for export to England. There, it would be sold – at a price higher than most impoverished Irish could pay. In fact, the Irish starved not for lack of food, but for lack of food they could afford.

The Irish planted over two million acres of potatoes in 1845, according to O Grada, but by 1847 potatoes accounted for only 300,000 acres. Many farmers who could turned to other crops. The potato slowly recovered, but the Irish, wary of dependence on one plant, never again planted it as heavily. The Irish had learned a hard lesson – one worth remembering.

Source: *EPA Journal* Vol. 20, Fall 1994, p. 44. Reprinted by permission.

which there exist few, if any, decomposers – continue to cause serious stresses on natural ecosystems. In other cases, relatively nontoxic wastes such as CO_2 may be produced in such large quantities that normal ecosystem processes cannot handle them, so they may accumulate (in this case potentially causing global warming and the altering of climate). The ultimate effect of such environmental stresses has been to lessen the productivity and diversity of natural ecosystems. Exhibit 2.4 shows how in Thailand waste resulting from a recent boom in commercial shrimp farming is causing ecological havoc. In this sense, purely from an ecological viewpoint, the natural disposition of the technological human has been to act as the breaker of climaxes. Such an act is clearly inconsistent with the sustainability of natural ecosystems.

To these broad implications should be added some important caveats.

In Chapter 1, a criticism was made of the economic perspective for treating the environment (the total of all ecosystems) as *external* to the human economy. In doing this, the *dynamic* links between the natural ecosystem and human economy are left out.

A closer look at the current paradigm in ecology reveals (as discussed above) that humans are treated as being an 'external disturbance' to natural ecosystems. O'Neill and Kahn (2000) recently wrote a rather interesting and thought-provoking article on the problem of ecology viewing human beings as just another biotic species within the ecosystem instead of an *external* influence. These authors suggest that humans should be viewed as an integral part of the total natural ecosystem (i.e. the biosphere). However, at the same time, on the basis of their interactions with other species and the environment, humans should be considered as a *keystone species*: a 'species that controls the environment and thereby determines the other species that can survive in its presence' (ibid.: 333).

What is notable here is a parallel between the treatment in ecology of humans as an external factor (disturbance) to natural ecosystems and the modern economic paradigm treatment of the natural environment as being external to the human economy. In both instances, the effect is to ignore the all-important *dynamic* links between the natural ecosystem and the human economy. The important message here is that human society and nature should be treated as *single dynamic entity*. This important subject will be addressed in some detail in Chapter 12.

2.6 Applying the tools: sustaining vision

This last section is an excerpt from an article by a well-known freelance writer on ecology and other related environmental issues, Michael Pollan, that appeared in the September 2002 edition of *Gourmet Magazine*. I decided to include this article in this chapter because it presents an illuminating case of applying the basic ecological principles discussed in this chapter.

> In the second day of spring, Joel Salatin is down on his belly getting the ant's-eye view of his farm. He invites me to join him, to have a look at the auspicious piles of worm castings, the clover leaves just breaking, and the two inches of fresh growth that one particular blade of grass has put on in the five days since this paddock was last grazed. Down here among the fescues is where Salatin makes some of his most important decisions, working out the intricate, multispecies grazing rotations that

Exhibit 2.4   Thailand's shrimp boom comes at great ecological cost

John McQuaid

Ban Lang Tha Sao, Thailand. Two years ago, Dulah Kwankha was toiling his life away in a rice paddy on the outskirts of his village, supporting his wife and three children with the $400 he earned each year. Then, in a story worthy of Horatio Alger, he became an entrepreneur and started earning six times that much. Dulah, 46, rode the economic wave that has swept up and down the Thai peninsula during the 1980s and 90s: shrimp farming.

With a $12,000 bank loan, backed by a Thai company, he converted his rice paddy into a shrimp pond that produces three crops a year, earning him $2,400. He now spends most of his time supervising the two villagers he pays to feed the shrimp, maintain the water flow and circulation, and harvest the black tiger prawns when they reach full size.

The succulent prawns, produced cheaply by farms like Dulah's, have flooded the US market in the past ten years and continue to gain popularity. To cash in, Thailand, Ecuador, China, Taiwan and other developing countries have thrown billions of dollars into shrimp farms. The shrimp-farming craze illustrates the power of the global marketplace to alter people's lives on opposite sides of the world, often for the worse.

Farmed shrimp has undercut the price of wild shrimp caught in the Gulf of Mexico, helping send a once-vital industry spiraling into economic decline. And it has brought the forces of capitalism to the doorsteps of subsistence farmers and fishers for the first time in history. Aquaculture has turned thousands of square miles of coastline in Thailand and other countries into humming engines of shrimp production.

But the price of this newfound wealth has been high. Cultures and values have been altered, often with devastating consequences. And in many places, the delicate ecologies that millions of people depend upon for their living are being ravaged by a headlong rush to collect on the world shrimp boom.

Every shrimp crop produces a layer of black sludge on the bottom of the pond – an unhealthy combination of fecal matter, molted shells, decaying food, and chemicals. It must be removed somehow – by bulldozer, hose or shovel – before the next crop cycle can begin.

There's no place to put it. So it is piled everywhere – by roadsides, in canals, in wetlands, in the Gulf of Thailand, on the narrow spits of land between the ponds. When it rains, the waste drains into the watershed, causing health problems. All along the coast, fishers say, the sludge, along with untreated or poorly treated shrimp farm waste water, has killed fish close to shore. Over time, a buildup of waste products from the ponds often renders them useless. When that happens, neither shrimp nor rice farming is possible.

The farms have other costs too, which may not become apparent for years. Nearly every tree in the shrimp farm zone has been uprooted or killed by polluted water. Many of those that remain are dying. There is literally nothing holding the land in place, and coastal erosion has increased dramatically in the past ten years, residents say. The intrusion of salt water has ruined rice paddies where they still exist.

have made Polyface one of the most productive, sustainable, and influential family farms in America.

This morning's inspection tells Salatin that he'll be able to move cattle into this pasture in a few days' time. They'll then get a single day to feast on its lush salad bar of grasses before being replaced by the 'eggmobile', a Salatin-designed-and-built portable chicken coop housing several hundred laying hens. They will fan out to nibble at the short grass they prefer and pick the grubs and fly larvae out of the cowpats – in the process spreading the manure and eliminating parasites. (Salatin calls them his sanitation crew.) While they're at it, the chickens will apply a few thousand pounds of nitrogen to the pasture and produce several hundred uncommonly rich and tasty eggs. A few weeks later, the sheep will take their turn here, further improving the pasture by weeding it of the nettles and nightshade the cows won't eat.

To its 400 or so customers – an intensely loyal clientele that includes dozens of chefs from nearby Charlottesville, Virginia, and Washington, DC – Polyface Farm sells beef, chicken, pork, lamb, rabbits, turkeys, and eggs, but if you ask Salatin what he does for a living, he'll tell you he's a 'grass farmer'. That's because healthy grass is the key to everything that happens at Polyface, where a half-dozen animal species are raised together in a kind of concentrated ecological dance on the theme of symbiosis. Salatin is the choreographer, and these 100 acres of springy Shenandoah Valley pasture comprise his verdant stage. By the end of the year, his corps de ballet will have transformed that grass into 30,000 pounds of beef, 60,000 pounds of pork, 12,000 broilers, 50,000 dozen eggs, 1,000 rabbits, and 600 turkeys – a truly astonishing cornucopia of food from such a modest plot of land. What's more, that land itself will be improved by the process. Who says there's no free lunch?

Sustainable is a word you hear a lot from farmers these days, but it's an ideal that's honored mostly in the breach. Even organic farmers find themselves buying pricey inputs – cow manure, Chilean nitrate, fish emulsion, biological insect controls – to replace declining fertility of the soil or to manage pest outbreaks. Polyface Farm isn't even technically organic, yet it is more nearly sustainable than any I've visited. Thanks to Salatin's deft, interspecies management of manure, his land is wholly self-sufficient in nitrogen. Apart from the chicken feed and some mineral supplements he applies to the meadows to replace calcium, Polyface supplies its own needs, year after year.

Salatin takes the goal of sustainability so seriously, in fact, that he won't ship his food – customers have to come to the farm and pick it up, a gorgeous adventure over a sequence of roads too obscure for my road atlas to recognize. Salatin's no shipping policy is what brought me here to Swoope, Virginia, a 45-minute drive over the Blue Ridge from Charlottesville. I'd heard rumors of Polyface's succulent grass-fed beef, 'chickenier' chicken, and the super-rich eggs to which pastry chefs attribute quasimagical properties – but Salatin refused on principle to FedEx me a single steak. For him, 'organic' is much more than a matter of avoiding chemicals. It extends to everything the farmer does, and Salatin doesn't believe food shipped cross-country deserves to be called organic. Not that he has any use for that label now that the USDA controls its meaning. Salatin prefers to call what he grows 'clean food', and the way he farms 'beyond organic'.

That it certainly is. The fact that Salatin doesn't spray herbicides and pesticides or medicate his animals unless they are ill is, for him, not so much the goal of his farming as proof that he's doing it right. And 'doing it right' for Salatin means simulating an ecosystem in all its diversity and interdependence, and allowing the species in it 'to fully express their physiological distinctiveness'. Which means that the cows, being herbivores, eat nothing but grass and move to fresh ground every day; and that chickens live in flocks of about 800, as they would in nature, and turkeys in groups of 100. And, as in nature, birds follow and clean up after the herbivores – for in nature there is no 'waste problem,' since one species' waste becomes another's lunch. When a farmer observes these rules, he has no sanitation problems and none of the diseases that result from raising a single species in tight quarters and feeding it things evolution hasn't designed it to eat. All of which means he can skip the entire menu of heavy-duty chemicals.

You might think every organic farm does this sort of thing as a matter of course, but in recent years the movement has grown into a full-fledged industry, and along the way the bigger players have adopted industrial methods – raising chickens in factory farms, feeding grain to cattle on feedlots, and falling back on monocultures of all kinds. 'Industrial organic' might sound like an oxymoron, but it is a reality, and to Joel Salatin industrial anything is the enemy. He contends that the problems of modern agriculture – from pollution to chemical dependence to food-borne illness – flow from an inherent conflict between, on one hand, an industrial mind-set based on specialization and simplification, and, on the other, the intrinsic nature of biological systems, whose health depends on diversity and complexity.

On a farm, complexity sounds an awful lot like work, and some of Salatin's neighbors think he's out of his mind, moving his cows every day and towing chicken coops hither and yon. 'When they hear "moving the cattle", they picture a miserable day of hollering, pick-up trucks, and cans of Skoal', Salatin told me as we prepared to do just that. 'But when I open the gate, the cows come running because they know there's ice cream waiting for them on the other side.' Looking more like a maitre d' than a rancher, Salatin holds open a section of electric fencing, and 80 exceptionally amiable cows – they nuzzle him like big cats – saunter into the next pasture, looking for their favorite grasses: bovine ice cream.

For labor, in addition to his six-foot, square-jawed, and red-suspendered self, the farm has Salatin's wife, Teresa (who helps run their retail shop and does the book-keeping), children Rachel and Daniel, and a pair of paid interns. (Polyface has become such a mecca for aspiring farmers that the waiting list for an internship is two years long.) Salatin, whose ever-present straw hat says 'I'm having fun' in a way that the standard monogrammed feed cap never could, insists, however, that 'the animals do all the real work around here'. So the chickens fertilize the cow pasture, the sheep weed it, the turkeys mow the grass in the orchard and eat the bugs that would otherwise molest the grapes, and the pigs well, the pigs have the sweetest job of all.

After we moved the cows, Salatin showed me the barn, a ramshackle, open-sided structure where 100 head of cattle spend the winter, every day consuming 25 pounds of hay and producing 50 pounds of waste. Every few days, Salatin adds another layer of wood chips or straw or leaves to the bedding, building a manure layer cake that's three feet thick by winter's end. Each layer he lards with a little corn. All winter the cake composts, producing heat to warm the barn and fermenting the corn. Why corn? There's nothing a pig likes more than 40-proof corn, and nothing he's better equipped to do than root it out with his powerful snout. So as soon as the cows go out to pasture in March, the 'pigerators', as Salatin calls them, are let loose in the barn, where they proceed systematically to turn and aerate the compost in their quest for an alcoholic morsel.

'That's the sort of farm machinery I like – never needs its oil changed, appreciates over time, and when you're done with it, you eat it.' Buried clear to their butts in compost, a bobbing sea of hams and corkscrew tails, these are the happiest pigs you'll ever meet. Salatin reached down and brought a handful of the compost to my nose; it smelled as sweet and warm as the forest floor in summertime, a miracle of trans-substantiation. After the pigs have completed their alchemy, Salatin spreads the compost on the pastures. There, it will feed the grasses so that the grasses might again feed the cows, the cows the chickens, and so on until the snow falls, in one long, beautiful, and utterly convincing proof that, in a world where grass can eat sunlight and food animals can eat grass, there is indeed a free lunch.

Did I mention that this lunch also happens to be delicious?

2.7 Chapter summary

- In this chapter it was noted that ecology studies the interrelationships between living organisms and their habitat, the physical environment. Since the key issue is always interrelation, the concept of a system is fundamental in any serious ecological study. Using the ecosystem as a framework, ecologists try to explain the general principles that govern the operation of the biosphere.
- The basic lessons of ecology are several. From a *purely* biophysical perspective (or biocentric view of the world), the most pertinent ones are:

    1   No meaningful hierarchical categorizations can be made among the living and nonliving components of an ecosystem because the physical environment and the living organisms are mutually interdependent.
    2   At a fundamental level, what goes on in 'living' natural ecosystems can be characterized as a continuous transformation of matter and energy. This transformation may be manifested in several ways, such as production, consumption, decomposition, recycling of matter, and the processes of life itself.
    3   Any ordinary transformation of matter–energy is governed by certain immutable natural laws, two of which are the first and second laws of thermo-dynamics. The first law informs us that there are *finite* stocks of resources (or a constant amount of matter) in the biosphere (the part of the universe where life as we know it is possible). The second law reminds us that since energy flows in only *one direction*, from useful to less useful forms, the continuing operation of any ecosystem requires a continuous input of energy from an external source. Usefulness is defined here in terms of the ability to do work – move or transform an object.
    4   Since matter is essentially constant in the biosphere, but used up in the process of transformation, the continuous functioning of an ecosystem requires that matter be recycled. In a natural ecosystem this is accomplished through a complex and interacting process of biogeochemical cycles.
    5   The species composition of a natural ecosystem undergoes gradual and evolutionary changes (succession). A mature ecosystem supports a great

        number of interdependent species. Although controversial, the conventional wisdom seems to suggest that ecosystems attain greater resilience as they continue to mature.

6   Ecosystems, however, are also systems of discontinuous changes. Disruptions resulting from external environmental factors (such as climate change) which affect extensive areas could have significant detrimental effects on species composition and the structure and functioning of the ecosystem.

•   Furthermore, in this chapter attempts were made to highlight some of the important links between ecology and economics. Among them are:

1   At a fundamental level, economics and ecology deal with common problems. That is, both disciplines deal with transformation of matter and energy.

2   However, this also means that, like that of the natural ecosystem, the operation of the human economy (as a subsystem of the entire Earth's ecosystem or the biosphere) must be subjected to the same natural laws governing the natural ecosystems. The implication of this is that the human economy must depend on the Earth's ecosystems for its basic material and energy needs.

•   Beyond this, on the basis of the materials discussed in this chapter, we were able to conclude the following:

1   Natural resources are finite. More specifically, the human economy is 'bounded' by a nongrowing and finite ecological sphere. This may be taken to imply that nature cannot be exploited without limits or the existence of a biophysical limit.

2   There are definite limits to conservation of energy through technological means (Second Law).

3   Throughout history, the tendency of humanity has been to lessen the resilience of the natural ecosystem, by either a *simplification* of the ecosystem (for example, modern agricultural practice) and/or the introduction and disposal of industrial wastes that are either persistent or totally foreign to a particular ecosystem(s). In the extreme cases, the threat here is loss of biodiversity and climate change.

4   The case study at the end of the chapter also shows that it is within human capability to design and practice agriculture that is sustainable – provided coexistence with nature is an important priority to humanity.

Review and discussion questions

1   Carefully review the following ecological concepts: ecosystem, primary producers, consumers, decomposers, photosynthesis, nitrogen fixation, ecological succession, biodiversity, ecological resilience, the first and second laws of thermodynamics, entropy, monoculture, keystone species.

2   What is the difference between an ecosystem structure and function? Could it serve any useful purpose except for that of pedagogical convenience?

3   State whether the following are *true*, *false* or *uncertain* and explain why.

    (a) Energy is the ultimate resource.

    (b) In principle, an ecosystem can continue to function without the presence of consumers.

(c) A mature ecosystem is complex, diverse, resilient and, as such, stable.

(d) Ecology and economics deal with production and distribution of valuable resources among complex networks of producers and consumers. Energy and material transformations underlie all these processes, and the fundamental constraints imposed by thermodynamics.

4   Identify three specific instances where human actions have led to what may be considered as losses of ecological resilience.

5   In his classic article 'The Historical Roots of Our Ecological Crisis' (1967), Lynn White, Jr. asserted that 'we shall continue to have a worsening ecological crisis until we reject the Christian axiom that nature has no reason for existence save to serve man'. Do you agree or disagree? Explain your position.

6   To what extent could a loss of biodiversity affect future potential for resource substitution possibilities? Do you think this potential economic value alone would be enough to pursue an aggressive biodiversity conservation initiative worldwide? Why or why not?

7   In the economic world, matter and energy are transformed for the purpose of creating utility (an enjoyment of life as understood and defined by humans) which is different from the biocentric perspective of the natural world where matter and energy are continually transformed for the purpose of sustaining life. Can these two perspectives be reconciled? Explain.

References

Botkin, D. B. and Keller, E. A. (2003) *Environmental Science*, 4th edn, John Wiley & Son, Inc.

Boulding, K. E. (1993) 'The Economics of the Coming Spaceship Earth', in H. E. Daly and K. N. Townsend (eds) *Valuing the Earth: Economics, Ecology, Ethics*, Cambridge, Mass.: MIT Press.

Commoner, B. (1974) *The Closing Circle: Nature, Man and Technology*, New York: Bantam Books.

Dasgupta, P., Levin, S. and Lubchenco, J. (2000) 'Economic Pathways to Ecological Sustainability', *BioScience* 54, 4: 339–45.

Georgescu-Roegen, N. (1993) 'The Entropy Law and the Economic Problem', in Daly, H. E. and Townsend, K. N. (eds) *Valuing the Earth: Economics, Ecology, Ethics*, Cambridge, Mass.: MIT Press.

Holling, C. S. (1997) 'The Resilience of Terrestrial Ecosystems: Local Surprise and Global Change', in Costanza, R., Perrings, C. and Cleveland, C. J. (eds) *The Development of Ecological Economics*, London: Edward Elgar.

Miller, T. G., Jr. (1991) *Environmental Science*, 3rd edn, Belmont, Calif.: Wadsworth.

Nordhaus, W. D. (1991) 'To Slow or Not to Slow: The Economics of the Greenhouse Effect', *Economic Journal* 6, 101: 920–37.

O'Neill, V. R. and Kahn, J. (2000) 'Homo economus as a Keystone Species', *BioScience* 50, 4: 333–7.

Pearce, D. W. (1978) *Environmental Economics*, 3rd edn, London: Longman.

Schneider, S. H. (1990) 'Debating Gaia', *Environment* 32, 4: 5–9, 29–30, 32.

White, L., Jr. (1967) 'The Historical Roots of Our Ecological Crisis', *Science* 55: 1203–7.

Part 2

The economics of the environment: theories and alternative public policy instruments

Part 2 comprises five chapters, Chapters 3–7. These chapters cover topics normally included in standard texts on environmental economics. Chapter 3 expounds two key elements of environmental economics: first, the key ecological and technological factors that are essential to understanding the trade-off between increased economic activity and environmental degradation; and second, the reasons why a system of resource allocation that is based on and guided by individual self-interest (hence, private markets) fails to account for the social costs of environmental damage – market failure. Chapter 4 develops theoretical models and economic conditions that can be used as a guide to control environmental pollution. In Chapters 5 and 6 a number of pollution-control policy instruments are thoroughly discussed and evaluated. Finally, Chapter 7 focuses on pollution problems with transboundary and global dimensions; more specifically, acid rain, the depletion of ozone and global warming.

As mentioned above, the chapters in Part 2 employ the same organizing principles as standard texts on environmental economics. However, while the general approaches used in these chapters have the appearance of following the standard treatment of these subjects in economics, a careful reading of each chapter reveals a departure of some significance from the norm. This difference stems from conscious efforts to insert ecological perspectives relevant to the main topics addressed in each chapter. These efforts were not made casually. In general, the approach taken is first to present the topic under consideration using the standard economic treatment, and then to follow this with critical appraisals of the main conclusions on the basis of their conformity or departure from what would have been realized if sufficient attention had been paid to ecological perspectives on this same subject matter.

3 Fundamentals of the economics of environmental resources

The 'optimal' trade-off between environmental quality and economic goods

3.1 Introduction

In Chapter 1, it was pointed out (see Figure 1.1) that the natural environment serves the human economy in three distinct ways: (i) as a source for both renewable and non-renewable extractive resources; (ii) as a provider of environmental amenities and ecosystem services; and (iii) as a decomposer and a place of storage for various types of wastes generated by normal economic activities.

In this chapter the focus is on developing fundamental ecological and economic principles to help us understand the extent to which the natural environment (in the form of water, air or landmass) can be used to assimilate or store industrial waste. 'Proper' management of the environment to this end requires two considerations be met. There should be:

1   A clear understanding of the nature of the *waste-absorptive capacity* of the natural environment under consideration. This issue is addressed in Section 3.2 using a simple model, with the objective of identifying certain key ecological and techno-logical factors that are essential in understanding the relationship between increased economic activity and the waste-absorptive capacity of the environment. This simple model also illustrates, at least theoretically, some of the factors involved in determining the *ecological threshold* of the natural environment in its capacity to absorb waste.

2   A mechanism by which to identify the *costs* (degradation of environmental quality) and the *benefits* (the production of more goods and services) resulting from the incremental use of the natural environment as a repository for industrial and municipal wastes. *In other words, what is involved here is the identification of the trade-off between economic goods and environmental quality at the margin.* This trade-off is vividly depicted in Figure 3.1. This shows on the one hand that economic well-being or *utility* is derived from the production of goods and services that are ultimately consumed by households. On the other hand, the production of goods and services necessarily causes emission of waste that causes the deterio-ration of the natural environment, hence, a negative utility. Therefore, on balance, economic well-being requires making a conscious trade-off between goods and services and environmental quality.

In this chapter, the trade-off between the production of goods and services and environmental quality is studied from both micro- and macroeconomic vantage points.

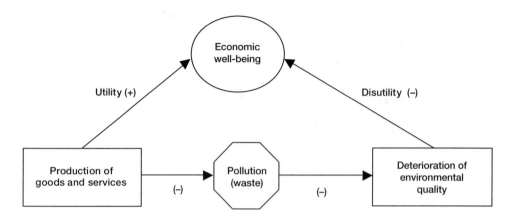

Figure 3.1 Trade-off between goods and services and environmental quality. An economic activity (production of goods and services) is expected to generate utility (economic well-being) when it is eventually consumed by households. At the same time, given that pollution is an undesirable byproduct of production activities, households' economic well-being would be negatively impacted due to a deterioration in environmental quality.

The microeconomic aspects of the issue deal with the development of the general theoretical condition for securing the 'optimal' environmental quality. This topic is dealt with in Section 3.3. At the macroeconomic level, the focus is on assessing the costs of ascertaining the 'desired' environmental quality in terms of unemployment and inflation. This is dealt with in Section 3.4.

3.2 The economic process and the assimilative capacity of the natural environment

We all want to protect the purity and vitality of our air and water, and the natural landscape. However, despite our desire to do so, as long as we are engaged in transforming material inputs (land, labor, capital, and raw materials) into economic goods, we cannot avoid creating residuals (the second law of matter and energy). These residuals (low entropic matter–energy) of the economic process are commonly referred to as *pollution*. Pollution then, is, an inevitable byproduct of economic activities.

Furthermore, by the first law of matter and energy, we know that this residual has to go somewhere. That 'somewhere' comprises the various media of the natural environment – air, water and/or the landscape. It is in this way that the natural environment is used as a repository for wastes generated through the economic process. In general, however, disposal in this way should pose no problem if done in moderation. This is because, as noted in Chapter 2, the natural environment has a decomposer population which, given adequate time, will transform the waste into harmless material, and/or return it as a nutrient to the ecosystem. *This self-degrading ability of the natural environment is commonly referred to as its assimilative capacity.* It should not be surprising, then, that from the viewpoint of environmental management, the quality of a particular environmental medium (air, water, land) is determined by its capacity to assimilate (degrade) waste.

In discussing the assimilative capacity of the natural environment, *three* important factors should be noted.

First, like anything else in nature, the assimilative capacity of the environment is *limited*. Thus, the natural environment cannot be viewed as a bottomless sink. With respect to its capacity to degrade waste, the natural environment is, indeed, a *scarce resource*.

Second, the assimilative capacity of the natural environment depends on the *flexibility* of the ecosystem and the *nature* of the waste. That is, the natural environment will not degrade any and all waste with equal efficiency (Pearce 1978). For example, the natural environment can deal with *degradable pollutants*, such as sewage, food waste, papers, etc., with relative ease. On the other hand, it is quite ineffective in dealing with *persistent or stock pollutants*, such as plastics, glass, most chemicals, and radioactive substances. For most of these waste elements there are no biological organisms currently in existence that can accelerate the degradation process. Thus, a very long period of time is required before these wastes can be rendered harmless.

Third, the *rate* at which the waste is discharged greatly affects the ability of the environment to degrade residuals. The implication of this is that pollution has a *cumulative* ecological effect. More specifically, *pollution reduces the capacity of an environmental medium to withstand further pollution* (Pearce 1978).

The obvious lesson is that, in managing the natural environment, it is crucial to give careful consideration to the *quality* of the waste, its *quantity* and the *rate* at which it is disposed of into the environment. To understand the significance of this point, the following simple model can be used. It is assumed that a *linear* relationship exists between waste and economic activity. Furthermore, this relationship is expected to be *positive* – that is, more waste is associated with increasing levels of economic activity. Mathematically, the general form of the functional relationship between waste emission into the environment and economic activity can be expressed as

$$W = f(X, t) \tag{3.1}$$

Or, in explicit functional form, as

$$W = \beta X \tag{3.2}$$

where W is the level of waste generated and X is the level of economic activity (i.e. production of goods and services). The variable t in equation (3.1) represents technological and ecological factors.

Equation (3.2) depicts the simple linear relationship we assumed between waste and economic activity, *holding the variable t at some predetermined level*. In equation (3.2), β represents the slope parameter, and is assumed to be positive. Also, the fact that the above linear equation has no intercept term suggests that only waste generated from economic activity, X, is considered relevant in this model. The relationship shown in equation (3.2) can be presented graphically, as shown in Figure 3.2A. In this figure, the x-axis shows the level of economic activity (in terms of production of goods or services) and the y-axis represents the quantity (volume) of waste disposed into the environment in some unspecified unit. The broken horizontal line, W_0, represents an additional assumption that was made to complete the basic framework of this simple model. This line is assumed to represent the total amount of waste that the environment could assimilate at a given point in time. Note also that to the extent that W_0 is positive, strictly speaking this model deals with *degradable* pollutants only. What general conclusions can be reached from this simple model? In response to this question, *four* points can be made.

First, given that the assimilative capacity is invariant at W_0, X_0 represents the maximum amount of economic activity that can be undertaken without materially affecting the natural environment. The waste generated at this level of economic activity will be completely degraded through a natural process. Thus, from this observation we can draw the general conclusion that a certain minimum amount of economic goods, such as X_0 in Figure 3.2A, can be produced without inflicting damage on the natural environment. Thus, X_0 indicates an *ecological threshold* of economic activity.

Second, increased economic activity beyond X_0 would invariably lead to an accumulation of unassimilated waste in the natural environment. Although it may not be fully captured by the above simple model, the effect of this accumulated waste on environmental quality (damage) will be *progressively higher* because, as indicated earlier, pollution reduces the capacity of an environment to withstand further pollution. As shown in Figure 3.2B, the ultimate impact of this dynamic ecological effect would be to shift the assimilative capacity of the environment – the broken horizontal line – downward.

The third point that can be conveyed using the above model is how *technological* factors may affect the ecological threshold of economic activity. The effect of techno-logical change could take two forms:

(a) Through technology the decomposition process may be accelerated. Note that in our simple model, this type of change is captured by the variable t. For example, using activated charcoal in a sewage treatment facility can accelerate the decompo-sition process of municipal waste. This amounts to an artificial enhancement of the assimilative capacity of the environment. Therefore, in Figure 3.2A the effect of this type of technological change would be to shift the dotted line upward, indicating an increase in the assimilative capacity of the environment. Other factors remaining equal, this would have the effect of increasing the ecological threshold of economic activity to something greater than X_0.

(b) A change in technology may also alter the relationship between the level of economic activity, X, and the rate at which waste is discharged into the natural environment. In our simple model this would be indicated by a change in the slope parameter, ß. For example, a switch from high to low sulfur content coal in the production of electricity would lower the amount of sulfur emitted into the environment per kilowatt-hour of electricity produced, X. In this case the ultimate effect would be to lower the value of the slope parameter, ß. As shown in Figure 3.2C, this entails a clockwise rotation of the line depicting the relationship between waste and economic activity. Again, if other factors are held constant, the overall effect of this type of technological change is to increase the ecological threshold of economic activity. *Thus, the implication here is that we can, to a certain degree, augment the ecological threshold of the natural environment by means of*

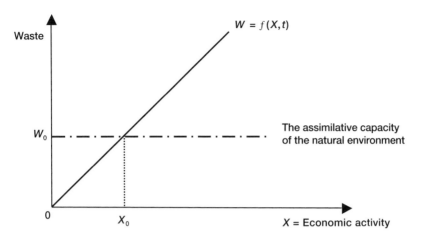

Figure 3.2A A simple relationship between economic output and waste discharge. Below X_0 level of economic activity, waste generated through economic activity is less than the natural assimilative capacity of the environment (W_0). Thus, economic activity up to the level X_0 would not lead to a deterioration of environmental quality. Environmental quality will start to suffer when economic activity is pursued beyond this threshold level of economic activity, X_0.

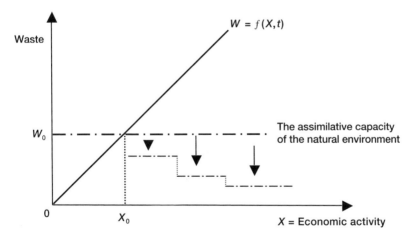

Figure 3.2B Possible dynamic effects on the assimilative capacity of the environment when waste accumulation is allowed to exceed the ecological threshold, holding all other factors constant. The reason for this apparent successive downwards tendency in the assimilative capacity of the environment is to reflect the notion that pollution tends to reduce the capacity of an environment to withstand further pollution.

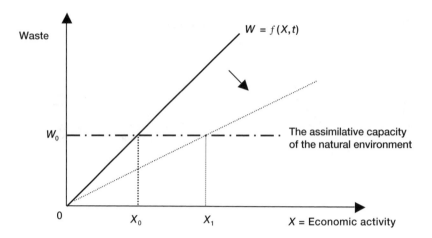

Figure 3.2C The effect of technology on the relationship between economic output and waste discharge *per unit* of output, β. A reduction in the value of β (lower environmental impact on a per unit basis) indicates an increase in the economic threshold activities from X_0 to X_1.

technology. As discussed above, the technological improvement could be triggered either by an improvement in waste processing or by input switching.

However, as Commoner (1971) warned us, technological solutions to environmental problems can have harmful side effects (more on this in Chapter 10). For example, at the local level, increasing the height of factory smokestacks can substantially alleviate the problem of acid deposition (acid rain in dry form) arising from sulfur dioxide emission. The intended effect of this is to emit a good share of the pollutants into the higher strata of the atmosphere. This would amount to solving the problem of pollution through *dilution*. However, as it turns out, what this does is to change the local pollution problem into a transboundary acid rain problem (more on this in Chapter 7). *The important lesson here is that technological projects intended to address environmental concerns should not be implemented without careful consideration of their potential side effects.*

The fourth and final point that should be noted is that, as discussed earlier, the natural environment will not degrade all waste with equal efficiency. In some instances the assimilative capacity of the natural environment could be, if not zero, then insignificant. In Figure 3.2, this situation would mean that the broken horizontal line representing the assimilative capacity of the natural environment would be closer to, or could even coincide with, the *x*-axis. In this situation, the ecological threshold of economic activity would, for all practical purposes, be *zero*.

We can draw a number of important lessons from the discussion in this section.

*   The natural environment has a limited capacity to degrade waste. The implication of this observation is that, in purely physical (not necessarily economic) terms, the waste assimilative capacity of the natural environment is a *scarce* resource.

- A certain minimum amount of economic goods can be produced without causing damage to the natural environment. Thus, zero pollution is not only a physical impossibility, but even on purely ecological considerations, it is an unnecessary goal to pursue.
- Although the above simple model does not adequately capture this, the cumulative effect of waste discharge into the natural environment is *nonlinear*. This is because pollution tends to reduce the capacity of an environment to withstand further pollution.
- The ecological threshold of economic activity (X_0 in Figure 3.2C) can be augmented by technological means.

These observations are based on a simple but careful conceptual analysis of the various factors affecting the relationships between the level of economic activity and the damage this action inflicts on the natural environment. However, so far nothing specific has been said about the trade-off between economic activity (the production of goods and services) and environmental quality. *This issue becomes relevant when the level of economic activity, as is often the case, extends beyond a certain ecological threshold* (e.g. X_0 in Figure 3.2A). This is, indeed, a key issue that will occupy much of the next section.

3.3 Why markets may fail to allocate environmental resources optimally

One important lesson we have learned from the discussion so far is that the natural environment has a limited capacity to degrade waste. To that extent, then, the natural environment is a scarce resource. Given this, it would be in the best interest of any society to manage its natural environment *optimally*. This entails that, as for any other scarce resource, the services of the natural environment as a repository of waste should be considered by taking full account of all the *social* costs and benefits. Could this be done through the normal operations of the market system? A complete response to this question, first and foremost, requires a clear understanding of certain complications associated with assignment of *ownership rights* to environmental resources. This is the subject of the next subsection.

3.3.1 Common property resources and the economic problem

In Appendix A, it was established that under a perfectly competitive market setting, resource allocation through a private market economy would lead to what is considered to be a socially optimal end. It was also demonstrated that the allocation of any scarce resource is socially optimal when, for the last unit of the resource under consideration, the marginal social benefit is equal to the marginal social cost ($MSB = MSC$).

How could a market economy that is primarily activated by decisions of private actors seeking to promote their own self-interest lead to a socially optimal result? In other words, what is the magic at work in transforming self-interest into social interest? To Adam Smith, *this magic is 'invisible' yet real, provided the actors in the market have indisputable rights to the use and disposal of all the resources that they are legally entitled to own.* In other words, for Adam Smith's Invisible Hand to operate, resource ownership must be clearly defined.

What exactly do we mean by a clearly defined ownership right? From the perspective of resource allocation, the ownership of a resource is said to be clearly defined if it satisfies four conditions (Randall 1987).

- First, the ownership rights of the resource are *completely specified*. That is, its quantitative and qualitative features as well as its boundaries are clearly demarcated.
- Second, the rights are completely *exclusive* so that all benefits and costs resulting from an action accrue directly to the individual empowered to take action.
- Third, the ownership rights of the resource are *transferable*. In other words, resources can be exchanged or simply donated at the 'will' of their owners.
- Finally, ownership is *enforceable*. That is, ownership of resources is legally protected.

When these four conditions are met, it can be shown that reliance on the self-interest-based behavior of individuals will ensure that resources are used where they are most valued.

An example of a resource that satisfies the above four criteria is the ownership of a private car. The ownership manual, together with the car registration, completely specifies the contents, model, color, and other relevant characteristics of the car. On the car's registration document, the authority of the state confirms the owner's exclusive legal right to the car. Therefore, no one else is allowed to use this car without proper permission from the owner. Once exclusive ownership is attained, it is in the owner's interest to adhere to a regularly scheduled maintenance program for the car, since failure to do so would cost no one else but the owner. Last but not least, the owner of the car can enter into voluntary trade or exchange of the car at any point in time. Furthermore, should the owner decide to sell the car, it would be in the owner's best interest to sell it at the highest possible price. *The ultimate effect of this process is to assure that ownership of a car will gravitate toward those individuals who value it the most (or are willing to bid the highest price).*

In the real world, not all resources satisfy the above ownership conditions. For example, a lake shared by all residents living in the surrounding area will not satisfy the second and third of the conditions set out above. In this case, the lake is a resource that is owned in common by all users living within a given geographic boundary line. Another example is the ambient air of a certain locality or region. In this case, none of the above four conditions could be completely satisfied. The ambient air is common property owned by everyone, and on practical grounds it is owned by no one – a clear case of *res nullius*. As you can see from these two examples, environmental resources, such as the ambient air and water bodies (lake, rivers, ocean shorelines, etc.), tend to be common property resources. By their very nature, the ownership of these resources cannot be clearly defined.

The question then is, what happens to private markets as a medium for resource allocation in situations where ownership rights of a resource(s) cannot be clearly delineated? The implications of this question can be seen by considering the hypothetical situation presented in Exhibit 3.1. This demonstrates how a valuable asset like a car can be reduced to valueless junk when it is perceived as a common property resource. In general, a closer look at a situation of this nature brings two important points into focus.

Exhibit 3.1   When a car turns into trash

Assume for a moment that you are a resident of a small island nation with a population of only 150,000. The families of this nation are economically well off and most of them own at least one car. The nation hardly uses public transportation. Now, imagine that one morning you wake up at your usual time, around 6:30 am, and you hear on the radio that the government has passed a law that completely revokes the private ownership of a car. The public announcement also states that the government has issued a master key that will run any car on the street, and such a key is to be found on the doorstep of each individual household. Of course, your first reaction would be to think that this is just a dream. However, the public announcement is so incessant and firm that it leaves you no chance of ignoring the event, of taking it as just a dream.

As shocking and disturbing as this event may be, let us assume that the people of this nation are so nonviolent that no visible disturbance occurs as a result of this draconian action. Instead, perhaps grudgingly, the people make the necessary efforts to deal with the prevailing situation. What is the situation? First, people still need a car to go to work, to shop, to visit friends and relatives, etc. Second, the citizens of this nation have no access to public transportation. Third, by government decree every citizen has free access to the cars that currently exist on the island. What will happen to the use and maintenance of cars in this society under these circumstances?

At first, people will start by driving a car that is within easy reach of them. Once they reach their destination, they will leave the car knowing full well that the same car may not be available for their next use. For how long would this pattern of car use continue? Not for long. This is because people would not have any incentive to properly maintain the cars. Who would fill a car with gasoline knowing that any amount left unused from a one-way trip might never be recouped? What would happen to cars should they run out of gas in the middle of a highway? Furthermore, who would have the incentive to pay for regularly needed maintenance, such as oil changes, tune-ups, etc.?

What would happen to the cars that simply ceased running because of mechanical problems? The answer to all these questions is that *in a short while, in this island nation cars would be transformed from being commodities of great value to valueless debris scattered all over the traffic arteries of the nation.* Of course, the root cause of this undesirable end is the treatment of cars as common property with free access for all. As Garrett Hardin (1968: 1244) elegantly puts it, 'Ruin is the destination toward which all men rush, each pursuing his own best interest in a society that believes in the freedom of the commons. Freedom in a commons brings ruin to all.' Clearly, from the perspective of environmental and natural resource management, the implications of this conclusion are quite significant. After all, what is at stake is the vitality and integrity of the global commons: the ambient air, most rivers, the shorelines, the oceans, etc.

First, for the commons, economic pursuit on the basis of individual self-interest would not lead to what is best for society as a whole. In other words, the principle of Adam Smith's Invisible Hand would be violated.

Second, if tragedy is to be averted, the use of commons needs to be regulated by a 'visible hand' (Hardin 1968).

At conceptual level, these two points represent the *core* issues of environmental economics. The next subsection provides the analytical and conceptual framework used to address these core issues at the very fundamental level.

3.3.2 Environmental externalities and their economic consequences

It was noted above that Adam Smith's fundamental theorem of the Invisible Hand would fail when resource ownership is defined in such a way that individuals could not take account of the full benefits or costs of their actions. This will happen *not* because the costs or benefits are not real. Instead, in this situation, the costs and benefits would be treated as incidental or external. A technical term used to describe this situation is *externality*. Formally, we define externalities as conditions arising when the actions of some individuals have direct (negative or positive) effects on the welfare or *utility* of other individuals, none of whom have direct control over that activity. In other words, externalities are incidental benefits or costs to others for whom they are not specifically intended.

Two classic examples of externality are described by the following cases. One is represented by the action of an *avid gardener* who invests in the beautification of her or his own property and, in so doing, raises the property values of the surrounding houses. A second example is represented by a *fish hatchery plant* that has to bear the cleanup costs for wastes discharged by a *paper mill* located upstream. In the first example, the neighbors are gaining *real* external benefits (positive externalities) without sharing the costs of the actions that yielded the beneficial result(s). In the second case, the cleanup cost to the hatchery is external (negative externality) because it is the result of an action imposed by a third party, in this case the paper mill.

What are the main sources of externalities? Let us use the classic examples above to answer this question. In the first example, no assumption is made that the benefits to the neighbors have resulted from a benevolent act by the gardener. On the contrary, the assumption is that the gardener's investment, in terms of both time and monetary outlays in the beautification of her or his property, is done on the basis of cost–benefit calculations that are consistent with any investor's self-interest. However, the fruit of this investment is an 'aesthetic enhancement' or 'environmental amenity' that has peculiar characteristics when viewed as an economic commodity. This commodity is *nonrival* in consumption. That is, once it is produced, the consumption of this commodity, say by the neighbors or any passers-by, would not reduce its utility for the gardener. Therefore, when such a commodity is produced, it makes no economic sense to exclude anyone from the use (consumption) of such an activity. Of course, in our simple example, the gardener, if she or he wishes, could exclude the neighbors by building a tall concrete wall around the house. However, this would not be achieved without additional cost. The most commonly used economic jargon to describe the costs associated with internalizing (remedying) externalities is *transaction costs*. In broad terms, transaction costs include any outlay expended for the purpose of specifying property ownership, excluding nonusers and enforcing property rights. This would be the intended effect if, in fact, the gardener in our example decided to erect a concrete wall around her or his clearly identified property line.

To summarize, the basic lesson we can draw from the first example, a private garden, is that an externality arises when the use by others of property (resources) is difficult to exclude. This difficulty may result from one of two possible sources. First, the resource by its very nature may be nonrival in consumption, and hence subject to *joint consumption*. Second, for either natural or technical reasons, the transaction cost of internalizing the externality may be excessively high (Coase 1960).

In the second example, the hatchery, the externality arises from the fact that the owners of the hatchery plant do not have the legal right to stop the operators of the paper mill from dumping their industrial wastes in the *river*. For that matter, since the river is viewed as *common property*, no one can be excluded from using it. Thus, similar to our first example, the nonexclusive use of the river is what causes an externality to persist. The only difference is the source of nonexclusiveness. In the first case, nonexclusiveness resulted from the fact that the resource under consideration is nonrival, and thus is subject to joint consumption. In our second example, non-exclusiveness resulted from the fact that the ownership of the resource under consideration (the river) was not clearly defined – that is, it is common property. Hence, from these two examples we can generalize that, in the final analysis, *lack of excludability* (nonexclusiveness) is the root cause of externality (Randall 1983). Most, if not all, environmental resources are externality-ridden for this very reason.

What is the economic consequence of an externality? Given what we have discussed so far, this is a simple question to answer. *In the presence of real externalities, there will be a divergence between private and social evaluations of costs and benefits* (Turvey 1963). In general, we can expect the following relationships to hold:

(a) In a situation where a *positive* externality is present (the first example above):

  Social benefits = Private benefits + External benefits

and

  External benefits > 0

Therefore,

  Social benefits > Private benefits

(b) In a case where *negative* externality prevails (the second example above):

  Social costs = Private costs + External costs

and

  External costs > 0

Therefore,

  Social costs > Private costs.

What we infer from the above series of relationships is that in the presence of an externality, we expect to observe a clear *divergence* between social and private benefits and social and private costs. Under these conditions, resource allocation through a

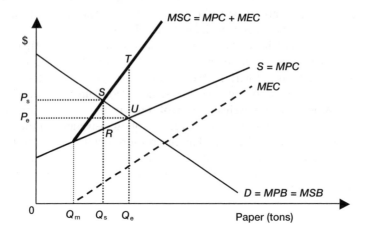

Figure 3.3 Social optimum in the presence of externality: the case of a hypothetical paper industry. Social optimum is attained when *MSC* = *MSB* and this does not coincide with the intersection point of the demand and the supply curves. The reason for this is the divergence between the marginal private cost (the ordinary supply curve) and the marginal social cost – which explicitly accounts for the cost of externality.

market mechanism – i.e. one that is based solely on consideration of private costs and benefits – would be inefficient when viewed from the perspective of society at large. This constitutes a clear case of *market failure* because the market, if left alone, lacks any mechanism by which to account for external costs and/or benefits.

Equipped with a clear understanding of the factors contributing to market failure, we are now in a position to examine why the allocation of environmental goods and services through market mechanisms leads to suboptimal results. This will be demonstrated using the hypothetical case of not just a single paper mill but all the firms of a paper mill industry. It is assumed that all firms in this industry are located along river banks and use rivers as a means of disposing of their industrial waste.

In Figure 3.3, curve *D* represents the market demand for paper. As discussed in Appendix A (Section 3), a demand curve such as *D* represents the marginal private benefit to consumers, *MPB*. In a situation where external benefit is zero (i.e. there are no positive externalities), a demand curve represents both the marginal private and the social benefits. This is assumed to be the case in Figure 3.3 (*D* = *MPB* = *MSB*).

The complication arises when considering the supply curve of paper. For the paper industry, the supply curve, *S*, represents the marginal private costs (*MPC*) of producing varying levels of paper. These costs represent the firms' expenditures on all priced inputs (i.e. labor, capital, raw materials, and the services of any resources owned by the owners of the firms in this industry). However, in the process of producing paper, firms are assumed to use rivers to dispose of their production waste at no cost. Thus, no such cost appears in the balance sheets of the firms in this hypothetical paper industry, and therefore no disposal cost forms part of the firm's supply curve, *S*, in Figure 3.3.

However, as explained in Section 3.2, the discharge of waste to a river would cause damage costs beyond a certain threshold level (see X_0 in Figure 3.2A). In Figure 3.3, this damage cost is represented by the broken curve labeled *MEC – marginal external cost*. This cost represents the monetary value of pollution damage imposed on society by the paper mill industry.

At this stage it is important to note the two important features of the *MEC* curve in Figure 3.3:

1   The marginal external costs do not start to materialize until the paper industry reaches a production level of Q_m. This is because, consistent with our earlier discussion, a certain minimum amount of output can be produced by the paper industry without materially affecting the quality of the environment (the river).
2   The marginal external cost curve, as shown in Figure 3.3, is expected to be positively sloped. That is, beyond Q_m, further increases in the production of paper (hence, more waste discharge) would be associated with external costs that tend to increase at an increasing rate. This is because, as discussed earlier, pollution reduces the capacity of an environment to withstand further pollution.

As shown in Section 4 of Appendix A, *efficiency* in resource allocation requires that *MSC* = *MSB*. In Figure 3.3 this condition would be met when the level of paper production was Q_s. Note that the marginal social cost curve (*MSC*) in Figure 3.3 is obtained by the vertical summation of the marginal private and marginal external cost curves (i.e. *MPC* + *MEC*). However, if decisions about production of paper were made through a freely operating market mechanism, the optimal level of production would have been Q_e, where *MPB* = *MPC*. Clearly, then, the market solution would fail to achieve the level of paper production that is consistent with what is considered to be socially optimal. More specifically, the tendency would be for the market to produce *more* paper than is socially desired. This can be explained by showing that society would stand to gain if, in fact, the production of paper were reduced from Q_e to Q_s. In other words, the market solution is *not* efficient.

If the production of paper were reduced from Q_e to Q_s, the total cost savings as a result of this move would be represented by the area under the social marginal cost curve, Q_eTSQ_s. This total social cost is composed of the total private costs as represented by the area under the marginal private cost curve, Q_eURQ_s, and the total external costs as represented by the area *UTSR*. On the other hand, by reducing the production of paper from Q_e to Q_s society would incur a loss in benefits. The lost benefits to society as a result of this particular move would be measured by the area Q_eUSQ_s – the area under the marginal social benefit curve. Stated differently, this represents the forgone consumers' benefit resulting from a reduction of paper production from Q_e to Q_s. Clearly, then, in reducing the production of paper from Q_e to Q_s, the total cost saving, area Q_eTSQ_s, exceeds the total forgone benefit area Q_eUSQ_s. Thus, the final outcome of this move represents a net cost saving measured by the area of the triangle *UTS*. Therefore, since a move away from the market solution represents a clear gain to society, the market solution, Q_e, is *not* Pareto optimal. Note that the market's inability to deliver the socially optimal solution arises from the fact that it has no automatic mechanism to account for the external costs. In Figure 3.3 area *UTSR* represents the total external costs that would be unaccounted for by the market. This cost is a measure of the imputed value of the additional environmental service (of the river) required if the production of paper is expanded from Q_s to Q_e.

What exactly is the implication of this analysis for environmental quality? The answer is rather straightforward. Assuming the amount of waste dumped in the river is directly proportional to the amount of paper produced, the market solution, Q_e, would be associated with a higher level of pollution than the socially optimal level of output, Q_s. *What this suggests is that the market, if left alone, would lead to lower environmental quality.*

At this stage it is instructive to see what general conclusions we can draw from the analysis presented thus far. In the presence of an externality, resource allocation through the guidance of a free-market system would lead to inefficiency. More specifically, because the market lacks a mechanism by which to account for external costs, it tends to favor more production of goods and services from industries inflicting damage to the natural environment. Thus, the presence of real externality results in a misallocation of societal resources.

The question, then, is what can be done to correct the misallocation of resources caused by environmental externalities? Does it require a minor or a major modification of the market system? In responding to these questions, the key issue at hand is to find the most effective way(s) of internalizing the externality. Some argue that, on the whole, there are *no* technical solutions to environmental externalities (Hardin 1968). In other words, externalities cannot be effectively internalized through voluntary private negotiation among the parties involved. Thus, according to this view, the only way to resolve environmental externalities effectively is through *coercive* methods (Hardin 1968). Among others, such methods include opting for public ownership of environmental resources, imposing environmental taxes or setting emission standards. These measures may entail direct or indirect interference with the operation of a private free market economy. For that reason, they are not generally favored by mainstream economists.

Mainstream economists would take the position that environmental externalities can be effectively remedied provided property rights are clearly defined. Thus, the role of a public agent (the government) is to assign rights to someone when an item of property lacks ownership. Once this is accomplished, the Invisible Hand will guide the market to allocate resources efficiently (Coase 1960). According to this view, then, internalization of environmental externalities requires minimal and very indirect government involvement. An extensive analysis of the various alternative methods of internalizing or correcting environmental externalities is given in Chapters 5 and 6.

This completes the exposition of the microeconomic aspects of the environmental issues to be presented in this chapter. We now turn to macroeconomic issues that attempt to explain the trade-offs society has to make between economic goods and higher environmental quality. Although, pedagogically, it makes sense to discuss the macroeconomic effects of environmental regulations right now, a good case can also be made to defer the discussion of this topic until a thorough analysis of environmental regulations is presented in Chapters 5 and 6. I will leave this choice to the individual reader.

3.4 The macroeconomic effects of environmental regulations: an overview

So far we have observed that, if not corrected, environmental externalities will cause a misallocation of resources. More specifically, from a societal viewpoint too many resources (labor, capital and raw materials) will be devoted to the production of goods and services (such as paper, cars, lawnmowers, television sets, restaurants, laundromats, etc.) and not enough resources to the preservation or protection of the environment (such as the atmosphere, the hydrosphere, wilderness areas, animal and plant species, etc.). This is generally recognized as the microeconomic effect of environmental externalities. As discussed above, one way of correcting (internalizing) this is by imposing a penalty on those who are directly responsible for polluting the environment. For our purposes here, the exact nature of the environmental regulation is not important (an exhaustive study of the various policy instruments used to protect the environment is deferred to Chapters 5 and 6).

However, policies used to internalize environmental externalities could have economy-wide effects. For example, as shown in Figure 3.3, the socially optimal level of paper production is associated with higher price (P_s instead of P_e) and lower level of output (Q_s instead of Q_e). If this is to be viewed as an economy-wide phenomenon, the implication would be that environmental policies may contribute to *inflation* (an increase in the aggregate price of goods and services) and *unemployment* (since less output means less use of labor and capital). These are the possible impacts of environmental regulations on macroeconomic performance. This can be a very serious consideration indeed during an inflationary and/or recessionary period such as the 1970s. A number of economic studies were conducted to offer an empirical estimate of the macroeconomic impacts of environmental regulations (Gary 1987; Portney 1981; Crandall 1981; Denison 1979). In general, the results of these studies were *inconclusive*. For a recent empirical study of this topic see Case Study 3.1. This case study offers a preliminary analysis of the macroeconomic impacts of the Clean Air Act amendments of 1990 in the United States.

Indeed, environmental regulation may have the effect of reducing output (hence, increasing unemployment) in the sectors of the economy that are directly affected by the regulation. For example, other factors remaining equal, a tax imposed on the automobile industry for the purpose of protecting the environment is likely to raise the price of cars and perhaps lead to an increase in industry-wide unemployment. However, because the ultimate purpose of the tax is to improve environmental quality, the sectors of the economy that are involved in the cleanup of the environment are likely to be expanding. Thus, the economy-wide effect of environmental regulation on unemployment is unclear since a decrease in employment in a certain sector of an economy could be offset by a gain in other sectors. Some economists even go as far as to claim that *cleaning up the environment creates more jobs than it destroys* (Hamrin 1975; Sullivan 1992). The reason for this is that, in general, pollution control is relatively more labor-intensive. Others argue that environmental regulations have negative effects on productivity (hence, on aggregate output, GNP) for a variety of reasons. For example, it is argued that pollution control expenditures displace investment in new plant and equipment, and require firms to use some inputs for compliance, hence adversely affecting the rate of increase in labor productivity (Crandall 1981). Furthermore, regulation is believed to increase the uncertainty climate of private industry, hence adversely affecting the level of industry-wide investment.

At least in theory, the price or inflationary effect of environmental regulation seems to be indisputable. This is because environmental policy forces society to take into account costs that would have otherwise been neglected. However, what is not clear is the magnitude of the inflationary effect of environmental regulation. In the United States, several empirical studies seem to suggest this effect has been minimal

Case Study 3.1   The economic impact of the 1990 Clean Air Act amendments

Keith Mason

In the recent debate in Congress and the media over a stronger Clean Air Act, questions about the economic implications of the proposed amendments figured prominently. Opinions were aired concerning the costs of the amendments, their potential impact on employment, and possible ramifications for US industry in international competition.

In large part, the economic debate was triggered by the costs of expanded air-pollution control programs. The Environmental Protection Agency (EPA) and the President's Council of Economic Advisors estimated that the new Clean Air Act would cost approximately $12 billion per year by 1995 – and approximately $25 billion per year when fully implemented in the year 2005. This is in addition to an already extensive level of air-pollution control: the EPA estimated that expenditures for air pollution control were approximately $27 billion annually in 1988.

Considered as a lump sum, this cost is enough to give anyone pause. In fact, however, economic impacts will be widely dispersed over the entire US economy and gradually incurred over a 15-year time period. When the new requirements are fully phased in, the estimated cost per day will be around 24 cents per person.

However, as with any cost estimate associated with a complicated piece of legislation that must be implemented over an extended period, uncertainty is the rule rather than the exception. Part of the difficulty lies in predicting future methods of pollution control. Air pollution control technology and the cost of that technology both change over time.

Given this, it is even more difficult to predict how increased pollution control expenditures will affect such economic indicators as employment, growth, productivity and trade. In terms of an approximate $7 trillion economy in the year 2005, $25 billion represents much less than 1 per cent of the size of that economy.

Real economic growth and productivity impacts are likely to be small, according to the Council of Economic Advisors. To the extent that productivity gains are decreased slightly, the impact is likely to be transitional and not permanent. The Council has said that some temporary unemployment will result from the Act (such as with high-sulfur coal miners), but the new law is not likely to have significant permanent negative effects on aggregate US employment.

Moreover, expenditures on pollution control bolster a growing US industry. The pollution-control industry is an important part of our economy. Expenditures on pollution control create domestic high-skilled jobs (some estimates are that for every $1 billion of air pollution control expenditure, between 15,000 and 20,000 jobs are created). As an added benefit, the reduced air pollution levels lead to improvements in worker health and productivity.

As for impacts on international trade, exact studies concerning the impact of the new act on competitiveness have not been completed. However, a preliminary comparison of selected industries among major trading partners indicates that other countries with strong national economies and trade surpluses have relatively greater degrees of air pollution control for some industries than will be required in the United

States under the new Clean Air Act. For instance, sulfur dioxide and nitrogen oxide emission control requirements that will apply to US power plants are less stringent than the controls already in place in Germany. The notion that additional environmental protection necessarily endangers international trade is to date unsubstantiated.

What have been substantiated are the enormous trade opportunities for pollution control equipment and expertise. The [former] Soviet Union's recent $1 billion order of General Motors pollution control equipment is just one example.

Source: *EPA Journal* Vol. 17, Jan./Feb. 1991, pp. 45–7. Reprinted by permission.

(e.g. Portney 1981). The main reason for this is that the aggregate expenditure on pollution control relative to GNP is quite small. However, for a given sector of the economy, the price effect of environmental regulation may be quite significant. For example, environmental regulation of the textile industry may require a significant increase in the price of textile products while having minimal effect on the aggregate price of goods and services taken as a whole.

To add to the above controversies, more recently Porter has (1990, 1991) hypothesized that strictly enforced environmental policy could have the effect of forcing firms to adopt more efficient production technologies. In the long run, the effect of this would be a reduction in production costs and a further stimulus to the economy (for actual evidence of what is now known as the 'Porter hypothesis' see World Resources Institute 1992 and the article by Jaffe, A. *et al.*).

The debate continues. In recent years as the economy slows down there appears to be a marked shift in public policy sentiment toward environmental deregulation in many state legislatures across the United States. The belief seems to be that three decades of creeping environmental controls have strangled the economy and in effect undermined economic competitiveness. In response to this growing sentiment towards deregulation, Stephen Meyer, director of the Project on Environmental Politics and Policy at MIT, has recently made the following observation on this controversial issue:

Given the high stakes involved the reader might find it unsettling to learn that credible evidence supporting this policy shift (deregulation) is virtually non-existent. To be sure, anecdotes about companies ruined by environmental regulation abound. Yet they provide no clues regarding the likely economic benefits from deregulation. Moreover there are an equal number of anecdotes about companies pulled back from the brink of bankruptcy by environmental efficiency. And stories about the growth of green companies continue to proliferate, giving rise to the argument that 'environmentalism' – vigorous policies of environmental protection – actually spurs economic growth.

[However] when we turn away from anecdotes and special interest (i.e. industry and environmental lobbies) 'studies', the result from rigorous, independent, economic analyses strongly suggest that no lasting macroeconomic gains will be forthcoming. Focusing on a number of different industries, using a variety of economic indicators and covering different time periods, these studies find that

Table 3.1 Business expenditures for pollution control as a percentage of total business capital expenditures and annual value of goods shipped, 1991

Industry sector	Pollution abatement expenditure vs. total capital expenditures, %	Pollution abatement operating expenditures vs. value of shipments, %	Employee payroll vs. value of shipment, %
All manufacturing	7.5	0.6	18.7
Petroleum and coal	24.8	1.8	3.0
Paper and allied products	13.7	1.3	15.0
Chemical and allied	12.5	1.4	10.6
Primary metals	11.4	1.5	16.3
Electrical machinery	2.9	0.4	21.0
Transportation equipment	2.8	0.3	16.5
Instruments amd related	2.3	0.2	25.0
Machinery (exc. electrical)	1.8	0.2	22.6
Electric utilities	5.0	–	–

Source: US Department of Commerce (1993; 12–13), *US Statistical Abstract*, 1993 (Table 1256).

neither national nor state economic performance have been significantly or systematically affected by environmental regulation.

Furthermore, in his forthcoming book entitled *Environmentalism and Economic Prosperity*, Meyer made an in-depth empirical analysis of the relationship between state and environmentalism and economic growth for the period 1982–92. Although they are slightly sensitive to the general economic conditions, overall his statistical findings *fail* to support the argument that states with stronger environmental policies suffer an economy penalty – lower rate of economic growth. However, when the focus of the study was on the period 1990–2 when the economy was in recession, there was evidence, albeit weak, that state environmentalism may increase the relative severity of recessions.

Thus, as a way of concluding this section, what can be said about the macroeconomic effects of environmental regulation in more definite terms?

First, at an aggregate level and under 'normal' economic conditions, there is compelling empirical evidence to suggest that environmental regulation has no discernible effect on long-run economic performance (in terms of aggregate output, price and productivity). The main reason for this is the simple fact that expenditure on pollution control at an aggregate level is very small. For example, as shown in Table 3.1, for the year 1991, total pollution abatement operating expenditure relative to the total value of the goods produced in the manufacturing sector was 0.6 per cent. Of course, as shown in the same table, the figure varies within the manufacturing sector from as low as 0.2 per cent to a high of 1.8 per cent. Note also that relative to pollution abatement expenditure, the expenditure on employment payroll exceeded the expenditure on pollution abatement by a factor of 31.

Second, for some industries, the investment requirement on pollution abatement capital expenditures could be quite burdensome and the effect on productivity during a time of economic slowdown considerable. For example, as shown in Table 3.1, in 1991 the total pollution abatement capital expenditures relative to the total value of goods produced and sold by the manufacturing sector of the economy was 7.5 per cent – which is not small. However, for some sectors of manufacturing industry, this percentage figure was in the double digits, approaching as high as 24.8 per cent for the manufacturing sector represented by petroleum and coal production. However, it is also very important to note that these highly impacted industries are the ones who stand to gain a great deal from advances on pollution abatement technology. Thus, taking a lead on the advancement of pollution abatement technology may have a considerable long-run payoff.

3.5 Chapter summary

- This chapter has dealt with concepts and principles fundamental to understanding standard environmental economics.
- It was postulated that the assimilative capacity of the environment (i.e. the ability of the natural environment to degrade waste arising from an economic activity) is in effect *scarce*, and is affected by a number of ecological and technological factors.
- It was observed that, for degradable pollutants such as most municipal wastes, a certain minimum amount of economic goods can be produced without causing damage to the natural environment. The exception to this is the emission of a highly toxic and persistent chemical compound such as DDT. In such a case, a *zero* level of pollution may be justified – like the ban on DDT in the United States. Thus, at least for degradable pollutants, *zero* level of pollution cannot be defended even on purely ecological grounds.
- However, given that most economic activities (production and consumption of goods and services) extend beyond the ecological thresholds necessary to keep the integrity of the natural environment intact (beyond X_0 in Figure 3.2A), *trade-off between increased economic activity and the level of environmental quality becomes unavoidable*.
- It was noted that the search for the 'optimal' trade-off between economic and environmental goods requires full consideration of all the relevant *social* costs and benefits. Unfortunately, for environmental resources, this cannot be done through the normal market mechanism for a number of reasons:

    1   Environmental resources, such as the atmosphere, all large bodies of water and public lands, are *common property resources*, and access to them has traditionally been open to all users.
    2   Consequently, environmental resources tend to be prone to *externalities* – incidental costs imposed by a third party.
    3   In the presence of externalities, economic pursuits on the basis of individual self-interest (hence, the private market) do not lead to what is best for society as a whole. This is because a freely operating private market has *no* automatic mechanism to account for external costs. Thus, scarce environmental resources are treated as though they are *free* goods.
    4   When external costs are unaccounted for, the production of economic goods and services is in excess of what is socially optimal, and the quality of the environment is compromised. That is, the market, if left alone, tends to favor the production of more economic goods at the expense of the quality of the environment.

- Alternatively, the above problem could be viewed this way. In the presence of an externality, market prices would fail to reflect 'true' scarcity value. As discussed in

Section 4 of Appendix A, price is a measure of true scarcity when the market equilibrium price, P_e, is equal to both marginal *social* cost and marginal social benefit (i.e. $P_e = MSC = MSB$). However, in the presence of an externality, the market equilibrium price, P_e, is equal to marginal private cost but not the marginal social cost ($P_e = MPC < MSC$). This is because the market has no mechanism to capture the external component of the social cost ($MSC = MPC + MEC$). Thus, since $P_e < MSC$, market price fails to reflect true scarcity value.

- Once this is understood, a possible solution to this type of externality problem is to find mechanisms that will account for external costs and correct the price distortion. How these work is the subject of Chapters 5 and 6.
- Finally, it was shown that taking any action to regulate the market to take into account environmental externalities implies a decline in economic goods and an increase in price (see Figure 3.3). Therefore, one often-raised concern is the *macroeconomic* effect of environmental regulations. In general, environmental regulations are suspected to have a negative effect on the economy for two reasons. First, they increase the private costs of firms. Second, they reduce the productivity of the economy because resources are diverted from the production of goods and services to investment in pollution control. Despite this claim, studies of the effects of environmental policies on macro variables such as GNP, inflation, productivity, and unemployment have been inconclusive. In general, the empirical evidence tend to suggest environmental regulations as having very limited macroeconomic effect. This is not to say, however, that effect of environmental regulations is evenly spread throughout an economy. Indeed, the main source of continued controversy in this area is the very fact that some industries (such as the textiles and chemicals) are significantly affected by measures taken to regulate the use of the environment. To makes matter worse, in the United States, the business sector and the public at large seem to have an inherent aversion to regulation – even if it is to protect the environment.

Review and discussion questions

1 Briefly review the following concepts: persistent pollutants, common property resources, transaction cost, joint consumption, externality, market failure, the polluter pays principle, internalizing externality, government failure, the Porter hypothesis.

2 State the *four* conditions for clearly defined ownership rights.

3 State whether the following statements are *true, false* or *uncertain* and *explain* why:

(a) Everybody's property is nobody's property.
(b) Waste emission should not exceed the renewable assimilative capacity of the environment.
(c) Environmental regulation creates more jobs than it destroys.

4 What is an externality? Provide two examples that are not given in the text. What are the root causes of environmental externalities? Please be specific. You are encouraged to use demand and supply analysis to answer this question.

5 It has been shown that the consequence of an environmental externality is a divergence between social and private costs. How would this cause market failure and what exactly is meant by market failure? Please be specific.

6   In some instances, consideration of 'transaction costs' alone could make internalizing an externality (positive or negative) economically indefensible. Can you provide three concrete examples of this nature?

7   Can you provide two good reasons why, in general, the business sector is unenthusiastic about environmental regulations? How would you reconcile this seemingly inherent reluctance of the business sector to invest in pollution abatement technology with the Porter hypothesis?

8   In the United States it was found that states with stringent environmental regulations did not perform (in terms of annual rate of economic growth) any less well than the states with relaxed environmental regulations. In fact, when the economy is operating under normal growth pattern (no recession), states with stringent environmental regulations outperformed the states that were not. How do you explain this?

9   Read the material in Exhibit 3.2 below and answer the three questions presented at the end of the exhibit.

Exhibit 3.2   What is the most desirable level of pollution?

Recently, the 'Society for Zero Pollution' sponsored a panel discussion on the topic 'Is Zero Pollution Viable?' The panelists included a well-known environmental economist and a very famous ecologist.

Probably to the dismay of their sponsor, both the economist and the ecologist agreed that zero pollution is neither viable nor desirable. On the other hand, both panelists were quite complimentary about society's efforts to initiate a timely and well-conceived public debate on general issues concerning the environment, and about the genuine concern society has shown for the growing deterioration of our environment.

In discussing his view on zero pollution, the ecologist stated that we must not forget that the environment has a limited ability to process waste. The concern for environmental pollution arises only when we emit wastes into the environment beyond its assimilative capacity. In his view, therefore, the socially desirable level of waste discharge (pollution) is that which is consistent with the assimilative capacity of the environment. In other words, waste emission should not exceed the renewable assimilative capacity of the environment.

In her turn, the economist disputed the assertion made by the ecologist by stating that it is quite consistent and rational for society to discharge waste (pollute) above and beyond the assimilative capacity of the environment in so far as society collectively values the benefit from the excess pollution (the extra value of the goods and services produced) at more than the cost of the damage to the environmental quality. Hence, the optimal (socially desirable) level of pollution is attained when the marginal social cost (MSC) of waste reduction – in terms of extra output and services sacrificed – is equal to the marginal social benefit (MSB) of waste reduction, in terms of the psychic and tangible benefits society may attain from improved environmental quality.

1   Do you agree that zero pollution is neither possible nor desirable? Why? Be specific.

2   How would you reconcile the views expressed by the ecologist and the economist? If you think they are irreconcilable, why so? Explain.

3   Recently, the Environmental Protection Agency proposed to ban the use of EDB (ethylene dibromide) to spray on domestically produced citrus fruits. Would this be consistent with either one of the above two views? Why, or why not?

References

Coase, R. (1960) 'The Problem of Social Cost', *Journal of Law and Economics* 3: 1–44.

Commoner, B., Corr, M. and Stamler, P. J. (1971) 'The Causes of Pollution', in T. D. Goldfarb (ed.) *Taking Sides: On Controversial Environmental Issues*, 3rd edn, Sluice Dock, Conn.: Guilford.

Crandall, R. W. (1981) 'Pollution Controls and Productivity Growth in Basic Industries', in T. G. Cowing and R. E. Stevenson (eds) *Productivity Measurement in Regulated Industries*, New York: Academic Press.

Denison, E. P. (1979) *Accounting for Slower Economic Growth: The United States in the 1970s*, Washington, DC: Brookings Institution.

Gary, W. (1987) 'The Cost of Regulation: OSHA, EPA and Productivity Slowdown', *American Economic Review* 5: 998–1006.

Hamrin, R. (1975) 'Are Environmental Regulations Hurting the Economy?', *Challenge* May–June: 29–38.

Hardin, G. (1968) 'The Tragedy of the Commons', *Science* 162: 1243–8.

Jaffe, A., Peterson, S. and Portney, P. (1995) 'Environmental Regulation and the Competitiveness of U.S. Manufacturing: What Does the Evidence Tell Us?' *Journal of Competitiveness*.

Meyer, S. M. (2002) 'The Economic Impact of Environmental Regulation', unpublished manuscript, 1–24.

—— (forthcoming) *Environmentalism and Economic Prosperity*, Cambridge: MIT Press.

Pearce, D. W. (1978) *Environmental Economics*, 3rd edn, London: Longman.

Porter, M. A. (1990) *The Competitive Advantage of Nations*, New York: Free Press.

—— (1991) 'America's Green Strategy', *Scientific American* 168.

Portney, P. (1981) 'The Macroeconomic Impacts of Federal Environmental Regulation', in H. M. Peskin, P. R. Portney and A. V. Knees (eds) *Environmental Regulation and the U.S. Economy*, Baltimore: Johns Hopkins University Press.

Randall, A. (1983) 'The Problem of Market Failure', *Natural Resources Journal* 23: 131–48.

—— (1987) *Resource Economics: An Economic Approach to Natural Resource and Environmental Policy*, 2nd edn, New York: John Wiley.

Seneca, J. J. and Taussig, M. K. (1984) *Environmental Economics*, 3rd edn, Englewood Cliffs, NJ: Prentice-Hall.

Sullivan, T. (1992) *The Greening of American Business*, Rockville, MD.: Government Institutes.

Tietenberg, T. H. (1992) *Environmental and Natural Resource Economics*, 3rd edn, New York: HarperCollins.

Turvey, R. (1963) 'On Divergence between Social Cost and Private Cost', *Economica*, August: 309–13.

World Resources Institute (1992) *World Resources 1992–93*, New York: Oxford University Press.

4 The economic theory of pollution control

The optimal level of pollution

4.1 Introduction

In Chapter 3 an attempt was made to address the issue of environmental quality by looking at the trade-off society has to make between economic goods and improved environmental quality. In addition to recognizing the existence of this trade-off, an attempt was made to formally establish the necessary condition for attaining the level of output (economic goods) that would be consistent with the socially optimal level of environmental quality. This approach (as it deals with market prices and outputs directly) also allowed us to see the implications of environmental regulation at the macro level.

However, the approach used in the previous chapter does not directly reveal the amount of waste emission associated with what is considered to be the socially optimal output. *This would pose no problem if there existed a stable and predictable relationship between waste emission and output, and if changes in market conditions did not have an independent effect on output.* Furthermore, the approach used in Chapter 3 does not say anything about either *pollution control technology* or the *demand* for environmental quality. However, these are technical and economic considerations that can hardly be taken for granted.

For these reasons, this chapter will discuss an alternative approach to the management of environmental quality by looking directly at the nature of *waste disposal costs*. Viewed this way, the economic problem will be to determine the volume of waste (not output as in Chapter 3) that is consistent with the socially optimal level of environmental quality, i.e. the optimal level of pollution. This approach, as will be seen shortly, provides a good many helpful new insights as well as a thorough evaluation of all the economic, technological and ecological factors that are considered significant in assessing pollution prevention (abatement) and pollution damage cost functions. Furthermore, the material presented in this chapter provides the basic analytical framework for the evaluations of alternative environmental public policy instruments (subjects covered in Chapters 5 and 6).

Finally, it should be noted at the outset that a section of this chapter (Section 4.6) is devoted to an ecological appraisal of the standard economic notion of the 'optimal' level of pollution control. This is primarily to note possible inconsistencies that may exist between the economic and ecological notions of optimal pollution.

4.2 Minimization of waste disposal costs

As discussed in Chapter 2, two principles, the first and second laws of thermodynamics, inform us that pollution is an inevitable byproduct of any economic activity. Furthermore, as discussed in Section 3.2 of Chapter 3, a certain minimum amount of economic activity can be pursued without causing damage to the natural environment. This is because the natural environment has the capacity, albeit a limited capacity, to degrade waste, although for persistent pollutants (such as DDT, mercury, radioactive waste and so on) the assimilative capacity of the environment may be, if not zero, quite insignificant.

Clearly, then, economic consideration of waste (pollution) becomes relevant when the amount of waste disposed exceeds the assimilative capacity of the environment. When this critical threshold is exceeded, what becomes immediately apparent is the trade-off between environmental quality and pollution. That is, further pollution beyond this threshold could occur only at the cost of reduced environmental quality. In other words, *pollution occurs at a cost*. This is, then, the rationale for a pollution control strategy or environmental management (a subject to be addressed in Chapters 5 and 6).

From a purely economic perspective, the management of pollution control or environmental quality is easily understood if the problem is viewed as minimizing *total* waste disposal costs. Broadly identified, waste disposal costs originate from two distinct sources. The first is the *pollution control* (abatement) *cost*: the cost that arises from society's cleanup effort to control pollution using some kind of technology. The second element is the *pollution damage cost*, which results from damage caused by untreated waste discharged into the environment. Thus:

Total waste disposal costs = Total pollution control (abatement) cost
+ total pollution damage cost.

Hence, the economic problem of interest is to minimize the total disposal costs, *with full recognition of the implied trade-off between its two components: control and damage costs*. This is because, from an economic viewpoint, a dollar's worth of investment (expenditure) on pollution control technology will make sense if, and only if, society is expected to be compensated by benefits to be realized from the avoidance of environmental damage that are worth more than a dollar. A good understanding of this economic logic requires, first of all, a clear and in-depth understanding of the nature of these two types of waste disposal costs to which we now turn.

4.2.1 Pollution control (abatement) costs and their salient properties

Pollution control (abatement) costs represent direct monetary expenditures by a society for the purpose of procuring resources to improve environmental quality or to control pollution. Expenditures on sewage treatment facilities, smokestacks, soundproof walls, and catalytic converters on passenger cars are just a few examples of pollution control costs. These expenditures may be incurred exclusively by private individuals, such as expenditures on soundproof walls by residents living in close proximity to an airport. In contrast, sewage treatment facilities may be undertaken as a joint project by local and federal government agencies. In this case the expenditures are shared by two government bodies. In some situations a project may be undertaken by a private firm with a subsidy

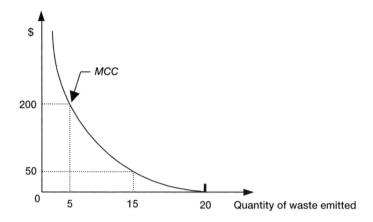

Figure 4.1 Marginal pollution control cost. Note that pollution control implies a movement
towards the origin from the benchmark level of waste of 20 units. Given this, it
is hypothesized that the *marginal* control cost increases with successive increase in
pollution cleanup. It cost a lot more to clean up the last unit of pollution than the
first.

from the public sector. Thus, as these examples illustrate, the bearers of the expenditures
on pollution control projects may vary, and in some instances are difficult to identify.
Despite this possible complication, the conventional wisdom is to view pollution
control cost in its entirety. To this extent the specific source of the expenditure is
irrelevant. What is relevant is that *all* components of the expenditure attributable to a
specific pollution abatement project are fully accounted for, regardless of the source of
the funds.

In general, we would expect the *marginal* pollution control cost to increase with
increased environmental quality or cleanup activities. This is because incrementally
higher levels of environmental quality require investments in technologies that are
increasingly costly. For example, a certain level of water quality could be achieved
through a primary sewage treatment facility. Such a facility is designed to screen out the
solid and visible material wastes, but nothing more. If a higher level of water quality is
desired, an additional expenditure on secondary or tertiary treatment may be required.
Such additional treatments would require implementation of new and costly technologies designed to apply either chemical and/or biological treatments to the water.
Graphically, we can visualize the marginal control cost (*MCC*) as follows.

Figure 4.1 represents the *marginal* pollution control cost in graphical form. Before
we proceed any further, it is very important to understand the exact reading of this
graph. First, the *benchmark* or total number of units of waste that is being considered
for treatment is 20. This is evident since the marginal cost of the twentieth unit of waste
(i.e. no waste treatment) is seen to be zero. Second, it is important to note that the
marginal pollution control cost increases at an *increasing rate* as a higher level of
cleanup or environmental quality (a movement towards the origin) is desired. The
numerical example in Figure 4.1 clearly indicates this. The marginal cost of controling
or treating the fifth unit of waste is seen to be $50. However, the marginal cost increases

to $200, a fourfold rise, to treat the fifteenth unit of waste. Note that given that the benchmark is 20 units, the treatment of the fifteenth unit is equivalent to leaving 5 units of waste untreated – which is what is shown in Figure 4.1.

At this stage it is important to specify certain important technological factors that determine the position of any marginal pollution control cost curve. More specifically, it is important to note that the marginal pollution control cost curves are constructed by holding constant such factors as the technology of pollution control, the possibility of input switching, residual recycling, production technology, etc. A change in any one of these predetermined factors will cause a shift in the entire marginal pollution control cost curve. For instance, an electric power plant that uses coal as its primary source of energy could reduce pollution (sulfur) emission by switching from coal with high sulfur content to low-sulfur coal. In this particular case, the effect would be to shift the marginal pollution control cost downward. Similar results would occur if there was a significant improvement in pollution control technology, such as the development of a new and more efficient catalytic converter for automobiles.

Finally, since pollution control costs are explicit or out-of-pocket expenditures, it is assumed that no apparent market distortion occurs as a result of a third-party effect, i.e. an externality. In other words, for pollution control costs, there will be no difference between private and social costs. However, this is not to suggest that market distortion in the assessment of pollution control costs cannot exist as a result of either market imperfection (monopoly power) or government intervention in the forms of subsidies and taxes.

As stated earlier, pollution control cost accounts for only one side of the total social costs of pollution. Let us now turn to a detailed examination of the second component of the total pollution disposal costs, namely pollution damage costs.

4.2.2 *Pollution damage costs and their salient properties*

Even if it is technologically feasible to get rid of all pollutants from a given environmental medium, such an undertaking may be difficult to justify on the basis of cost considerations. However, as discussed in Chapter 3, when the volume of waste discharged exceeds the assimilative capacity of the environment, and is left untreated, it can contribute to deterioration in environmental quality. *The total monetary value of all the various damages resulting from the discharge of untreated waste into the environment is referred to as pollution damage cost.*

Such damage to environmental quality may be manifested in a variety of ways, largely depending on the *amount* and the *nature* of the untreated waste. For example, when *biodegradable* pollutants, such as sewage, phosphate-containing detergents and feedlot waste are emitted into a lake, they can lead to the development of a process known as eutrophication. Over time, the outcome of this process is to cover a substantial portion of the lake with green organic matter, primarily algae and weeds. One immediate effect is a reduction in the scenic appeal of the lake. In addition, there is a negative impact on the population of aquatic organisms, because the ability of a body of water to support fish and other organisms depends on how much dissolved oxygen it contains. Thus, if biodegradable pollutants were discharged into a lake and left untreated, the damage to environmental quality would be identifiable in terms of reduced scenic attraction and decreased population of certain aquatic organisms, such as fish. The monetary value of these adverse environmental effects constitutes pollution damage cost.

   The identification and estimation of pollution damage costs are more complicated in the case of *persistent* pollutants. Examples of such pollutants include toxic metals, such as lead and mercury, radioactive wastes, and inorganic compounds such as some pesticides and waste products produced by the petrochemical industry. *What is particularly significant about these types of pollutant is not the mere fact that they are patently dangerous to living organisms and the ecosystem as a whole, but that because of their very slow decomposition processes they tend to persist in the environment for a very long period of time.* In other words, their adverse environmental effects transcend present action. For example, radioactive elements leaking from nuclear power plants today will have detrimental effects over several generations. This makes the estimation of damage costs arising from persistent pollutants extremely difficult.

   In general, then, *pollution damage costs are identifiable in terms of the losses of or damage to plants and animals and their habitats; aesthetic impairments; rapid deterioration of physical infrastructures and assets; and various harmful effects on human health and mortality.* In order to estimate damage costs, however, we need to go beyond accounting for the physical damage. More specifically, damage identified in physical terms needs to be expressed in monetary terms as much as possible (see Case Study 4.1).

   As the above discussion indicates, estimation of pollution damage costs is a formidable task and requires a good deal of imagination and a creative approach. Furthermore, other factors being equal, the more persistent the pollutants, the harder the task of evaluating damage costs. In fact, as we will see in Chapter 8, *some aspects of pollution damage are simply beyond the realm of economic quantification.* Regardless of these difficulties, pollution damage does occur. Hence, as a society striving for a better life, we need to develop a procedure that will provide us with a framework designed to enhance our understanding of pollution damage costs.

   Conceptually, Figure 4.2 represents the general characteristics of the marginal pollution damage cost (*MDC* curve). More specifically, as discussed above, the damage cost curve measures the social cost of damage to the environment in monetary terms, resulting from each additional unit of waste emission. A basic assumption in the construction of this curve is that damage cost is an increasing function of pollution emissions. In other words, the damage caused by a unit of pollution increases progressively as the amount of pollution (untreated waste) emitted increases. As the numerical example in Figure 4.2 indicates, the marginal damage cost increases from $125 (the cost of the tenth unit of waste) to $500 (the cost of the fifteenth unit of waste) as the amount of waste emissions increases from 10 to 15 units. *This is, of course, in accord with the ecological principle discussed in Chapter 2, the cumulative (nonlinear) effect of pollution on the environment.*

   Several factors affect the position of the marginal pollution damage cost curve. These include changes in people's preferences for environmental quality, changes in population, discovery of new treatment(s) of damage caused by environmental pollution – such as a medical breakthrough in a treatment of a certain cancer, or a change in the nature of the assimilative capacity of the environment. Alterations in any one of these factors will cause the marginal pollution damage costs to shift. With other factors held constant, a preference for a higher level of environmental quality will shift the marginal damage cost curve in Figure 4.2 upward or move it to the left. This is rather straightforward once it is understood that, as demonstrated in Exhibit 4.1, *the marginal pollution damage cost curve actually represents what people are willing to pay to avoid damage, or the demand function for environmental quality.* It makes sense, then, that a

Case Study 4.1   Economic effects of poor indoor air quality

Curtis Haymore and Rosemarie Odom

Poor indoor air quality (IAQ) takes its toll in a variety of ways. It damages our health and our possessions; it lowers our productivity at work; and it diverts resources to diagnosing and solving problems that result from it. Although the economic costs of some of these damages are fairly tangible and easy to quantify, a large portion are hidden. The cumulative impact can easily reach into the billions of dollars.

The cost of diagnosing, mitigating and litigating IAQ problems is evidenced by the burgeoning number of businesses providing these services. A recent EPA survey indicated that over 1,500 firms specialize in IAQ services, a 25 per cent increase from 1988. The median price for evaluating and balancing ventilation systems ranges from $250 to $1,500. The median for duct-cleaning services is about $500 and for asbestos abatement and construction/renovation about $5,000. Costs can be as high as $50,000 for some of these services. In addition, the cost of fees, awards and settlements is also growing as an increasing number of IAQ-related cases are litigated. Although most IAQ complaints are resolved through settlements, enormous sums of money have to be invested in investigations, testing and expert testimony, in addition to legal fees. The settlements themselves are often in the hundreds of thousands to millions of dollars.

The economic costs of poor IAQ also include actual damage to property caused by contaminants. Indoor air pollutants can damage metals, paints, textiles, paper, and magnetic storage media, and can cause increased soiling, deterioration of appearance and reduced service life for furniture, draperies, interiors, and heating, ventilation and air conditioning (HVAC) equipment. Some objects and materials are 'sensitive populations' that are particularly susceptible to damage. For example, antique leather-bound books and fine art are particularly vulnerable to a number of contaminants. Electronic equipment, which is particularly susceptible to corrosion, represents a large investment at risk from poor IAQ.

Injury to people represents an even larger cost of poor IAQ. The Environmental Protection Agency ranks IAQ problems as one of the largest remaining health risks in the United States. Health effects range from the mildly irritating, such as headaches and allergies, to the life-threatening, such as cancer and heart disease. Medical costs due to excess cancer cases caused by indoor air contaminants are estimated to range from $188 million to $1.375 billion nationwide. Heart disease caused by exposure to environmental tobacco smoke can equal another $300 million. One study indicated that for every 100 white-collar workers, poor IAQ would cause an extra 24 doctor visits per year. This amounts to another $288 million.

One of the 'invisible' costs of poor IAQ is the lost productivity of workers who experience headaches, eye irritation and fatigue, among other symptoms. Productivity drops as employees are less effective at their task, spend more time away from their workstations, or require more frequent breaks. Even a seemingly minor activity such as taking a pain reliever or opening a window can disrupt productivity. In more severe cases, increased absenteeism and plummeting morale result. One study found that

14 minutes are lost per eight-hour day due to poor IAQ. In addition, for every ten workers, poor IAQ causes an additional six sick days per year. If this is true, the resulting cost of the lost productivity for the United States is $41.4 billion.

Source: *EPA Journal* Vol. 19, No. 4, 1993, pp. 28–9. Reprinted by permission.

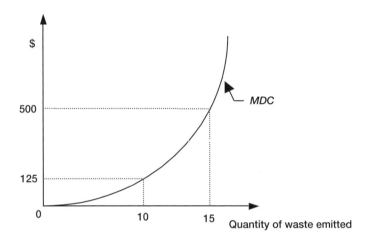

Figure 4.2 Marginal pollution damage cost. It is hypothesized that the environmental damage of each successive unit of pollution increases incrementally. The justification for this relies on the notion that pollution has a cumulative effect of reducing the capacity of the environment to withstand further pollution, hence hastening the process of environmental damage.

preference for higher environmental quality is consistent with an increase in society's willingness to pay to avoid damage.

One last issue of considerable significance to be discussed is the fact that *pollution damage costs are externalities*. By definition these are costs incurred by members of a society after the pollution damage has already occurred. This is an important factor in the determination of the optimal level of pollution – the subject matter of the next section.

4.3 The optimal level of pollution

At the outset of this chapter it was stated that the management of environmental quality is easily understood if the problem is viewed as the minimization of total disposal costs. It was also made clearer that the total disposal costs are composed of two parts: pollution control and pollution damage costs. In Subsections 4.2.1 and 4.2.2 we made a considerable effort to understand the nature of these two components. Equipped with this information, we are now in a position to formally specify what exactly is meant by an optimal level of pollution and how it is associated with the minimization of total disposal cost.

Exhibit 4.1   Marginal damage cost as the demand function for environmental quality

Conceptually it can be shown that Figure 4.3A (which is exactly the same as Figure 4.2) and Figure 4.3B are two alternative representations of the marginal pollution damage costs (*MDC*). The only difference between these two figures is in the labeling of the *x*-axis. In Figure 4.3A, the *x*-axis represents units of untreated waste emitted into the environment, and in Figure 4.3B the same axis represents the units of treated waste or cleanup.

However, it is also important to note that these two alternative presentations offer different interpretations regarding the damage cost curve. In Figure 4.3A, as discussed earlier, the damage cost curve measures the social cost of the damage to the environment in monetary terms resulting from each additional unit of waste emission. This cost increases as the volume of waste emitted increases. For example, as the numerical example indicates, the

marginal cost increases from $125 to $500 as the amount of waste emissions increases from 10 to 15 units. On the other hand, the damage cost curve represented by Figure 4.3B depicts the amount society is *willing to pay to avoid damage* (or cleanup) at the margin. In other words, it measures society's willingness to pay for improved environmental quality on an incremental basis, or the *demand* for environmental quality.

To gain a clearer understanding of this concept, let us assume a benchmark of 20 units of waste that needs to be treated or cleaned up. This unit is shown in Figure 4.3B, and the marginal damage cost is zero at this level of treatment. That is, no damage is done given that all the 20 units are treated. At this point, people will not be willing to pay for any further treatment beyond the 20 units. Now, suppose the amount of waste treated is reduced to 5 units – which is equivalent to saying that $(20 - 5)$ or 15 units

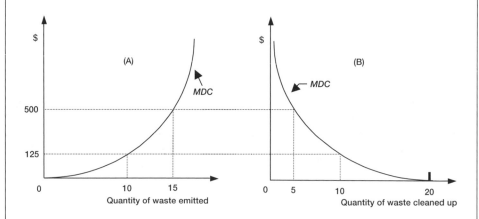

Figure 4.3 An alternative interpretation of the marginal pollution damage cost curve (*MDC*). Note the only difference between these two graphs is the reading on the *x*-axis (waste emission versus waste cleanup). For example, in Figure 4.3B, the marginal cost for cleaning up the fifth unit of waste is $500. Given the benchmark of waste is 20 units, a cleanup of 5 units of waste implies the emission of 15 units of waste. As shown in Figure 4.3A, the emission of the fifteenth unit of waste is $500. Similar interpretations can be given for each of the corresponding points between these two graphs. The main point for exploring this issue is, as discussed in Exhibit 4.1, to show that the marginal damage cost curve in fact represents the *demand* for environmental quality.

of untreated waste are emitted into the environment. With this in mind, the $500 in Figure 4.3B is a measure of what society is willing to pay to clean up the fifth unit of waste. When viewed this way the *MDC* curve represents society's demand for environmental quality. Furthermore, as shown in Figure 4.3B, society's willingness to pay declines as higher levels of environmental quality (more cleanup) are sought. For example, society's willingness to pay for the cleaning up of the tenth unit of waste is $125, which is less than what society is willing to pay for the fifth unit, $500 – an observation that is consistent with the law of demand.

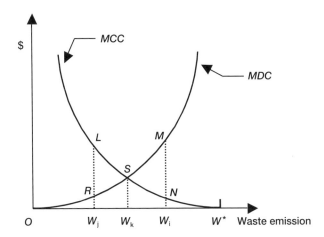

Figure 4.4 The optimal level of pollution. The optimal level of pollution, W_k, is achieved at a point where $MDC = MCC$. Any deviation from this level of pollution in either direction would not be cost-effective. For example, at W_i level of waste emission, $MDC > MCC$, suggesting that the cost of dumping untreated waste in the environment is greater than what it costs to use clean up technology. Thus, there is something to be gained taking action to clean waste – a movement towards W_k. Similar argument can be made for the case of waste disposal W_j, which is to the left of W_k.

In Figure 4.4 the marginal damage cost (*MDC*) and the marginal control cost (*MCC*) curves are drawn on the same axes. From this graph it is evident that if a pollution control measure is not undertaken, the total amount of waste discharged would be W^*. However, the socially optimal level of waste discharge is W_k, where the usual equimarginal condition is satisfied, i.e. *MDC* is equal to *MCC*. At this level of waste discharge, the total control cost is represented by the area W^*SW_k (the area under the *MCC* curve) and the total damage cost is depicted by the area OSW_k (the area under the *MDC* curve). The total disposal cost, which is the sum of these two costs, is shown by the area OSW^*. The question, then, is how do we know that this total cost represents the minimum? Or, stated another way, how do we know that W_k represents the Pareto optimal level of waste emission?

We can easily demonstrate that W_k is Pareto optimal (see Section 3 of Appendix A for an extended discussion of Pareto optimality) by showing that any attempt to set the level of waste emission either above or below W_k would lead to an increase in the total disposal cost. First, suppose that the level of waste emission is increased from W_k to W_i. As shown in Figure 4.4, the total damage cost for this incremental emission, W_k to W_i, is indicated by the area $W_k SM W_i$, the area under the *MDC* curve. However, as a result of the emission of this additional amount of untreated waste, there will be a reduction in pollution control cost. This incremental cost saving is shown by area $W_k SN W_i$, the area under the *MCC* curve. The net result of increasing the level of waste emission from W_k to W_i is an increase in the total disposal cost by area *SMN*. A similar argument can be made to show that lowering the level of the waste emission from W_k to W_j would result in an increase in the total disposal cost by area *SLR*. Thus, the pollution level at W_k is Pareto optimal. In other words, the optimal level of pollution emission is attained when the marginal damage cost is equal to the marginal control cost, and hence the total disposal cost is minimized when this condition is met. A numerical illustration of this optimality concept is presented in Exhibit 4.2.

4.4 Changes in preferences and technology and their effects on the optimal level of pollution

Let us start by examining how changes in preferences for environmental quality and technology may affect the socially optimal level of pollution by using Figures 4.6A, 4.6B and 4.6C. In Figure 4.6A, let us assume that MDC_0 and MCC_0 represent the initial marginal damage and control cost curves. Given this, the optimal level of pollution would be W_k. Suppose now, because of a new environmental awareness campaign, people's demand for higher environmental quality has increased. The effect of this would be to shift the *MDC* curve to the left since, as explained in Exhibit 4.1, the

---

Exhibit 4.2   Pareto-optimal pollution: a numerical illustration

To illustrate the condition for Pareto-optimal pollution using a numerical example, let us assume that the marginal damage and control costs are represented by the straight lines shown in Figures 4.5A and 4.5B. According to Figure 4.5A, the optimal level of pollution will be 150 tons. This means, given that a total of 250 tons of waste needs to be disposed of to attain the optimal level of pollution, 100 tons (250 − 150) of waste must be cleaned up using some kind of pollution control technology.

In Figure 4.5A the total cost for controlling or cleaning up the 100 tons is represented by the area of triangle *B* (the relevant area under the marginal control cost curve). This will be $2,500 [½ (100 × 50)].

The damage cost associated with the 150 tons of untreated waste (the optimal level of pollution) discharged into the environment is represented by area of triangle *A*. Its monetary value will be $3,750 [½ (100 × 50)].

Thus, the total cost is $6,250 ($2,500 + $3,750), i.e. the sum of the total control and damage costs. Since this is the optimal level of pollution, it suggests that the total cost is the minimum at this level. To verify this, let us now look at Figure 4.5B. Suppose the amount of the untreated waste discharged into the environment is increased from 150 tons (the optimal pollution) to 180 tons. This entails a reduction in the amount of waste that needs to be treated from 100 to 70 tons (250 − 180). As a result, the total pollution control (cleanup) cost will decrease from $2,500 (the area of triangle *B* in Figure 4.5A) to $1,225 (the area of triangle *D* in Figure 4.5B).

However, because of the increase in the pollution level from 150 to 180 tons, the total damage cost will escalate from $3,750 (the area of triangle *A* in Figure 4.5A) to $5,400 (the area of the triangle that is composed of (*A* + *C* + *E*) in Figure 4.5B). Thus, when the level of pollution is raised to 180 tons, the total waste disposal cost equals $6,625 ($1,225 + $5,400). This total cost is $375 ($6,625 − $6,250) more than the cost at the optimal level of pollution, 150 tons. As can be easily verified, the $375 is the area of triangle *E* in Figure 4.5B.

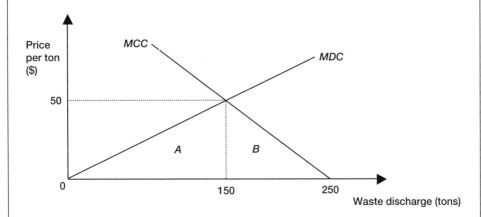

Figure 4.5a The optimal level of pollution: a numerical illustration.

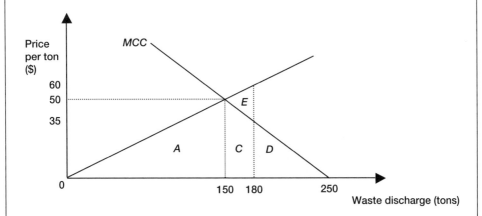

Figure 4.5b What happens when optimality is not attained?

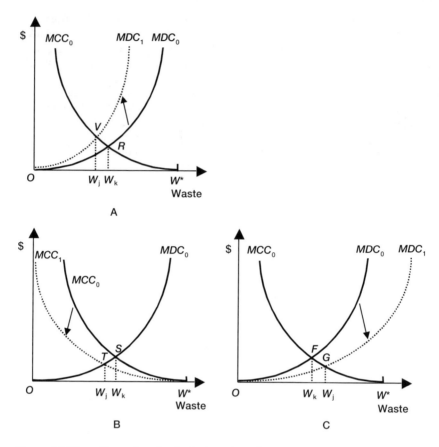

Figure 4.6 The effect of technological and preference changes on the optimal level of pollution. Given that the marginal damage cost represents the demand for environmental quality, Case A indicates an upward shift in this demand curve due to people's preference for higher environmental quality. Case C on the other hand shows a reduction (downward shift) in the demand for environmental quality due to a reduction in damage costs resulting from a medical breakthrough in treating ailments arising from pollution. Case B presents a case where technological improvement in waste treatment facilities allows firms to treat any given level of waste at a lower cost than before.

MDC curve shows what people are willing to pay to avoid damage. In Figure 4.6A this is shown by the shift of the marginal damage cost curve from MDC_0 to MDC_1. Other factors being held constant, this change in the marginal damage cost will alter the position of optimal level of pollution from W_k to W_j. Hence, we can conclude from this that, other factors being equal, a preference for a higher level of environmental quality would lead to a lower tolerance for pollution or a higher level of environmental quality – which makes a good deal of sense. However, *it is important to note that the higher environmental quality was realized at some cost*; the total disposal cost is higher at the new equilibrium (area *OVW** instead of *ORW**).

A similar approach could be used to analyze the effect of technology on the level of pollution that society is willing to tolerate at a point in time. To show this, suppose that there is a technological breakthrough in the control or treatment of a specific type of waste. Since this implies a cost saving in waste treatment, the marginal control cost curve will shift downward to the left. This is shown in Figure 4.6B by a shift in the marginal control cost curve from MCC_0 to MCC_1. Assuming no changes in other factors, this shift will have the effect of reducing the level of pollution from its initial level W_k to W_j. Here again the conclusion we reach is that improvement in waste treatment technology would allow society to reduce its level of pollution or improve its environmental quality. *Moreover, the improvement would be accomplished without an additional increase in the total disposal cost.* As seen in Figure 4.6B, when the level of pollution is W_k, the total waste disposal cost is shown by area OSW^*. However, with the new level of pollution, W_j, the total waste disposal cost is reduced to OTW^*. In this particular case, therefore, there is not only a decline in pollution, but also a reduction in waste disposal costs. This is more like 'you can have the cake and eat it too'. Indeed, it is a good example of the miracle of technology!

Technology may also affect the level of pollution that society would like to have in some other ways. To see this, let us assume that there is a technological breakthrough in the treatment of a cancer caused by exposure to a certain pollutant. Other factors being equal, the obvious effect of this is to shift the marginal damage cost downward and to the right. In Figure 4.6C, this is shown by a shift in the marginal damage cost curve from MDC_0 to MDC_1. As a result, the new optimal level of pollution, W_i, will exceed the level of pollution present before the change in technology occurred, W_k. Here is a case, then, where *improvement in technology would lead to an increase, rather than a decrease, in the level of pollution or a deterioration of environmental quality.* However, even under this condition, improvement in technology would lead to a reduction in total waste disposal costs. This can easily be verified using Figure 4.6C. The total disposal cost was area OFW^* before the technological breakthrough in cancer treatment occurred, but this cost is now reduced to area OGW^*.

Clearly, as the above two cases illustrate, a technological improvement that causes a shift in either the MCC curve or the MDC curve leads to a reduction in total disposal cost. *A saving in disposal cost, then, is the unambiguous result of improved technology.* However, the effect of technological improvement on the level of pollution or environmental quality is not so straightforward. If the MCC curve were to shift to the left due to technological advances in waste treatment, other factors being equal this would lead to a decline in pollution, hence improved environmental quality. On the other hand, if the effect of the change in technology were to shift the MDC curve to the right, then if other factors remained constant, the outcome would be an increase in the level of pollution, and hence a further deterioration in environmental quality. These are important observations to keep in mind since they provide us with a clear warning that technology does not provide an unequivocal resolution to environmental problems.

4.5 An alternative look at market failure

This section revisits market failure – a subject that was explored in Chapter 3. The main objective here is to demonstrate how the phenomenon of market failure can be explained using the model developed in this chapter. This is done using Figure 4.7. According to this figure, the optimal level of pollution is W_k, where the equality of

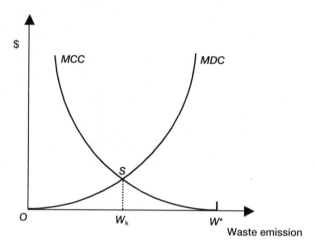

Figure 4.7 Optimal level of pollution.

marginal damage and marginal control costs is satisfied. The question is, could this level of pollution be attained through the free operation of the market? The answer is rather straightforward once we recognize one important difference between damage and control costs. That is, as discussed earlier, *damage costs are externalities, while control costs are not*. Given this, what is cheapest for private firms would not be cheapest for society as a whole. In other words, with respect to the damage costs there will be a divergence between private and social costs. In general, the tendency is for private firms to totally ignore the damage costs. This point is illustrated in Figure 4.7. At the socially optimal level of pollution, W_k, the total waste disposal cost is represented by area OSW^*. This total cost is composed of the total damage costs, area OSW_k, and the total control costs, area $W_k SW^*$. However, if this were done through the market, it would be in the best interest of private firms to minimize control costs and ignore damage costs altogether (since damage costs are externalities). This would move the market solution closer to W^*. Thus, the optimal solution, W_k, could not be attained unless measures were taken to make private firms internalize the externality. Hence, this is a clear case of market failure.

4.6 The optimal level of pollution: an ecological appraisal

> Pollution cleanup is better than doing nothing, but pollution prevention is the best way to walk more gently on the earth.
>
> (Miller 1993: 15)

This section addresses whether or not basic ecological realities are consistent with the concept of an economically optimum level of pollution. Let us start by looking at an extreme case where no pollution is permitted, such as DDT in the United States. While the ecological justification for this is easy to see, how can this ban be addressed using the

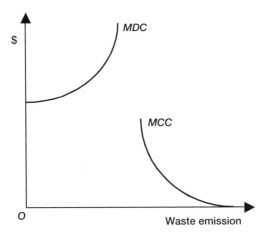

Figure 4.8 A case where zero level of waste emission is considered as optimal. The key issue here is that the marginal damage cost is everywhere above the marginal damage cost. Hence, waste emission should be reduced to zero.

economic model discussed in this chapter? If a zero level of pollution is deemed socially optimal, then as shown in Figure 4.8, at every level of pollution the *MDC* is greater than the *MCC*, and the ban on any substance generating such waste is economically justified. In such an instance, no inconsistency exists between the economic and ecological resolutions of pollution.

Yet that is an extreme case. In most instances, the economic optimum is associated with a positive level of pollution emission. This is to be expected, and it is not necessarily inconsistent with ecological reality (refer to Section 3.2 in Chapter 3). However, there are several reasons why the economic optimum may not be ecologically desirable. This issue will now be explored using three specific cases. The first case suggests that basing the 'optimum' solely on *human preferences* (willingness to pay) is not appropriate, especially when it is applied to the environment. The second case implies that the standard economic approach to pollution control may *put more emphasis on pollution cleanup than pollution prevention*. The third uses the results of three specific empirical studies to illustrate situations, in this case global warming, *where the 'optimum' pollution does not adequately safeguard the interests of future generations and the Earth's ecosystems as a whole*.

Case 1

As the discussion so far reveals, in estimating the damage function, only human preferences are considered. What is troubling is the extent to which a purely anthropo-centrically based preference ordering adequately accounts for future human life (i.e. ensures intergenerational equity) and the integrity of the natural ecosystems (Funtowicz and Ravetz 1994). Without such assurance, a divergence between economically and ecologically optimum pollution may be inevitable. In this respect, the bias is expected to be toward more pollution, since the economic estimate of the damage function is likely to understate the welfare of the future generations and the diversity and resilience of natural ecosystems (more on this in Chapter 8).

Case 2

As is evident from the discussion throughout this chapter, the economic criterion for an optimal level of pollution is developed with the implicit assumption of a predetermined level of waste – a benchmark. For example, in each of the cases where the determination of optimal pollution level has been demonstrated, W^* was identified as the benchmark – the maximum level of a particular waste under consideration for cleanup. In searching for the optimum level of cleanup, no economic considerations are made concerning the absolute size of the benchmark itself. *The focus is simply on the cheapest way of disposing of a predetermined level of waste.* Thus, optimum pollution is calculated without any consideration of what it would be worth to society if a reduction in the benchmark pollution W^*, were to take place. Given this, the standard economic approach to pollution control is most likely to stress pollution cleanup, rather than pollution prevention. A strategy of pollution prevention emphasizes waste reduction at source or reducing the amount of waste before it enters any waste system. To the extent that this is ignored or underemphasized, the economic approach to pollution control may yield a suboptimal ecological outcome. The discussion in Exhibit 4.3 presents some of the difficulties as well as the opportunities involved in applying pollution prevention to manage environmental problems.

Case 3

In determining the optimal level of pollution, we assume that we have all the relevant information needed to obtain a good estimate of both the pollution control and pollution damage costs. As discussed earlier, while estimates of pollution control cost may be relatively easy to obtain, it is extremely difficult to evaluate all aspects of the damage costs. This is especially true when the pollution under consideration involves irreversible ecological change and the risk of major adverse surprises over a long time horizon. This is illustrated in the results of two studies by Nordhaus and one by Cline, as summarized in the remainder of this section. All three were motivated by a desire to find the best possible strategies to slow global warming over the coming century.

First, it may be instructive to provide a brief background to global warming and its expected consequences. According to the second report (1995) of the United Nations-sponsored Intergovernmental Panel on Climate Change, human activities have already caused global mean temperatures to rise by one half of a degree celsius since 1860 – about the beginning of the industrial period in the United States. The same report projects an increase in the range of 1–3.5°C in average temperatures over the next century if concentrations of greenhouse gases (GHGs) – carbon dioxide, methane, chlorofluorocarbons (CFCs), and nitrous oxides – continue to rise at current rates. If present trends continue, global warming is expected to trigger many changes in the natural environment, such as damage to world agriculture and forestry, and a rise in sea level, and to affect the adjustment capacities of many species (for more on the causes and consequences of global warming see Chapter 7, Section 4). In the three economic studies of global warming that follow, the emission of greenhouse gases is viewed as a global externality.

Exhibit 4.3   An ounce of pollution prevention?

It is Benjamin Franklin who is usually credited with the maxim 'an ounce of prevention is worth a pound of cure', although Franklin himself conceded that the sayings in *Poor Richard's Almanack* were derived from the wisdom of many ages and nations. Poor Richard also said: ''Tis easier to prevent bad habits than to break them'. Was he troubled by the vision thing and trying to tell us something? Forewarned, forearmed? The trouble with pollution prevention is that it wears many faces and is not always easily recognized. (What's more – bite thy tongue – it's not always feasible. How, for example, should we apply it to the problem of radon?) Designing an automobile engine to burn gasoline more completely, and thereby emit less carbon monoxide, is pollution prevention; hanging a catalytic converter on the tailpipe is not. Similarly, EPA's 'green' programs, which conserve electricity, prevent pollution (electricity generation accounts for 35 per cent of all US emissions of carbon dioxide); planting trees does not.

The Pollution Prevention Act of 1990 sets up a hierarchy of preferred approaches to protecting the environment. First and foremost, pollution should be prevented at the source whenever feasible. Pollution that cannot be prevented should be, in order of preference, recycled, treated or, as a last resort, disposed of in an environmentally safe manner. Operationally speaking, then, pollution prevention is source reduction, which is further defined in the Act as any practice that reduces the amount of any pollutant entering any waste stream. This applies to all activities in our society,

including those carried out in the energy, agriculture, consumer, and industrial sectors. Restricting development to protect sensitive ecosystems like wetlands is pollution prevention, as is cultivating crops that have a natural resistance to pests. Wrapping a blanket around your water heater is pollution prevention, and so is using energy-efficient light bulbs.

Sounds easy. Pollution prevention is not one of the many tools that can be applied to manage environmental problems (see the May/June 1992 issue of *EPA Journal*); rather, it is the ideal result that all management programs should try to achieve. The trouble is we've had so little experience pursuing pollution prevention that when we get down to making real choices it sometimes eludes us. We may have to compare products over their entire life cycle – mining, manufacturing, use, reuse, disposal. Now that they are both recyclable, which should we use, paper or plastic grocery bags? Paper biodegrades, but not in most landfills, and it is both bulkier and heavier to handle. Plastic manufacture has an image as a pollution-intensive industry, but papermaking is too. In fact, when pollution prevention has been the result, it has sometimes been inadvertent. It is the rising cost of landfilling, for example, that has persuaded many companies to reduce the solid waste they generate. As Poor Richard advised: 'Would you persuade, speak of Interest, not of Reason'.

Source: *EPA Journal* Vol. 19, No. 3, 1993, p. 8. Reprinted by permission.

The first study (Nordhaus 1991) was based on an analytical framework identical to that presented in this chapter. Thus, the primary aim of the study was to find an 'efficient' strategy for coping with global warming. In this study, the environmental damage function is defined as the cost to society due to climate change (such as effects on crop yields, land lost to oceans, human displacement, etc.). The control cost function reflects the added expenditures incurred by the economy for the purpose of reducing

GHG emissions in order to slow the greenhouse effect. These costs include, but are not limited to, the changes required to switch from fossil to nonfossil fuels, the search for substitutes for CFCs, and the protection of coastal properties and structures.

Additionally, this study assessed the impact of climate change assuming a doubling of pre-industrial (before 1860) CO_2 concentration. This benchmark level of CO_2 concentration is projected to increase global mean temperatures by 3°C. If nothing is done, the full impact of this climate change will start to be realized by 2050.

The results of this study depended on several factors, notably the estimation of the damage function. Thus, three different levels of the damage costs were considered, and on the basis of the medium damage function, the optimal reduction (where $MDC = MCC$) was shown to be 11 per cent of total GHG emissions. If this materialized, damage from the climate change would be roughly 1 per cent of the world's gross national product, and for this reason a modest program of international abatement is warranted.

The study by Cline (1992) considered the above assessment to be too modest. This study also used a cost–benefit framework for determining the efficient control of GHG emissions. However, the Cline study estimated the damage function differently. Cline argued that Nordhaus's study underestimated the damage cost from the greenhouse effect because it was based on a relatively short time horizon. That is, Nordhaus suggested that if policies to reduce GHGs emission were undertaken now, the global warming trend would stabilize by the year 2050 or so. However, this may not be the case because 'global warming is cumulative and irreversible on a time scale of centuries' (Cline 1992: 4).

Thus, a much longer time should be considered, perhaps as much as three hundred years. When this is done, 'global warming potential in the very long term is far higher than the 2°C to 3°C range usually considered – simply because the process does not stop at the conventional benchmark of a doubling of carbon dioxide' (ibid.). The estimate of the damage cost should account for this dynamic effect of global warming.

In addition, Cline was quite deliberate in considering the uncertainty associated with the damage cost. He considered society to be risk-averse and computed his final result after accounting for this risk factor. As a whole, the Cline study was based on a framework consistent with the precautionary principle, discussed at some detail in Chapter 9. As would be expected, the Cline study recommends an aggressive program of global reduction in GHG emissions. This is how the summary of the study reads:

> In sum, for several reasons, but especially because of the inclusion of more dramatic effects associated with nonlinear damage and very long-term warming, the policy conclusion in this study differs from that found in the Nordhaus steady-state analysis. The results here indicate that a program holding global carbon emissions to 4 [gigatons of carbon] per year – which would amount to a 71 per cent reduction from baseline by 2050, an 82 per cent reduction by 2100 and a 90 per cent reduction by 2200 – is warranted under risk aversion.
>
> (Cline 1992: 309)

The third study (Nordhaus 1992) was based on what is known as the dynamic integrated climate–economy (DICE) model of global warming. One of the advantages of this model is it allows a comparative analysis of the impact of alternative policy measures designed to slow climate change. Nordhaus investigated five alternative policies, one of which was called the ecological, or climate stabilization, policy. This policy option attempts 'to slow climate change to a pace that will prevent major ecological impacts. One proposal is to slow the rate of temperature increase to 0.1°C per decade from 1950' (p. 1317). Thus, the goal is to achieve this ecological end without regard to cost.

As it turned out, the 'ecological policy' favors a much higher emissions control rate than the policy based on economic efficiency – the optimal path. This is how Nordhaus described the result:

> Emissions control rates differ greatly among the alternative policies. In the optimal path, the rate of emissions reduction is approximately 10 per cent of GHG emissions in the near future, rising to 15 per cent late in the next century, whereas climate stabilization requires virtually complete elimination of GHG emissions.
>
> (Nordhaus 1992: 1318)

4.7 Chapter summary

- The primary objective of this chapter was to derive the condition for an 'optimal' level of pollution. This was done by closely examining the trade-off between two categories of costs associated with pollution: pollution control and damage costs.
- Pollution control costs refers to all the direct or explicit monetary expenditures by society to reduce current levels of pollution, e.g. expenditure on sewage treatment facilities. This cost function primarily reflects the *technology* of pollution control.
- Pollution damage costs denote the total monetary value of the damage from discharges of untreated waste into the environment. Pollution damage costs are difficult to assess since they entail assigning monetary values to harms done to plants and animals and their habitats; aesthetic impairments; rapid deterioration to physical infrastructure and assets; and various harmful effects on human health and mortality.
- Furthermore, it was noted that pollution damage costs are externalities.
- A trade-off exists between pollution control and damage costs. The more spent on pollution control, the lower will be the damage costs, and vice versa.
- In view of these trade-offs, it would be beneficial to spend an additional dollar on pollution control only if the incremental benefit arising from the damage avoided by the additional cleanup (waste control) exceeded one dollar. It can then be generalized from this that it would pay to increase expenditure on pollution control, provided that at the margin the control cost is less than the damage cost, i.e. $MCC < MDC$.
- It follows, then, that the optimal level of pollution (waste disposal) is attained when at the *margin* there is no difference between control and damage costs, i.e. $MCC = MDC$. When this condition is met, as demonstrated in this chapter, the total waste disposal cost (the sum of the total control and damage costs) is minimized.
- Further analysis of the nature of the two categories of costs of pollution revealed the following:

  1 The marginal pollution control cost (MCC) increases with an increase in pollution cleanup activities. This is because, incrementally, a higher level of environmental quality requires investments in technologies that are

increasingly costly. In the extreme case, taking the first visible waste from a body of water will cost much less than the last remaining waste, provided it is feasible at all!

2   The marginal pollution damage cost (*MDC*) is an increasing function of pollution emission. This can be explained by the ecological principle that pollution reduces the capacity of a natural ecosystem to withstand further pollution, i.e. a gradual loss of ecological resilience, so to speak.

3   The marginal damage cost can be interpreted as depicting society's willingness to pay for pollution cleanup, and hence, the demand for environmental quality.

• Another important issue addressed in this chapter is the possible divergence between economic and ecological optima. Three specific cases were examined to illustrate the significance of this issue:

1   It was observed that since the economic problem is stated as finding the cheapest way to dispose of a predetermined level of waste, *W**, in searching for the economic optimum the emphasis has been on *pollution cleanup* rather than *pollution prevention*. This difference matters because the focus on pollution prevention is *reduction of waste at the source*, whereas in the case of pollution cleanup the goal is to find the cheapest way of disposing of a predetermined level of waste.

2   Inconsistency between the economic and the ecological optimum may arise when the pollution under consideration is likely to impose environmental damage that is *irreversible* in the long term. This was demonstrated using empirical studies dealing with the economic effects of climate change.

3   Because damage costs are anthropocentrically determined, there is no assurance that the economic optimum level of pollution will adequately protect the well-being of other forms of life and the Earth's ecosystems as a whole.

Review and discussion questions

1   Briefly define the following concepts: pollution control cost, pollution damage cost, persistent pollutants, eutrophication, pollution prevention as opposed to pollution cleanup.

2   Explain how the damage cost function represents the demand function for environmental quality.

3   State whether the following statements are *true*, *false* or *uncertain* and explain why. Answer these questions using a graph of marginal damage and control cost curves.

(a) Improvement in pollution control technology reduces pollution while at the same time allowing society to realize savings in its expenditure on waste control. A 'win–win' situation, indeed!

(b) An increase in the living standard of a nation (as measured by an increase in per capita income) invariably leads to increased demand for environmental quality and consequently to a reduction in environmental deterioration.

(c) The real pollution problem is a consequence of population. (Hint: note that the damage cost is the demand for environmental quality.)

4   Fundamentally, the economics of pollution control deals with 'proper' accounting for the trade-off between control and damage costs. Explain the general nature of

the trade-off using the concepts of *MCC* and *MDC*. More specifically, explain what happens in each of the following three situations: $MCC > MDC$, $MCC < MDC$ and $MCC > MDC$.

5   Examine the following two statements. Are they equivalent?

(a) Pollution damage costs are externalities.
(b) Not all aspects of pollution damage costs can be evaluated in monetary terms.

6   Evaluate the relative merit of each of the following environmental management strategies. Identify a real-world case(s) in which one of these strategies is more appropriate than the others.

(a) Pollution should be 'prevented' at the source whenever feasible.
(b) Pollution should be 'controlled' up to a point where the total social cost for disposing it is minimized.
(c) Pollution should be controlled to prevent major long-term and irreversible ecological impacts.

References

Cline, W. R. (1992) *The Economics of Global Warming*, Washington, DC: Institute for International Economics.

Funtowicz, S. O. and Ravetz, J. R. (1994) 'The Worth of a Songbird: Ecological Economics as a Post-Normal Science', *Ecological Economics* 10: 197–207.

Intergovernmental Panel on Climate Change (1995) *Climate Change 1994: Radiative Forcing of Climate Change*, Cambridge: Cambridge University Press.

Miller, T. G., Jr. (1993) *Environmental Science*, 4th edn, Belmont, Calif.: Wadsworth.

Nordhaus, W. D. (1991) 'To Slow or Not to Slow: The Economics of the Greenhouse Effect', *Economic Journal* 101: 920–48.

——(1992) 'An Optimal Transition Path for Controlling Greenhouse Gases', *Science* 258: 1315–19.

5 The economics of environmental regulations

Regulating the environment through judicial procedures

> The tragedy of the commons as a food basket is averted by private property, or something formally like it. But the air and waters surrounding us cannot readily be fenced, and so the tragedy of the commons as a cesspool must be prevented by different means, by coercive laws or taxing devices that make it cheaper for the polluter to treat his pollutants than to discharge them untreated.
>
> (Hardin 1968: 1245)

5.1 Introduction

In Chapter 4 the focus was on developing a theoretical framework that would direct us to the conditions under which a socially optimal level of environmental quality could be attained. One of the major revelations in that chapter (see Section 5) was that environmental resources are externality-ridden. For this reason, the socially optimal level of environmental quality cannot be achieved through the unbridled operation of private markets. What this suggests is, as discussed earlier, a clear case of market failure and consequently a justification for public intervention.

Exhibit 5.1   Ore-Ida Foods to pay $1 million for polluting the Snake River

After pleading guilty to five criminal violations of the Clean Water Act, Ore-Ida Foods Incorporated was fined $1 million and placed on three years' probation by the US District Court in Portland, Oregon. The violations included discharging potato and other vegetable wastes into the Snake River from the wastewater treatment plant at Ore-Ida's facility in Ontario, Oregon, in violation of the company's permit issued under the National Pollutant Discharge Elimination System (NPDES). The EPA's [the US Environmental Protection Agency] Criminal Investigation Division initiated the complaint after being tipped off by an employee about data manipulation, illegal discharges and tampering with monitoring devices at the treatment plant. Ore-Ida will pay $250,000 of the fine immediately; it has until the end of the probation period to pay the rest or spend it on wastewater-recycling equipment at the treatment plant. The company has already spent $12 million on upgrading the plant. Ore-Ida Foods is headquartered in Boise, Idaho; it is a wholly owned subsidiary of H. J. Heinz Corporation.

Source: *EPA Journal* Vol. 20, 1994, p. 5. Reprinted by permission.

However, as will be evident throughout the next two chapters, public intervention is *not* a necessary nor sufficient condition for attaining the optimal allocation of environmental resources. Sufficiency requires that we attain the optimal environmental quality through means (policy instruments) that are *cost-effective* – that involve the least cost. Hence, on practical grounds, resolving environmental problems requires more than mere recognition of market failure or of the necessity of public intervention to correct an externality.

With this important caveat in mind, in this chapter we evaluate three legal approaches for regulating the environment, namely *liability laws*, *property rights* or *Coasian methods*, and *emission standards*. The unifying theme of these three approaches is their focus on the legal system to deter abuse of the environment. In the case of liability laws, the court would set monetary fines on the basis of the perceived damage to the environment. The Coasian method uses the legal system to assign and enforce property rights. Emission standards are set and enforced through legally mandated laws. Each of these policy instruments is evaluated on the basis of the following specific criteria: efficiency, compliance (transaction) cost, fairness, ecological effects, and moral and ethical considerations.

5.2 Environmental regulation through liability laws

In many countries, including the United States, liability laws are used as a way of resolving conflicts arising from environmental damage. The main idea behind this type of statutory enactment is *to make polluters liable for the damage they cause*. More specifically, polluters are the defendants and those who are affected by pollution, the pollutees, are the plaintiffs. Thus, since polluters are subject to lawsuits and monetary payments if they are found guilty (see Exhibit 5.1), it is in their best interest to pay special attention to the way they use the ambient environment as a medium for waste disposal. In this sense, liability laws can be used as a means of internalizing environmental externalities. The question then is, how effective is the use of liability laws in internalizing environmental externalities?

We can address this question using a hypothetical example, the environmental dispute between two firms, a paper mill and a fish hatchery. As in Chapter 3, the problem is a river that is used jointly by these two firms. The paper mill uses the river to discharge the byproducts of its manufacturing process, and the fish hatchery relies on the same river to raise juvenile fish. By virtue of its upstream location, the production activity of the paper mill will have a negative impact on the operation of the hatchery. However, since neither of these firms can claim sole ownership of the river, there is no mechanism to make the paper mill pay for the damage it is imposing on the operation of the hatchery. As we have seen in Chapter 3, if this third party effect of the paper mill's production activity is not corrected, it will inevitably cause a misallocation of societal resources. In particular, there will be an overproduction of paper (hence, a higher level of waste discharge into the river) and an underproduction of fish, relative to what is considered socially optimal. How can a situation like this be rectified using liability laws?

As stated above, liability laws hold polluters accountable for the damage they cause to third parties (pollutees). This means that polluters are required to pay financial compensation in direct proportion to the damage they inflict on those third parties. For our two firms, this suggests that the paper mill, through a specific statutory mandate, will be ordered to compensate the owner of the fish hatchery. Ideally, for problems

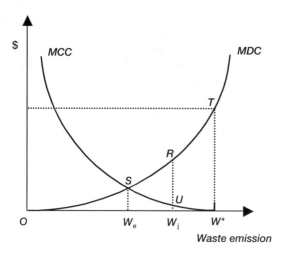

Figure 5.1 The optimal level of pollution under strictly enforced liability law. If compensation is awarded in direct proportion to damage, the *MDC* would represent the legally sanctioned compensation the paper mill has to pay to the hatchery. Given that the *MCC* represents the marginal cost to the paper mill for an alternative way to dispose of its waste, it will be in this firm's best interest to limit its pollution to W_e – which is less than what it would have been (W^*) if the liability law was not effected at all.

related to the environment, the court sets the level of compensation on the basis of the *damage cost function*. Let us assume that the court has free access to detailed and accurate information about the damage costs relevant to our two firms. We can then draw the marginal damage cost curve (*MDC*), shown in Figure 5.1, using this information.

If the river is considered a free good, amount W^* of waste will be discharged by the paper mill. This corresponds to the situation in which the river is treated as a 'common' property resource; hence, the paper mill has free access to its use. However, at this level of waste emission the paper company is causing damage to the fish hatchery with a *total* monetary value equal to the area OTW^* – the area under the marginal damage cost curve when amount W^* of waste is emitted. Thus, under a strict liability law the court will use this monetary value as a *benchmark* for the compensation to be awarded to the fish hatchery. Suppose the paper mill is actually ordered to pay this amount of compensation to the owner of the fish hatchery. This order then will force the owner of the paper mill to re-evaluate the mill's decision concerning waste disposal, using reasoning we shall now set out.

Since compensation is awarded in *direct proportion* to the damage, the owner of the paper mill knows that the mill can always reduce its penalty by decreasing the amount of waste it is discharging into the river. For example, if the amount of waste emitted into the river is reduced from W^* to W_j, as shown in Figure 5.1, the monetary value of the penalty that the paper mill has to pay (in terms of damage compensation) will be area ORW_j – which is less than area OTW^*. However, this firm also faces additional nonlegal costs. The reduction of its waste emission from W^* to W_j would require cleanup costs measured by area W^*UW_j – the area under the relevant MCC curve. Hence, the net saving from reducing waste discharge from W^* to W_j to this firm would be area W^*URT. Is this the best this firm can do?

The answer to this question is *no*. In fact it can be shown that it would be in the best interest of the paper mill to reduce its waste discharge from W^* all the way to W_e. This is because, for any level of waste greater than W_e, the MDC (the legally sanctioned compensation the paper mill has to pay to the hatchery) is greater than the MCC – the amount the paper mill has to pay for using waste treatment technology. Thus, under this scenario the maximum waste that the paper mill will emit into the river will be W_e. Interestingly, this result is identical to the condition for an optimal level of pollution that was obtained in Chapter 4, i.e. $MDC = MCC$. The implication of this is that, *in an ideal setting (where the regulators have full and accurate information about damage costs), environmental regulation through liability laws could force polluters to pay for an environmental service that would be consistent with its scarcity (social) value.*

The above result clearly suggests that, at least conceptually, if environmental regulations are carefully designed and strictly enforced through liability laws, an optimal level of pollution will be secured. Furthermore, this optimal level of pollution is *not* determined by a government decree; rather, it is reached by a decision-making process of private concerns reacting only to *a financial disincentive* imposed on them by a fully enforced liability law. How effective are liability laws as an instrument for regulating the use of environmental resources?

On the positive side, at least theoretically, liability laws are capable of causing private decision-makers to gravitate toward the socially optimal level of pollution. Furthermore, this can be accomplished without the need for prior identification of the optimal level of pollution, provided the court has detailed and accurate information on damage costs. In this sense, then, liability laws basically operate on the premise of *economic incentives*. In addition, liability laws tend to have *moral appeal*, since they are based on the premise of punishing the perpetrator of the damage. In other words, 'the polluter-pays' principle is strictly applicable.

However, using the courts to enforce victims' rights in relation to pollution damage has several disadvantages. First, legal remedies are generally slow and costly. Second, relying on dispute resolution by means of lawsuits may be *unfair* if the damaged individual does not have the resources to bring a suit. Third, when the number of affected parties (polluters and pollutees) is large, it may be difficult to determine who harmed whom, and to what exact degree. For instance, lawsuits would face almost insurmountable difficulties (or high transaction costs) in solving problems concerning fouled air in crowded industrial areas. This approach seems to work best where the number of polluters is small and their victims are few and easily identified.

In most nations, including the United States, liability laws were probably one of the earliest forms of public policy tools used to internalize environmental externalities. The use of this approach was perhaps justifiable at this early stage of environmental litigation because the problems tended to be local and, generally, the parties involved in the dispute fewer. Furthermore, at that time, courts tended to deal with cases that were considered more as *environmental nuisance* (such as littering) rather than environmental damage with considerable risk to human health and ecological stability.

However, as environmental concerns became complex, fresh approaches to solving these problems were sought. An approach that generated considerable excitement in the economics profession in the 1960s was the property rights or Coasian approach, named after economist Ronald Coase. The initial impetus for this approach was its implication that the role of public intervention was limited. Let us now turn to the discussion and evaluation of this approach.

5.3 The property rights or Coasian approach

As discussed in Chapter 3, environmental resources are externality-ridden because they lack clearly defined property rights. Once this is acknowledged, any effort to internalize (remedy) environmental externalities requires an effective scheme for assigning property rights. This captures the essence of the property rights approach. More specifically, the approach requires that property rights should be assigned to one of the parties involved in an environmental dispute. Furthermore, according to Coase (1960), the assignment of property rights could be completely arbitrary and this would have no effect on the final outcome of the environmental problem under consideration. For example, in the case of environmental pollution, *the Coasian approach suggests that the optimal level of pollution can be achieved by an arbitrary assignment of property rights to either the polluter(s) or the pollutee(s).* This proposition that the assignment of property rights to a specific party has no effect on the optimal level of pollution is the core concept of what is widely known as the Coase theorem. To demonstrate the essence of this theorem in a simple manner, we shall again use the two familiar firms, the paper mill and the fish hatchery.

As noted earlier, the problem between these two firms arises because their economic activities involve the joint use of a river. To demonstrate how this problem can be remedied using a property rights approach, let us start by assuming that the legal rights to the use of the river belong to the hatchery. Given this, the hatchery, if it wishes, could completely deny the paper mill access to the river. That is, the paper mill would not be permitted to use the river to discharge its waste. In Figure 5.2, this situation is represented by the origin *O*, where the amount of waste emitted into the river from the paper mill is *zero*. This means that the paper mill has to find an alternative way of disposing the waste from its current operation – a total of 200 units. The key question is, then, will this be a stable situation? Given the *MDC* and *MCC* curves presented in Figure 5.2, the answer to this question would be a *no*, for the following reason.

When the waste discharged by the paper mill is less than W_e (110 units), we observe that the *MCC* (the incremental cost of cleanup for the paper mill using other means than the river) is greater than the *MDC* – the incremental damage cost to the hatchery. For example, as shown in Figure 5.2, for the 70th unit of the waste that is emitted into the river, the marginal damage cost to the hatchery is $20. However, to achieve this same result, the cost to the paper mill is $50. Note that this $50 is the marginal control cost of treating (cleaning) the 130th unit of waste (200 − 70). Thus, given this situation, the paper mill will clearly have an incentive to offer a financial bribe to the fish hatchery for the right to use the river for discharging its industrial waste. For example, as shown in Figure 5.2, to discharge the 70th unit of waste the paper mill will be willing to pay the hatchery a fee of between $20 and $50. This should be acceptable to both parties. For the hatchery, a payment exceeding $20 more than compensates for the damage caused to its fish operation from the dumping of the 70th unit of waste into the river. Similarly, this situation should also be advantageous to the paper mill because the cost of using an alternative technology to dispose of the 70th unit (i.e. to clean up the 130th unit)

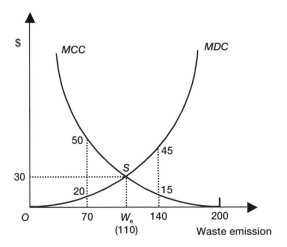

Figure 5.2 Graphical illustration of the Coase theorem. This graph can be used to explain the notion that pollution problems can be resolved optimally by an arbitrary assignment of property rights.

of waste to this firm is at least $50. In general, then, these two firms will be in a position to engage in a mutually beneficial transaction provided that, at the point where the negotiation is taking place, $MCC > MDC$. Furthermore, the negotiation between these two parties ceases when, for the last unit of waste discharged by the paper mill, $MCC = MDC$. This is indeed the condition for the optimal level of pollution. In Figure 5.2, this is attained at W_e, or 110 units of emission.

As discussed earlier, the Coase theorem goes beyond the mere recognition of optimality. It also states that *this optimal outcome is completely independent of the two parties who have rights to the river*. To demonstrate this, let us now consider the case where the paper mill has exclusive legal rights to the use of the river. Under these circumstances the paper mill, if it wishes, can dispose of all its waste into the river. If this strategy is followed, then as shown in Figure 5.2, the paper mill will discharge a total of 200 units of waste into the river. However, this company is not limited to this option only. As shown in Figure 5.2, for each unit between 110 and 200 units of waste discharged, the MDC is greater than the MCC. This situation will allow the fish hatchery and the paper mill to engage in a mutually beneficial transaction. To see this, let us focus on what happens when the emission is at 140 units. When this unit of waste is discharged, the MDC to the fish hatchery is $45, but the cost to the paper mill of treating this same unit is $15. Note that the $15 is the marginal cost to the paper mill for controlling the 60th unit of emission (200 − 140). Thus, when the emission level is at 140 units the MDC is *greater* than the MCC. Given this, the hatchery will have an incentive to offer a financial bribe to the paper mill of anywhere between $15 and $45 to withhold this unit of waste. It is easy to see that the paper mill will most likely take this offer seriously since the cost of controlling the 60th unit of waste (200 − 140) is only $15. Thus, to the extent that the offer of the hatchery exceeds $15, the paper mill will abide by the wishes of the hatchery. A similar situation prevails for all the units where the *MDC* exceeds the *MCC*, i.e. between 200 and 110 units. Thus, the optimal level of pollution is again reached at W_e or 110 units, where *MDC* = *MCC*. This result verifies the validity of the Coase theorem.

In the 1960s, for most economists the Coase theorem was an exciting and appealing revelation. *The profound implication of this theorem has been that pollution problems can be resolved by an arbitrary assignment of property rights. What is appealing about this is that it reduces the role of public regulators to a mere assignment of enforceable ownership rights. Once this is done, as discussed above, the optimal level of pollution is attained through voluntary negotiation of private parties – which is consistent with the spirit of the private market.*

Despite its appeal, however, the Coasian approach has several weaknesses. First, in our example above, the source of the pollution as well as the parties involved in the dispute are easily identifiable. However, in many real-world situations, the sources of the pollution are likely to be multifaceted and their impacts quite diffuse. In addition, environmental disputes normally involve several parties. In a typical real-world situation, then, the cost of negotiation and enforcement – the *transaction cost* (the monetary outlays for specifying, defining and enforcing property rights) – could be quite high. As discussed earlier, a high transaction cost could distort the final outcome of an environmental dispute in a rather significant manner. In such a situation, a resolution reached using the property rights approach might be far removed from what is considered to be socially optimal.

The above consideration would be even more serious when pollution problems (such as acid rain, global warming and ozone depletion) transcend national boundaries, involve irreversible changes and considerable uncertainty, and call for a coordinated and multifaceted response by a large number of nations that are involved.

Second, a property rights approach, especially its Coasian variation, seems to support the ethos that 'the end justifies the means'. As is evident from the above discussion, in this approach the focus is singularly placed on attaining an optimal outcome. Whether the optimal outcome is attained by assigning property rights to the polluters or assigning them to the pollutees is considered entirely irrelevant. Clearly, this seems to be counter to what appears to be the conventional wisdom – 'the polluter-pays' principle.

Third, according to the Coase theorem, the optimal level of pollution can be achieved irrespective of which party was given the initial property rights, the polluters or the pollutees. However, what the theorem does not address is the impact the initial assignment of property rights has on *income distribution*. In general, the income position of the party empowered with property rights is positively impacted. To see this, let us refer back to Figure 5.2. Furthermore, let us assume that the hatchery has exclusive rights to the use of the river. Given this scenario, we have already demonstrated that W_e will be the optimal level of effluent. Let us suppose that this outcome was reached on terms stipulating that the paper mill would pay a uniform compensation of $30 dollars per unit of pollution discharged into the river. Note that the paper mill would be willing to pay $30 for each unit of untreated waste it discharged into the river until the emission level reached W_e or 110 units. This is because along this relevant range of waste emission, $30 < *MCC* – what the paper mill would have paid to control its waste using alternative means. Under this arrangement the hatchery will receive a total payment equal to $3,300 ($30 × 110). However, by letting the paper mill discharge 110 units of waste into the river, the hatchery incurs a damage cost represented by the area OSW_e

(the area under the *MDC* curve). The dollar value of this damage will be approximately $1,650 [½ (110 × 30)]. This represents a net gain of approximately $1,650 to the hatchery – a gain realized at the expense of the paper mill. Therefore, in terms of total societal income, the gain of the hatchery was offset by the loss of the paper mill. The reverse would be the case if the initial assignment of property right were switched from the hatchery to the paper mill.

Fourth, in the above analysis it is assumed that transferring the property rights from one party to another would not cause either party to cease to function. What if this is not the case? What if giving the property rights to the hatchery makes the paper mill go out of business or vice versa? Under this situation, as Starrett and Zeckhauser (1992) have demonstrated, the Coasian approach will not yield a unique optimal solution.

So far we have examined two possible mechanisms by which a society could attempt to control pollution, namely liability laws and property rights regimes. In both of these types of pollution control scheme, the regulatory roles of public authorities were viewed as something to be minimized. In the case of liability laws, the principal role of the court is reduced to simply setting the fine (compensation) polluters have to pay to the damaged parties. Under the property rights approach the sole responsibility of the public authorities is to assign property rights to one of the parties involved in an environmental dispute. Once these steps have been taken, at least theoretically it is presumed that the interaction of the relevant parties involved in the dispute will lead to an efficient outcome. In this sense, then, both liability laws and property rights exemplify a *decentralized* approach to pollution control.

While this may be appealing in some professional circles, especially among economists, the fact remains that the above two approaches are of limited use in a real-world situation. This is because modern environmental problems are generally widespread in their scope, varying in their ecological impacts, and involve a large number of people with varying socioeconomic circumstances. For this reason, one of the most widely used methods of regulating environmental damages has been based on direct regulation – a *centralized* form of pollution control. How such a regulatory instrument works and its limitations are the subjects of the next section.

5.4 Emission standards

An emission standard is a *maximum* rate of effluent discharge that is legally permitted. Emission standards can take a variety of forms. The form that is intuitively most obvious is, of course, a standard expressed in terms of *quantity* or *volume* of waste material released into the ambient environment per unit time. For example, it might be the case that in any given week, no more than 100 tons of untreated sewage waste is allowed to be released into a given river stream. In some cases, in setting emission standards the focus is on maintaining the overall quality of a more diffuse environmental medium. This is normally done by setting an *ambient standard* on the basis of an allowable concentration of pollution. For example, the ambient standard for dissolved oxygen in a particular river might specify that the level must not be allowed to drop below 3 parts per million (ppm). One other commonly used regulatory practice is *technology standards*. In this case, regulators specify the technologies that potential polluters must adopt (see Exhibit 5.2).

In principle, the emission standard mandated is supposed to reflect the public interest at large; any violators are subjected to legal prosecution. Moreover, if found guilty,

---

Exhibit 5.2   Emission standards proposed for marine engines

Working in cooperation with the marine industry, the EPA [the US Environmental Protection Agency] has proposed the nation's first emissions standards for marine engines. The standards proposed would apply to all new outboard, inboard, stern-drive and personal watercraft engines (such as Jet Skis and Wave Runners). Manufacturers would begin phasing in the new standards over a nine-year period, beginning with the 1998 model year. The technology developed will create a new generation of low-emission, high-perform-ance engines. Older models would be unaffected by the new standards. The 12 million marine engines now in the United States give off about 700,000 tons per year of hydrocarbon (HC) and nitrogen oxide (NO_x) emissions; the new generation of marine engines is expected to reduce NO_x emissions to 37 per cent and HC emissions by more than 75 per cent. HC and NO_x emissions create ground-level ozone, which can irritate the respiratory tract, causing chest pain and lung inflammation. Ozone can also aggravate existing respiratory conditions such as asthma.

Of all 'non-road' engines, only lawn and garden engines emit higher levels of HC, a 1991 EPA study found; only farm and construction equipment emit higher levels of NO_x. New standards for lawn and garden engines were proposed in May. Standards for land-based, non-road diesel engines such as those in farm and construction equip-ment were finalized in June.

It is expected that the design changes necessary to reduce emissions will also improve performance and fuel economy, making starting easier and acceleration faster, and produce less noise, odor and smoke.

Source: *EPA Journal* Vol. 20, 1994, p. 3. Reprinted by permission.

---

violators are punished by a monetary fine and/or imprisonment. In this sense, then, emission standards are environmental policies that are based on 'command-and-control' approaches.

In the United States, the Environmental Protection Agency (EPA) is responsible for implementing environmental laws enacted by Congress. Table 5.1 provides a list of some of these laws. In implementing them, the EPA, which is a federal agency, works in partnership with state, county and local municipality governments to use a range of tools designed to protect the environment. State and local standards may exceed federal standards, *but cannot be less stringent*. All states have environmental agencies; some are separate agencies and others are part of state health departments. Although the EPA sets the minimum standards, these state agencies are responsible for implementing and monitoring many of the major environmental statutes, such as the provisions of the Clean Air Acts. Enforcement of the standards is usually a state or local responsi-bility, but many enforcement actions require the resources of both federal and state authorities.

The basic economics of emission standards can be briefly discussed using the familiar graph presented in Figure 5.3 (see p. 98). Suppose the amount of waste that would have been emitted in the absence of regulation is 300 units. If we assume that the public authorities have full information about the damage and control cost functions, then they will be in a position to recognize that the socially optimal level of pollution

Table 5.1 Some of the major environmental laws enacted by the United States Congress, 1938–90

1938	Federal Food, Drug, and Cosmetic Act (last amended 1988)
1947	Federal Insecticide, Fungicide, and Rodenticide Act (last amended 1988)
1948	Federal Water Pollution Control Act (or the Clean Water Act; last amended 1988)
1955	Clean Air Act (last amended 1990)
1965	Shoreline Erosion Protection Act
1965	Solid Waste Disposal Act (last amended 1988)
1970	National Environmental Policy Act (last amended 1975)
1970	Resource Recovery Act
1970	Pollution Prevention Packaging Act (last amended 1983)
1971	Lead-Based Paint Poisoning Prevention Act (last amended 1988)
1972	Coastal Zone Management Act (last amended 1985)
1972	Marine Protection, Research, and Sanctuaries Act (last amended 1988)
1972	Ocean Dumping Act
1973	Endangered Species Act
1974	State Drinking Water Act (last amended 1994)
1974	Shoreline Erosion Control Demonstration Act
1975	Hazardous Materials Transportation Act
1976	Resource Conservation and Recovery Act
1976	Toxic Substances Control Act (last amended 1988)
1977	Surface Mining Control and Reclamation Act
1978	Uranium Mill-Tailing, Radiation Control Act (last amended 1988)
1980	Asbestos School Hazard Detection and Control Act
1980	Comprehensive Environmental Response, Compensation, and Liability Act
1982	Nuclear Water Policy Act
1984	Asbestos School Hazard Abatement Act
1986	Asbestos Hazard Emergency Response Act
1986	Emergency Planning and Community Right to Know Act
1988	Indoor Radon Abatement Act
1988	Lead Contamination Control Act
1988	Medical Waste Tracking Act
1988	Ocean Dumping Ban Act
1988	Shore Protection Act
1990	National Environmental Education Act

Source: *EPA Journal* Vol. 21, No. 1, 1995, p. 48. Reprinted by permission.

is 150 units, which is less than 300. To attain the socially optimal level of pollution, public authorities would now set the emission standard at 150, and strictly enforce it.

The ultimate effects of this are as follows. First, if the standard is successfully implemented, the socially optimal level of pollution is preserved. Second, polluters will be forced to internalize the cost of controlling pollution emissions up to the socially optimal level. As shown in Figure 5.3, polluters will be forced to reduce their waste from 300 to 150 units, and given their *MCC* curve, the total cost of doing this will be area W_eFW^*. *Note that if it were not for the emission standard, polluters would have been in a position to entirely avoid this cost.*

In our discussion we have explicitly assumed that the public authorities somehow have perfect information concerning the damage and control costs. That is a very strong assumption, given what we know about the nature of these two cost functions, especially, as discussed in Chapter 4, the difficulty associated with estimating marginal damage cost. Is this assumption absolutely necessary? The short answer to this question

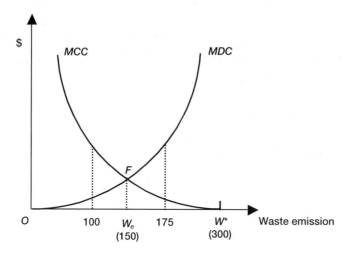

Figure 5.3 Emission standards as a policy tool to control pollution. The argument presented via this graph is that through the competing voices of various opposing special interest groups (i.e. pro-environmental versus pro-business groups), public authorities would, in the long-run, gravitate toward setting a standard that will lead to the attainment of the optimal level of pollution, W_e.

is *no*. However, without the assumed perfect information there is no guarantee that the outcome will be socially optimal. Nevertheless, in the absence of full information on damage and control costs, the public authorities may set the initial emission standard on the basis of what appears to be *the best available information* about these costs at the point in time the decision is made. For example, in Figure 5.3, suppose that the emission standard is initially set at 100 – a standard stricter than the socially optimal level, W_e or 150 units. Clearly, this policy is likely to anger the polluters and cause a request for re-evaluation of the emission standard. If, after a careful re-evaluation of the damage and control costs, the outcome of the initial standard setting is judged to be too stringent, then the public authorities will revise their standard in such a way that more pollution will be permitted. Similarly, if the authorities set emission standards that are below what is considered to be socially optimal, such as 175 units, this mandate will be vehemently challenged by advocates of the environment. The news account in Exhibit 5.3 illustrates typical public reactions to proposed changes in emission standards. In this case the specific issue involves public reactions to a stricter air quality standard proposed by the EPA.

The broader implication of the above analysis is that through trial and error and the competing voices of various special interest groups, the public authorities gravitate toward setting a standard that will, in the long run, lead to the attainment of the optimal level of pollution. In this respect, then, at least in principle, emission standards appear to provide room for flexibility.

In addition to its presumed flexibility, emission standards are sought to have the following advantages. First, in principle, emission standards can be simple and direct – to the extent that they aim at the attainment of clearly defined numerical or techno-

Exhibit 5.3   EPA proposes strict new air quality standards

Washington – To the consternation of many state and business leaders, the Environmental Protection Agency proposed stringent new air quality standards Wednesday that would cost more than $6.5 billion a year to meet. The new rules would tighten pollution limits that many cities already fail to meet and regulate more of the tiny particles from smokestacks.

After reviewing more than 200 studies – its most extensive scientific peer review ever – the agency concluded that current standards do not adequately protect public health, especially for children. 'Today, EPA takes an important step for protecting public health and our environment from the harmful effect of air pollution', said EPA Administrator Carol Browner.

But opponents criticized the agency for failing to consider the high cost of the proposals and said it lacked data to support some assumptions. 'The US EPA is putting a huge mandate on the state, on local governments and on consumers without having fully evaluated the cost, the relative health benefits and the technical feasibility of meeting the standards', said Donald Schregardus, director of the Ohio Environmental Protection Agency.

But Browner said the EPA's mandate called for it to ensure that health standards meet current science regardless of cost. She estimated that meeting the new standards would cost between $6.5 billion and $8.5 billion annually. However, she claimed that would be offset by up to $120 billion in health benefits, such as fewer hospital stays or missed work. The decision was a setback for industry, which mounted a massive lobbying campaign against the proposal.

A coalition of industry and business groups predicted that states and cities would have to impose drastic pollution controls, including travel restrictions, mandatory car pooling and restrictions on pleasure boats, lawn mowers and outdoor barbecues. Owen Drew of the National Association of Manufacturers predicted that the restrictions would have 'a chilling effect on economic growth'.

But the EPA called that a scare tactic, and said most areas could meet the standards using smog-reduction programs already on the books. Also, in those areas needing changes, most will come in factories and refineries, not in changed driving or other habits, the agency said.

The new standards would require communities to cut ozone levels by one third to 0.08 parts per million cubic feet of air from 0.12 ppm, the current standard. The readings, however, will be taken over an average of eight hours, rather than during a single one-hour period, making it somewhat easier to meet the new standard.

The EPA also wants to regulate tiny particles of dust down to 2.5 microns in diameter. Currently standards apply only to particles of 10 microns or larger. It would take about 8 microns to equal the width of a human hair. Health experts argue that the minuscule particles – many of which come from industrial or utility smokestacks – cause the most harm because they lodge deep in the lungs.

Source: *Kalamazoo Gazette/The Associated Press*, November 28, 1996. Copyright © 1996 The Associated Press. Reprinted by permission.

logical objectives. Second, they can be effectively used to keep extremely harmful pollution, such as DDT and industrial toxic wastes, below dangerous levels. In other words, when a given pollutant has well-known and long-lasting adverse ecological and human health effects, command-and-control approaches may be the most cost-effective. Last but not least, they tend to be politically popular because they have a certain *moral appeal*. Pollution is regarded as a 'public bad', therefore the activities of polluters should be subject to considerable public scrutiny.

However, despite their simplicity, flexibility and political appeal, emission standards as a policy instrument for environmental regulation have several flaws. Moreover, some of these flaws are considered to have serious adverse economic and social implications. First, standards are set solely by government fiat. To this extent they are highly interventionist and signify a major departure from the cherished spirit of the 'free market'. Second, pollution control practices applied through administrative laws, such as emission standards, generally require the creation of a large bureaucracy to administer the program. If this is so, the administrative and enforcement costs (i.e. the transaction costs) of applying emission standards can be considerable.

Third, in setting standards, a strong tendency may exist for the regulators and the established firms to cooperate. The end result of this may be a 'regulatory capture', where regulators are influenced to set standards in ways that are likely to benefit the existing firms. Thus, standards have the potential to be used unjustly as barriers to entry.

Fourth, while the administrative and enforcement costs of pollution control laws are real and in some instances considerable, the regulatory agency is not designed to generate its own *revenue*, except for the occasional collection of fines from violators of the law.

A fifth problem with emission standards is that the administrative process that is used to set the standard may neglect consideration of *economic efficiency*. This manifests itself in two ways.

First, economic efficiency requires that in setting a standard, *both* damage and control costs should be taken into account. Public regulators, in their desire to please a particular special-interest group, may be inclined to set standards on the basis of either damage or control cost, but not both. For example, administrators wishing to please their environmentally conscious constituents would be inclined to set emission standards on the basis of damage cost only. This action might overly sensitize regulators to the risk of environmental damage (pollution) – which could ultimately result in a recommendation of excessively stringent emission standards. The opposite would have been the case if emission standards are set solely on considerations of control costs.

Second, emission standards are typically applied *uniformly* across emission sources. This happens for two practical reasons. First, the administrative and enforcement costs of designing and implementing standards that vary with the different circumstances of each pollution source could be quite costly. Second, from a purely administrative viewpoint, it is much easier to monitor and enforce standards that are uniform across emission sources

When there are several emitters with a wide range of technological capabilities, however, pollution control policy based on a uniform emission standard would *not* be *cost-effective*. The reason for this is rather straightforward, as is shown in Figure 5.4. In this example, for the sake of simplicity we are considering the activities of only two firms or sources. As is evident from the curvatures of their respective marginal control cost curves, these firms employ different emission control technologies. Furthermore, let us assume that the emission standard is set so that a total of 200 units of waste will be controlled by these two firms. In addition, the government authorities have decided to accomplish this through a uniform emission standard that splits the responsibilities for cleanup equally between the two parties. In Figure 5.4, this suggests that each firm would be responsible for cleaning up 100 units of waste. Under this mandate, the *total*

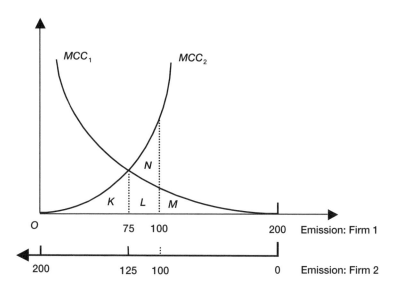

Figure 5.4 The cost effectiveness of emission standards. What this graph explains is the simple fact that unless the firms under consideration operate using identical waste processing technology (MCC_1 and MCC_2 are identical), pollution control policy based on a *uniform* emission control will not be cost-effective.

waste control cost for these two firms would be represented by area $K + L + M + N$. This total is composed of the waste control costs of Firms 1 and 2, which are represented by areas M and $K + L + N$ respectively. Could this total control cost be reduced by using a non-uniform assignment of emission standard setting? In other words, is a policy based on a uniform emission standard cost-effective?

The answer to the above question is clearly *yes*, as can easily be seen using Figure 5.4. Suppose the government authorities order Firm 2 to clean up only 75 units of the total waste, and Firm 1 is charged to clean up the rest, which will be 125 units (200 − 75). Under this scenario, the total waste control cost (the combined costs of both firms) is measured by area $K + L + M$. Note that this cost is smaller than the cost the two firms incurred when a uniform emission standard was applied – area $K + L + M + N$. Furthermore, careful observation indicates that with the new allocation, the marginal control costs of the two firms are equal, i.e. $MCC_1 = MCC_2$. This condition is signifi-cant because it suggests that area $K + L + M$ is the minimum cost of cleaning up the desired level of total waste emissions, 200 units. This is the case because, at this level of emission, the marginal control costs for the two firms are equal, and hence there is no opportunity left to further reduce costs by reallocating resources from one firm to the other. *Thus, we can conclude that the total cost of controlling (cleaning up) a given amount of waste is minimized when the marginal control costs are equalized for all emitters. Awareness of this condition clearly reveals that unless the firms under consider-ation operate using identical waste processing technology, pollution control policy based on a uniform emission control will not be cost-effective.* This is an important lesson to note for policy-makers dealing with environmental pollution control.

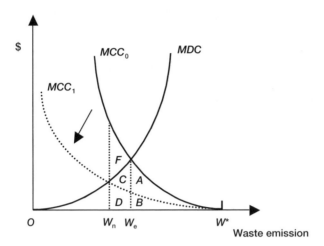

Figure 5.5 Emission standards and the incentive to improve pollution control technology. This graph shows how emission standards could have the potential to undermine firms' incentive to invest in new pollution control equipment. The effect of an investment in pollution control technology is illustrated by a downward shift in the *MCC*. The net saving from such a project initially appeared to be represented by area *C + A*, it is argued that a change in emission standards to reflect the new reality may reduce the saving to area (*A – D*).

The sixth and the last weakness of emission standards to be discussed in this chapter is that the unintended effect of setting a standard may in reality be to discourage investment in new and improved pollution control technology. Figure 5.5 can be used to illustrate the essence of the above two points. In this figure, let MCC_0 and MDC_0 represent the initial marginal control and damage cost curves, respectively. To be more specific, let us assume these are costs associated with waste emissions from one of our familiar firms, the paper mill. Given this information, the efficient level of pollution will be W_e. Let us further assume that, using an economic efficiency criterion as a policy guide, the current emission standard is set at W_e. That is, by law, W_e is the maximum amount of waste that the paper mill is allowed to emit into the river. Under this condition the total expenditure to the firm for complying with this law is represented by area *A + B*: the area under curve MCC_0 corresponding to emission level W_e. Note that if the firm were not regulated at all, it would have emitted amount W^* of waste into the river and its cleanup cost would have been zero.

At this point, the paper mill knows that it cannot do much to change the law. However, it is still at liberty to find a way of reducing its cleanup cost by some technological means. What economic conditions need to be met in order for this firm to have an incentive to invest in new waste controlling technology? The simple answer is that the paper mill will insist that the cost savings from the use of the new technology be sufficiently large to recoup a fair rate of return from its initial investment expenditure. To see this logic clearly, suppose we assume that the paper mill is contemplating the introduction of new waste processing technology. If this were implemented, as shown in Figure 5.5 the impact of the new technology would be to shift the marginal control cost curve from MCC_0 to MCC_1. Given the current level of emission standards, W_e, with the new technology the pollution control cost to the paper mill would be measured by area B – the area under MCC_1 given that the emission standard is set at W_e. When compared with the old technology, this represents a cost saving indicated by area A. It should be noted, however, that this amount of saving can be realized if, and only if, the emission standard is kept at the current level, W_e. There is no guarantee that the regulatory authorities will not revise their decision when the firm's technological condition becomes fully apparent to them. That is, when policy-makers become aware of the new waste processing technology available to the firm, they may decide to change the emission standard to reflect this change. In Figure 5.5 the new standard would be W_n. Under this tighter emission standard, the total waste control cost to this firm would be represented by area $B + D$ – the area under curve MCC_1 when the emission standard is set at W_n. This result implies an increase in the pollution control cost for this firm by area D. Hence, as a result of this further tightening of the emission standards, the net savings from implementing the new technology would now be reduced from what would have been area A, to the difference between the areas of A and D. *The implication here is that emission standards could have the potential to undermine firms' incentive to invest in new pollution control equipment. Furthermore, given the above scenario, firms subject to emission standards would have an incentive to hide technological changes from the regulatory authorities.*

5.5 Chapter summary

This chapter discussed *three* alternative policy approaches used to internalize environmental externalities: liability laws, Coasian methods and emission standards. The unifying feature of these approaches is their direct dependence on the *legal system* to resolve environmental litigation.

- Liability law was one of the earliest methods used to deter abuses of the environment. This approach uses statutory acts that are specifically intended to make polluters liable for the damage they cause. If found liable, polluters are ordered to pay to the plaintiff (in this case the pollutees) financial compensation in *direct proportion* to the damage they have inflicted.
- The principal advantages of liability laws are:

  1   They are effective in deterring environmental nuisance (such as littering).
  2   They have moral appeal since they are based on the polluter-pays principle.

- The main disadvantages of liability laws are:

  1   They are subject to high transaction costs when the number of parties involved is large and when getting reliable information about the damage is not easy.
  2   They are 'unfair' if the individual damaged does not have the resources to bring a lawsuit.

- The property rights or Coasian approach is conceptualized on the fundamental premise that the root cause of environmental externalities is the lack of clearly defined ownership rights. The legal system is then used to assign enforceable ownership rights.

- The Coase theorem affirms that the final outcome of an environmental dispute (in terms of pollution reduction) is *independent* of the decision made regarding the assignment of the property rights to a specific party: the polluter or pollutee.
- The principal advantages of the property rights approach are:

  1   It minimizes the role of regulators to a mere assignment of enforceable property rights.
  2   It encourages the resolution of environmental disputes through private negotiations. In other words, it advocates a *decentralized* approach to pollution control.

- The primary disadvantages of the property rights approach are:

  1   The transaction costs are high when the parties involved in the negotiation process are large in number.
  2   It appears to be indifferent to the polluter-pays principle.
  3   It has the potential to affect the income distribution of the parties involved in the negotiation. In this respect, the final outcome may be judged to be 'unfair'.

- Emission standards represent a form of 'command-and-control' environmental regulation. The basic idea involves restricting polluters to a certain predetermined amount of effluent discharge. Exceeding this limit subjects polluters to legal prosecution, resulting in monetary fines and/or imprisonment. This has been a widely used method of environmental regulation in many countries of the world.
- The main advantages of emission standards are:

  1   Generally, less information is needed to introduce regulations. As a standard represents a government fiat, it is simple and direct to apply.
  2   They are effective in curbing or controlling harmful pollution, such as DDT.
  3   They are morally appealing and politically popular since the act of polluting is declared a 'public bad'.
  4   They are favored by environmental groups because standards are generally aimed at achieving a predetermined policy target.

- The primary disadvantages of emission standards are:

  1   They are highly interventionist.
  2   They do not generate revenue.
  3   They may require the establishment of a large bureaucracy to administer programs.
  4   They are generally *not* cost-effective.
  5   They do not provide firms with sufficient incentive to invest in new pollution control technology.
  6   There is a strong tendency for regulatory capture: cooperation between the regulators and polluters in ways that provide unfair advantages to established firms.

Review and discussion questions

1   Quickly review the following concepts: liability laws, the polluter-pays principle, the Coase theorem, regulatory capture, transaction cost, cost-effective.

2   State whether the following are *true, false* or *uncertain* and *explain* why.

   (a) Whether one likes it or not, the abuse of the environment cannot be effectively deterred without some degree of regulation of the free market. Thus, public intervention is *both* a necessary *and* a sufficient condition for internalizing environmental externalities.

   (b) The air pollution problem can be solved by simply specifying or assigning exclusive rights to air.

   (c) Environmental advocacy groups generally favor command-and-control approaches because these unambiguously convey the notion that pollution is bad and as such ought to be declared illegal.

3   Despite the impeccable logic of the Coase theorem, private actors on their own often would fail to resolve an externality problem because of transaction costs. Comment on this statement using two specific examples.

4   Provide four reasons why economists generally do not advocate a command-and-control approach to environmental policy.

5   The core problem of a command-and-control approach to environmental policy is its inherent bias or tendency to standard-setting practice that is *uniformly* applicable to all situations. For example, the ambient-air quality standards in the United States are basically national. This may have serious efficiency and ecological implications because regional differences in the factors affecting damage and control cost relationships are not effectively captured. Comment. Would considerations of transaction costs have a bearing on your response to this question? Why, or why not?

References

Coase, R. (1960) 'The Problem of Social Cost', *Journal of Law and Economics* 3: 1–44.

Hardin, G. (1968) 'The Tragedy of the Commons', *Science* 162: 1243–8.

Starrett, D. and Zeckhauser, R. (1992) 'Treating External Diseconomies – Market or Taxes', in A. Markandya and J. Richardson (eds) *Environmental Economics: A Reader*, New York: St Martin's Press.

United States Environmental Protection Agency (1994) *EPA Journal*, Fall issue.

——(1995) *EPA Journal*, Winter issue.

6 The economics of environmental regulations

Pollution taxes and markets for transferable pollution permits

> Thrust a price theorist into a world with externalities and he will pray for second best – many firms producing and many firms and/or consumers consuming each externality, with full convexity everywhere. No problem for the price theorist. He will just establish a set of artificial markets for externalities, commodities for which property rights were not previously defined. Decision units, being small relative to the market, will take price as given. The resulting allocation will be competitive outcome of the classical type. If artificial markets do not appeal, an equally efficient taxing procedure is available.
>
> (Starrett and Zeckhauser 1992: 253)

6.1 Introduction

The subject of this chapter is environmental regulations. In this respect, it is an extension of the previous chapter. However, here we shall examine cases where the legal system is used only *indirectly*, and primarily to correct price distortions. This can be done by imposing a financial penalty or pollution tax, or by creating artificial market conditions that would allow pollution trading. Two approaches are used to address these issues: effluent charges and transferable emission permits. Effluent charges and transferable emission permits are alike in one important way. They represent a *decentralized* and, at least in theory, *cost-effective* approach to pollution control.

6.2 Effluent charges

An *effluent charge* is a tax or financial penalty imposed on polluters by government authorities. The charge is specified on the basis of dollars or cents per unit of effluent emitted into the ambient environment. For example, a firm may be required to pay an effluent charge of $0.30 per unit of waste material it discharges into a lake.

As public policy instruments, effluent charges have a long history and have been used to resolve a wide variety of environmental problems. For example, to address the concern of global warming, several prominent scholars in recent years have been proposing a global carbon tax (Pearce 1991). As will be evident from the discussions to follow, there are three major attractions of an effluent charge. First, it is less interventionist than emission standards and operates purely on the premise of financial incentive or disincentive, not on a command-and-control principle. Second, it can be relatively easy to administer. Third, it provides firms with incentives to reduce their pollution through improved technological means – quite the opposite to what we noted in discussing emission standards.

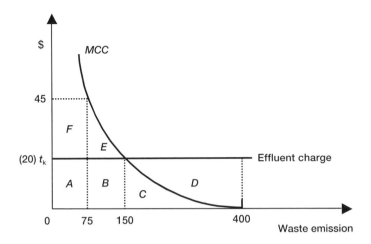

Figure 6.1 Pollution control through effluent charges. When a profit-maximizing firm is confronted with an effluent charge such as t_k, it would be in its best interest to treat its waste whenever the cost of treating an additional unit of waste was less than the effluent tax (i.e. $t_k > MCC$). The firm would cease its effort to control waste when no gain could be realized from any additional activity of this nature (i.e. $t_k = MCC$).

How does the effluent charge approach work? This question can be addressed using Figure 6.1, which portrays a situation where a firm is discharging waste into a particular environmental medium (air, water or land). The firm is required to pay an effluent tax of amount t_k, or $20 per unit of waste discharged. We are also provided with the *MCC* curve of this firm. Given this information, it is fairly easy to draw the conclusion that a private firm interested in minimizing its cost would discharge 150 units of waste. Note that this means that the firm will control 250 units of waste (400 − 150) using its facility to clean the waste. This is cost-minimizing because at 150 units, the usual equimarginal condition is attained. More specifically, the marginal control cost is equal to the predetermined effluent tax; $MCC = t_k = 20.

When this condition is met, the firm has no incentive to reduce its waste discharge to less than 150 units. To see this, suppose the firm decided to reduce its emission to 100 units. At this level of emission, as shown in Figure 6.1, $MCC = $45 > t_k = 20. Thus, paying the tax to discharge the waste would be cheaper for the firm than using its facility to clean the waste. A similar argument can be presented if the firm decides to increase its waste discharge to a level exceeding 150 units. However, in this case it would be cheaper for the firm to clean the waste using its waste-processing facilities than pay the tax, i.e. $MCC < t_k$. Simply stated, when a profit-maximizing firm is confronted with an effluent charge, it would be in its best interests to treat its waste whenever the cost of treating an additional unit of waste was less than the effluent tax (i.e. $t_k > MCC$). The firm would cease its effort to control waste when no gain could be realized from any additional activity of this nature (i.e. $t_k = MCC$).

At this stage, it is important to note two points. First, without the effluent charge, this firm would have had no incentive to employ its own resources for the purpose of cleaning up waste. In other words, in Figure 6.1, since the service of the environment is considered a free good, this firm would have emitted a total of 400 units of effluent into the environment. This implies that *an effluent charge reduces pollution because it makes the firm recognize that pollution costs the firm money* – in this specific case, $20 per unit of effluent. This shows how an externality is internalized by means of an effluent charge. Second, as shown in Figure 6.1, when the effluent charge is set at t_k, the total expenditure by the firm to control pollution using its own waste-processing technology is represented by area C – the area under the MCC curve when the emission level is 175 units or the firm chooses to control 225 units of its waste (400 − 175). In addition, the firm has to pay a tax ($20 per unit) on the amount (175 units) of untreated waste it decided to emit into the environment, which is indicated by area $A + B$. In this specific case this will be $3,500. Thus, the total cost for this firm to dispose its 400 units of waste will be the tax plus the total control cost, i.e. area $A + B + C$. *Note that under an effluent charge regime, the public authorities will not only make the firm clean up its waste to some desired level, but also be able to generate tax revenue that could be used to further clean up the environment or for other social objectives.* This is an important advantage that an effluent charge has over emission standards.

It is important to note that the firm has the option not to engage in any waste cleanup activity. However, if the firm decides to exercise this option, it will end up paying an effluent tax of an amount represented by area $A + B + C + D$, which will be $8,000 ($20 × 400). Clearly, this will not be desirable, since it entails a net loss equivalent to area D when compared to the effluent charge scheme.

So far we have discussed effluent charge on a purely conceptual level and considering only a single firm. We have yet to inquire how the 'optimal' level of effluent discharge is determined. *Ideally, what we would like the effluent charge to represent is the social cost, on a per unit basis, of an environmental service when it is used as a medium for receiving emitted waste.* For this to happen, the effluent charge needs to be determined by taking both the damage and control costs into consideration at an aggregate level. In Figure 6.2, the MCC curve represents the aggregate (sum) of the marginal control costs for all the relevant firms (or polluting sources). Given this, the optimal effluent charge, t_e, is attained at the point where $MCC = MDC$. In other words, t_e is the uniform tax per unit of waste discharged that we need to impose on all the firms under consideration so that collectively they will emit a total amount of waste of no more than W_e – the optimal level of waste. This level of waste is achieved after full consideration of all the damage and control costs and from the perspective of society at large.

However, obtaining all the information that is necessary to impute the ideal effluent charge would be quite costly (Baumol and Oates 1992). Thus, *in practice, policy-makers can view this ideal only as a target to be achieved in the long run.* In the short run, government authorities determine effluent charge using a trial-and-error process. Initially, they will start the motion by setting an 'arbitrary' charge rate. This rate may not be totally arbitrary, to the extent that it is based on the best possible information about damage and control costs available at that point in time. Moreover, this initial rate will be adjusted continually after observing the reaction of the polluters and as new and refined information on damage and control costs becomes available. The ultimate objective of the government authorities in charge of setting the tax rate is to realize the optimal rate as expeditiously as possible. This, more than anything else, requires the use of a carefully crafted trial-and-error process and flexible administrative programs and procedures.

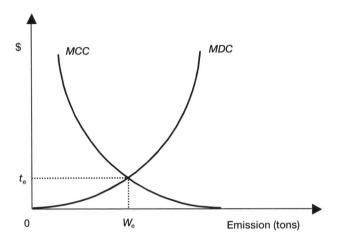

Figure 6.2 The optimal level of effluent charge. The optimal effluent charge, t_e, should be the tax-rate which when implemented would tend to yield the socially optimal level of waste discharge (W_e). When this level of waste is emitted, $t_e = MCC = MDC$. Note that t_e may or may not be equal to t_k, the effluent tax imposed on firms at a point in time.

However, Roberts and Spence (1992) basically rejected the idea that the regulatory authorities, simply by means of an iterative process, could arrive at the optimum solution when they are uncertain about the actual costs of pollution control. They showed that, in the presence of *uncertainty*, government authorities base their decision on what they expect to be the MCC of the firm. When control costs turn out to be greater than expected, environmental policy based on effluent taxes would allow waste discharges in excess of what is considered to be socially optimal, and the opposite result (excessive cleanup) will occur if control costs turn out to be less than expected. In either case, optimality is not attained.

One of the most heralded advantages of an effluent charge is that it is cost-effective. A public policy instrument, such as an effluent charge, is cost-effective when the implementation of this instrument guides private concerns to allocate their resources in such a way that they are minimizing their pollution control costs. In Chapter 5 we developed the economic criterion for cost-effectiveness. To restate this criterion, the total cost of cleaning up a given amount of waste is minimized *when the marginal control costs are the same for all the private concerns engaged in pollution control activities* (see Figure 5.5). In that chapter, using this criterion, we saw that emission standards are not cost-effective.

Why is effluent charge cost-effective? Under the effluent charge regime, each firm (polluting source) is charged a uniform tax per unit of waste discharged, such as t_k in Figure 6.1. As discussed earlier, each firm would independently determine its emission rate by equating its marginal control cost with the predetermined emission tax, t_k. Suppose we have ten firms; since they all are facing the same effluent charge, then, at equilibrium, $MCC_1 = MCC_2 = MCC_3 = \ldots = MCC_9 = MCC_{10} = t_k$. As mentioned earlier, this is precisely the condition for a cost-effective allocation of resources, and

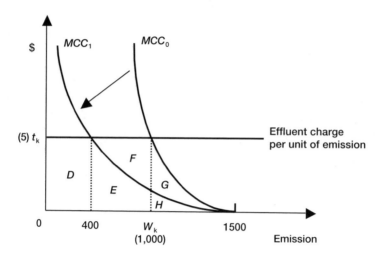

Figure 6.3 An effluent charge and a firm's incentive to invest on a new pollution control technology. This graph shows how under the effluent charge regime firms would have greater incentive to invest in pollution control technology than under emission standards. Under the effluent charge regime, the firm's cost savings include not only the gains from efficiency in its waste processing plants (area *G*) but also from what the firm avoided having to pay to the government authorities in the form of effluent tax (area *F*). (Compare this result with that in Figure 5.5.)

it results in the effluent charge that automatically minimizes the cost of pollution control. This is indeed a startling and desirable result. Nonetheless, *it is important to note that a cost-effective allocation of resources does not necessarily imply a socially optimal allocation of resources.* This is because a cost-effective allocation of pollution control requires only that all the parties involved in pollution cleanup activities face the same effluent charge; and nothing more. On the other hand, a socially optimal allocation of pollution cleanup presupposes a single and uniquely determined effluent charge. As shown in Figure 6.2, this unique rate, t_e, is attained when the condition $MCC = MDC$ is met. It is important to note, however, that t_e is *not* necessarily equal to t_k.

At the onset of this section, a claim was made that an effluent charge provides firms with an incentive to improve their waste control technology. How? Using Figure 6.3, suppose we have a single firm (polluter) that is subjected to an effluent charge of t_k per unit of emission. The shift of this firm's marginal control cost curve from MCC_0 to MCC_1 is caused by the introduction of a new and improved method of pollution control. Of course, since the innovation and implementation of the new technology costs money, the firm will undertake this project if, and only if, the expected cost savings from the project under consideration are substantial. In general, other factors being equal, the higher the expected cost savings from a given project, the higher the firm's likelihood to adopt the new and improved pollution control technology. Having stated this, using the information in Figure 6.3 we can vividly illustrate two points: (a) the potential cost savings of our hypothetical firm resulting from new pollution control technology; and (b) the fact that, when compared to emission standards, a policy based on effluent charges will provide greater financial incentives (cost savings) to investors in pollution control technology.

Given that t_k represents the effluent charge per unit of emission, before the introduction of the new technology the firm is discharging 1,000 units of its waste. This means that the firm is controlling or cleaning up 500 units (1,500 − 1,000) of its waste. For discharging 1,000 units, the regulatory agency would be able to collect effluent tax (revenue) of $5,000, which is represented by area $D + E + F$. In addition, this firm incurs a further expenditure for cleaning up or processing 500 units of its waste. The expenditure for controlling this amount of waste is measured by area $G + H$. Thus, area $D + E + F + G + H$ represents the combined expenditure on effluent tax and waste processing for this firm.

By applying logic similar to that above, it can be shown that if the new waste processing technology is adopted, area $D + E + H$ represents the total (effluent charge plus waste processing) expenditure of this firm. Note that the relevant MCC curve is MCC_1. Thus, area $F + G$ represents the cost-saving directly attributable to the adoption of the new technology. Is this cost-saving large enough to warrant the adoption of the new technology? Unfortunately, the answer to this question cannot be addressed here. However, what we are able to demonstrate at this stage is that this cost saving from the new technology would have been smaller if the firm's activity had been regulated using an emission standard instead of an effluent charge. In other words, an effluent charge provides stronger financial incentives to the firm to adopt new technology than does an emission standard.

To see this clearly, suppose the emission standard is set at 1,000, i.e. at the level of the firm's operation prior to introducing the new technology. To process the required waste, 500 units, the firm's total expenditure for controlling its waste is represented by area $G + H$. However, provided the emission standards remain unchanged, this cost can be reduced to area H if the firm decides to adopt the new technology. Thus, the area G represents the cost saving to this firm as a result of adopting the new waste processing plant. Clearly, the magnitude of this saving is smaller than the cost saving that was gained under the effluent charge system – area $F + G$. Thus, under the effluent tax regime the saving is greater by area F.

Of course, there is no great mystery about this result. Under the effluent charge regime, the firm's cost saving is limited not only to the efficiency gains in its waste processing plants, but also by what the firm is obliged to pay to the government authorities in the form of effluent tax. To see this, first note that, with the new technology, the firm is able to reduce its waste from 1,000 to 400 units – a reduction of 600 units. In doing this, the firm is able to reduce its tax by $3,000 (5 × 600). This tax saving corresponds to area $E + F$. However, the firm's expenditure to clean up the 600 units using the new technology is only area E. Thus, the net saving to the firm is area F. Note that under emission standards, there is no saving from tax.

The discussion so far clearly indicates that, as a public policy instrument, an effluent charge has a good many attractive features. However, no policy tool can be free of weaknesses, and effluent charge is no exception. The following are some of the major weaknesses of an effluent charge.

First, the waste monitoring and enforcement costs of a pollution control policy based on an effluent charge could be high, especially when a large number of polluters are scattered over a wide geographical area. That is, when compared to an emission standard setting, an effluent charge requires the gathering and monitoring of more refined and detailed information from each pollution source, since the effluent charge requires the processing of both financial and technological information. Unlike emission standards, it is not based on purely physical considerations.

Second, an effluent charge can, and rightly so, be viewed as an emission tax. The question is then, who actually ends up paying this tax? This is a relevant issue because firms could pass on this tax to the consumers by charging a higher price to the consumers of their products. Furthermore, how does the tax impact consumers in a variety of socioeconomic conditions, for instance, the poor versus the rich, and black versus white? What this warns us is that we need to be aware of the *income distribution* effect of effluent charges. It is important to note, however, *that an effluent charge generates revenue*. If government adopts a policy that is fiscally neutral, the revenue raised by taxes on pollution can be used to correct the income distribution or any other negative effects caused by the tax. Some argue that it is important to be mindful about the *double-dividend feature of pollution tax*. That is, pollution tax can be used to correct market distortion (i.e. externalities arising from excessive use of environmental services) and raise revenues which could be used to finance worthwhile social projects, such as helping the poor, providing an incentive to firms to undertake environmentally friendly projects, etc. (Pearce 1991).

Third, we have already seen that an effluent charge automatically leads to the minimization of pollution control costs. However, while an effluent charge is cost-effective in this specific way, this result in itself does not imply *optimality*. Whether an effluent charge produces an optimal outcome or not depends entirely on the choice of the 'appropriate' effluent tax. The determination of this tax requires not just pollution control, but the simultaneous consideration of both control and damage costs.

Fourth, because of the amount of detailed information needed to estimate the appropriate charge, in practice an effluent charge is set on a trial-and-error basis. If nothing else, this definitely increases the uncertainty of private business ventures concerning pollution control technology. Furthermore, in some situations (such as where significant regional differences in ecological conditions exist), *optimality may require imposing a nonuniform effluent charge policy*. For example, the correct level of carbon tax imposed to control greenhouse-gas emissions may vary in different countries of the European Union. Situations of this nature clearly add to the problems of imposing the appropriate absolute level of charges in relation to the level and nature of emissions caused by each source.

Fifth, effluent charges are a financial disincentive given to polluters. This system of charge does not say that it is *morally* wrong to knowingly engage in the pollution of the environment. It simply states that one is permitted to pollute provided one pays the assessed penalty for such an activity. Of course, the justification for this is that damage to the environment can be restored using the money generated by penalizing polluters. To some people, this conveys a perverse logic. There is a big difference between protecting the natural environment from harm and repairing it after it has been damaged.

The fact that an effluent charge is set on a trial-and-error basis (i.e. it is not market-determined from the outset) has been a source of considerable concern to economists. The upshot of this concern has been the development of an alternative policy instrument to control pollution, namely transferable emission permits. This policy tool, the subject of the following section, has all the advantages of effluent charges and treats pollution as a commodity to be traded piecemeal using the *market*.

6.3 Transferable emission permits

Essentially, the main idea behind transferable emission permits is to create a market for *pollution rights*. A pollution right simply signifies a permit that consists of a unit (pound, ton, etc.) of a specific pollutant. Under the transferable emission permit approach, government authorities basically have two functions. They determine the *total allowable permits*, and decide the mechanism to be used to *distribute* the initial pollution permits among polluters.

How do government authorities determine the total number of permits or units of pollutants? Ideally, the total should be set by considering both the damage and the control costs from the perspective of society at large. Accordingly, W_e in Figure 6.2 would satisfy such a condition. In practice, however, accurate estimates of damage and control costs may not be readily available because they may involve astronomically high transaction costs. Thus, generally, the total number of permits is determined by government agencies using the best information available about both damage and control costs at a point in time. *It is important to note that, as a policy instrument designed to curb the abuse of the natural environment, the success of a transferable permit scheme very much depends on the total size of pollution permits.* Thus, this is not a decision that should be taken lightly, although government authorities can always adjust the number of pollution permits issued to a polluter at any point in time.

Once the total number of emission permits is determined, the next step requires finding a mechanism by which the permits are initially distributed among polluters. No single magic formula exists that can be used to distribute the initial rights among polluters, especially if 'fairness' (equity) is an important consideration. Despite this concern for equity, provided pollution permits are freely transferable, the initial distribution of rights will have no effect on how the permits are eventually allocated through the market mechanism. In other words, as we shall soon see, the efficient allocation of permits will be independent of the initial distribution of pollution rights provided permits are freely transferable. Is this the Coase theorem in disguise?

From the discussion so far, it is important to observe that a system of transferable permits operates on the basis of the following postulates:

1   It is possible to obtain a legally sanctioned right to pollute.
2   These rights (permits) are clearly defined.
3   The total number of permits and the initial distribution of the total permits among the various polluters are assigned by government agencies. In addition, polluters emitting in excess of their allowances are subject to a stiff monetary penalty.
4   Pollution permits are freely transferable. That is, they can be freely traded in the marketplace.

These four attributes of a system of transferable permits are clearly evident in Exhibit 6.1. This describes the actual procedures that the United States Environmental Protection Agency (EPA) was proposing to use to limit sulfur dioxide emissions from the major electric power plants in Eastern and Midwestern states, by means of a program of market-based trading of allowances.

To illustrate how a resource allocation system that is based on transferable permits is supposed to work, let us consider some simple examples. Suppose that after careful consideration of all the relevant information, government agencies in some hypothetical

---

Exhibit 6.1   Acid rain emission limits proposed for over 900 power plants

Proposed plant-by-plant reductions in acid rain emissions have been listed by the EPA for most of the electric-power generating plants in the United States. One hundred and ten of the largest plants, mostly coal-burning utilities in 21 eastern and midwestern states, will have to make reductions beginning in 1995; at the turn of the century, over 800 smaller plants must also cut back on their emissions, and the larger plants must make further reductions. Electric power plants account for 70 per cent of sulfur dioxide (SO_2) emissions in the United States; SO_2 is the chief contributor to acid rain.

Under the 1990 Clean Air Act, each power plant is to be issued emissions allowances. Each allowance equals one ton of SO_2 emissions per year. The number of allowances a plant gets is determined by formula and is based in large part on the plant's past consumption of fuel. As the program gets under way in 1995, each plant must hold enough allowances to cover its annual emissions. It can meet its requirement either by reducing emissions or by purchasing allowances from other utilities. For every ton of SO_2 a plant emits in excess of its allowances, it will pay a penalty of $2,000 and will forfeit on allowance. This program of market-based trading in allowances, combined with tough monitoring and enforcement, is believed to have significant advantages over traditional 'command-and-control' regulations. By allowing utilities that can reduce emission cheaply to sell excess allowance to those whose control costs are high, total reductions can be achieved most cost-effectively. As a safeguard, no utility – no matter how many allowances it holds – will be allowed to emit SO_2 in amounts that exceed federal health standards.

Source: *EPA Journal* Vol. 18, no. 3, 1992, pp. 4–5. Reprinted by permission.

---

state issue a total of 300 permits for a period of one year. Each permit entitles the holder to emit a ton of sulfur dioxide. There are only two firms (Firm 1 and Firm 2) emitting sulfur dioxide. Using a criterion that is considered to be 'fair', government authorities issue an equal number of permits to both firms. That is, the maximum that each firm can emit into the air is 150 tons of sulfur dioxide per year. Finally, let us suppose that in the absence of government regulation *each* firm would have emitted 300 tons of sulfur dioxide (or a total of 600 tons of sulfur dioxide for both firms). Thus, by issuing a total of 300 permits, the ultimate objective of the government policy is to reduce the current level of total sulfur emission in the region by half (300 tons). Figure 6.4 incorporates the hypothetical data presented so far. However, in this figure the marginal control costs for the two firms are assumed to be different. Specifically, it is assumed that Firm 1 uses more efficient waste processing technology than Firm 2.

Given the conditions described above, the two firms can engage in some form of mutually beneficial negotiations. To begin, let us look at the situation that Firm 1 is facing. Given that it can discharge a maximum of 150 units of its sulfur emission, Firm 1 is operating at point *R* of its *MCC* curve. At this point it is controlling 150 units of its sulfur emission. For this firm, the *MCC* for the last unit of sulfur dioxide is $500. On the other hand, Firm 2 is operating at point *S* of its *MCC* curve, and it is controlling 150 units of its waste and releasing the other 150 units into the environment. At this level of operation, point *S*, the *MCC* of Firm 2, is $2,500. What is evident here is that at their current level of operations, the marginal control costs of these two firms

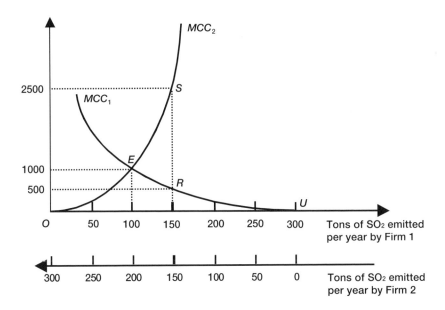

Figure 6.4 How transferable emission permits work. This graph shows that once a clearly
defined pollution permit is created (i.e. commodification of environmental
pollution is achieved), individual firms will be guided via an Invisible Hand to use
environmental resources in a manner that is considered socially optimal.

are different. More specifically, to treat the last unit of emission, it costs Firm 2 five
times as much as Firm 1 ($500 versus $2,500). Since permits to pollute are freely
tradeable commodities, it would be in the best interest of Firm 2 to buy a permit from
Firm 1 provided its price is less than $2,500. Similarly, Firm 1 will be willing to sell a
permit provided its price is greater than $500. This kind of mutually beneficial exchange
of permits will continue as long as, at each stage of the negotiation between the two
parties, $MCC_2 > MCC_1$. That is, as long as the MCC of Firm 2 exceeds that of Firm 1,
Firm 1 will be in a position to supply pollution permits to Firm 2. This relationship will
cease to occur when the MCC of the two firms attain equality, i.e. $MCC_2 = MCC_1$. In
Figure 6.4, this equilibrium condition is reached at point E. At this equilibrium point,
Firm 1 is emitting 100 tons of sulfur (or controlling 200 tons of sulfur). This means that
Firm 1 is emitting 50 tons of sulfur less than its maximum allowable permits. On the
other hand, at the equilibrium point, Firm 2 is emitting 200 tons of sulfur, 50 tons more
than its maximum allowable pollution permits. However, Firm 2 is able to fill the deficit
in its allowance by purchasing 50 tons worth of pollution permits from Firm 1. Note
also that at equilibrium the total amount of sulfur emitted by these two firms is 300 tons,
which is exactly equal to the total pollution permits issued by government authorities.

What exactly is the difference between the initial position of these two firms (points
R and S) and the new equilibrium condition established through a system of transferable pollution permits, point E? In both cases, the total units of sulfur emission are
the same: 300 tons of sulfur. However, what is desirable about the new equilibrium
position (point E) is that it is cost-effective. First, note that it satisfies the usual

condition for cost-effective allocation of resources, i.e. the marginal control costs of the firms under consideration are equal. Using Figure 6.4, it is also possible to show that both firms are better off at the new position. At the initial level of operation (points R and S), the *total* pollution control cost for these two firms is represented by area *OESRU*. The *total* pollution control cost at the new equilibrium position (point E) is measured by area *OEU*. Therefore, by moving to the new equilibrium, the total control cost is reduced by area *ERS*. This clearly constitutes a Pareto improvement since – by moving from the old to the new position – no one is made worse off. This is because the movement is brought about by a voluntary and mutually beneficial exchange between the two firms.

Furthermore, like an effluent charge system, the use of transferable permits would provide strong incentives to encourage investment in new pollution control technologies. For those who are curious, this can easily be demonstrated using an approach similar to that in the previous section, using Figure 6.3.

As a public policy instrument, perhaps the most remarkable feature of transferable permits is that, once the size of the total number of permits is determined, the allocation of these permits among competing users is based entirely on the market system. This was demonstrated above using a rather simple case of only two firms. However, *the remarkable feature of the transferable pollution permits system is that it works even better when the number of parties involved in the exchange of permits increases.* The only thing that this system requires, as discussed earlier, is the creation of clearly defined new property rights: pollution permits. Once this is accomplished, as in the case for the markets for goods and services (see Appendix A), individual firms will be guided, via an Invisible Hand, to use environmental resources in a manner that is considered 'socially' optimal. *Furthermore, this system of allocation creates an actual market price for the environmental commodities under consideration.* For example, in Figure 6.4 the market equilibrium price is $1,000 per permit.

Given these features of transferable pollution permits, it is not difficult to see why such a system should command the enthusiastic support of economists. Since the early 1980s, economists have been strongly lobbying the EPA to adopt transferable pollution permits as the primary policy tool for regulating the environment. As a result of this effort, in recent years there have been increasing applications of transferable permits in a wide variety of situations. In some sense, the growing application of transferable permits is creating what amounts to a revolutionary reform not only of the way the EPA has been conducting its regulatory affairs, but also of how the general public is reacting to environmental concerns. The reading in Case Study 6.1 is a good illustration of this.

Is such an enthusiastic endorsement of the EPA and the economics profession justified? It would be fine provided the enthusiasm were tempered with proper qualifications. For one thing, it should be recognized that transferable pollution permits are not panaceas. Like many other systems of resource allocation, in some instances they can have high administrative and transaction costs. Furthermore, it is extremely important to note that *what a system of transferable pollution permits guarantees is a cost-effective allocation of the total number of permits that are issued by the government authorities. Whether such a system leads to an optimal use of environmental resources depends largely on how government authorities determine the total number of permits to be issued.* As stated earlier, this requires the compiling of detailed and accurate information about damage costs – a very difficult and costly task to accomplish (more on this in Chapter 8). Without such information, we can never be sure that the market price for

Case Study 6.1   Purchasing pollution

Meg Sommerfield

What can $20,500 buy?

More than 1,800 reams of photocopier paper, 6,833 pints of Ben and Jerry's ice cream, or a new car, among other things.

How about 290 tons of sulfur dioxide? At least that's what students at Glens Falls (NY) Middle School want to buy with money they have raised.

The students have raised $20,500 to buy so-called pollution allowances at the US Environmental Protection Agency's annual auction at the Chicago Board of Trade this week.

Each credit allows the purchaser to emit a ton of sulfur dioxide, a colorless, suffocating gas. The students would retire the allowances they buy, thereby reducing the amount of sulfur dioxide that is released into the air. The EPA will auction about 22,000 credits this year.

The school in upstate New York raised about $13,640 from a community auction, more than $4,000 from a letter-writing campaign, and $3,860 through 25-cent 'gum allowances' and 50-cent bubble-blowing permits.

While gum is usually verboten, a Glens Falls teacher had permission to sell gum for one day. The teacher sold 1,000 pieces of gum before 8:30 am.

Leading the charge was sixth-grade teacher Rod Johnson.

'We study the problem, and buying the pollution allowances gives us a solution', he said.

Glens Falls and fifteen other elementary, middle and secondary schools participating in the pollution auction got involved with the help of the National Healthy Air License Exchange, a Cleveland-based nonprofit environmental group. Most of the other schools have raised a few hundred dollars.

Last year, Glens Falls Middle School was the first K-12 school to buy allowances, raising $3,200 to buy 21 tons. And though the 290 tons of emissions the school hopes to buy this year is small relative to the total being auctioned, Mr Johnson says it's a significant learning experience for his students.

Source: *Education Week Library*, March 27, 1996. Copyright © 1996 Editorial Projects in Education. Reprinted by permission.

permits accurately reflects the 'true' scarcity value of the environmental resource under consideration.

In fact, Roberts and Spence (1992) demonstrated that, in the presence of uncertainty, a regulatory scheme based on transferable pollution permits would yield results that differ from the socially optimal outcome. When control costs turn out to be higher than expected, a policy based on transferable permits will tend to yield an outcome that suggests a cleanup cost more than the socially optimal level and vice versa. Note that this result is the opposite of what is stated with regard to effluent charges. For this reason, Roberts and Spence (1992) advocate using a combination of effluent charges and transferable pollution permits when uncertainty is prevalent.

In addition, as mentioned earlier, we need to be aware that the mechanism by which government agencies eventually decide to distribute the permits among potential users can have significant equity implications. Should permits be distributed equally among the potential users? Should they be distributed in proportion to the size of the firms under consideration? Should they be distributed by means of a lottery? Should permits be publicly auctioned? Since each one of these allocation systems has varying impacts on the various users of the permits, it will be impossible to completely avoid the issue of fairness or equity. For example, in the United States, permits are allocated on the *grandfathering principle* (where permits are allocated relative to the size of a firm's historical level of emissions), which favors the existing major polluters. Evidence of this is the permit allocation formula the EPA used in Exhibit 6.1, which is based on the utility companies' past consumption of fuel (coal) – the primary source of sulfur dioxide pollution.

Pollution permits can be subject to abuse by special-interest groups. What if an environmental group decides to buy a number of permits for a certain pollutant and retires them? Of course, this action may serve conservation-minded souls very well, but will this be true for society at large? Furthermore, what this entails is that any group with a considerable amount of money can influence the market price and hence the quantity of pollution permits traded. For example, established firms can deter new entrants by hoarding permits. Ultimately, unless suitable mechanisms are used to deal with such abuses, the notion of protecting the environment through marketable pollution permits may be far less satisfactory than theory suggests. Note also that any effort to curb market abuses entails transaction costs – which is problematic if they are too high.

Finally, to some individuals the very idea of pollution rights or permits to pollute promotes reprehensible *moral* and *ethical values*. As discussed above, a system of allocation based on transferable permit entrenches the notion that the environment is just another commodity to be traded piecemeal using the market. Here the fear is that since several aspects of environmental amenities are not subject to market valuation (a subject to be discussed in Chapter 8), such a system of allocation would eventually lead to the abuse of the natural environment.

6.4 Applying the tools: an evaluation of the emissions trading programs in the United States

Emissions trading programs began to be implemented by the EPA in the mid-1970s. Until the mid-1980s, the experiments with this market-based environmental policy measure were limited in their scope and were primarily designed for controlling local air pollutants (Tietenberg 1998). In general, market-based environmental policy instruments are favored because they promise to be flexible and as such cost-effective, especially when compared with the traditional command-and-control type of environmental regulation.

6.4.1 Programs to phase out leaded gasoline and ozone-depleting chlorofluorocarbons

In the mid-1980s the EPA used emissions trading programs to phase out leaded gasoline from the market (Stavins 1998). In adopting this method, the EPA's primary aim was to provide greater flexibility to refiners in how the deadlines were met, without increasing the amount of lead used. Under this program, over the transition period a fixed amount of lead was allocated to the various refiners. Refiners were then permitted to trade (buy and sell), provided that the total amount of lead emitted did not exceed the authorized lead permits issued by the EPA. However, the fact that these permits were freely transferable allowed some refiners to comply with the deadlines with greater ease and without having to fight the deadlines in court. In this respect, the lead permits program was quite successful in facilitating the orderly adoption of more stringent regulations on lead in gasoline in the United States. Furthermore, the program ended as scheduled on December 31, 1987.

Another area where transferable permits programs were used in the United States was in phasing out ozone-depleting chlorofluorocarbons (CFCs). The United States initially adopted such a program to comply with the ozone international agreement at the Montreal Protocol in September 1988 (more on this in the next chapter). The Montreal Protocol required the signatory nations to restrict their production and consumption of the chief ozone-depleting gases to 50 per cent of 1986 levels by June 30, 1998. In response to this, on August 12, 1988, the EPA officially instituted a tradeable permit system to meet its obligations. To achieve the targeted reductions, all major producers and consumers of ozone-depleting substances in the United States were rationed to baseline production or consumption permits (allowances), using 1986 levels as the basis. These permits were transferable within producer and consumer categories. In general, the EPA's efforts to achieve the reductions of ozone-depleting substances have been quite successful both in terms of cost-effectiveness and in meeting the deadlines. However, what may not be clear at this stage is how much of this success can be attributed to the EPA's use of a tradeable permits program. More specifically, in large part the success of this program might have come from the fact that it has been relatively easy to find *substitutes* for CFCs.

6.4.2 The acid rain control program

The first large-scale use of tradeable pollution permits in the United States was introduced with the passage of the 1990 Clean Air Act Amendments. More specifically, Title IV of this act was responsible for initiating a nationwide use of market-based approaches primarily designed to reduce sulfur dioxide (SO_2) emissions from power plants by about half the amount of the 1980 levels by the turn of the century. Why was SO_2 emission a major concern?

In the 1980s, acid rain was a hotly debated worldwide environmental concern. In the United States, emissions of SO_2 from power plants were the chief precursor of *acid rain*. SO_2 emissions were steadily increasing during the 1970s and the 1980s. By the late 1980s, in the United States alone the total SO_2 emission was approaching 25 million tons per year. Accumulated over time, acid rain depositions on lakes, streams, forests, buildings, and people are believed to cause substantial damage to aquatic organisms and trees, erode and disfigure stone buildings and historical monuments, and impair the lungs of people (more on this in the next chapter).

Confronted with the prospect of growing acid rain related problems, the United States government started Phase I of its ambitious SO_2 emissions reduction program in 1995. The goal of the program has been to cut the annual SO_2 emissions from power plants by 10 million tons from 1980 levels by the year 2000 (see Exhibit 6.1). The acid rain reduction programs in Phase I involved 110 mostly coal-burning plants. Phase II is expected to start in the year 2000, immediately following the end of Phase I. In Phase II, the goal will be to further reduce SO_2 emissions by another 10 million tons per year by 2010. This will be achieved by increasing the number of power plants participating in the acid rain reduction programs and by further tightening emissions standards – SO_2 emitted per million British thermal units. The projection is that by 2010, total SO_2 emissions in the United States will dwindle to 8.95 million tons per year.

However, when Congress passed the 1990 Clean Air Act Amendments, the cost of the acid rain control programs was a major concern. The cost estimates for Phase I alone were running as high as $10 billion a year, which is equivalent to $1,000 per ton of SO_2 controlled (Kerr 1998). This cost estimate was based on the assumption that SO_2 emissions will continue to be regulated through 'command-and-control' approaches. Given this, considerable attention was given to searching for cost-effective ways of operationalizing the acid rain control programs. One outcome of this was the adoption of a flexible system of emissions trading.

Under the system of emissions trading, the EPA still retains the power to set the upper limits on the annual levels of SO_2 emissions for the nation. Furthermore, to achieve the total annual emissions goal, the EPA limits individual power plants under the acid rain programs by issuing a fixed number of tradeable permits (allowances) on the basis of historical emissions and fuel use (see Exhibit 6.1). Each allowance is worth one ton of SO_2 released from the smokestack, and to obtain reductions in emissions, the number of allowances declines yearly. A small number of additional allowances (less than 2 per cent of the total allowances) are auctioned annually by the EPA (Tietenberg 1998). At the end of each year, utilities that have emitted more than their pollution permits allow them will be subjected to a stiff penalty, $2,000 per ton. In addition, all power plants under the acid rain program are required to install continuous emission monitoring systems (CEMS), machines that keep track of how much SO_2 the plant is emitting.

However, although each participant in the acid rain reduction program is given a fixed number of allowances, power plant operators are given complete freedom on how to cut their emissions. On the basis of cost considerations alone, a plant operator might install scrubbers (desulfurization facilities that reduce the amount of SO_2 exiting from the stack), switch to a coal with a lower sulfur content, buy or sell allowances, or save allowances for future use. As we shall see shortly, these are the unique features that greatly contributed to the overall flexibility and cost-effectiveness of the acid rain reduction programs. Note that the overall flexibility of these programs is not limited to a consideration of allowance trading. The options available to plant operators with regard to the types of scrubber and the different qualities of coal that they can purchase are significant contributors to the overall flexibility and cost-effectiveness of the acid rain reduction programs.

Allowance trading can be effected using the *offset*, the *bubble* or the *banking* policies. The *offset policy* is designed to permit allowance trading in a geographic region known as a nonattainment area – a region in which the level of a given air pollutant (SO_2, in the case of the acid rain reduction program) exceeds the level permitted by the federal standards. Under this policy, an increase in SO_2 emissions from a given smokestack can be offset by a reduction (of a somewhat greater amount) of the same pollutant from any other smokestack owned, by the purchase of allowances equal to the offset amount from other companies in the nonattainment area. Hence, trading offset among companies is permitted, provided the permit requirements are met and the nonattainment area keeps moving toward attainment. This is feasible because companies are required to more than offset (by an extra 20 per cent) any pollution they will add to the nonattainment area through new sources. Under the offset policy, the new sources could be new firms entering into the nonattainment area – hence allowing economic growth (Tietenberg 1998).

By contrast, the *bubble policy* allows emissions trading opportunities among multiple emission sources (collectively recognized as forming a bubble) to be controlled by existing emitters. Provided the total pollutants leaving the bubble is within the federal standards, polluters are free to pursue a cost-effective strategy for controlling pollution. In other words, not all sources are held to a uniform emission standard; thus, within a given bubble, emitters are allowed to control some pollution sources less stringently than others, provided a sufficient amount of emission reduction is realized from the other sources within the same bubble.

The emissions *banking policy* simply allows polluters to save their emission allowances for use in some future year. These saved allowances can be used in offset, bubble or for sale to other firms. This is an important feature of the United States SO_2 reduction program as it allows firms an opportunity for intertemporal trading and optimization (Schmalensee *et al.* 1998).

As stated earlier, Phase I of the United States acid rain reduction program has been in effect since 1995. Early indications are that the use of tradeable allowances has been quite successful. According to a recent study by Schmalensee *et al.* (1998), for the first two years the reduction in SO_2 emissions from participating power plants was, on average, about 35 per cent below the legal limit – the total allowances issued or auctioned for each of these two years. Furthermore, this was done at a cost of less than $1 billion per year (Kerr 1998). Note that this cost figure is far below the initial cost estimate of the acid rain control program, which, as pointed out earlier, was expected to run as high as $10 billion per year. Thus, the preliminary empirical evidence indicates that, so far, the SO_2 allowance trading programs have been remarkably economical. Furthermore, the costs for Phase II, although likely to be higher than the costs for Phase I, are also expected to be much lower than initial estimates.

To what factor(s) can the successes of the acid rain reduction programs, so far, be attributed? It is important to note that not all the cost savings can be attributed to the allowance-trading program. According to some estimates, 30 per cent of the overall cost savings from the acid rain reduction programs can be attributed to allowance trading, which is by no means insignificant (Kerr 1998). However, the contribution of allowance trading would have been higher than 30 per cent if it had not been for the low volume of allowance trading during the first two years of Phase I. This situation is expected to improve in future years as the market conditions for allowance trading develop further.

At this point, therefore, the bulk of the cost savings stem from the overall flexibility of the acid rain reduction programs. This means that other external factors, such as the unexpected decline in prices for scrubbers and substantial fall in coal transportation costs due to railroad deregulation, were important contributing factors to the overall cost savings realized by the program during its first two years of operation.

The early success of the acid rain reduction experiment is raising hope that allowance trading could be similarly applied to several major environmental programs, including carbon dioxide (CO_2) reduction programs intended to slow down the trend in global warming. For example, during the 1997 Kyoto Protocol on global warming, the United States insisted on the use of tradeable permits to limit global CO_2 emissions (more on this in Chapter 7). This was also a hotly contested issue in the Buenos Aires conference held exactly a year after the Kyoto conference.

However, so far the United States' push for international CO_2 trading has been greeted with a great deal of skepticism and resistance for two reasons. First, in general, tradeable permits work best when transaction costs are low, which may not be the case for the proposed CO_2 reduction programs because the compliance (monitoring and enforcement) costs are likely to be high for any environmental program that relies heavily on international accords involving countries from diverse cultural, political and economic orientations. Second, as Stavins (1998: 83) rightly pointed out,

> the number and diversity of sources of carbon dioxide emissions due to fossil fuel combustion are vastly greater than in the case of sulfur dioxide emissions as a precursor of acid rain, where the focus can be placed on a few hundred electric utility plants.

Thus, the success in the SO_2 emission reduction program in the United States does not provide a blanket endorsement for the use of allowance trading programs for cutting CO_2 emissions designed to reduce the risk of global climate change.

6.5 Chapter summary

This chapter discussed *two* alternative policy approaches that can be used to correct environmental externalities: effluent charges and transferable emission permits. The common feature of these two policy instruments is that they both deploy market incentives to influence the behavior of polluters. Effluent charges and transferable emission permits are alternative forms of market-based environmental policy instruments.

- Effluent charges represent a tax per unit of waste emitted. Ideally, a tax of this nature reflects the imputed value or shadow price (on a per unit basis) of the services of an environment as a repository for untreated waste. Thus, the idea of the tax is to account for external costs so that price distortion will be corrected. For some philosophical and cultural reasons, effluent charges seem to be used more widely in Europe than in the United States. In general, Americans seem to exhibit considerable intolerance of any form of tax.
- The principal advantages of the effluent charges are:
  1 They are relatively easy to administer.
  2 They are generally cost-effective.
  3 They generate revenues while correcting price distortions – the double-dividend feature of effluent charges.
  4 They tend to provide firms with incentives to invest in pollution control technology.
- The main disadvantages of the effluent charges are:
  1 Monitoring and enforcement costs tend to be high.
  2 They could have a disproportionate effect on income distribution.
  3 They do not condemn the act of polluting on purely moral grounds. It is acceptable to pollute, provided one pays for it.

4   Firms are philosophically against taxes of any form, especially when they are perceived to cause increased prices and an uncertain business environment.

5   Environmental organizations generally oppose effluent charges for both practical and philosophical reasons. Pollution taxes are 'licenses to pollute'. Taxes are generally difficult to tighten once implemented.

- The transferable emission permits approach to pollution control requires, first and foremost, the creation of *artificial* markets for pollution rights. A pollution right represents a permit that consists of a unit of a specific pollutant. The role of the regulator is limited to setting the total number of permits and the mechanism(s) by which these permits are distributed among polluters. Once they receive their initial allocation, polluters are allowed to freely exchange permits on the basis of market-established prices. This pollution control instrument is gaining popularity in recent years, especially in the United States.

- Primary advantages of transferable emission permits are:

1   They are least interventionist.

2   They are cost-effective, especially when the number of parties involved in the exchange of permits is large.

3   They provide observable market prices for environmental services.

4   They can be applied to a wide range of environmental problems.

- The principal disadvantages of transferable emission permits are:

1   The mechanisms used to distribute permits among potential users could have significant equity implications.

2   The idea of permits to pollute promotes, to some, reprehensible moral and ethical values.

3   Their applicability is questionable for pollution problems with international scope, such as global warming.

4   They are ineffective when there are not enough participants to make the market function.

5   Permits can be accumulated by firms for the purpose of deterring entrants or by environmental groups for the purpose of attaining the groups' environmental objectives.

- Preliminary empirical evidence indicates that the United States SO_2 emissions trading program has performed successfully. Targeted emissions reductions have been achieved and exceeded, and at costs significantly less than what they would have been in the absence of the trading provisions.

- This success would not necessarily apply in cases of international pollution. For example, could an emissions trading program be effective in cutting CO_2 emissions intended to reduce the risk of global warming? It will most likely be less effective than the United States' experiment in SO_2 emissions reduction programs because of high enforcement and monitoring costs of a pollution problem with a global dimension. Despite this, during the Kyoto summit on climate change one of the most contentious events was the insistence by the United States government to allow the use of transferable emission permits as an instrument to control global CO_2 emissions.

Review and discussion questions

1 Briefly describe the following concepts: effluent charges, transferable pollution permits, the grandfathering principle, the Clean Air Act Amendment of 1990, the bubbles, offsets and emissions banking policies.

2 State whether the following are *true, false* or *uncertain* and explain why.

   (a) To say that an effluent charge is cost-effective does not necessarily mean that it is socially optimal. This is because cost-effectiveness does not account for damage costs.
   (b) The remarkable feature of tradeable permits is that they work best when the parties involved in the trade are large in numbers.
   (c) Pollution taxes and tradeable permits are 'licenses to pollute'.
   (d) Effluent charges and permits provide unfair competitive advantages to existing firms.

3 Some economists argue that a policy instrument to control pollution (such as effluent charges and transferable pollution permits) should not be dismissed on the basis of 'fairness' alone. Issues of fairness can always be addressed separately through income redistribution. For example, tax revenue from effluent charges can be used to compensate the losses of the damaged parties. Critically evaluate this claim.

4 As you have read in this chapter, since the mid-1980s the Environmental Protection Agency (EPA) in the United States has seemingly come to rely increasingly on transferable emission permits.

   (a) In general, do you support this fundamental shift in policy from the traditional 'command-and-control' regulations to market-based trading of pollution allowances? Why, or why not?
   (b) Why do you think the rest of the world is rather slow or not enthusiastic in adopting this type of pollution control policy? For example, the United States is the principal country pushing for the use of CO_2 permits to regulate greenhouse gas emission while the rest of the world seems to be somewhat reluctant to endorse the use of such a pollution regulation mechanism. Speculate.

5 Environmental organizations have opposed market-based pollution control policies out of a fear that permit level and tax rates, once implemented, would be more difficult to tighten over time than command-and-control standards. Is this fear justifiable? Why, or why not?

6 Which environmental policy options discussed in this and previous chapters would you recommend if a hypothetical society were facing the following environmental problems? In each case, briefly explain the justification(s) for your choice.

   (a) A widespread problem of campground littering
   (b) Pollution of an estuary from multiple-source irrigation runoffs
   (c) Air pollution of a major metropolitan area
   (d) The emission of a toxic waste
   (e) Damage of lakes, streams, forests, and soil resulting from acid rain
   (f) A threat to human health due to stratospheric ozone depletion
   (g) A well-founded fear of a gradual extinction of an endangered species, for example, the rhinoceros.

References

Baumol, W. J. and Oates, W. E. (1992) 'The Use of Standards and Prices for Protection of the Environment', in A. Markandya and J. Richardson (eds) *Environmental Economics: A Reader*, New York: St Martin's Press.

Kerr, R. A. (1998), 'Acid Rain Control: Success on the Cheap', *Science* 282: 1024–7.

Pearce, D. W. (1991) 'The Role of Carbon Taxes in Adjusting to Global Warming', *Economic Journal* 101: 938–48.

Roberts, M. J. and Spence, M. (1992) 'Effluent Charges and Licenses under Uncertainty', in A. Markandya and J. Richardson (eds) *Environmental Economics: A Reader*, New York: St Martin's Press.

Schmalensee, R., Joskow, P. L., Ellerman, A. D., Montero, J. P. and Baily, E. M. (1998) 'An Interim Evaluation of Sulfur Dioxide Emissions Trading', *Journal of Economic Perspectives* 2, 12: 53–68.

Starrett, D. and Zeckhauser, R. (1992) 'Treating External Diseconomies – Market or Taxes', in A. Markandya and J. Richardson (eds) *Environmental Economics: A Reader*, New York: St Martin's Press.

Stavins, R. N. (1998) 'What Can We Learn from the Grand Policy Experiment? Lessons from SO_2 Allowance Trading', *Journal of Economic Perspectives* 2, 12: 69–88.

Tietenberg, T. (1992) *Environmental and Natural Resource Economics*, 3rd edn, New York: HarperCollins.

——(1998) 'Ethical Influences on the Evolution of the US Tradable Permit Approach to Air Pollution Control', *Ecological Economics* 24: 241–57.

7 Global environmental pollution

Acid rain, ozone depletion and global warming

Contributed by Marvin S. Soroos

Most of the world's climate scientists say global warming is a real and serious threat. Market forces won't solve the problems, because markets treat pollution as a costless byproduct and under price it. 'Free-market' advocates are promoting a complex scheme of tradable (transferable) emission rights. But this 'market' does not exist in nature; it must first be constructed – by government diplomats and regulators. And these emissaries must resolve complex policy questions: how much overall pollution to allow; how to allocate the initial stock of tradable permits; whether to have waivers or subsidies for poor countries; and whom to empower to police the system. Here, globalization demands more statecraft, not more market.

(*Business Week*, November 11, 1997)

7.1 Introduction

Chapter 4 explained that the atmosphere is one of the four components of the Earth's ecosystems, along with the hydrosphere, lithosphere and biosphere. The atmosphere is a mixture of gases, primarily nitrogen and oxygen, which circulates around the Earth up to an altitude that is equal to only about 1 per cent of the radius of the planet. The atmosphere moderates the flow of energy coming from the Sun, including intense ultraviolet radiation that is harmful to plant and animal species. Gases in the atmosphere also capture some of the heat radiated from the Earth toward space, and in doing so maintain a climate that has been hospitable to a multitude of species.

Human beings pollute the atmosphere when they use it as a medium for disposing of a vast array of waste substances in the form of gases or tiny liquid or solid particles. Pollutants contribute to two types of environmental problem that may take on international or even global dimensions. First, certain types of pollutant are transported by air currents over hundreds, if not thousands, of miles before they are washed out of the atmosphere by rain or snow, or fall to Earth in a dry form. In the process, some of these pollutants pass over international boundaries. Such is the case with sulfur dioxide (SO_2) and nitrogen oxides (NO_x), which form acids when they combine with water vapor in the atmosphere or with moisture on the Earth's surface after being deposited in a dry form. Other pollutants pose a problem when they alter the chemical composition of the atmosphere in ways that modify the flow of energy to and from the earth. Scientists have linked chlorofluorocarbons (CFCs) and several other synthetic chemicals to a thinning of the stratospheric ozone layer that intercepts ultraviolet radiation from the sun. Human additions to naturally occurring concentrations of greenhouse gases such as carbon dioxide (CO_2) and methane (H_4) are believed to be raising the average temperature of the planet, which is triggering other climatic and environmental changes.

7.2 Causes and consequences of acid rain

Acid rain is a term commonly used to refer to several processes through which human-generated pollutants increase levels of acidity in the environment. The problem arises when pollutants such as SO_2 and NO_x are released into the atmosphere, primarily from power plants, metal smelters, factories, and motorized vehicles. Some of these pollutants, which are known as precursors of acid deposition, quickly precipitate to the Earth in a dry form near their source, where they combine with surface moisture to form acidic solutions. Under certain circumstances, however, these pollutants remain in the atmosphere for periods of up to several days, during which they may be carried by wind sources over considerable distances. While in the atmosphere, the pollutants may undergo a complex series of chemical reactions in the presence of sunlight and other gases, such as ammonia and low-level ozone, which are also generated by human activities. The resulting chemicals may be absorbed by water vapor to form tiny droplets of sulfuric and nitric acids that are washed out of the atmosphere in the form of rain, snow, mist, or fog (Park, 1987: 40–8).

Acid rain was largely a localized problem near the source of the pollutants until well into the twentieth century. The problem became increasingly regional as governments began mandating taller smokestacks to disperse pollutants more widely as a strategy for relieving local air pollution problems. Originally, it was thought the pollutants would become so diluted as they were dispersed that they would pose no further problems. By the 1960s, however, it had become apparent that pollutants from the industrial centers of Great Britain and mainland Europe were causing increasingly serious acidification in southern Sweden and Norway. Subsequent studies soon revealed that large amounts of air pollution were flowing across national frontiers throughout the European region, and between the United States and Canada as well. More recently, much of the pollution responsible for Japan's acid rain has been traced to China and Korea.

Acid rain has several harmful effects. The most visible of its consequences is corrosion of the stone surfaces of buildings and monuments, as well as of metals in structures such as bridges and railroad tracks. In Scandinavia and eastern North America, the heightened acidity of rivers and lakes has been linked to the disappearance of fish and other forms of aquatic life. The severity of the impact of acid rain on freshwater environments varies considerably depending on the extent to which the rocks and soils of the region neutralize the acids. Acid rain also appears to have been a cause of the widespread damage to trees that was observed in the forests of Central Europe by the early 1980s, a phenomenon known by the German word *Waldsterben*, which means 'forest death'. A similar pattern of forest decline has been observed in eastern North America, especially at the higher levels of the Appalachian Mountains. Scientists have had difficulty, however, isolating the natural processes through which pollution causes widespread damage to trees (Schütt and Cowling, 1985).

7.3 Causes and consequences of depletion of the ozone layer

Low-level ozone resulting from human pollutants is undesirable because not only is it one of the principal components of the health-threatening photochemical smog that plagues many large cities, but it is also an oxidant that contributes to the production of acid rain. Thus, it is ironic that ozone created by natural processes, which resides in the stratosphere at altitudes of 10–40 km in concentrations of only a few parts per million, is critical to the survival of most life forms that have inhabited the planet. Ozone is the only chemical in the atmosphere which absorbs certain frequencies of intense ultraviolet (UV) radiation that are damaging to plants and animals. Microscopic organisms at the bottom of the food chain, such as phytoplankton and zooplankton, are especially vulnerable to increased doses of UV radiation.

In 1974 scientists Mario Molina and F. Sherwood Rowland called attention to the possibility that CFCs posed a threat to the stratospheric ozone layer. CFCs are a family of chemical compounds that were widely used in refrigeration, aerosol sprays, foam insulation, and the computer industry. These chemicals had proved to be useful for numerous applications because they do not react with other chemicals under normal conditions and thus are non-corrosive, nontoxic and nonflammable. Noting that CFCs were apparently not precipitating out of the atmosphere, Molina and Rowland hypothesized that the highly stable CFC molecules would rise slowly through the atmosphere until they reached the stratosphere, where they would encounter intense solar radiation that would finally break them apart. In the process, highly unstable chlorine molecules would be released, which would break ozone molecules apart in a catalytic reaction that would leave the chlorine molecule available to attack other ozone molecules. Thus, a single CFC molecule reaching the stratosphere might lead to the destruction of hundreds of thousands of ozone molecules (Molina and Rowland 1974).

The first evidence of a significant decline in stratospheric ozone came from a team of British scientists, who in 1985 reported that concentrations of ozone over Antarctica during several preceding spring seasons were down 40 per cent from what they had been two decades earlier (Farman *et al.* 1985). By 1988, further research conclusively attributed the Antarctic 'ozone hole' to human-generated substances, including CFCs. By then, other commercially used chemicals, including halons, carbon tetrachloride and methyl chloroform, were also believed to threaten the ozone layer. Moreover, evidence was mounting that stratospheric ozone concentrations were declining at other latitudes, although not nearly to the degree seen over Antarctica, where each year the ozone hole showed signs of expanding and deepening (Watson *et al.* 1988).

Scientists have had greater difficulty determining the extent to which declining ozone concentrations have resulted in an increase in the amount of UV radiation passing through the atmosphere and reaching the surface of the planet. Likewise, evidence of damage to plant and animal species has been slow to accumulate, although a worldwide decline in populations of amphibians, such as frogs, toads and salamanders, may be attributable in part to the effects of increased doses of UV radiation on the eggs of these species (Blaustein *et al.* 1994).

7.4 Causes and consequences of global warming

Nearly half of the solar energy that approaches the planet Earth is reflected or absorbed by gases and aerosols in the atmosphere, with the greatest amount, approximately 22 per cent, being intercepted by the white tops of clouds. The remaining solar radiation, most of which is in the form of infrared or visible light waves, passes through the atmosphere to the surface of the planet. There it is either reflected off light surfaces such as snow and ice, or absorbed by land, water or vegetation. Much of this energy that is absorbed by the Earth is reradiated out from the planet toward outer space in the form of longer-wave infrared rays. A portion of this escaping energy is absorbed by certain gases found in the atmosphere, in particular CO_2, CH_4 and NO. In the process, heat is released that warms the lower atmosphere (Anthes 1992: 50–4). These substances that are so critical to the Earth's climate account for only about 0.03 per cent of atmospheric gases. Water vapor, which occurs in concentrations of from 0 to 4 per cent of the atmosphere, also intercepts outgoing infrared radiation. This process has become known as the 'greenhouse effect', because as with the glass walls of a greenhouse, the atmosphere allows solar energy to pass inwards while blocking its escape, thus keeping the space within it warm compared to outside conditions. Thus, it is the so-called greenhouse gases (GHGs) – CO_2, CH_4 and NO – along with water vapor, that account for the Earth's moderate climate. Much larger amounts of CO_2 in the atmosphere of Venus explain its intensely hot climate, while the frigid conditions on Mars are attributable to lesser concentrations of GHGs (Fisher 1990: 18–20).

Human activities are adding significantly to the concentrations of the principal GHGs in the Earth's atmosphere. The burning of fossil fuels, in particular coal and petroleum, releases CO_2, which can remain in the atmosphere for a century or longer. The clearing of forests not only releases the carbon stored in the trees, but also removes an important sink for CO_2, as trees absorb CO_2 from the air through the process of photosynthesis. Concentrations of CO_2 in the atmosphere have risen from approximately 280 ppm prior to the industrial age to 371 ppm by 2001 (Keeling and Whorf, 2002). Levels of CH_4, a gas that is shorter-lived in the atmosphere, have also been rising even more sharply due to a variety of human activities, such as wet rice cultivation, livestock raising and the production and transport of natural gas. Atmospheric scientists are concerned that human-generated pollutants are responsible for an 'enhanced greenhouse effect' that is reflected in a significant rise in global mean temperatures (Trenberth 2001).

Long ice cores extracted from deep in the glaciers of Greenland, Antarctica and the Andes mountains provide a record of the composition of the Earth's atmosphere and climate as far back as 400,000 years. By analyzing the chemical composition of gases trapped in air pockets in the ancient ice, scientists have been able to determine that there is now substantially more CO_2 in the atmosphere than at any other time during the era covered by the ice cores. Their research also reveals that over this extended period there is a striking relationship between major shifts in climate and fluctuations in concentrations of CO_2 (Barnola *et al.* 1987).

There are already indications that human additions to GHG concentrations in the atmosphere are having an impact on global temperatures. The United Nations-sponsored Intergovernmental Panel on Climate Change concluded in its third report, released in 2001, that global mean temperatures had risen by 0.6°C over the past century. Moreover, the 1990s appears to be the warmest decade since 1860 and 1998 was the warmest year for that period. The report concludes that most of the warming that had occurred during the last 50 years can be attributed to human activities. The same report projects an increased global mean temperature of 1.4 to 5.8°C for the period 1990 to 2100 if concentrations of GHGs continue to rise at current rates (IPCC 2001: 10–13). To put this amount of change in perspective, global mean temperatures were about 1°C lower during the Little Ice Age from approximately 1400 to 1850 and about 5°C colder during the most recent major glacial era, which ended about 10,000 years ago (Oeschger and Mintzer 1992: 63).

A significant warming of the atmosphere is likely to trigger substantial climatic changes. These impacts are expected to vary considerably by region. Some areas will experience warmer and drier climates, while others may become cooler and moister. Substantial changes in temperature and rainfall patterns would have significant implications for agriculture. Reductions in stream flows might trigger water shortages, jeopardize irrigation and limit the production of hydroelectric power. Unusually dry conditions in some areas might set the stage for immense, uncontrollable forest and range fires, which would generate large amounts of smoke and release additional CO_2 into the atmosphere. At the other extreme, abnormal precipitation events are likely to become more frequent, causing increasingly destructive floods. As ocean waters warm, potentially destructive tropical storms, such as hurricanes, cyclones and typhoons, may become more frequent and intense Stevens 1999).

Global warming is likely to trigger many other changes in the natural environment. If present trends continue, sea levels are projected to rise by between nine and 88 cm over the next century due to both thermal expansions of the ocean waters and the melting of polar and mountain glaciers (IPCC 2001: 16). Rising sea levels pose a threat to low-lying coastal zones, where many of the world's major cities are located. Small island states, many of which are located in the Caribbean Sea and western Pacific Ocean, are especially vulnerable to sea level rises as well as to tropical storms and associated storm surges. Shifts in climate zones may exceed the adjustment capacity of many species, while other, more adaptable species, including agricultural pests and disease vectors, may be able to spread more widely. Forests are especially vulnerable to climatic changes because trees migrate very slowly and are susceptible to infestations (Stevens 1999).

The greatest amount of warming is expected to take place in the polar regions. With the shrinking of glaciers and ice packs, less solar energy will be reflected while more is absorbed, thus contributing to further warming (McCarthy and McKenna 2000). Warmer conditions may also accelerate the melting of permafrost, which would release large amounts of the GHG CH_4 into the atmosphere. A lessening of the temperature gradients between the equator and the poles could strongly influence the prevailing weather patterns in the temperate mid-latitude regions. It could also weaken major ocean currents that distribute heat around the planet. If the warm, northward-flowing Gulf Stream were to weaken considerably, the climate of northern Europe might cool significantly (Calvin 1998).

While there is a general convergence of opinion among scientists that human additions to atmospheric concentrations of GHGs are likely to trigger significant climatic and environmental changes, considerable uncertainties remain about how much change will take place and how these changes will play out in specific regions. Questions remain about key factors such as the amount of atmospheric CO_2 that will ultimately be absorbed by the oceans and the impacts that clouds will have on future climates. Furthermore, it is difficult for scientists to isolate the causes of recent weather and environmental anomalies that appear to bear out the global warming scenario, such as the spate of unusually warm years since 1990 and an increased incidence of floods resulting from unusually heavy precipitation. Are these a consequence of a human-enhanced greenhouse effect? Or simply naturally occurring fluctuations in the climate of the planet?

7.5 International responses to acid rain, ozone depletion and climate change

International responses are needed to effectively address environmental problems that transcend the boundaries of individual nations. There is no world government with the authority to impose and enforce solutions to such problems. Nations claim the sovereign right to regulate what takes place within their borders without interference from outside. Thus, it is up to the community of nations, which currently numbers more than 190, to enter voluntarily into agreements with one another to limit the flow of pollutants that contribute to environmental problems of international and global scope. Such agreements normally take the form of treaties, or what are commonly called conventions, which are negotiated among interested countries, usually under the auspices of an international institution such as the United Nations. Only those countries that formally become parties to a treaty, in accordance with their constitutionally specified ratification procedures, are legally obliged to comply with its provisions.

International responses to environmental problems typically take the form of a series of treaties. The initial agreement is a vaguely worded framework convention, which acknowledges the emergence of a potentially important problem that warrants international attention while encouraging the parties to cooperate on additional scientific research that will further illuminate the nature of the problem and its possible consequences. Most framework agreements call upon the parties to take voluntary steps to control or limit activities within their jurisdictions that are contributing to the problem. Finally, such a treaty establishes procedures for the parties to meet periodically to consider adopting additional measures to address the problem. These supplemental agreements commonly take the form of protocols that set target dates for limiting the emission of certain air pollutants, or even reducing them by specified amounts. As with other treaties, protocols are binding only on the countries that formally ratify them. This multiple-stage process involving framework conventions and a succession of protocols has proven to be a flexible format for negotiating progressively stronger agreements as scientific evidence mounts on the severity of the threat and political support grows for adopting more stringent international regulations.

Sweden and Norway made the case for international rules that would stem the flow of acid-forming air pollutants across international boundaries as early as the United Nations Conference on the Human Environment, which was held in Stockholm in 1972. The first treaty on the subject was adopted in 1979 at a meeting convened in Geneva by the United Nations Economic Commission for Europe (ECE). At the time, few countries shared the sense of urgency that the Scandinavian nations had about the problem of acidification. Thus, there was little support for the adoption of a schedule for mandatory reductions of emissions of SO_2 and other acid-forming pollutants. The outcome of the conference was a weakly worded framework agreement known as the Convention on Long-Range Transboundary Air Pollution (LRTAP). The LRTAP Convention contains the vague expectation that states will ensure that activities taking place within their boundaries do not cause damage in other countries. It goes on to suggest that the parties should 'endeavor to limit and, as far as possible, to gradually reduce and prevent air pollution', using 'the best technology that is currently available' (see Jackson 1990).

The alarming spread of the *Waldsterben* syndrome through the forests of central Europe prompted West Germany and several neighboring countries to abruptly shift from being staunch opponents to becoming strong advocates of international regulations on air pollution. A 1985 meeting of the parties to the LRTAP Convention adopted a protocol that required ratifying states to reduce their emissions of SO_2 by 30 per cent from 1980 levels by 1993. Each country was left to decide on the measures it would adopt to accomplish this reduction. Several of the parties to the original LRTAP Convention refused to become parties to the Sulfur Protocol, most notably the United Kingdom, the United States, Poland, and Spain. Eleven countries, however, felt that the Sulfur Protocol did not go far enough and made individual commitments to reduce their emissions of SO_2 by more than 50 per cent by dates ranging from 1990 to 1995. Sweden, followed by Norway and Finland, set out to achieve 80 per cent reductions by 1995 (Soroos 1997: 127–30).

The parties to the LRTAP Convention went on to negotiate several additional protocols. In 1988 they concluded a protocol that would limit emissions of NO_x to 1987 levels after 1994. Disappointed that the protocol failed to mandate any reductions in NO_x emissions, 12 countries signed a separate declaration setting out a goal of cutting their emissions by 30 per cent by 1998, using any year between 1980 and 1986 as a base. The next in the series of protocols, which was concluded in 1991, targeted volatile organic chemicals (VOCs), a broad category of substances that is responsible for ground-level ozone and photochemical smog. The parties to the protocol were expected to cut their VOC emissions by 30 per cent by 1998. The recommended base year was 1988, although the parties had the option of selecting any year between 1984 and 1990. The parties also had the option of achieving the reduction for their country as a whole, or only in certain designated regions within the country, which contribute significantly to ozone problems in other countries (Soroos 1997: 130–2).

The parties to the LRTAP Convention adopted a Revised Sulfur Protocol in 1994. This agreement is based on the concept 'critical load', which is the amount of acidic deposition that a geographical region can absorb without significant environmental damage. As the negotiations got under way, each country was given its own target percentage for reducing its sulfur emissions. These targets were derived from a computer model which took into account how much the emissions of each country contributed to acidic deposition in excess of the critical loads in other countries, as well as the costs that would be entailed in reducing the emissions. The initial objective of the negotiations was to secure commitments that would reduce excess acidic deposition in the European region by 60 per cent by 2000. Austria, Denmark, Germany, Sweden, and Finland agreed to reductions of 80 per cent or more from 1990 levels by 2000. Other countries were not willing to commit themselves to the full sulfur reduction goals that were assigned them or pushed the target date back to 2005 or 2010. Thus, only a 50 per cent reduction in excess acidic deposition is projected if all countries follow through on their commitments (Soroos 1997: 132–6). Further negotiations led to the Protocol to Abate Acidification, Eutrophication, and Ground Level Ozone, which was adopted in Gothenburg, Sweden, in 1999. It is designed to achieve additional reductions in emissions of four pollutants – SO_2, NO_x, VOCs, and NH_3 – by 2010.

International efforts to address the problem of depletion of the ozone layer took a similar track in the early stages, although in this case the negotiations were global in the sense of being open to all countries. A strong public reaction to the initial warnings of

Molina and Rowland about the threat that CFCs may pose to the ozone layer prompted the United States in 1978 to ban nonessential uses of the chemicals, such as in aerosol sprays. Several other countries followed suit – most notably Canada, Norway and Sweden. However, other nations, including major users and producers of CFCs, were not persuaded that such action was necessary, given the state of knowledge about the threat to the ozone layer. The first international treaty on the subject, the Vienna Convention on the Ozone Layer of 1985, was a typical framework agreement. It called upon the parties to control, limit, reduce or prevent activities that may be found to diminish the ozone layer. However, as with the LRTAP Convention, the initial treaty on the ozone layer did not set a timetable for mandatory limits or reductions in the production or use of substances linked to ozone depletion (see Benedick 1998).

The announcement of the Antarctic ozone hole in 1985 lent greater urgency to efforts to preserve the ozone layer. Even before scientists had definitively linked the ozone hole to human causes, agreement was reached in 1987 on the landmark Montreal Protocol on Substances that Deplete the Ozone Layer. The protocol requires the parties to reduce their production and use of CFCs by 20 per cent by 1993 and by 50 per cent by 1998, with 1986 being the base year. Production and consumption of halons, a family of chemicals used widely in fire extinguishers, were not to exceed 1986 levels after 1993 (Litfin 1994: 78–119).

When it was adopted, the Montreal Protocol was viewed as a major breakthrough toward preservation of the ozone layer. Its adequacy quickly came under question, however, as scientific evidence mounted that ozone loss was taking place more rapidly than had been anticipated, not only over Antarctica, but also at other latitudes. Accordingly, the parties to the Montreal Protocol met in London in 1990 and adopted amendments to the document that would require a complete phasing out of CFCs and halons by the year 2000. Carbon tetrachloride and methyl chloroform, two other chemicals linked to ozone loss, would be banned by 2000 and 2010, respectively. Even more ominous reports on the ozone layer prompted the adoption of another set of amendments at a meeting of the parties to the Montreal Protocol in Copenhagen in 1992. The date for discontinuing halons was advanced to 1994, while production of CFCs, carbon tetrachloride and methyl chloroform would end by 1996. Use of HCFCs, a substitute for CFCs that poses less of a threat to the ozone layer, would be gradually phased out by 2030 (Litfin 1994: 119–76). Additional amendments were adopted in Montreal in 1997 and Beijing in 1999.

The Montreal Protocol of 1987 and the amendments adopted in 1990 and 1992 have drastically cut back the flow of CFCs and other ozone-destroying chemicals into the atmosphere. If there is full compliance with existing international agreements, concentrations of stratospheric ozone are expected to bottom out in the next few years and then gradually to return to previous natural levels by about 2050 (UNEP 2001: 6). However, there are two reasons for caution about whether the ozone layer will begin recovering so soon. The first is a disturbing level of illicit trade in the banned substances, in particular CFCs. Second, methyl bromide, another significant contributor to ozone depletion, remains to be fully controlled due to the resistance of agricultural interests who depend upon the chemical to fumigate their fields (see French 1997).

The success in concluding the Montreal Protocol and its amendments offers reason for hope that decisive action can also be taken to limit human-induced climate change, the other major global atmospheric problem confronting humanity. The threat of significant global warming was first taken up at high-level international conferences in the late 1980s, following a series of years with unusually warm global average temperatures. Negotiations begun in 1991 led to the signing of the Framework Convention on Climate Change at the Earth Summit in Rio de Janeiro the next year. At the time, many of the industrial countries and a coalition of nearly 40 small island nations strongly favored inclusion of a schedule for mandatory limits, if not actual reductions, in emissions of GHGs such as CO_2. No such provision was included in the convention, however, due largely to the refusal of the United States to commit itself to limits that might be costly to implement, while in its view significant scientific uncertainties remained on the need for such measures.

Though similar to the framework agreements that address the problems of transboundary pollution and depletion of the ozone layer, the Climate Change Convention is a stronger document in certain respects. It establishes an ambitious goal of stabilizing concentrations of GHGs in the atmosphere at a level that would prevent dangerous anthropogenic interference with the climate system. The developed countries are called upon, but not required, to limit their GHG emissions to 1990 levels by the year 2000. Finally, developed countries were expected to submit periodic reports on the steps they are taking to reduce GHG (see Bodansky 1993). As the decade wore on, however, GHG emissions in most developed countries continued to increase. Thus, there was little prospect that they would accomplish the goal of reducing emissions to 1990 levels by the year 2000.

The nations that have ratified the Framework Convention on Climate Change meet each year as the Conference of the Parties (COP) to the treaty. The nations attending COP1, which was held in Berlin in 1995, agreed that the original treaty did not go far enough and committed themselves to negotiate a schedule for binding reductions that would be ready for adoption when they gathered for COP3 in Kyoto in 1997. On the eve of the Kyoto meetings, it appeared unlikely that the United States and the European nations could resolve their contrasting positions on emission reductions. However, to the surprise of most observers, COP3 adopted a protocol committing the developed countries to achieve an average 5.2 per cent reduction in their GHG emissions from 1990 levels by the average of the years 2008 to 2012. Most of the European countries, and the European Union as a whole, agreed to reduce GHG emissions by 8 per cent, while the United States and Japan committed to 7 per cent and 6 per cent cutbacks, respectively. Several countries, including Russia and Ukraine, simply promised a return of GHGs emissions to 1990 levels, while Norway and Australia insisted on being allowed to increase their emissions by 1 and 8 per cent, respectively. The protocol does not call upon developing countries to restrain their emissions of GHGs, which are on course to exceed those of the developed countries by about 2025 ('Kyoto Protocol . . .' 1997).

The Kyoto Protocol included several so-called 'flexible mechanisms', which offer developed countries several options that could make it easier for them to achieve their emission targets. Steps taken to increase carbon sinks, such as by expanding forest cover, can be used to offset mandated emissions reductions. Nations may purchase emission credits from countries whose emissions are below their Kyoto targets, with Russia and Ukraine being the most likely sources of credits because their emissions dropped significantly as their economies shrank during the 1990s. There is also the possibility of 'joint implementation' projects, which would entail investing in projects in developing countries that would achieve a net saving in GHG emissions. Finally, a group of developed countries could agree to a collective reduction, but among themselves agree on differentiated targets, an option that has been adopted by the European Union (EU).

Thus, Germany and the United Kingdom have committed to greater than 8 per cent reductions to allow other members of the EU to have lesser targets.

The original Kyoto Protocol left many details to be worked out later. Little progress was made at COP4 in Buenos Aires in 1998 and COP5 in Bonn in 1999. At these meetings, the United States pushed for the developing countries to begin restraining their GHG emissions to improve the prospects for ratification of the protocol by the US Senate. COP6 in The Hague in 2000 broke down in disarray as the United States insisted upon receiving at least some credit for its existing carbon sinks, while resisting efforts of the Europeans to limit the extent to which the flexible mechanisms could be used to achieve its emission reduction target. In March 2001, the new Bush administration summarily rejected the Kyoto Protocol, leaving it up to the other nations to decide whether to continue work on finalizing the document without the participation of the United States, the leading emitter of GHGs. A reconvened COP6 in the summer of 2002 achieved key compromises among the remaining countries and a finalized protocol was adopted at COP7 in Marrakech, Morocco, later in the year. Many countries have ratified the protocol and begun taking steps to reduce their GHG emissions.

The Kyoto Protocol is more significant as a political accomplishment than an environmental one. At best it would have achieved little more than a 5 per cent reduction in the GHG emissions of the developed countries, while emissions were growing rapidly in the developing countries, which have resisted all efforts thus far to make any commitments to limiting their emissions. The rejection by the United States will substantially reduce the impact of the protocol, as will many compromises that were struck in working out the details of the flexible mechanisms. Even if a 5 per cent reduction in the emissions of the developed countries could be achieved, it would be a small step toward the 60–80 per cent reduction that would be necessary to stabilize concentrations of GHGs in the atmosphere at prevailing levels.

7.6 The economics of atmospheric pollution

Nations negotiate international treaties and other agreements to achieve preferred outcomes that would be more costly, if not impossible, to achieve on their own. Treaties are contracts in which each party to the agreement accepts certain obligations in return for commitments from others to limit or curb activities that are damaging to its interests. Thus, the terms of the agreement determine how the cost of producing certain benefits will be divided among the parties. In the give-and-take of the negotiating process, countries normally pursue their national interests by seeking to incur as few obligations as possible, especially those that would be costly to fulfill, while obtaining the greatest possible concessions from other states.

The task of negotiating international agreements on transboundary acid-forming pollution would have been less complicated if the pollutants circulated equally in all directions. In most cases, however, prevailing winds carry much more pollution in some directions than in others. Thus, upwind countries are net 'exporters' of pollution to other countries, while downwind states are net 'importers' of acid pollutants from other states. Canada, for example, receives approximately four times the volume of acid-forming air pollutants from the United States as flows in the opposite direction from Canada to the United States (Cowling 1982: 118). Likewise, in the European region, the United Kingdom contributes far more to the problem of acidification in Scandinavia and mainland Europe than they do in the reverse direction.

The predominantly upwind countries such as the United States and United Kingdom have little incentive to become parties to international agreements that obligate them to reduce emissions of acid-forming pollutants. They would incur the substantial cost of preventing air pollution, such as smokestack scrubbers, while the principal benefactors of these expenditures would be their downwind neighbors. Alternatively, whatever downwind countries agreed to do to limit their emissions would do very little to diminish any problems the upwind country had with acidification. Thus, it is not surprising that the United States and United Kingdom were unwilling to become parties to the 1985 Sulfur Protocol, which would have required them to reduce their SO_2 emissions by 30 per cent by 1993.

Numerous countries in Europe, such as Germany, Switzerland and Austria, are both major exporters and major importers of air pollution. Much of the acidic deposition within their territories originates in other countries, while a large proportion of their emissions is deposited outside their borders. For these countries the costs of complying with international limits are offset by the benefits of less acidic deposition within their boundaries. Thus, these centrally located countries have been willing to join the Scandinavian countries and Canada in advocating international controls on emissions of acid-forming air pollutants.

Who should bear the costs of reducing the transnational flow of air pollutants? Should it be the polluting countries? Or should they be paid by the countries that are victims of acidic deposition originating beyond their borders? The predominant principle in international law is that the polluter should pay the costs of reducing its emissions or, alternatively, for the damage that its pollution causes beyond its borders. The polluter-pays principle was affirmed in the landmark Trail Smelter case, in which the United States brought a complaint against Canada for pollution from a large smelter operation in Trail, British Columbia, which was alleged to have damaged orchards across the border in the state of Washington. In deciding the case in 1941 an international tribunal sided with the United States. Canada was not only required to take steps to reduce the pollution in the future, but was also instructed to compensate the United States for past damages (see Wirth 1996).

The polluter-pays doctrine was reaffirmed by the declaration adopted at the Stockholm Conference in 1972. The frequently cited Article 21 of the declaration provides that states 'have the sovereign right to exploit their resources in accordance with their environmental policies'. The article also suggests, however, that states have an obligation to 'insure that activities within their own jurisdiction or control do not cause damage to the environment of other states or areas beyond the limits of national jurisdiction' (*Declaration on the Human Environment . . .* 1972). The series of protocols that limit emissions of SO_2, NO_x and VOCs also place the burden of complying with these limits on the countries where the pollutants originate.

The alternative is for the victim of pollution to pay for its reduction. The victim-pays doctrine presumes that nations have a right to engage in activities that generate reasonable amounts of pollution, some of which may be deposited beyond their borders. Accordingly, if the benefits from stemming this flow of pollution are substantial enough to the countries that receive the pollutants, it should be up to them to absorb the costs entailed in reducing them. Thus, a downwind country might compensate its upwind neighbors for the expenses they incur in curbing their emissions. The victim-pays principle has not been widely applied in international law. One notable example, however, is the payments that The Netherlands and Germany made to the

French government to invest in measures to reduce chloride pollution entering the river Rhine from France's upstream potash mines (see Bernauer 1996).

The circumstances are somewhat different in the cases of ozone depletion and climate change. Here the problem is one not of pollutants simply being transported by air currents from one country to another, but of pollution altering the chemistry of the atmosphere in ways that modify the flow of energy to and from the planet. No country or region of the world will fully escape the impacts of these atmospheric changes. Thus, any steps taken to limit the magnitude of these changes go toward the creation of global public goods in the form of a protected ozone layer and the maintenance of desirable climates. The challenge for negotiators is to induce nations to invest in the creation of global public goods that they can enjoy even if they do not shoulder their fair share of the cost of producing them. The temptation for nations is to be 'free riders', taking advantage of the sacrifices of others while shirking their own responsibility to contribute to the creation of a public good.

The willingness of states to enter into international agreements to mitigate global atmospheric problems depends in part on the stakes that are involved for them. Some countries are likely to be more heavily impacted than are others. The amount of observed ozone loss, and consequently increased exposure to damaging UV radiation, varies considerably by latitude, with the far northern and far southern regions being the most affected. Likewise, the amount and type of climate change will differ considerably by region, with the largest amount of warming being expected in the higher latitudes. Other areas, however, may see greater changes in the frequency and intensity of storms and rainfall patterns. Countries with low-lying coastal areas are especially vulnerable to rises in sea level caused by warmer climates.

How should the cost of producing these global public goods be divided? The polluter-pays doctrine would place most of the responsibility on the advanced industrial countries, which are the source of the lion's share of the pollutants that are causing stratospheric ozone depletion and climate change. Over time, however, the proportion from the developing countries has been increasing. Most of the advanced industrial countries have indicated their willingness to shoulder this responsibility by advocating international rules that would require developed countries to reduce emissions of the pollutants responsible for these problems. There have been notable exceptions, however, most notably the United States which has refused to make binding commitments to reduce its emissions of GHGs. In effect, the United States plays the role of free rider in that it will benefit from whatever moderation of climate change trends occurs as a result of the emission reductions of other countries.

Developing countries have been reluctant to agree to limits on their release of the pollutants responsible for global atmospheric changes. For them, economic development and reducing poverty are more immediate priorities than limiting ozone depletion and global warming. There is also the issue of fairness. If the developed countries are largely responsible for most of the human-generated pollutants that have accumulated in the atmosphere thus far, then presumably they should take the first major steps to address the problems that arise. By cutting back sharply on their emissions of pollutants such as CFCs and CO_2, the advanced industrial countries would make it possible for the developing countries to increase their relatively low level of emissions to further their economic development, without seriously aggravating the atmospheric problems such emissions trigger. Furthermore, if the cooperation of the developing countries in limiting pollutants is desired, then the richer countries should be willing to compensate them for the costs that they incur in controlling pollution.

While the industrial countries have been largely responsible for past emissions of the pollutants responsible for depletion of ozone layer and climate change, the share of the developing countries has grown rapidly in recent decades. Thus, the future success of the international responses to these problems will depend on the willingness of developing countries to limit their emissions of these pollutants to levels that are considerably lower than they have been in the developed countries. To encourage their participation in the 1987 Montreal Protocol and its subsequent amendments, the developing countries were allowed ten-year grace periods for complying with schedules for reducing and phasing out the chemicals linked to ozone loss. The London amendments of 1990 provided for a special multilateral fund of $160–$240 million to assist developing countries to reduce their use of CFCs and other ozone-depleting substances. Technologies related to the production and use of suitable substitutes were to be provided to developing countries 'under fair and most favorable conditions'.

The 1992 Framework Convention on Climate Change explicitly acknowledged that emissions of GHGs by the developing countries are relatively low, but could be expected to increase as these countries meet the social and developmental needs of their people. The agreement placed the primary responsibility for limiting GHG emissions and preserving carbon sinks on the developed countries, which were asked, but not required, to reduce their net emissions to 1990 levels by the year 2000. While the Kyoto Protocol of 1997 obligates developed countries to reduce their GHG emissions by more than 5 per cent over the next decade, there are no provisions requiring the developing countries to limit their emissions. The absence of limits on the GHG emissions of the developing countries, which it is feared may offer them a competitive advantage in international trade, has been seized upon by opponents of the Kyoto Protocol in the United States who seek to prevent its ratification by the Senate.

There are limits to how hard a bargain the developing countries should try to drive with the advanced industrial countries over dividing up the costs that would be entailed in limiting global atmospheric changes. If negotiations fail, developing countries are likely to be the most seriously impacted. Many of them have large coastal cities and low-lying agricultural regions that are especially susceptible to rising sea levels and tropical storms. Some are highly vulnerable to changing rainfall patterns that could lead to the expansion of deserts. Numerous developing countries are located in tropical regions where heat stress would become more prevalent and disease vectors flourish. The economies of developing countries are more dependent on agricultural exports that may be jeopardized by climate changes. Finally, developing countries have significantly fewer resources with which to adapt to whatever environmental changes take place, such as to rebuild after being struck by tropical storms. Reducing these environmental threats may not yet be a high priority for developing countries, but to ignore them could prove to be very costly over the long run.

7.7 Chapter summary

*   This chapter discussed three atmospheric pollution problems that have inter-national or even global consequences: acid rain, depletion of the stratospheric ozone and climate change.

- Acid rain has become a serious problem affecting forests and freshwater aquatic life in Europe, North America and, increasingly, in developing regions. The problem takes on international dimensions when pollutants such as SO_2 and NO_x are emitted in one country and are then transported by air currents over national boundaries before being deposited in other countries.
- Two other atmospheric pollution problems, depletion of the stratospheric ozone layer and climate change, are global in scope. They arise because human-generated pollutants have the effect of altering the chemical composition of the atmosphere in ways that alter the flow of energy either to or from the planet Earth. The thinning of the ozone layer allows greater amounts of damaging ultraviolet radiation to reach the surface of the Earth. Human additions to atmospheric concentrations of GHGs keep more of the heat radiated from the Earth from escaping into outer space, thus warming the world's climate.
- Each of the three atmospheric problems discussed in this chapter is the subject of a series of international agreements, beginning with a general framework convention that was followed by one or more protocols which specify target dates for mandatory reductions of emissions of pollutants.
- The transboundary flow of acid-forming pollutants in Europe has been partially stemmed by a series of protocols that target emissions of CO_2, NO_x and VOCs.
- Agreements on transboundary air pollutants causing acid rain have been difficult to conclude because upwind countries, such as the United Kingdom and the United States, have been reluctant to bear the costs of reducing emissions largely for the benefit of downwind states. Their resistance to regulations on these pollutants runs counter to the principle of 'polluter pays', which was established in international law by the Trail Smelter case of 1941.
- The production and consumption of CFCs and other principal ozone-destroying chemicals have been sharply diminished by the 1987 Montreal Protocol as amended in 1990, 1992 and 1995. Much of the success is attributable to the availability of substitutes for the banned chemicals.
- Under the terms of the Montreal Protocol and its amendments, developing countries were given ten additional years to phase out ozone-depleting substances and promised economic and technical assistance to facilitate their use of substitutes for the banned chemicals.
- The threat of climate change has been addressed by the 1997 Kyoto Protocol, which provides for reductions in GHG emissions by developed countries and acknowledges the historical responsibility of the advanced industrial countries for the enhanced greenhouse effect. Some industrial countries, however, have been reluctant to make a commitment because the Protocol asks them to limit their GHG emissions, while imposing no similar expectations on the developing countries.

References and further reading

Anthes, R. A. (1992) *Meteorology*, 6th edn, New York: Macmillan.

Barnola, J. M., Raynaud, D., Korotkevich, Y. S. and Lorius, C. (1987) 'Vostok Ice Core Provides 160,000-Year Record of Atmospheric CO_2', *Nature* 329: 408–14.

Benedick, R. E. (1998) *Ozone Diplomacy: New Directions in Safeguarding the Planet*, revised edition, Cambridge, Mass.: Harvard University Press.

Bernauer, T. (1996) 'Protecting the Rhine River against Chloride Pollution', in R. O. Keohane and M. L. Levy (eds) *Institutions for Environmental Aid: Pitfalls and Promise*, Cambridge: Cambridge University Press.

Blaustein, A. P. *et al.* (1994) 'UV Repair and Resistance to Solar UV-B in Amphibian Eggs: A Link to Population Decline', *Proceedings of the National Academy of Sciences* 91: 1791–5.

Bodansky, D. (1993) 'The United Nations Framework Convention on Climate Change: A Commentary', *Yale Journal of International Law* 18: 451–558.

Calvin, W. H. (1998) 'The Great Climate Flip-Flop', *Atlantic Monthly* 281, 1: 47–64.

Cowling, E. B. (1982) 'Acid Precipitation in Historical Context', *Environmental Science and Technology* 16, 2: 110–22.

'Declaration on the Human Environment of the United Nations Conference on the Human Environment' (1972) *International Legal Materials* 11: 1462.

Farman, J. C., Gardiner, B. G. and Shanklin, J. D. (1985) 'Large Losses of Total Ozone in Antarctica Reveal Seasonal ClO_x/NO_x Interaction', *Nature* 315: 207–10.

Fisher, D. (1990) *Fire and Ice: The Greenhouse Effect, Ozone Depletion, and Nuclear Winter*, New York: Harper & Row.

French, H. (1997) 'Learning from the Ozone Experience', in Lester Brown *et al. State of the World 1997*, New York: Norton, 151–71.

Intergovernmental Panel on Climate Change (2001) *Climate Change 2001: The Scientific Basis, Summary for Policy Makers*, http://www.ipcc.ch/pub/spm22-01.pdf.

Jackson, C. I. (1990) 'A Tenth Anniversary Review of the ECE Convention on Long-Range Transboundary Air Pollution', *International Environmental Affairs* 2: 217–26.

Keeling, C. D. and Whorf, T. P. (2002) 'Atmospheric Carbon Dioxide Record from Mona Loa', http://cdiac.esd.ornl.gov/trends/co2/sio-mlo.htm

'Kyoto Protocol to the United Nations Framework Convention on Climate Change' (1997) UNDOC. FCCC/CP/L.7/Add.1.

Litfin, K. T. (1994) *Ozone Discourses: Science and Politics in Global Environmental Cooperation*, New York: Columbia University Press.

McCarthy, J. J. and McKenna, M. C. (2000) 'How the Earth's Ice is Changing', *Environment* 42, 10: 8–18

Molina, M. J. and Rowland, F. S. (1974) 'Stratospheric Sink for Chlorofluoromethanes: Chlorine Atom-Catalyzed Destruction of Ozone', *Nature* 249: 810–12.

Oeschger, H. and Mintzer, I. M. (1992) 'Lessons from the Ice Cores: Rapid Climate Changes during the Last 160,000 Years', in I. M. Mintzer (ed.) *Confronting Climate Change: Risks, Implications and Responses*, Cambridge: Cambridge University Press.

Park, C. C. (1987) *Acid Rain: Rhetoric and Reality*, New York: Routledge.

Schütt, P. and Cowling, E. B. (1985) 'Waldsterben, A General Decline of Forests in Central Europe: Symptoms, Development, and Possible Causes', *Plant Disease* 69: 548–58.

Soroos, M. S. (1997) *The Endangered Atmosphere: Preserving a Global Commons*, Columbia, SC: University of South Carolina Press.

Stevens, W. K. (1999) *The Change in the Weather: People, Weather, and the Science of Climate*, New York, Delacorte Press.

Trenberth, K. (2001) 'Stronger Evidence of Human Influences on Climate: The 2001 IPCC Assessment', *Environment* 43, 5: 8–19.

United Nations Environment Programme (2001) *Backgrounder: Basic Facts and Data on the Science and Politics of Ozone Protection*, http://www.unep.org/ozone/pdf/Press-Backgrounder.pdf.

Watson, R. T., Rowland, F. S. and Gille, J. (1988) *Ozone Trends Panel Executive Summary*, Washington, DC: NASA.

Wirth, J. D. (1996) 'The Trail Smelter Dispute: Canadians and Americans Confront Transboundary Pollution, 1927–41', *Environmental History* 1, 2: 34–51.

Part 3

Valuing the environment

Part 3 consists of two Chapters, 8 and 9. These deal with economic valuation of environmental services. Some of the key concepts and issues addressed in these chapters include: the methodological issues of imputing values to environmental resources; the various standard techniques used by economists to measure the monetary values of environmental damage or amenities; cost–benefit analysis and the ethics of discounting the future.

Valuation of the environment is one of the most important topics in environmental economics and, as will be evident from the discussions in these two chapters, economists have been making significant advances in this area over the past two decades. Conceptually, this area of environmental economics, while challenging and controversial, could lead to very exciting learning experience for the curious mind. In my judgement, this area of environmental economics constitutes the most fertile ground for future contributions by economists to the management and protection of valuable environmental resources. People are more likely to care about the well-being of the natural environment once its value becomes more apparent to them. The two chapters in Part 3 explore the efforts economists have been making towards the achievement of this worthwhile objective.

In these chapters, consistent with the theme of this book, deliberate efforts are taken to evaluate the various standard valuation techniques through an ecological lens. Furthermore, attempts are made to offer alternatives to traditional cost–benefit analysis. These alternatives include cost effectiveness, the precautionary principle and environmental impact analysis. Part 3 also discusses at some length risk assessment and management, intergenerational equity and environmental justice.

Finally, I would like to leave you with this suggestion, for what it is worth. Chapters 8 and 9 are rather long. For this reason, it may be helpful to read the chapter summaries first. The chapter summaries are written in such a way that the reader will get a full picture of the important material covered in the chapters.

8 Economic valuation of environmental services

According to the current paradigm in economics 'The ecosystem is viewed as external to society, providing goods and services, unoccupied territory in which to expand, and assimilative capacity to handle by-products. . . . Economics seeks to integrate this externalized environment into its own paradigm through the concept of 'valuation.' This approach sounds reasonable on the surface. Society should place a monetary value on the goods and services provided by the ecosystem and also on the effects of human activity on the ability of the ecosystem to provide these goods and services. Values for these 'externalities' can then be inserted into the economic model. Within the economic model, these externalities would provide the self-regulation needed to manage society's use of the environment.

(O'Neill and Kahn 2000: 333)

8.1 Introduction

The primary objective of this chapter is to investigate the various methods by which economists *attempt* to measure the benefits of environmental improvement or the preservation of the services of the natural environment. Generally, environmental improvement arises from *damages avoided* by taking certain well-defined action(s). For example, an environmental 'project' undertaken to clean up a lake could trace its benefits from the mere fact that, among others, such action would lead to an improvement (or a reversal of the damages) to the natural aesthetic value of the lake. As another example, the benefits of a public policy measure intended to preserve a wetland area may come from the contributions this action would have on biodiversity, flood control and enhanced environmental amenities. (In this chapter, a project refers to any intentional actions undertaken by a private or public body for the purpose of changing the quality of the natural environment.)

The above discussions indicate that the benefits from environmental improvement are inferred from assessment of avoided environmental *damages*. However, as discussed in Chapter 4, environmental damage costs are *externalities*. Thus, in most instances, their monetary values cannot be readily and directly obtained through the usual market mechanism. Despite this apparent difficulty, economists do attempt to measure the benefits from environmental improvement. How this is done is the central theme of this chapter. In the next section the methodological basis for measuring the benefits arising from improved environmental quality is examined. The focus is on understanding the exact context in which economists attempt to measure the *value* of improved environmental quality or avoided environmental damage.

8.2 Valuation of benefits: the methodological issue

Economists use *willingness to pay* as the standard measuring stick of benefit. Willingness to pay is measured by the demand price at the margin. For example in Figure 8.1, P_1 represents what consumers' are willing to pay for the tenth unit of good or service, Q. Similarly, P_e would be a measure of consumers' willingness to pay for the twenty-fifth unit of output. For products where a market exists, individuals exercise choice by comparing their willingness to pay with the price of the product under consideration. They purchase the good or service when their willingness to pay equals or exceeds the price, and not otherwise. For example, in Figure 8.1, if we assume P_e to be the market equilibrium price, all those consumers whose willingness to pay is represented by P_1 will be expected to decide to purchase this good or service. Thus, viewed this way, decision-making based on willingness to pay must reflect individuals' preferences for the good in question. What does all this mean for our task at hand, the measurement of social benefits from an environmental project?

To answer this question more clearly, let us assume that the specific project under consideration is a government mandate to control sulfur emissions from electric power plants located in certain regions of a nation. In this case, the benefit is a direct result of improved air quality or the environmental damage avoided as a result of reduced sulfur emissions. Benefits of this nature are measured by using a *demand curve* as shown in Figure 8.2. Note that, as discussed in Chapter 4 and specifically in Exhibit 4.1, the *marginal damage cost curve represents the demand curve for environmental quality*.

Suppose point A on the demand curve represents the situation that prevailed before the project was initiated. Note that the project here is the legislative mandate to control sulfur emissions. Thus, before the legislative mandate, individuals were willing to pay price t_1 to avoid the last unit of sulfur emission, Q_1. Now, suppose that due to the new government initiative, sulfur emission is reduced from Q_1 all the way to Q_2. That is, with the stricter sulfur pollution control, society is allowed to move from point A to B along its demand curve for environmental quality. At the new position, point B, individuals are willing to pay the price t_2 in order to avoid the last unit of emission, i.e. Q_2. Given this, what is the *total* social benefit of this project? This total benefit is represented by the area under the demand curve – area Q_1ABQ_2, which represents the sum of society's willingness to pay for moving from its initial position, point A to the new position point B.

A total benefit derived in this fashion is subject to several interesting interpretations. One interpretation is to view it as a measure of the *maximum* sum of money members of a given society are willing to pay to reduce sulfur emission from Q_1 to Q_2. Hence, viewed this way, it is a measure of *willingness to pay* (WTP). Alternatively, it could be interpreted as the *minimum* monetary compensation that members of a given society need in order to voluntarily accept that the proposed project (reduction in sulfur emission from Q_1 to Q_2) is *not* undertaken. This is a measure of *willingness to accept* (WTA).

To consider that WTP and WTA are equivalent would suggest that people value gains and losses similarly. If people do not in fact do this, for instance if they weigh losses more heavily than gains, there may be a higher value on preserving environmental amenities than the economic estimates based purely on willingness to pay would indicate. This would also be a result consistent with the usual assumption of the

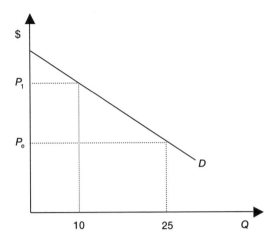

Figure 8.1 The concept of willingness to pay. Demand measures the price households are willing to pay in aggregate for a specified quantity provided in the market at a point in time.

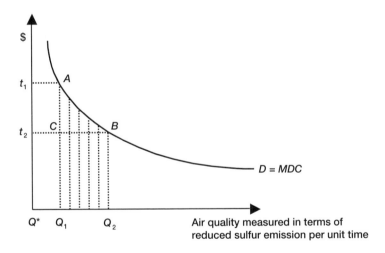

Figure 8.2 How to impute the total value of environmental project(s) using the demand curve for environmental quality.

convexity of consumers' preference function [For a detailed discussion on this subject matter see Hanemann (1991).]

Furthermore, it is important to note that since economic valuation of benefit is based on the concept of willingness to pay, the shaded area measures people's 'preferences' for changes in the state of their environment (Pearce 1993). What this suggests is that *when economists attempt to measure the benefits from improved environmental quality, they are measuring not the value of the environment but the preferences of people for an environmental good or environmental bad.* To further clarify this, consider this: one effect of a higher air quality standard may be improvement in human health, which causes a decrease in the average mortality rate. Thus, in this particular case, benefit is synonymous with increased quality of life or increased 'life' expectancy. Despite this, the economic measure of benefit makes no pretension of valuing 'life' as such. Instead, the measure is of people's preferences for a healthier and longer life. *Essentially, then, economists do not and cannot measure the value of life or the environment as such. Instead, what they attempt to measure is the preferences of people for a healthier life or for a preservation of environmental amenities.* This, indeed, represents one of the key methodological foundations of the economic valuation of environmental quality.

At this stage it is very important to note the following three points regarding the above approach to the estimation of benefits arising from environmental damage avoidance. First, valuation of the environment is based on human preferences alone, and it is assumed that all aspects of environmental damage can be valued in monetary terms. This means that a dollar value should be assigned to species and ecosystems that are considered to be irreplaceable. The alternative is, of course, to assume that nothing in life is irreplaceable (or has substitutes). Second, as shown in Figure 8.2, the estimation of benefit is not time-specific. This approach either assumes perfect foresight or simply neglects to address the *uncertainty* involved in environmental damage. This is an important point to keep in mind since many relevant environmental concerns (such as acid rain, ozone depletion, climate change, species preservation, etc.) involve a considerable degree of uncertainty (Krutilla 1967). Third, it is assumed that the changes in the environmental quality (such as the move from *A* to *B* in Figure 8.2), are reasonably *small*. In other words, what is being contemplated to measure is the value (benefit) of incremental change in environmental service. Thus, when viewed from a larger perspective, losses from environmental damage are too small to count (Johansson 1990). It is important to understand, however, that small changes would not precipitate major disturbance only if one assumes a convex world – in both its economic and ecological contexts (O'Neill and Kahn 2000).

Furthermore, it is also important to note here that the standard environmental valuation technique as described above precludes the attempt by Costanza and his associates to measure the *total* annualized value of the flow of environmental services to the human economy, which was estimated to be approximately $33 trillion (1997). As Dasgupta *et al.* (2000: 342) put it,

> The standard approach 'is meaningful because it presumes that humanity will survive in the incremental change and be there to experience and assess the change. However, the latter [Costanza's approach] estimate should cause us to balk because if crucial environmental services were to cease, life would not exist. But who would be there to receive $33 trillion of annual benefits if humanity were to exchange its very existence for them? Almost paradoxically, perhaps, the total value of the world's ecosystem services has no meaning and, therefore, is of no use, even though the value of incremental changes to those ecosystems not only has meaning – it also has use.

Thus far the discussion has focused on the methodological basis for measuring environmental benefits (avoided damage). In this regard, it is established that economic benefits should be measured on the basis of individuals' 'willingness to pay.' However, to say that benefit is measured on this basis will not be sufficient, since the actual measurement of 'willingness to pay' requires *information on the prices (demand)*, which in the case of environmental assets, are, if not impossible, difficult to obtain directly through the usual market mechanism. *Therefore, economists have no choice but to look for various alternative techniques of directly and indirectly eliciting willingness to pay for environmental assets.* In recent years considerable advances have been made in this area, and a fairly wide range of techniques are now available for eliciting willingness to pay for various aspects of environmental assets – which are the subject of the next section.

It should also be pointed out that the presentation in this chapter goes beyond an analysis of the various techniques present-day economists' attempts to elicit willingness to pay in order to measure the value of environmental service. The last section of the chapter (Section 8.4), consistent with what has been the main feature of the book, presents a critical assessment of the standard approaches of environmental valuation.

8.3 Practical methods for measuring the benefits of environmental improvement

In the previous section we explored the methodological issues pertaining to the measurement of benefits from environmental improvement. *The consensus within the economic profession appears to be that such benefits or avoided damage costs should be measured by eliciting individuals' willingness to pay for incremental changes in environmental quality.* Once the issue of interest is identified this way, then the challenge becomes a matter of discovering methods of eliciting this information under conditions where market failure is the rule rather than the exception. This section deals with discussions of the techniques most commonly used by economists for the purpose of eliciting people's willingness to pay for changes in the quality of environmental services or assets.

The choice of the specific technique used for the purpose of eliciting willingness to pay depends on the specific nature of the types of environmental damage that are being avoided in order to achieve the desired environmental quality. Among others, the avoided damage may include impairment to human health – a higher risk of mortality and morbidity; loss of economic outputs, such as fish harvest and extraction of certain minerals; increased exposure to environmental nuisance, such as noise, odor and debris; amenity and aesthetic losses; simplification of natural habitats; and irreversible damage to an ecosystem. While several techniques may be used to elicit a willingness to pay from which the demand for avoiding a particular type of environmental damage (e.g. noise) can be derived, *economists have yet to develop a single technique that could be used effectively in all circumstances.* Also, in a specific situation some techniques tend to be better than others. Thus, in many cases the choice of technique could be an important issue in itself. For this reason, the rest of this section is devoted to highlighting the salient features of the most widely used techniques for the purpose of eliciting a willingness to pay for improvement in environmental assets.

Finally, it is important to note that economists view the environment as an *asset* that provides a variety of services. A specific wetland area, for example, may provide aesthetic, ecological, recreational, industrial, and life-sustaining services. Hence, as we will observe shortly, measuring the benefits of an environmental asset may require the use of *several* different techniques for the purpose of eliciting *total* willingness to pay (i.e. total benefit) of a project, such as the preservation of a specific wetland area.

8.3.1 The market pricing approach

The market pricing approach is used when the environmental improvement under consideration causes an increase or decrease in real outputs and/or inputs. Examples may include a decrease in timber harvest and/or extraction of minerals resulting from a legislative enactment that effectively expands the acreage set aside as a wilderness area; the expected increase in fish harvest due to the implementation of a new water pollution control technology; or an increase in crop yield arising from a legislative mandate of a higher air quality standard.

In the above examples, benefits from environmental improvement (avoided damage) are identified in terms of changes in outputs or inputs; more specifically, timber, minerals, fish, and crops. These outputs or inputs are expected to have market prices that accurately reflect their scarcity values or, where this is not the case, *shadow prices* (i.e. values of similar goods in private markets) can be easily imputed. Thus, *where environmental improvement is directly associated with changes in the quantity or price of marketed outputs or inputs, the benefit directly attributable to the environmental improvement in question can be measured by changes in the consumers' and producers' surpluses.*

Consumer surplus refers to any benefit that consumers may receive when purchasing goods and services at the prevailing market prices. Clearly, consumers would benefit more when market prices are lower than what they are willing to pay. On the other hand, *producer surplus* refers to any benefit (including profits) suppliers receive when they sell the goods and services they produce at market price. Evidently, producers benefit more as production costs decrease relative to the market price (refer to Section 3 of Appendix A for an expanded discussion of both consumer and producer surplus).

To illustrate how consumer and producer surpluses are used in environmental policy concern, consider our earlier example, the effect of a higher air quality standard on crop yield. As shown in Figure 8.3, the actual effect of the higher air pollution standard is a shift in the supply curve from S_0 to S_1, indicating an improvement in crop yield. In other words, since improved air quality enhances crop yield, other things equal, at every level of output farmers are now willing to sell their crop at a lower price than prior to the legislative enactment to improve environmental quality. As a result of the shift in the supply curve, the market price for the agricultural commodity will fall from P_0 to P_1. Obviously this would lead to an increase in consumers' surplus. Furthermore, if the shift in supply is associated with significant cost saving, the producers' surplus will also be rising. As shown in Figure 8.3, this benefit (to both consumers and producers) from improved air quality is measured by the difference in consumers' and producers' surpluses before and after the mandated change in air quality standard – area $ABCE$ (the difference in the net social benefits between the original, triangle ABP_m, and the new position, area ECP_m).

One of the major concerns when conducting this kind of analysis is the need to accurately account for all the factors that affect the supply and demand of the goods and services under consideration. For instance, in our example above, it is important to carefully isolate the effect of other factors on the supply curve, such as technological change. In general, this can be done using statistical analysis that may require time series data for several key variables affecting demand and supply.

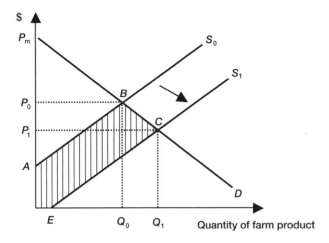

Figure 8.3 Change in consumers' surplus as a measure of social benefit. Originally, at Q_0, the social surplus was measured by area of the triangle ABP_m (the sum of the consumers' and producers' surpluses). When output is increased from Q_0 to Q_1, the social surplus was expanded to area ECP_m. Hence, the shaded area represents the *net* gain in social surplus.

For an excellent case study that uses this approach see Dixon and Hufschmidt (1986: 102–20). These authors attempted to place a value on the loss of the fishery resource caused by the coastal development of Tokyo Bay using the market value of lost marine products (shrimp and crab, seaweed and fish) production.

Another variation of the market pricing approach is the use of the opportunity cost scenario. For example, in a case study that dealt with forest conservation and development program in Madagascar, Kremen *et al.* (2000) used the opportunity cost method this way. The case study specifically dealt with preserving a 33,000 ha area of tropical forest (Masoala National Park and the surrounding buffer zone). The opportunity cost approach simply looks at the land use that produces the highest alternative return. At the national level, it was estimated that the highest return would result from large-scale industrial logging concession, implying that the Masoala Peninsula should become a forestry concession instead of a national park.

8.3.2 The replacement cost approach

This approach is used as a measure of benefit when the damage that has been avoided as a result of improved environmental conditions can be approximated by the market value of what it cost to *restore* or *replace* the damage in question. For example, acid rain, among its other effects, is known to accelerate the deterioration of a nation's infrastructure, such as highways, bridges and historic monuments. Suppose a given nation passed a bill that reduces the emissions of acid rain precursors (sulfur and nitrates) by 50 per cent. For the sake of simplicity, assume that all the sources of these pollutants emanate from within the boundary of the nation. One obvious outcome of a legislative mandate of this nature is to slow down the deterioration of the nation's physical infrastructure. If the replacement cost approach is used to measure this benefit from avoided environmental damage, it will be assessed on the basis of the savings realized from reduced expenditures on repairing, restoring and replacing the nation's infrastructure.

In exactly what way does the replacement cost approach measure people's willingness to pay? It can elicit people's willingness to pay to the extent that the reduction in replacement and restoration costs (due to improved environmental conditions) closely reflects people's willingness to pay to avoid environmental damage (Pearce 1993). This qualified response to the question raised earlier is prompted because *replacing lost services rests on the assumption that the public is willing to accept a one-to-one tradeoff between a unit of services lost due to damage and a unit of service gained due to restoration.*

However, in some cases, environmental damage may not be capable of being completely repaired or replicated. Even if it could be, the replicas would probably be of little worth compared to the original. An example of this would be an attempt to estimate the value of a wetland area that is ear-marked for housing development by what it would take to restore or replicate it somewhere else in the vicinity of the original site. In this instance, other methods of benefit assessment, such as contingent valuation (to be discussed later) would be more appropriate. For this reason, the replacement cost approach should be used with some care. Despite this apparent weakness, *the use of this method could be quite tempting because it is generally easy to find what appears to be rough but fairly adequate estimates of replacement costs.*

As an example, in one case study (Dixon and Hufschmidt 1986: 63–82) this approach was used to estimate the cost of recovering and replacing eroded soil from an agricultural project in Korea. In this case study the productive asset that had been damaged was the soil in the upland areas. The costs of physically replacing lost soil and nutrients was used as a benchmark by which to measure the replacement costs. These replacement costs were then viewed as measures of the minimum benefits to be realized from preventive steps (new soil management techniques) that could be undertaken to restore and maintain the original productivity of the damaged soil.

8.3.3 Hedonic pricing approaches

A Environmental amenities associated with property values

Environmental features can increase land and house values if they are viewed as attractive or desirable, or they can reduce values if they are viewed as nuisances or dangerous, and therefore undesirable. For example, because of the associated odor, noise, debris, and health risks, people in search of housing sites would tend to equate a landfill site's proximity with diminished environmental quality. Given a choice between two houses offered for the same price and identical in every other respect, except that one is closer to a landfill site, home buyers will choose the house that is further away. Only when the closer house is offered for less money will families consider it a suitable alternative. At some lower market price of the closer house, home buyers will become indifferent in choosing between that site and a higher-priced one further away from the landfill site. In this way, then, people are *implicitly* revealing their willingness to pay for avoiding the nuisances associated with a landfill by paying higher prices for houses located further away from such a site. *This is the typical case of a hedonic price where the value or price of an environmental feature (neighborhood amenities, clean air, clean water, serenity, etc.) is imputed by looking at the effect that its presence has on relevant market-priced goods (such as, property value).* Other examples where hedonic prices can be effectively used include noise pollution from a point source (an airport, say), which can reduce the nearby residential property values; the effect of the construction of a nuclear plant on the property values of nearby residential areas; and urban residential development and its effect on nearby agricultural land value. How in such cases is hedonic valuation carried out in practice?

Hedonic valuation uses statistical methods to estimate how much of the overall price (say of housing) is due to a given environmental attribute or amenity. The analysis starts by realizing functional relationship between a set of *independent* and *dependent* variables. In the case of housing, the attributes constituting the independent variables may include location, lot size, scenery, number of rooms, floor space, mechanical systems, age, school district, and property tax level, etc. The dependent variables are observed market prices for housing. The analyst collects data on these variables for as many parcels of property as is practical. These data are fitted statistically to produce estimated coefficients for an equation called the *hedonic price function*. The coefficients of the price function express a unit dollar value (marginal price) associated with a unit of measurement of each attribute.

For example, Nelson *et al.* (1992) conducted an empirical study to estimate the price effects of landfill sites on house values. Using a sample of 708 single-family homes in the Ramsey, Minnesota, area that were located within close proximity to a landfill site, they found that the site adversely affected home values. More specifically, according to the empirical results of this study, 'house value rises by nearly $5,000 for each mile it is located away from the landfill. On a percentage basis, house value rises by about 6.2 per cent per mile from the landfill' (p. 362).

A problem with the above finding is that it assumes that the unit dollar value revealed by hedonic price function will remain constant regardless of the level of the environmental quality; in the above example, it is assumed to be $5,000 for each mile away from the landfill site. However, in many instances, one would expect the unit value to be higher for homes closer to the landfill site. Economists approach this problem by applying a statistical technique known as *a second stage of the hedonic valuation methods* (a discussion of this method is beyond the scope of this text). Thus, the two-stage hedonic valuation method produces values for both a one-unit change and a multi-unit change from the sample average value for the environmental amenity (Songhen, 2001). In our earlier example, Nelson *et al.* (1992) applied the second stage of the hedonic valuation method and reported that, as would be expected, the effect on house values of a landfill site varied with distance. The adverse effect on home values was 12 per cent for homes located at the landfill boundary and 6 per cent at about one mile. The adverse effect on home values was negligible for homes that were located beyond two miles from the landfill site.

The above discussion limits the application of a hedonic price approach to cases where environmental attributes can be, in some way, inferred by looking at the market prices for housing and/or land or, in general, property values. In cases where such data are easily available, *a hedonic price approach of this nature can be of great utility because it is based on people's actual behavior.* In other words, the values derived reflect real commitments of consumer resources to achieve specific environmental quality improvement. Hedonic valuation of this nature is also significant because the transaction of a house purchase represents a large share of most consumers' income (welfare). Thus, the value attached to the residential environment should represent a large share of the overall value attached to environmental quality. However, its major drawback also stems from the fact that the approach is completely dependent on property values and as such has a limited application. For example, it will not be applicable to measuring benefits relating to national parks, endangered species, ozone depletion, and so on.

B Valuation of health risks stemming from exposure to workplace environmental hazards

Another area where the hedonic price method can be used is the economic valuation of changes in human health conditions, such as *mortality* (premature death) and *morbidity* (illness) primarily associated with occupational choices. In these cases, as we will observe shortly, willingness to pay is inferred from available data on medical expenditures and income or wages.

Pollution is often perceived as an environmental factor that exposes humans to some degree of health risk. For example, groundwater contamination caused by toxic waste disposal on a landfill site that is not properly sealed may be a serious human health hazard. This health hazard, over time, may result in a significantly higher than average incidence of disease and premature death among the population in the nearby community. Similar results can also occur from workplace exposure to toxic chemicals, carcinogens, or other environmental hazards. How can we measure, in monetary terms, an environmental effect that increases the mortality and morbidity rates of a community? Are we not here implicitly measuring such things as human 'life', pain and suffering? After all, is not life priceless?

These are all legitimate questions to raise. However, as stated in Section 8.2, if the objective is to measure benefits from avoiding environmental damage by means of individuals' willingness to pay, *what is being measured is not values of 'life' or 'pain' but people's preferences for health risk – how much damage they are willing to avoid*. We all take risks of this nature on a daily basis. What else can explain people's behavior when they drive a car, especially on congested highways such as the Los Angeles freeways? Accordingly, then, the 'life' that is measured is a 'statistical life'. With this caveat, how do we measure morbidity and mortality using the hedonic price approach?

When applying the hedonic price approach, *morbidity* risks associated with work-place environmental hazards are assumed to be factored into wages paid by different occupations. That is, jobs which are associated with a higher than average health risk, such as mining, tend to pay risk premiums in the form of higher wages. Such wage–risk differentials can be used for measuring changes in morbidity resulting from environ-mental pollution. For example, let us assume that the average wage rate of coal miners is $15 an hour, whereas the average wage of blue-collar workers in the manufacturing sector is only $10 an hour. The $5 wage premium offered in the mining industry can be used as a measure of the relatively higher health risk associated with this industry. In other words, the *compensating wage differential*, in our example $5, is presumed to be sufficient to entice a worker to accept a less desirable or a more hazardous job such as mining rather than a work in an assembly-line with less risk to worker safety. One obvious problem with this approach is the fact that it assumes that workers do have the economic freedom to choose among alternative occupations. The issue at stake is how well a compensating wage differential can be used as a measure of 'preferences' for reducing mortality risk.

In similar fashion to what was done for housing, statistical methods are used to construct a functional relationship between the level of workers' compensation and environmental risk. In this case, the dependent variables are wage rates for similar occupational categories and the independent variables are attributes of risk, such as different exposure levels to environmental hazards. The major challenge here is to control statistically for all the non-safety related differences between the different occupational categories under consideration in order to isolate the difference in wage associated with difference in safety. If this is successfully accomplished, the final statistically fitted *hedonic wage function* would reveal how much compensation, on average, workers require in order to accept more environmental risk.

Another area where hedonic valuation may be considered is in the economic evaluation of *premature mortality*. Here, the economic value of interest is approximated by society's loss of labor productivity (lost real income) as a result of an individual's premature death caused by specific pollution-related ailments. The specific valuation approach used in this case relies on a calculation of the *present discounted value* (to be discussed in the next chapter) of future earnings that were lost due to premature mortality. An empirical study conducted by Peterson (1977) may help to clarify how this method actually works.

This study dealt with estimating the social cost of discharges by Reserve Mining Corporation of nonmagnetic rock or tailings into Lake Superior. The tailings contaminated the lake's water with asbestos-form fibers – a known carcinogen. This incident exposed the North Shore citizens to serious health risks since these communities draw their public water from the lake. It was estimated that contamination of the lake water would increase the average annual number of deaths in the North Shore region by 274 over the 25 years of remaining operation of the plant. It was also determined that the mean age at death of the North Shore victims would be 54 years of age, or 12.8 years less than the average life expectancy of a male in the United States, which was 66.8 years.

In addition, the social cost caused by each individual premature death was computed by estimating the annual present value of the lost productivity society suffers from each victim. This was estimated to be $38,849 (at 1975 prices) per victim. Then, given the projected 274 deaths per year, the total social cost imposed by Reserve's pollution to the North Shore community was estimated to be $10,644,626.

At this point, it is important to note that the estimate of $38,849 does not represent the value of the 12.8 extra years of living (life) to an individual. Can you imagine anyone willing to sacrifice 12.8 years of her or his life for as little as the above sum of money, or even ten or more times that figure? To an individual, life, however short, is perhaps priceless. Therefore, what the above estimate measures is the economic value of 12.8 years of statistical life and nothing else (Mishan 1971). Hence, from the perspective of society at large, an individual, in terms of her or his economic contribution, is nothing more than a statistical entity.

In some instances, the above valuation method has been used as the basis for actual compensation for job-related fatalities. This method when used for individual cases implies that death of individuals who differ only in their annual income would lead to different levels of compensation. In fact, this has been one of the major contentious issues in the discussion between the United States government and the lawyers representing relatives of the September 11 fatalities in New York City. As would be expected, there is a great deal of discomfort in using this approach, primarily due to *equity* considerations.

Measuring the economic value of changes in morbidity and mortality is much more involved, however. Prior to even starting the economic valuation process, it is necessary to establish a clear understanding of the various ways in which the specific pollutant(s) in question impair human health. Formally, this is done by using a technique known as the *dose–response* approach. In general, the steps required to carry out an effective dose–response analysis include measuring emissions and determining the resulting ambient quality, estimating human exposure and measuring impacts on human health (more on this in the next chapter). These are biological and ecological relationships that need to be established before estimating the economic value of changes in mortality and morbidity arising from environmental pollution. In several situations, dose–response analysis could be, although necessary, an expensive procedure to undertake. Thus, economic valuation of mortality and morbidity using the hedonic price approach could be an expensive proposal.

8.3.4 The household production function approach

A Aversive expenditures

In the household production function approach benefits from improvement in environmental quality are measured by looking at households' expenditures on goods and/or services that are *substitutes* or *complements* for the purpose of avoiding environmental damage. Examples of such types of household expenditure include installing sound-proof walling to reduce noise; purchasing radon-monitoring equipment to protect oneself from exposure to radon gas; purchasing water filters to reduce the risk of drinking contaminated water; frequent hospital visits to reduce the chance of serious ailments from prolonged exposure to air pollution; frequent painting of residential dwellings due to smoke emissions from a nearby factory; and so on. In each of these cases, we observe that households are willing to pay a certain amount of money (price) to avert specific environmental damage(s). Therefore, these expenditures, commonly known as aversive expenditures, can be used as a measure of households' willingness to pay for a certain level (standard) of environmental quality (quietness, clean water, clean air). Note that in many cases, in order to attain a given change in environmental quality, several types of aversive expenditures may be undertaken simultaneously. In this situation, total benefit is measured by summing the various expenditures needed to attain the desired level of environmental attribute(s).

B Travel cost method

Another variation of the household production function approach involves the valuation of environmental services from *recreational sites*, such as national parks. A special technique that is used to estimate the benefit from changes in the environmental amenities of recreational sites is known as the travel cost method. *This method measures the benefit (willingness to pay) stemming from a recreational experience, by looking at households' expenditures on the cost of travel to a desired recreational site.* The basic idea behind this approach is this. The services of a recreation site, for example a camping ground, cannot be adequately measured by the gate price, which is usually very low. However, users of this campsite come from various locations. Therefore, instead of the gate price, the price or the willingness to pay of each user can be approximated by her or his travel cost. This method originated in the 1950s, and ever since then it has been used widely and with considerable success to empirically estimate the demand (hence willingness to pay) for recreational sites.

For example, in one study (Dixon and Hufschmidt 1986), the recreational value of Lumpinee Park in Bangkok was estimated using the travel cost approach. Lumpinee is a public park located in the middle of Bangkok, the capital of Thailand. As the population and the economic activities around this city continued to grow, the opportunity cost (the commercial value of the park for other activities) of maintaining this park had been increasing steadily. What this prompted was a doubt in the minds of the public about the economic viability of the park. How did the recreational and amenity value of the park compare with its commercial value for other activities?

If the value of the park were to be assessed on the basis of the entrance fee (which was zero or nominal), its value would be virtually nothing. The alternative was to use the travel cost approach, and this was done to get a more accurate measure of consumers' surplus for the park. The use of this approach basically entails the construction of an empirical demand function for the public park. As discussed above, this was done by hypothesizing that the costs in money and time spent traveling to a free or nominally priced recreational site could be used to approximate consumers' willingness to pay for the site. For people living close to the recreational site the travel cost was low, and the expectation was that they would tend to visit the site more often. The opposite would be the case for those visitors traveling to the site from more distant places. Thus, other things remaining constant, the general expectation would be that *an inverse relationship between the travel cost and the number of visits to the given recreational site would be observed. In essence, this would represent the demand for a recreational site.*

There are two types of travel cost model: single-site and multiple-site models. *The difference between these two approaches arises from the fact that individuals are able to make trips to alternative recreational sites is explicitly considered in the multiple-site models.* This consideration is important to the extent that omitting the prices and quantities of relevant substitutes will bias the resource valuations.

The basic data needed to use travel cost methods include: the characteristics of individuals; the number of visits they make to the site; and information about their travel costs. As would be expected, more data are needed for multiple-site models. In addition to the characteristics of individual sites, data are needed to delineate the set of sites that is to be included in the model. Further, if the travel cost method is to be used to value changes in environmental quality, then site-quality data that vary over or across individuals are needed.

As an extension of our earlier example, the demand was estimated for Lumpinee Park using *single-site* survey data. The survey to obtain the basic needed data was conducted through interviews with 187 randomly selected visitors arriving from 17 different administrative districts. The actual interviews took place at the park on two separate occasions, one in August and the other in November 1980. Afterwards, on the basis of this survey data and using statistical demand analysis, the demand for Lumpinee Park was estimated. Given this demand estimate, the consumers' surplus enjoyed by visitors to the park was estimated to be 13,204,588 baht annually. This was equivalent to $660,230 annually at the 1980 exchange rate of US$1 = 20 baht. At 10 per cent the capitalized value of the park would be $6.6 million. Thus, even though visitors did not pay an admission fee, the large consumers' surplus realized by its users clearly indicated that Lumpinee Park was a very valuable environmental asset.

However, the travel cost method has two glaring drawbacks. First, application of the method is limited to the valuation of recreational sites. Second, the valuation itself is incomplete, since this method does not account for a recreational site's *existence value*. People may still value a recreational area even if they themselves have never been in the area. A simple example would be people who value the Grand Canyon even though they have never been there and have no plans to visit it in the near future. In this case the primary motivation to protect it may be for future use by themselves or their offspring. It could also be derived from the strong ethical and moral commitment that some people have to preserve nature. As important as this issue is in environmental and resource economics, the travel cost method does not capture existence value. In the case of Lumpinee Park, when an explicit effort was made to account for the existence value of the park, the capitalized value was increased from $6.6 million to $58 million. The particular method used to capture the nonuse value of an environmental asset such as Lumpinee Park is the subject of the next subsection.

8.3.5 *The contingent valuation method*

The four approaches considered so far share two common features. First, willingness to pay is measured by using market prices either *explicitly* (in the case of the market pricing approach) or *implicitly*, such as via the prices of substitutes and complementary goods and services traded through the ordinary market. Second, in these approaches the stress has been exclusively on estimating *use values*. These are benefits or satisfactions received by individuals who are directly utilizing the services (amenities) provided by the natural environment. For example, as discussed above, the travel cost method measures the value of wilderness only from the very narrow perspective of its recreational value to identifiable current users.

However, there are several attributes of the natural environment from which individuals obtain satisfaction and hence benefits. For example, the value of wilderness cannot be measured only by its recreational values to current users; it has *nonuse values* to the extent that there are people who are willing to pay to preserve wilderness for future uses. *Such nonuse value may not be captured by approaches that are anthropocentric in their focus and confined to measuring the willingness to pay of resource users at a particular point in time*. This could be a serious problem when the resources under consideration involve long-time horizons, considerable uncertainty and/or irreversibility (Krutilla 1967; Arrow and Fisher 1974). Unfortunately, these are characteristics common to many environmental assets. Thus, any effective method designed to measure benefits arising from changes in the condition of environmental assets cannot afford to simply dismiss the need to account for nonuse values. As much as possible, a serious effort should be made to measure both the use and the nonuse values. *Contingent valuation* represents the general techniques or procedures used to elicit willingness to pay in this broad and inclusive sense.

Before we discuss the specific procedures associated with contingent valuation, it will be instructive to have a clear understanding of the principal components of nonuse values associated with environmental assets. In the environmental and resource economics literature, nonuse values are hypothesized as having *three* separable components, namely option, bequest and existence values or demands.

Option value refers to a sort of insurance premium individuals may be willing to pay to retain the option of possible future use. For example, people will be willing to pay some amount of money for the preservation of wilderness or the protection of a unique site – such as the Grand Canyon or Yosemite – not because they are currently using it but because they want to reserve an option that would guarantee their future access to such a resource. Note here that people behave this way because of their uncertainty regarding the future demand for or supply of these natural resources (Krutilla 1967; Johansson 1990). In this sense, consideration of option value is important when uncertainty is prevalent (Johansson 1990).

Bequest value refers to the satisfaction that people gain from the knowledge that a natural resource endowment is being preserved for future generations. Strictly speaking, bequest value is an intergenerational component of the option value. Bequest value would have considerable relevance in a situation where the natural resources under consideration are unique and damage will be irreversible, and there exists uncertainty regarding future generations' demand for and/or the supply of these resources. Examples are national parks, wilderness, tropical forests, aquifers, blue whales, coastal wetlands, coral reefs, and so on. *Basically, bequest demand exists to the extent that the present generation is willing to pay for preserving natural resources for the use of future generations.*

Existence value refers to the satisfaction that some people derive from the preservation of natural resources so that there remains a habitat for fish, plants, wildlife, and so on. In other words, it refers to what people are willing to pay (demand) for preserving the ecological integrity of the natural environment, i.e. for stewardship. Recent debt-for-nature swaps by several internationally renowned conservation organizations for the purpose of protecting the tropical forest are examples of such stewardship activity.

The general conceptual model that captures the essence of the above discussion can be presented by the following identities:

(a) Total value = Use value + Nonuse value

and

(b) Nonuse value = Option value + Bequest value + Existence value.

Thus, the total value of an environmental asset is composed of not one, but several kinds of willingness to pay. This is because in many instances environmental assets are characterized by economic factors, but also by special attributes such as uniqueness, irreversibility and uncertainty as to future demand and supply. When any one of the above attributes is relevant, the economic value of a natural resource should include both use and nonuse values. To ignore this fact and focus exclusively on use value could lead to severe underestimation of benefits and, as a result of this, unwarranted exploitation of valuable natural resources. For example, if the decision to preserve wilderness is to be based solely on benefit derived from recreational use (use value), the result could be the allocation of an insufficient amount of public land to wilderness protection. The real challenge, then, is to find ways of eliciting a willingness to pay for option, bequest and existence values so that nonuse value will be adequately considered. How can this be done, when the environmental attributes under consideration (such as aesthetic properties, survival of species, variety of ecosystems) have no substitutes or complements traded through the ordinary market? *This question suggests that it is impossible to assess nonuse values by using implicit prices. Therefore, a technique designed to estimate nonuse values cannot use real market information. The best it can do is to create hypothetical or artificial market conditions that elicit willingness to pay for the purpose of estimating nonuse values.*

In the contingent valuation approach, willingness to pay is elicited by conducting a *survey*. A carefully selected sample from the relevant population is asked to respond to a series of meticulously worded questions about their willingness to pay, contingent on changes in the availability and/or quality of an environmental amenity, such as the preservation of coastal wetlands or wilderness. The survey is designed in such a way that individuals are faced with a *hypothetical* market-like choice and are then asked about their willingness to pay for a specific end. In the contingent valuation method, the design of the questionnaire is crucial. It requires an in-depth knowledge of statistical survey methods, economics, ecology and, most importantly, a good deal of creativity and imagination. Hence, normally, a good contingent valuation survey involves a collaborative effort of people from different fields of studies; environmental scientists, economists, policy analysts and statisticians.

Normally, a contingent valuation survey is composed of two major phases: the *scenario* and the *valuation questions*. The main objective of the scenario phase is to explain to study participants the exact nature of the proposed action and how their involvement in the survey might influence the proposed activity under consideration. For example, in a case involving a local nature center, the contingent valuation scenario would describe the attributes of the particular nature center in detail, including the services it provides, the habitats and species it protects, as well as available alternative recreation sites. Photographs and maps should be provided as supplements to this information in order to make sure each respondent has the same basic knowledge of the Center. The scenario should also include the current condition of the Nature Center, and what conditions might result if a proposed action is or is not implemented. For instance, the scenario might describe what the Center is like now, and what would happen to the area if the Nature Center had to close or substantially reduce services due to lack of funds. The purpose of the scenario is to give respondents enough information about the relevant effects of the proposed actions so they will be able to consider how valuable those effects are to them.

The next important task to be performed after describing the scenario is the *valuation question*. This phase of the contingent valuation survey deals with the design of the specific format(s) of the questions to be posed to the respondents for the purpose of revealing their values. Two issues are involved here: the context of the payment mechanism and the format of the valuation question.

An important issue regarding the context of valuation is the mechanism through which payments would be collected. Would the payment be in the form of taxes or increased fees? If taxes, what kind of tax? Income or property taxes? In general, the objective is to find payment mechanisms that will seem *realistic* to respondents yet be neutral in their effects on responding to the valuation question.

Because of its familiarity to respondents, the valuation question is often framed as *referendum*. For instance, respondents may be asked if they would vote *yes* or *no* on a ballot that would increase their taxes in order to keep the nature center in their locality. The increase in taxes may be varied from respondent to respondent in order to understand willingness to pay across a wide range of possible values. An alternative format for this may be to ask respondents to record the maximum increase in taxes they

Exhibit 8.1   Valuation questionnaire: the case of the Kalamazoo Nature Center

When answering the questions provided in this survey, please make sure to keep in mind the following three situations: (i) The Kalamazoo Nature Center is only one among many recreational opportunities in the Kalamazoo Area. (ii) Your income is limited and has several alternative uses. (iii) The following set of questions asks you to focus solely on KNC and not on other environmental issues or other parks and nature centers in the state.

1 What aspects of Kalamazoo Nature Center do you value?

(a) Quietude/get-away from the city
(b) Aesthetic/scenic beauty
(c) Protection of native plants and animals, including some rare habitats and species
(d) Availability to next generation
(e) Educational value
(f) I benefit from just knowing it exists
(g) I hope to visit KNC in the future

2 How concerned are you about the possibility of the KNC/s closure?

(a) Very concerned
(b) A little concerned
(c) Not concerned at all

3 As a taxpayer, how much of an increase in your annual taxes would you be willing to pay to support the continuation of the services currently provided by the KNC?

(a) $50
(b) $100
(c) $500
(d) Other (please specify) $_____

4 What is the maximum annual amount that you would be willing to pay to prevent closure of KNC?

5 Have you ever considered bequesting money to KNC to ensure its continued existence? If so, how much are you willing to give?

6 Would you be willing to act as a volunteer at the Nature Center in one of its educational programs, secretarial duties, maintenance, animal care, or other? If so, how many hours per week are you willing to spend?

You may revise your willingness to pay value at any point. Please tell me now if you wish to do so.

Thank you Sir/Madam. The Kalamazoo Nature Center thanks you for taking time to complete this survey as your responses will help their research efforts greatly.

(Sarah Rockwell).

would accept and still vote positively on the proposed change. In general, given the unfamiliarity of most people with placing a monetary value on an environmental amenity, the result of the valuation exercise would be more accurate if a *closed-end* choice of willingness to pay is used. Exhibit 8.1 offers a simple illustration of how the valuation question was actually framed. The material in this exhibit is extracted from a class project written by one of my students. The project under consideration was the Kalamazoo Nature Center.

Finally, although they have not been discussed so far, it is important to be aware of the following four important issues that a good contingent valuation survey should ideally address.

1   Most contingent surveys include additional questions that provide data on the respondents' demographic characteristics and socioeconomic circumstances. This information could be used to enrich the final analysis of the study.

2   Contingent valuation surveys may include questions specifically designed to determine the actual motivation of a respondent's vote. Is the vote of a respondent to a valuation question an expression of *preference* or *opinion* or *protest*? This matters because the primary goal of a contingent survey is to elicit an individual preference and nothing else.

3   Identification of the relevant population and the determination of sample size are also important issues that need to be addressed.

4   Whether the survey should be conducted in personal or telephone interviews or mail surveys (or in some combination of these three survey mechanisms) is also another important and unavoidable issue to be considered.

What all these additional considerations indicate is that contingent valuation studies can be *expensive*. But expense aside, the major advantage of the contingent valuation approach is its potential as a general procedure for assessing the *total* economic value (use values plus nonuse values) of any type of environmental asset. A mere three decades have passed since the concept of nonuse value started to receive serious attention in environmental and resource economics.

Applications of contingent valuation are even more recent. So far, some empirical work has been done using this method, with mixed but encouraging results (e.g. Schulze *et al.* 1981; Walsh *et al.* 1983, 1984). *What is even more encouraging about the growing use of the contingent valuation method in the field of natural resources is that it is promoting an enduring awareness – within the discipline of economics – that the economic value of the natural environment goes beyond what can be captured by direct and/or indirect observations of market information.* In other words, natural resources have intrinsic values that cannot possibly be captured through market or extramarket information – which, as discussed in Chapter 1, has never been the natural belief of mainstream economists. It remains the case, however, that even the most sophisticated design of contingent valuation instruments cannot fully capture the total value of environmental assets, for several reasons (more on this in the next section).

On technical grounds alone, several potential biases may arise that could undermine the validity of the preference information gathered using the contingent valuation method. Among others, these include:

1   *Strategic bias*: respondents may refuse to respond to survey question(s) or will not reveal their 'true' willingness to pay for strategic reasons. They may do this if they think there is a 'free rider' situation. However, evidence of strategic bias appears to be limited (Bohm 1979). In some instances, people may refuse to respond to survey question(s) not because of 'free rider' considerations, but because they simply refuse to put monetary value on environmental services that they consider to be priceless (more on this later).

2   *Information bias*: the survey result is not independent of the information provided to respondents. Thus, what people are willing to pay for environmental assets depends on the quantity and quality of the information provided to them, including the way questions are constructed. For example, many empirical studies reveal a marked divergence between willingness to pay (WTP) and willingness to accept (WTA). That is, it matters a great deal whether respondents are asked how much they are willing to pay to preserve a wilderness in its pristine condition, or how much they are willing to accept in compensation for its loss. Furthermore, as Gatto

and De Leo (2000: 350) pointed out, information bias with regard to 'existence value' could be more pronounced and entails a considerable risk because 'species with very low or no aesthetic appeal or whose biological role has not been properly advertised will be given a low value, even if they play a fundamental ecological function'. For example, the protection of 'the Big Five' (lions, elephants, buffalo, hippos, and tigers) is the major driving force in the wilderness conservation movements in many African countries. However, this is based largely on the considerations of perceived commercial values and emotional attachments of people to these animal species rather than on the significance of the ecological roles of these species in maintaining the dynamic balance of the ecosystems which they are a part of.

3   *Hypothetical bias*: This refers to the fact that respondents are not making 'real' transactions. Respondents tend to be sensitive to the instruments used for payment (such as entrance fee, sales tax, payroll tax, income tax, and so on.) There is also considerable doubt about the extent to which a simulated market can fully capture the dynamic feedback that characterizes a real competitive market. Is it possible to generate efficient price information from an artificially constructed market? The most likely answer to this question is 'no'.

4   *Difficulties with the reference group for pricing*: This refers to the notion that valuation of environmental damage based on contingent valuation methods could be significantly influenced by the group of people that is taken as a reference for valuation – particularly on their income (Gatto and De Leo 2000). For instance, using the population of the United States as a reference group, the existence value of the affected species and ecosystems from the 1989 Exxon Valdez oil spill incident in Alaska was calculated to be of the order of $5 billion – a figure that was then used to compensate the people of Alaska for their losses (Van der Straaten 1998). The issue here is whether this level of compensation would have been warranted if this same incident had occurred in a country with similar ecological conditions but where people had incomes much lower than in the United States. This question has very important implications for how we use contingent valuation methods to estimate the existence values of fragile but *globally* important natural resources (such as tropical forests) that are largely found in the poorest regions of the world.

At this stage, it may be helpful to illustrate the use of the contingent valuation approach in a real-world situation. Walsh *et al.* (1984) sought to estimate the preservation value of incremental increases in wilderness designations in Colorado. For this case study, a mail survey was conducted during the summer of 1980, covering a sample of 218 Colorado households. These participants were shown four maps of the state of Colorado, and on each map a different acreage was designated as wilderness. One of the maps showed the 1.2 million acres of land currently (1980) designated as wilderness in Colorado. This represented 2 per cent of the land of the state. The other three maps showed hypothetical wilderness designations, of areas 2.6, 5 and 10 million acres respectively. As far as possible, every effort and precaution were taken to provide the respondents to the survey with realistic and credible information about the contingent market. This information was intended to offer a solid background to the scientific, historical and economic significance of wilderness areas for the current and future citizens of Colorado.

With the above information in hand, each respondent was asked to write down the maximum amount of money they would be willing to pay annually for the preservation of four increments in designated wilderness depicted on the four maps. This was followed by asking the respondents to allocate their reported willingness to pay among the four categories of value: recreational use; option; existence; and bequest demands. Note that option, existence and bequest values are measures of nonuse and hence of the preservation value of wilderness. Viewed this way, total preservation value is the residual after recreational use benefits have been subtracted from the total willingness to pay for wilderness preservation.

Once all the necessary survey data had been gathered and processed, statistical demand analysis was used to estimate preservation values. This involved estimating a separate demand for each component of the preservation value, namely option, existence and bequest values. It would be beyond the scope of this book to go into the details of the procedures used to estimate these demand functions. The final result of the study is presented in Table 8.1.

The last row of Table 8.1 shows the estimate of the total values for each of the four wilderness designations. For example, for the existing (1980) level of designated wilderness areas of 1.2 million acres, the total value was estimated to be $28.5 million. The total values for each designation level are split into two major groups, namely use value (which represents the recreational use of the wilderness) and nonuse value (which corresponds to the preservation value of the wilderness). For example, again focusing on the existing wilderness designation areas of 1.2 million acres, the total value ($28.5 million) was obtained by summing recreational use value ($13.2 million) and the preservation or nonuse value ($15.3 million). The preservation value was further broken down into its three major components, namely option, existence and bequest values. For the existing wilderness area, these values were reported to be $4.4, $5.4 and $5.5 million, respectively. All categories of the preservation value are reported on both a per household and total basis.

Several inferences can be drawn from these results. For example, increasing the area of designated wilderness from 1.2 to 2.6 million acres (which amounted to slightly more than a doubling of the existing wilderness designation areas) was shown to increase the total value by 46 per cent (from $28.5 to $41.6 million). Thus, doubling the areas of the wilderness designation does not double the total value. As interesting as this observation may seem to be, however, for our purpose here what is important to notice is this: for all four wilderness designation categories, the nonuse or preservation values represented a significant portion of the total value. Even at the lower end (which was associated with the wilderness area of 10 million acres), nonuse value was 37 per cent of the total value. What this shows, at least in principle, is the significance of valuation techniques (such as the contingent valuation approach) that seek to incorporate the estimation of nonuse values (benefits) in their analysis. Failure to account for such benefits may lead society to take decisions that could cause irreversible damage to wilderness areas and other environmental resources of a similar nature.

This concludes the discussion of the various techniques modern economists are currently using to assess benefits arising from an improvement in the condition of the natural environment (clean air, water, etc.). Before embarking on the next section – critical appraisal of the economic approach to environmental valuation, it is worth looking at Table 8.2, which is an effective way of summarizing the salient characteristics and functions of *all* the valuation techniques discussed in this chapter.

Table 8.1 Total annual consumer surplus from recreation use and preservation value to
Colorado households from increments in wilderness designation, Colorado, 1980

| | Existing and potential wilderness designation | | | |
Value categories	*Wilderness areas, 1980, 1.2 million acres*	*Wilderness areas, 1981, 2.6 million acres*	*Double 1981 wilderness areas 5 million acres*	*All potential wilderness areas 10 million acres*
Recreation use value				
Per visitor day	$14.00	$14.00	$14.00	$14.00
Total, million	13.2	21.0	33.1	58.2
Preservation value to Colorado residents				
Per household	13.92	18.75	25.30	31.83
Total, million	15.3	20.6	27.8	35.0
Option value				
Per household	4.04	5.44	7.34	9.23
Total, million	4.4	6.0	8.1	10.2
Existence value				
Per household	4.87	6.56	8.86	11.14
Total, million	5.4	7.2	9.7	12.3
Bequest value				
Per household	5.01	6.75	9.10	11.46
Total, million	5.5	7.4	10.0	12.5
Total annual recreation use value And preservation value to Colorado households, million	$28.5	$41.6	$60.9	$93.2

Source: *Land Economics*, Vol. 60, No. 1, February 1984. © 1984. Reprinted by permission of the University of Wisconsin Press.

8.4 Critical assessment of the economic approach to environmental valuation

In the previous section a concerted effort was made to point out some of the major drawbacks associated with each of the techniques that economists use to assess the benefits of environmental projects. However, this was done without questioning the fundamental premises of the neoclassical economic valuation methodology. This section will highlight *four* of the most serious criticisms of the neoclassical approaches to valuing the environment. These are as follows. First, environmental values should not be reducible to a single one-dimensional standard that is ultimately expressed only in monetary terms. Second, high levels of uncertainty make the measurement and the very concept of *total value* meaningless. Third, survey techniques used to elicit willingness to pay confuse preferences with beliefs. Fourth, important ecological connections may be missed when valuing components of a system separately. The rest of this section discusses these four issues one at a time.

Table 8.2 A grand summary of the economic methods for valuing ecosystem services discussed in this chapter

Specific nature of the environmental damage	Examples	Primary economic method(s) used for valuations	Type of uses
1 Loss of economic outputs and inputs	Fish, crops and wood products	Market valuation approach	Use value
2 Increased exposure to environmental nuisance	Noise, odor and debris	Hedonic pricing and household production approaches	Use value
3 Impairment to human health	Risk of mortality and morbidity	Hedonic pricing approach	Use value
4 Recreational, amenity and aesthetic losses	Bird watching, camping, etc.	Travel cost and contingent valuation methods	Use value
5 Simplification of natural habitats	Loss of biodiversity	Contingent valuation (?) and precautionary approach	Nonuse value
6 Irreversible damage to an ecosystem function and/or structure	Species extinction and climate change	Precautionary approach*	Nonuse value

*Extensive discussion of the precautionary approach is provided in the next chapter, Chapter 9.

1 Environmental values should not be reducible to a single one-dimensional standard that is ultimately expressed only in monetary terms

The conventional approaches to valuations assume that a monetary value can be assigned to all aspects of environmental amenities. Furthermore, as Funtowicz and Ravetz (1994: 199) put it:

> the issue is not whether it is only the marketplace that can determine value, for economists have long debated other means of valuation; our concern is with the assumption that in any dialogue, all valuations or 'numeraires' should be reducible to a single one-dimensional standard.

They described this whole effort as a 'commodification of environmental goods'.

It is argued that this principle should not be accepted because *it blatantly denies the existence of certain intangible values of the natural environment that are beyond the economic*. They are unmeasurable and can be described only in qualitative terms that are noneconomic in nature. Improved quality of life, the protection of endangered species and ecosystems, the preservation of scenic or historic sites (such as the Grand Canyon), and the aesthetic and symbolic properties of wilderness are examples of this. The main message here is that it would be wrong and misleading to ignore intangibles in an effort to obtain a single dollar-value estimate for benefits. There are irreplaceable and priceless environmental assets whose values cannot be captured either through the market or by survey methods designed to elicit people's willingness to pay. *However, it is important to note that to describe an environmental asset as priceless cannot mean that such a resource has an infinite value.* This would imply that it would be worth devoting the whole of a nation's GNP (and beyond) to the preservation of its environmental assets.

2 High levels of uncertainty make the measurement and the very concept of total value meaningless

The conventional measure of environmental damage stems from the difficulties associated with the uncertainty inherent in certain uses of environmental resources. Uncertainties of this nature are particularly important when the resources in question are difficult or impossible to replace and for which no close substitute is available (Krutilla 1967). Under these circumstances the potential costs of current activities could be, although uncertain, very high. This is particularly significant where the outcomes are expected to be irreversible. Contemporary examples are global warming, biodiversity loss, ozone destruction, and so forth.

There are important implications from uncertainties of this nature. Among them are the following.

(a) Uncertainty compounds the difficulty of evaluating environmental damage.
(b) Where irreversibility is a serious concern, the damage may be unmeasurable or infinitely high (Johansson 1990). In such a case, the very notion of total value may be meaningless.
(c) As Krutilla (1967) effectively argued, *the maximum willingness to pay could be less than the minimum amount that would be necessary to compensate for the loss of the natural phenomenon in question*. This is because the more difficult it is to replace a loss of environmental goods with other goods, the higher the compensation needed for people to accept the loss. Under this condition, attempts to determine individuals' willingness to pay for nonuse values (i.e. existence, option and bequest values) using the contingent valuation method could have misleading outcomes.
(d) When the potential for catastrophic outcomes in the future is a major concern, proper management of the underlying uncertainty requires explicit consideration of the interest of the future generations – intergenerational equity. According to Perrings (1991), this can be done using the *precautionary principle* as a guide for decision-making. This approach assigns a worst-case value to the uncertain outcome of current activities. The 'optimal' policy is then the one that minimizes the worst imaginable outcome. Under this approach it makes perfect sense to opt for preservation of the natural environment if costs are potentially large and very long-term (more on this in the next chapter).

3 Survey techniques used to elicit willingness to pay confuse preferences with beliefs

Sagoff (1988b) wrote a stinging criticism of the whole approach of evaluating environmental damage on the basis of survey data that purport to reflect the respondents' willingness to pay. His main objection is based on what is or is not conveyed by people's preferences, which are used as a means of eliciting willingness to pay. More specifically, he argued that the conventional wisdom in economics is to treat judgements (or beliefs) expressed about the environment as if they are preferences (or desires). According to Sagoff, judgements (ethical or otherwise) involve

> not desires or wants but opinions or views. They state what a person believes is right or best for the community or group as a whole. These opinions may be true or false,

and we may meaningfully ask that person for the reasons that he or she holds them. But an analyst who asks how much citizens would pay to satisfy opinions that they advocate through political association commits a category mistake. The analyst asks of beliefs about objective facts a question that is appropriate only to subjective interests and desires.

(Sagoff 1988b: 94)

This consideration is especially significant when property rights are not clearly delineated (such as in the case of the environment). The main reason for this is that *people's preferences for these kinds of resources include aspects of their feelings that are not purely economic*. These feelings may be based on aesthetic, cultural, ethical, moral, and political considerations. Therefore, under this condition, it is quite possible that some people may prefer not to sell publicly owned resources at any price. This perhaps explains why some respondents in contingent valuation surveys refuse to indicate the price at which they are willing to buy or sell environmental resources; their refusal is not, as often claimed, for strategic reasons.

The implication is that environmental policy should be based not only on market information (prices) but also on a decision-making process that includes open dialogues on the basis of democratic principles (see Sagoff 1988a). In this way, the various dimensions of environmental policy (aesthetic, cultural, moral, and ethical) may be adequately incorporated.

4 Important ecological connections may be missed when valuing components of a system separately

Another drawback particularly relevant to the contingent valuation method results from a potential failure to account for certain ecological factors. More specifically, to the extent that total value (use values plus nonuse values) is based on economic values, it may fail to account for *primary values*: 'system characteristics upon which all ecological functions are contingent' (Pearce 1993). In this sense, total value may not really be total after all! As discussed in Chapter 2, one of the lessons of ecology is that all elements of a natural ecosystem are mutually interrelated. Therefore, strictly from an ecological viewpoint, the value of a particular entity in the natural environment (an animal species, a valley, a river, humans, etc.) should be assessed on the basis of its over-all contribution to the sustainability (health) of the ecosystem as a whole. Essentially, assessing the total value of a particular natural environment (such as wilderness) as the sum of the values of the parts or individual attributes does not account for the whole. However, this is the underlying premise of the contingent valuation approach (see Exhibit 8.2).

Using a similar line of reasoning, O'Neill and Kahn (2000: 333) also argued that the current economic concept of *valuation* 'is of limited use because the *dynamic* responses of the ecosystem itself are not included within the economic model. The economic model assumes, incorrectly, that the environment is the constant and stable background for economic activity. The feedback loop between the human species and its ecosystem remains incomplete.'

Exhibit 8.2   Toward ecological pricing

Alan Thein Durning

Ecological pricing is [a] . . . necessary condition of a sustainable forest economy. Virgin timber is currently priced far below its full costs. For instance, the price of teak does not reflect the costs of flooding that rapacious teak logging has caused in Myanmar; nor does the price of old-growth fir from the US Pacific Northwest include losses suffered by the fishing industry because logging destroys salmon habitat. Those losses are estimated at $2,150 per wild Chinook salmon in the Columbia River, when future benefits to sports and commercial fishers are counted.

Few attempts have been made to calculate the full ecological prices of forest products but they would undoubtedly be astronomical for some goods. A mature forest tree in India, for example, is worth $50,000, estimates the Center for Science and Environment in New Delhi. The full value of a hamburger produced on pasture cleared from rain forest is about $200, according to an exploratory study conducted at New York University's School of Business. These figures, of course, are speculative. Calculating them requires making assumptions about how many dollars, for instance, a species is worth – perhaps an imponderable question. But the alternative to trying – failing to reflect the loss of ecological functions at all in the price of wood and other forest product – ensures that the economy will continue to destroy forests.

The full economic value of a forest ecosystem is clearly huge. Forests provide a source of medicines worth billions of dollars. Their flood prevention, watershed stabilization and fisheries protection functions are each worth billions more. Their scenic and recreational benefits also have billion-dollar values for both the world's growing nature tourism industry and local residents.

The full value of forests includes each of these components, from sources of medicines to pest controls. But, again, market prices count only the direct costs of extracting goods, not the full ecological costs. In accounting terms, the money economy is depleting its natural capital without recording that depreciation on its balance sheet. Consequently, annual losses come out looking like profits, and cash flow looks artificially healthy. For a business to do this – liquidate its plant and equipment and call the resulting revenue income – would be both self-destructive and, in many countries, illegal. For the money economy overall, however, self-destruction generally goes unquestioned.

How can we move toward ecological pricing? By changing government policies. A primary responsibility of governments is to correct the failures of the money economy, and global deforestation is surely a glaring one. Yet forest policies in most nations do the opposite: They accelerate forest loss. The first order of business for government, therefore, is to stop subsidizing deforestation. The second is to use taxes, user fees and tariffs to make ecological costs apparent in the money economy. Until the money economy is corrected in these ways, forest conservation will remain an uphill battle.

Source: Worldwatch Institute, *States of the World 1993*, Copyright © 1993. Reprinted by permission.

8.5 Chapter summary

- This chapter dealt with economic approaches to the evaluation of benefits arising from improvement in environmental quality or avoidance of environmental damage.

- Following standard practice in economics, in theory the benefit (or avoided damage cost) from a project to improve environmental quality is captured by individuals' *willingness to pay* at the *margin*. Total benefit is then measured by the sum of society's willingness to pay – the area under the relevant range of the demand curve for an environmental good or, more specifically, the marginal damage cost curve.

- When environmental benefit is measured in this manner, *three* important issues require particular notice:

  1   The benefit from improved environmental quality is not intended to measure the 'value' of the environment as such. Instead, what is measured is people's preferences or willingness to pay for an environmental good or to avoid an environmental bad (damage).

  2   The estimation of the total benefit includes consumers' surplus. In other words, total benefit is not computed by simply multiplying equilibrium market price and quantity.

  3   It is understood that the motivation of estimating environmental benefit is not to value the environment as a whole (as the recent study by Costanza *et al.* indicates), but to evaluate the benefits and/or costs associated with changes made to the environment due to human activities. Most importantly, the changes are assumed to be not large enough to cause a major modification to the future circumstances of humanity – life, as we know it, will go on.

- Because measuring the area under the marginal damage cost curve entails assessment of benefits (in monetary terms in so far as this is possible) of environmental services normally not traded through ordinary markets, mechanisms must be developed to *implicitly* measure willingness to pay. This is done by using shadow prices, i.e. prices of substitutes and complementary goods and services that are traded through the ordinary market.

- In this chapter, we examined the *three* most common approaches to measuring *implicit* willingness to pay, namely the replacement cost approach, the hedonic price approach and the household production function approach – which incorporates, among other things, the travel cost method. Considerable efforts were made not only to explain these alternative measures of the value of environmental services but also to assess their apparent strengths and weaknesses. In addition, some case studies were either cited or directly used to show how the estimates of values are done empirically.

- These approaches have one common feature: they measure benefits on the basis of *use values*. These are benefits or satisfactions received by individuals who are directly utilizing the services or amenities provided by the natural environment. But some environmental assets, such as wilderness, have *nonuse values*; for instance, the value of preserving wilderness so that it will be available for the use of future generations. Three distinctively different features of future uses were discussed in this chapter, namely option, bequest and existence values.

- The economic value of the natural environment goes beyond what can be captured by direct and/or indirect observations of market information or use value. Thus, the total benefit from environmental assets (such as wilderness) should reflect *total* value – the sum of use and nonuse values. (It is important not to confuse efforts to estimate this total value with measuring the value of the flow of environmental services on a global scale.)
- However, techniques designed to estimate nonuse values can *not* use real market information, which means that willingness to pay for nonuse values must be estimated by means of a *hypothetical* market condition. This is done using the contingent valuation method. The main feature of this method is that it attempts to elicit willingness to pay by conducting an extensive *survey*. Contingent valuation is being increasingly used by economists and appears to hold the key to further progress in the estimation of *total* values of environmental services.
- In general, economic approaches to environmental valuation have been criticized for a number of reasons. Chief among them are:

  1 The 'commodification' of environmental goods – the idea that environmental values are reducible to a single one-dimensional standard that is ultimately expressed only in monetary terms – is objectionable to some.
  2 Survey techniques used to elicit willingness to pay confuse preferences with belief. This is a serious criticism given that economists (as serious 'scientists' who are engaged in an effort to measure value as objectively as possible) never have the desire to enter into the realm of measuring belief, even unintentionally.
  3 Where uncertainty and irreversibility are serious concerns, the damage may be unmeasurable or infinitely high. In this case, the very notion of *total* value may be meaningless.
  4 Important ecological connections may be missed when valuing components of a system separately. In this case, the *total* value may not be 'total' after all!

Review and discussion questions

1 Briefly explain the meaning of the following concepts: statistical life, aversive expenditure, use value, intangibles, incommensurable, option values, bequest value, existence value, total value, commodification of environmental goods, debt-for-nature swaps.
2 State whether the following are *true*, *false* or *uncertain* and explain why.

   (a) To describe an environmental asset as 'priceless' does not mean that it has an infinite value.
   (b) Economists do not attempt to measure the value of the environment. What they attempt to measure is the preferences of people for an environmental good or environmental bad.
   (c) The estimation of benefits from environmental assets would be unaffected by whether the method used to measure benefit was based on willingness to pay (WTP) or willingness to accept (WTA).

3 According to a study conducted in 1977, excessive tailings discharge into a lake is expected to reduce the average life expectancy of those in a nearby community

by approximately 12 years (from 66 to 54 years). The monetary value to the community of this premature death was estimated to be $40,000 per victim annually. Let us suppose that because of a general price increase over the past 25 years, $40,000 in 1977 is worth $150,000 currently. Does this mean the value of 12 years of life for an individual in this community (at current prices) is $1,800,000? If your answer to this question is no, then what does this figure represent? If your answer is 'yes', would you be willing to trade 12 years of your life for $1,800,000? Explain.

4   In this chapter, we discussed five commonly used techniques for measuring the monetary values of environmental damage (benefit), namely market pricing, replacement cost, hedonic pricing, household production function (which includes the travel cost method), and contingent valuation. Below, you are given a hypothetical situation where environmental damage of some kind has occurred. For each of these cases choose the best technique(s) to estimate the cost of the damage in question, and provide a brief justification for your choice of the particular technique(s).

(a) Excessive soil erosion due to deforestation
(b) Decline in property values due to groundwater contamination
(c) Loss of habitats for rare plant species due to a development project for ecologically sensitive wetlands
(d) Excessive noise from a nearby industrial complex
(e) Damage to the scenic value of a lakeshore due to eutrophication.

5   A colleague said to me, 'I have my own personal doubts about contingent valuation when respondents are ethically committed to environmental preservation. If they are asked a willingness-to-accept question, then they may respond with an infinite or very large price. In essence, they see the resource as priceless or incommensurable with respect to monetary values. If they are asked a willingness-to-pay question, they may object on grounds that they are being forced to pay for something that has ethical standing and on moral grounds should not be damaged or destroyed; or they might simply offer what they can afford in order to meet what they see as their moral obligation to save the environment. The point is that contingent valuation analysis, while interesting, could be conceptually problematic.' Do you agree or disagree with my colleague? Why, or why not?

6   Economists are difficult to understand. They claim they can put a monetary value on premature death, but not on human life. They also claim they can value ecosystem services (such as wetland area) in a certain locality, but not the value of the world's ecosystem services. How could this be? Discuss.

References

Arrow, K. and Fisher, A. C. (1974) 'Environmental Preservation, Uncertainty, and Irreversibility', *Quarterly Journal of Economics* 88: 312–19.

Baumol, W. J. (1968) 'On the Social Rate of Discount', *American Economic Review* 58: 788–802.

Bohm, P. (1979) 'Estimating Willingness to Pay: Why and How?', *Scandinavian Journal of Economics* 84: 142–53.

Carson, R. and Mitchell, R. (1991) *Using Surveys to Value Public Goods: The Contingent Valuation Method*, Baltimore: Resources for the Future.

Costanza, R. *et al.* (1997) 'The Value of the World's Ecosystem Services and Natural Capital', *Nature* 387: 253–60.

Dasgupta, P., Levin, S. and Lubchenco, J. (2000) 'Economic Pathways to Ecological Sustainability', *BioScience* 50, 4: 339–45.

Dixon, J. A. and Hufschmidt, M. M. (eds) (1986) *Economic Valuation Techniques for the Environment: A Case Study Workbook*, Baltimore: Johns Hopkins University Press.

Funtowicz, S. O. and Ravetz, J. R. (1994) 'The Worth of a Songbird: Ecological Economics as a Post-Normal Science', *Ecological Economics* 10: 197–207.

Gatto, M. and De Leo, A. G. (2000) 'Pricing Biodiversity and Ecosystem Services: The Never-Ending Story,' *BioScience* 50, 4: 347–55.

Hanemann, W. M. (1991) 'Willingness-to-Pay and Willingness-to-Accept: How Much Do They Differ?' *American Economic Review* 81: 635–47.

Johansson, P-O. (1990) 'Valuing Environmental Damage', *Oxford Review of Economic Policy* 6, 1: 34–50.

Kneese, A. (1984) *Measuring the Benefits of Clean Air and Water*, Washington, DC: Resources for the Future.

Kremen, C., Niles, J. O., Dalton, M. G., Daly, G. C., Ehrlich, P. R., Fay, J. P., Grewal, D., Guillery, R. P. (2000) 'Economic Incentives for Rain Forest Conservation Across Scales', *Science* 288: 1828–31.

Krutilla, J. V. (1967) 'Conservation Reconsidered', *American Economic Review* 57: 787–96.

Loomis, J. and White, D. (1996) *Economic Benefits of Rare and Endangered Species: Summary and Meta-analysis*, Colorado State University, CO: Fort Collins.

Mishan, E. J. (1971) 'Evaluation of Life and Limb: A Theoretical Approach', *Journal of Political Economy* 79: 687–705.

Nelson, A. C., Genereux, J. and Genereux, M. (1992) 'Price Effects of Landfills on House Values', *Land Economics* 68, 4: 359–65.

O'Neill, V. R. and Kahn, J. (2000) 'Homo economus as a Keystone Species', *BioScience* 50, 4: 333–7.

Pearce, D. W. (1993) *Economic Values and the Natural World*, Cambridge, Mass.: MIT Press.

Perrings, C. (1991) 'Reserved Rationality and the Precautionary Principle: Technological Change, Time, and Uncertainty in Environmental Decision Making', in R. Costanza (ed.) *Ecological Economics: The Science and Management of Sustainability*, New York: Columbia University Press.

Peterson, J. M. (1977) 'Estimating an Effluent Charge: The Reserve Mining Case', *Land Economics* 53, 3: 328–40.

Sagoff, M. (1988a) 'Some Problems with Environmental Economics', *Environmental Ethics* 10, 1: 55–74.

——(1988b) *The Economy of the Earth*, Cambridge, Mass.: Cambridge University Press.

Schulze, W. D., d'Arge, R. C. and Brookshire, D. S. (1981) 'Valuing Environmental Commodities: Some Recent Experiments', *Land Economics* 57: 11–72.

Shogren, J. F. (1997) 'Economics and the Endangered Species Act', *Endangered Species Update*, School of Natural Resources and Environment, University of Michigan.

Songhen, B. (2001) 'Case Study of a Market-Based Analysis: Soil Erosion in the Maumee River Basin', in Allegra Cangelosi (ed.) *Revealing the Economic Value of Protecting the Great Lakes*, Washington, DC: Northeast-Midwest Institute and National Oceanic and Atmospheric Administration.

Van der Straatan J. (1998) 'Is Economic Value the Same as Ecological Value?' Paper presented at the Seventh International Congress of Ecology (INTECOL), 19–25 July, Florence, Italy.

Walsh, R. G., Miller, N. P. and Gilliam, L. O. (1983) 'Congestion and Willingness to Pay for Expansion of Skiing Capacity', *Land Economics* 59, 2: 195–210.

Walsh, R. G., Loomis, J. B. and Gillman, R. A. (1984) 'Valuing Option, Existence, and Bequest Demands for Wilderness', *Land Economics* 60, 1: 14–29.

9 A framework for assessing the worthiness of an environmental project

Cost–benefit analysis and others

9.1 Introduction

In Section 8.3 of the previous chapter, we discussed the various techniques that economists employ to assess the benefits of a project implemented to avoid environmental damage. A *project* in this case is defined as a concrete action taken to alter the state of the natural environment – generally, against its deterioration. A case in point is an intentional plan taken by a given society to control SO_2 emissions from an electric power plant. As shown in Figure 9.1 (which is a replica of Figure 8.2), undertaking this project allows society to move from the status quo, point A, to a new position, point B. Furthermore, in this particular case, the total benefit resulting from the implementation of the project is identified by the shaded area under the society's demand curve for environmental quality.

However, if a society wants to evaluate the worthiness of this project, information about a project's benefit alone will not be sufficient. Undertaking a project requires the use of scarce societal resources. Thus, in order to determine a project's worthiness, the benefit of the project has to be weighed against its cost. The basic technique economists use for appraisal of *public* projects is popularly known as *cost–benefit analysis* (CBA). Cost–benefit analysis is commonly used to appraise a wider range of public projects. Highways, bridges, airports, dams, recycling centers, emission control technology, and a legislative mandate to conserve or preserve resources are just a few examples of projects that can be evaluated using cost–benefit analysis (see Mishan 1982). In general, the process involved in conducting a full-scale cost–benefit analysis uses *four* steps (see Exhibit 9.1).

From the outset, it is important to note that cost–benefit analysis involves making a *value judgement*. This is because, in assessing the relative worthiness of a project, it is necessary to declare that a given state of nature is either 'better' or 'worse' than another. For example, in Figure 9.1 we moved from state A (the status quo) to state B – a position attained after the sulfur emission control technology has been implemented. *In cost–benefit analysis, what we want to develop is a 'norm' by which we can judge that state A is 'better' or 'worse' than state B.* Thus, cost–benefit analysis falls directly into the province of what is known as *normative (welfare) economics*.

It is very important to say from the onset that this chapter is not limited to a discussion of cost–benefit analysis. In the last section of the chapter, several other alternative methods that can be used either as a complement or a substitute for the traditional cost–benefit analysis for assessing the worthiness of environmental projects

Exhibit 9.1   The four steps involved in conducting cost–benefit analysis

1 **Specify the social values of concern.** There are actually many publics and many social values. The first step in CBA is to decide on the values and perspectives of concern to the decision-makers. . . . If one is conducting a CBA for a national agency, the public normally would be the population of the entire country. But if an employee of a city or regional planning agency conducts a CBA of a local environmental program, a more appropriate focus would be on the costs and benefits accruing to people living locally in those areas. The first step also includes a complete specification of the main elements of the project or program: location, timing, groups involved, connections with other programs, and the like.

2 **Identify and measure the physical and biological changes that should be measured.** All that public money for environmental monitoring could really pay off if quality data could be fed into CBAs in this step. For some projects, determining the changes for concern including both input and output flows, can be reasonably easy. For example, in planning a water treatment facility, the engineering staff will be able to provide a full physical specification of the plant, together with the inputs required to build it and keep it running. For other types of programs, such determinations can be much harder. For example, a restriction on development in a particular region can be expected to reduce runoff locally. But what could be the actual environmental consequences? Could the restrictions deflect development into surrounding 'green fields'? In this step, we become acutely aware of the time it can take to complete large environmental projects and the even greater time involved as their impacts play out. Uncertainty manage-ment becomes a major factor in the process because the job of specifying inputs and outputs involves predictions of future events, sometimes many years after an intervention begins.

3 **Estimate the costs and benefits of changes resulting from the program.** Assigning economic values to input and output flows is done to measure social costs and benefits. Typically, costs and benefits are measured in monetary terms. This does not mean relying on market value because in many cases, particularly on the benefit side, the effects are not registered directly in markets. Neither does it imply that only monetary values count. It means we need a single metric to translate all of the effects on an intervention to make them comparable among themselves and with other public activities. When we cannot find a way to measure how much people value these effects, it is important to supplement monetary results of a CBA with estimates of intangible effects.

4 **Compare costs and benefits.** In this final step, total estimated costs are compared with total estimated benefits. However, if benefits are not to be realized until some time in the future, first they must be converted to the present-day value, factoring in the selected discount rate. . . . This judgement call deserves special examination and discussion and is closely linked to Step 1, in which social values of concern are identified. The present value of the stream of benefits minus the present value of costs give the present value of net benefits.

Source: *Revealing the Ecological Economic Value of Protecting the Great Lakes*, Northeast-Midwest Institute and National Oceanic and Atmospheric Administration (2001), pp. 60–1.

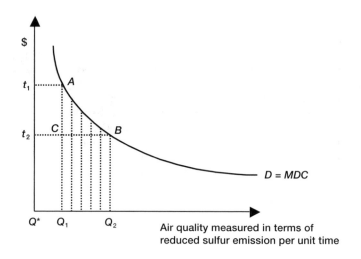

Figure 9.1 Total value of environmental project(s) and the demand curve for environmental quality.

are discussed. More specifically, the discussion in this section includes the following well-known environmental project evaluation criteria: the precautionary principle; cost-effectiveness analysis; environmental impact studies; risk assessment and risk management; and environmental justice and ethics. In addition, as far as possible, the discussion examines the compatibility of each of these alternative environmental project evaluation methods with traditional cost–benefit analysis procedures.

9.2 The welfare foundation of cost–benefit analysis

Welfare economics deals with economic methodologies and principles indispensable to policy-makers engaged in the design and implementation of collective decisions. Two principles of welfare economics are specially important, since they form the foundation on which economists base their judgement of the relative desirability of varying economic states of nature.

Principle I: 'actual' Pareto improvement states that if by undertaking a project no members of a society become worse off and at least one becomes better off, the project should be accepted.

Principle II: 'potential' Pareto improvement states that a project should be considered if, by undertaking it, the gainers from the project can compensate the losers and still remain better off in their economic conditions than they were before.

Let us examine the implications of these two principles using Figure 9.2. The hypothetical production possibility frontier describes the choices that a given nation is facing between *conservation* (setting aside more land for wilderness) and *development* (using land to produce consumption goods and services or to increase the production capacity of the economy). Suppose point *M* on the production possibility frontier represents the status quo. Recently, the government of this hypothetical nation has

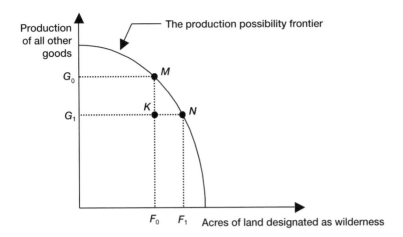

Figure 9.2 The choice between conservation and economic development.

passed legislation that mandates the expansion of the public land holding specifically designated for wilderness. The expected effect of this legislative mandate on the economic state of this nation is shown by a movement along the production possibility frontier from point *M* to *N*.

According to the criterion outlined by Principle I, the move from point *M* to *N* should be accepted if, and only if, not a single member of this hypothetical nation becomes worse off and at least one becomes better off as a result of such a move. However, it is highly unlikely that a situation of this nature could occur in the real world. In the case of our hypothetical nation, some individuals who are pro-development are likely to be made worse off by the move from *M* to *N*. This is because such a move could be attained only at the sacrifice of goods and services (the move from G_0 to G_1) that are appealing to these particular members of this nation. *'Actual' Pareto improvement would be possible if, and only if, our hypothetical nation has been operating inefficiently to begin with, such as at point* K. In this case, it is possible to move from *K* to *N* without violating Principle I.

On the other hand, according to Principle II, the move from *M* to *N* should be accept- able if, and only if, the gain by the pro-conservation individuals (the monetary value of $F_1 - F_0$) is greater than the loss by the pro-development individuals (the monetary value of $G_0 - G_1$). Thus, at least conceptually, the gainers could be able to compensate the losers and still remain ahead. *It should be noted, however, that Principle II does not require that compensation actually has to be made.* What is stressed is merely that the 'potential' for compensation exists. Essentially, then, Principle II simply states that the move from *M* to *N* would be considered economically 'efficient' provided that the aggregate benefit from such a move exceeded the aggregate cost. That is, the net benefit of the project is positive. In other words, if we let the letters *B* and *C* represent aggregate benefit and cost, respectively, then, according to Principle II, the move from *M* to *N* would be economically *efficient* provided $B - C > 0$. In short, real income is higher at point *N* than at *M*. However, *it is important to note that this criterion does not even pretend to address the income distribution effect of a project.* That is, who gains or loses from undertaking a project is considered irrelevant (or something to be addressed after the fact), provided that the net benefit from the project in question is positive.

9.3 The net present value criterion

The fundamental normative (welfare) criterion of cost–benefit analysis is based on 'potential' Pareto improvement. To understand this, let us see how a project appraisal is ordinarily performed using a cost–benefit analysis approach.

First, this approach requires information on the flow of expected benefits and costs from the project in question. Let B_t and C_t represent the streams of benefits and costs in year t, where $t = 0, 1, 2, 3, \ldots, n - 1, n$. Thus, for examples, B_1 and C_1 would represent the benefit and the cost of the project in year 1, and similarly B_5 and C_5 are the benefit and the cost relating to year 5. The letter n represents the expected lifetime of the project under consideration. If $n = 30$, the project has an expected lifetime of 30 years, and B_{30} and C_{30} would represent the benefit and the cost of the project in its final year.

Second, we need to know what is called the *discount rate*, the rate at which the streams of time dated benefits and costs are weighted. A more systematic and detailed discussion of discount rates will follow later. For now, let the variable r represent the discount factor, and assume $r > 0$.

Given these two pieces of information (streams of the expected benefits and costs from a project, and the discount rate), a typical cost–benefit analysis arrives at a decision using the following rule:

(1) Compute the *net* present value (*NPV*) using the formula

$$NPV = \Sigma\{(B_t - C_t)\,[1/(1 + r)^t]\}$$

(2) A project should be *accepted* if its *NPV* is greater than 0.

The *net* present value formula above is composed of two components: the *net* benefit for year t, $(B_t - C_t)$, and an expression used for weighting the *net* benefit of year t, $[1/(1 + r)^t]$. Thus, accordingly, net present value is calculated by summing (Σ) the weighted net benefits of a project over its entire lifetime. [The formula used to weight the flow of future benefits, $1/(1 + r)^t$, and the rationale behind it may require further explanation. The discussion in Exhibit 9.2 is designed for this purpose.]

As stated above, *according to the* NPV *criterion a project is declared acceptable if the sum of the net discounted benefit over the lifetime of the project is positive.* This is consistent with potential Pareto improvement, according to which a project is worthy of consideration provided the *net* benefit from the project is positive, i.e. $B - C > 0$. *It is in this sense, then, that potential Pareto improvement serves as the theoretical foundation for cost–benefit analysis that is based on the* NPV *criterion.* However, this also means that a cost–benefit analysis that is based on the *NPV* criterion has the same pitfalls as the potential Pareto improvement.

Exhibit 9.2 The discount factor and the rationale behind it

This exhibit is designed to probe a bit deeper into the nature of the weighing factor, i.e. the expression $1/(1 + r)^t$ and the rationale behind it. It can be shown that what this expression represents is *the present value of a dollar of net benefit coming at the end of* t *years*. Let us demonstrate what this concept entails using a simple numerical example. Suppose the value of the discount rate, *r*, is given to be 0.05 or 5 per cent, and let $t = 5$. This would suggest that the present value of $1 of net benefit coming five years from now would be $1/(1.05)^5$, or roughly 78 cents. It can be also shown, with the same discount rate, that the present value of a $1 net benefit coming 10 and 15 years from now would be 61 and 48 cents, respectively. Consistent with the results in this numerical demonstration, it can be shown that as long as the discount rate is positive, $r > 0$, the present value of a dollar *net* benefit declines as time passes. If this is the case, a positive discount rate would suggest putting less weight on the value of net benefit in the future relative to the present, hence, *discounting* the future. *This has a very important implication for the subject matter of this chapter since a positive discount rate means giving less weight to environmental benefits (amenities) that accrue in the long term* (more on this later).

What economic rationale can be given for discounting future benefits? According to conventional wisdom, this behavior expresses the simple fact that people typically have *a positive time preference*, i.e. other things remaining equal, people prefer their benefit now rather than later. This preference is evidenced by the fact that financial institutions must offer interest payments in order to get people to deposit money, thereby foregoing current consumption. Viewed this way then, discounting reflects the *opportunity cost* of not having access to money or any other benefits immediately. What does this all mean to *intertemporal* choice of environmental amenities, the subject that is of particular interest to us here? Taken literally, discounting suggests that people would value environmental amenities (for example, recreational experiences such as water rafting, fishing, skiing, etc.) more highly now than if they were provided the *same* experience twenty years from now. Why so?

Two explanations have been given for this behavior: people tend to discount the future because they are *myopic* or impatient (Mishan 1988), and people are *uncertain* about the future (Mishan 1988; Pearce and Nash 1981). Discounting is an important issue in cost–benefit analysis, and will be further discussed in Section 9.5.

---

1 When a *net* present value criterion is used for a project appraisal, the acceptability of the project is based purely on *economic efficiency*. In other words, a positive *NPV* means nothing more than an improvement in real income.
2 The *net* present value criterion does not address the issue of *income distribution*. It focuses exclusively on the project's contribution to aggregate real income of a society. In other words, the impact that the project may have on income distribution is simply ignored.

As is evident from the above discussion, the use of *NPV* for project appraisal requires three concrete pieces of information: estimates of both the annual *benefits* and *costs* over the expected lifetime of the project and the *discount rate*. Since the *NPV* criterion is used to assess public projects, these three variables need to be assessed from the perspective of *society* at large. To fully understand what this actually entails, it is worthwhile to compare and contrast how benefits, costs and discount rates are treated in project appraisals in the *private* and *public* sectors.

9.4 Private versus public project appraisal

As noted above, cost–benefit analysis is primarily used for project appraisal in the public sector. An analogous approach used in the private sector is called *financial appraisal* or *capital budgeting*. When the *NPV* is used, both cost–benefit analysis and financial appraisals follow the same criterion for accepting or rejecting a project, i.e. a project is accepted if *NPV* > 0. *However, the two approaches differ significantly in the methods used to estimate the costs and benefits of a project and the choice of the discount rate.* Why this is so is the subject of this section.

9.4.1 Estimation of benefits

In the private sector, benefit is identified as *revenue* or *cash flow*, and it is obtained by simply multiplying market price and quantity. However, as we have already seen in Chapter 8, *for public projects, benefit is measured by the sum of individuals' willingness to pay along the relevant range of the demand curve for a product or a service under consideration.* These two approaches to measuring benefit could result in markedly different outcomes. To see this, let us revisit our earlier example of a project designed to control SO_2 emissions from electric power plants located in a certain region. As shown in Figure 9.1, for society at large in any given year, the total benefit from this project is represented by the area under the demand curve. (The value of this area is obtained by summing the willingness to pay along the relevant range, Q_1 to Q_2, of the demand curve for environmental quality.) However, if the project's benefit is to be evaluated using the demand price, t_2, associated with Q_2 level of environmental quality, the incremental benefit of increasing the environmental quality from Q_1 to Q_2 would be $t_2 (Q_2 - Q_1)$ or the area of the rectangle $Q_1 CBQ_2$. This would have been the case if the project had been viewed as a private concern. Accordingly, the benefit estimate by the public sector would be greater than for the private concern by the area of the triangle ABC – the consumers' surplus realized by this particular society as a result of improving its environmental quality from Q_1 to Q_2. In summary, *the estimate of benefit from a public project includes the cash flows plus consumers' and producers' surpluses, whereas in the private sector the estimate of benefit from a project includes only cash flows received by private concerns.* Thus, unless the size of the project is *very small*, the difference in the estimates of benefits using these two approaches could be quite significant.

There is one other important issue that is worth mentioning regarding the nature of the benefits of a public versus a private project. As discussed in Chapter 8, because most public projects, especially those associated with the environment, tend to be *externality-ridden*, estimation of their benefits poses a major challenge and often requires the use of valuation techniques that are subject to major controversy. Exhibit 9.3 shows general guidelines for cost–benefit analysis that incorporates environmental valuation, i.e. valuation of benefits that are indirectly traded in markets or not traded at all. In

Exhibit 9.3   Guidelines for cost–benefit analysis that incorporates environmental valuation

Principles for valuing benefits that are indirectly traded in markets

Examples of such benefits are reduction in health and safety risks, the use values of environmental amenities, and the enjoyment of scenic vistas.

1 To estimate the monetary value of such indirectly traded goods, the willingness-to-pay valuation method is considered the conceptually superior approach.
2 Alternative methods may be used when there are practical obstacles to the accurate application of direct willingness-to-pay methods.
3 A variety of methods have been developed for estimating indirectly traded benefits. Generally these methods apply statistical techniques to distill from observable market transactions the portion of willingness to pay that can be attributed to the benefit in question. Examples include estimates of the value of environmental amenities derived from travel cost studies, hedonic price models that measure differences or changes in the value of land, and statistical studies of occupational risk premiums in wage rates.
4 For all these methods, care is needed in designing protocols for reliably estimating benefits by adapting the results of previous studies to new applications.
5 Reliance on contingent valuation methods depends on hypothetical scenarios. The complexities of the goods being valued by this technique raise issues about its accuracy in estimating willingness to pay, compared to methods based on (indirect) revealed preferences.

6 Accordingly, value estimates derived from contingent valuation studies require greater analytical care than studies based on observable behavior. For example, the contingent valuation instrument must portray a realistic choice situation for respondents – where the hypothetical choice situation corresponds closely to the policy context in which the estimates will be applied.

Principles and methods for valuing goods that are not traded, directly or indirectly, in markets

Examples of such goods are preserving environmental or cultural amenities apart from their use and direct enjoyment by people.

1 For many of these goods, particularly goods providing nonuse values, contingent valuation methods may provide the only analytical approach currently available for estimating values.
2 The absence of observable and replicable behavior with respect to the good in question, combined with the complex and often unfamiliar nature of the goods being valued, argues for great care in the design and execution of surveys, rigorous analysis of the results, and a full characterization of the estimates to meet best practices in the use of this method.

Source: *Revealing the Ecological Economic Value of Protecting the Great Lakes*, Northeast-Midwest Institute and National Oceanic and Atmospheric Administration (2001), pp. 59–60.

Case Study 9.1   Economics and the Endangered Species Act: the costs of species protection

Jason F. Shogren

When Congress passed the Endangered Species Act (ESA) in 1973, it was explicit in stating that economic criteria should play no role in species listings or in the designation of critical habitat. It was not until the amendments to the ESA in 1978 that economics first entered the ESA.

Today it does not take an economist to see that economic issues are critical to the ESA debate. With a large fraction of endangered or threatened species inhabiting private land (75 per cent according to a 1993 estimate by The Nature Conservancy), a significant portion of the ESA costs are borne by private property owners, while the ESA benefits accrue to the entire nation. Assessing costs and benefits in endangered species protection, however, is not simple.

This exhibit illustrates the difficulties associated with assessing the costs of species preservation. These costs include the transaction costs of species protection, opportunity costs to property owners of restricted property rights, and opportunity costs of public funds used in species recovery.

The best measure of economic loss is opportunity cost. Opportunity costs include the reduced economic profit from restricted or altered development projects, including agriculture production, timber harvesting, minerals extraction, and recreation activities; wages lost by displaced workers who remain unemployed or who are re-employed at lower pay; lower consumer surplus due to higher prices; and lower county property and severance tax revenue.

Opportunity costs have been estimated for a few high-profile, regional ESA conflicts, such as the northern spotted owl. One study estimated that an owl recovery plan . . . would decrease economic welfare by between $33 and $46 billion (Montgomery *et al.* 1994). Another study estimated the short-run and long-run opportunity costs of owl protection to Washington and Oregon at $1.2 billion and $450 million (Rubin *et al.* 1991).

Opportunity costs also exist with public programs, because resources devoted to species conservation could have been spent on something else viewed as potentially more valuable to the general public. The US Department of the Interior estimated that the potential direct costs from the recovery plans of all listed species were about $4.6 billion (US Fish and Wildlife Service 1990).

The General Accounting Office (1995) compiled estimates of the predicted direct outlays needed to recover selected species, including the costs of implementing the most important, 'high-priority' recovery actions. The total for the 34 plans with complete cost estimates was approximately $700 million.

Of the money actually expended on endangered species recovery by federal and state agencies between 1989 and 1991 (1989 was the first year data were published), over 50 per cent was spent on the top ten species, including the bald eagle, northern spotted owl, and Florida scrub (Metrick and Weitzman 1996).

In addition to direct public spending, private expenditures add to the cost of ESA implementation. These expenditures include the time and money spent on applications for permits and licenses, redesign of plans, and legal fees. National estimates for these expenditures do not exist for the ESA. As a possible benchmark, private firms fighting over Superfund spent an estimated $4 billion through 1991 (Dixon 1995).

contrast, most often, estimation of the benefits from private projects tend to be a straightforward exercise because it is based on easily observable market information about price and quantity changes.

9.4.2 Estimation of costs

The approaches used to assess the costs of a project are also materially different for the private compared to the public sector. In the private sector, the cost estimate of a project is obtained in such a way that it reflects all the *direct* costs associated with the implementation and operation of the project in question. In other words, in the private sector, cost estimates include all the monetary expenditures by private firms to acquire resources to make the project operational. These costs are considered relevant to the extent that they directly affect the interests of the private firms under consideration. Furthermore, *these costs are 'financial' to the extent that their estimate is based on market prices; therefore, they may or may not reflect opportunity costs.* On the other hand, in the public sector, costs are measured in terms of forgone opportunities (see Case Study 9.1). Moreover, both the internal and the external costs of the project should be included. In short, *an estimate of a cost for a public project should reflect social costs, which include both the internal and the external costs of a project evaluated in terms of opportunity costs.*

   However, we have to be extremely cautious in evaluating the *social cost* of a project. In an attempt to include all the relevant internal and external costs, it is quite easy to count some costs more than once. *Double counting*, therefore, is a very serious problem in cost–benefit analysis of public projects. To illustrate this let us go back once more to the example dealing with a legislative mandate enacted for the purpose of conserving wilderness. As shown in Figure 9.2, the effect of this project or legislative mandate has been to move this society from its initial position, M, to a new position, N. The new position is associated with less consumption of goods and services, and more wilderness. More specifically, the opportunity cost of expanding the acreage allotted to wilderness from F_0 to F_1 is measured by a decrease in the production of conventional economic goods and services from G_0 to G_1.

   Let us now suppose that lumber is one of the conventional goods affected negatively. That is, one effect of the new conservation initiative is a decline in lumber production. How should we measure this as part of the social cost to the conservation initiative? One way to do this would be to impute the market value of the decline in lumber that is directly attributable to this particular conservation initiative. To more clearly show how this can be done, let the variables L_0 and L_1 represent the output of lumber (in cubic feet) before and after the conservation project is implemented. Since we have already postulated that $L_0 > L_1$, $(L_0 - L_1)$ represents the amount in cubic feet by which lumber output is reduced. Then, let P_0 and P_1 represent the real prices of lumber (in cubic feet) before and after the conservation initiative. Other things being equal, we expect that $P_1 > P_0$. Given this information on the changes of the prices and outputs for lumber, we can impute the market value of the decline in lumber that is directly attributable to the wilderness conservation project to be $P_1(L_0 - L_1)$.

However, the decline in lumber from L_0 to L_1 may have additional economy-wide effects. For example, a shortage of lumber may cause an increase in the price of new housing construction, and household and office furniture. Should cost increases of this nature be imputed as part of the overall cost of the decline in lumber output? If so, the social cost of the wilderness conservation project should include not only the market value of the decline in lumber, namely $P_1(L_0 - L_1)$, but also the increase in the cost of new houses and household and office furniture. *Although at first glance this idea may seem to make sense, a closer look would suggest that only the market value of the decline in real output of lumber should be counted.* The *inflationary* impact of lumber shortages on the construction of new houses and office furniture should not be counted as part of the cost of the new conservation initiative. Otherwise, it would amount to counting cost twice: once by the increase in the price of lumber (from P_0 to P_1), and then again by the *inflationary or secondary effects* of this same price increase throughout the economy.

It is important not to confuse secondary effects of the above nature with externalities or external effects. Unlike environmental externalities (see Chapter 3), secondary effects are not associated with changes in *real* output. For instance, in the example above, no indication was given that the increase in the price of lumber had caused a decline in new housing starts and/or the output of the furniture industry.

On the other hand, if the decrease in lumber production has caused an actual decline in new housing construction and/or the output of the furniture industry, then the market value of these real output effects should be a part of the overall cost attributable to the wilderness conservation project. *To sum up, in imputing the costs of a public project, all real output effects should be included. However, in cost–benefit analysis, special care should be taken not to include inflationary or secondary effects of price changes as part of the cost of a project. Otherwise, for reasons already stated above, we will be double-counting costs.*

9.4.3 Choice of the discount rate

A third difference between public and private project appraisal is the choice of the discount rate. Both the private and public sectors use positive discount rates, i.e. $r > 0$. The difference is that, in general, the public or social discount rate, r_s, is lower than the private discount rate, r_p. There are *two* justifications for this difference.

1   Individuals (or private concern) will not view the future in the same way as society, which represents the collective concern of individuals. In general, individuals are seen as being *selfish* and *shortsighted* (Mishan 1988). They seem to be mostly concerned with their own welfare in the present or in the very near future. Hence

they do not assign much importance to benefits that might be forthcoming in the future, i.e. they tend to discount benefit coming at some future date heavily. On the other hand, the public sector, which represents society as a whole, is believed to have a longer-term perspective. Thus, the discount rate used in the public project should be lower than that used in the private sector.

2   Individuals are more *risk averse* or *uncertain* about the future than society at large. After all, for all practical purposes society can be viewed as having an eternal life. What this means is that private projects are exposed to more risk while public projects are virtually immune. Under this circumstance, efficient allocation of societal resources would dictate that a relatively higher discount rate should be applied to private investment projects (Pearce and Nash 1981). In other words, the discount rate should be adjusted upward to reflect the greater risk associated with undertaking private projects.

A pertinent question, then, is how large should be the difference between *social* and *private* discount rates? From past empirical studies, both in the United States and elsewhere, the difference between these two discount rates can range between 3 and 5 percentage points. For social projects, although no consensus view exists, a discount rate of 4 per cent (net of inflation) is generally recommended. On the other hand, the private discount rate (net of inflation) could be as high as 10 per cent. If this is the case, would a difference of 3 to 5 percentage points matter much? *From the viewpoint of resource allocation over time, the answer to this question depends on the time horizon of the project under consideration.* For more on this read Exhibit 9.4 – a 'must read' for those who want to understand the pervasive nature of discounting.

9.5 Discounting and intergenerational equity

In the discussion in the previous section, we noted that projects dealing with the conservation of environmental assets (such as coastal wetlands, wilderness, national parks, estuaries, etc.) are highly sensitive to discounting. Moreover, *while the decision about project appraisal is made on the basis of the preferences of the current generation, a particular feature of environmental costs and benefits is that they often accrue to people in generations yet to come.* Under these circumstances, since discounting implies that gains and losses to society are valued less the more distant they are in the future, can the use of a positive discount rate be ethically justifiable? What restraints, if any, should the current generation voluntarily accept for the benefit of the future? As would be expected, even within the economics profession the responses to this question vary widely depending on one's view of humankind's future predicament.

For many economists, the use of a positive discount rate *per se* is not an issue of significance. It simply reflects the fact that people have a *positive time preference*; this is considered to be normal (for more on this refer back to Exhibit 9.2). The implication of this is that if present consumption is preferred to later consumption for any reason, positive discounting is appropriate. Thus, for most economists (primarily neoclassicist), what is important in appraising any project is the appropriate discount rate to be used. More specifically, in the case of public projects, which include most projects of an environmental nature, the *social* discount rate should be used. For reasons discussed in the previous section, in most instances the social discount rate tends to be *lower* than its private counterpart. In this sense, then, *the preference for social rather than private*

Exhibit 9.4   The pervasive nature of discounting

This exhibit shows precisely how project appraisal is sensitive to small changes in the discount rate, depending on the time horizon of the project under consideration. To do this we can use the *NPV* formula given below together with Figures 9.3a and 9.3b.

$$NPV = \Sigma\{(B_t - C_t)[1/(1 + r)^t]\}$$

First, let us examine the term in the above *NPV* formula known as the *discount factor*, $(1 + r)^t$. The value of this depends on two variables, t and r. The higher the discount rate, r, and the longer the time horizon, t, the larger the value of the discount factor. In other words, the discount factor increases as r and/or t increases. This is illustrated in Figures 9.3a and 9.3b. In both figures, it is evident that for a given discount rate, the discount factor increases with increase in time t. For example, in Figure 9.3a, where the discount rate is held constant at 5 per cent, the value of the discount factor increases from 1 to 80.7 over a period

of 90 years. Similarly, as shown in Figure 9.3b, when the interest rate is 10 per cent, over the same time interval – 90 years – the value of the discount factor increases from 1 to 5,313.

These results on their own are neither surprising nor particularly interesting. *What will be more intriguing will be to observe the rate at which the discount factor increases over time for a given discount rate.* When the discount rate is 5 per cent – Figure 9.3a – in the first 15 years the interest factor grows from 1 to 2.07, i.e. slightly more than doubled. In the second 15 years (year 15 to year 30) the discount factor increases from 2.07 to 4.32 – again slightly more than doubled. Thus, when the interest rate is 5 per cent, it takes the same number of years, 15 to be exact, to double the discount factor from 1 to 2 as it does to raise it from 2 to 4. It follows, then, that every 15 years the discount factor is growing geometrically, i.e. as 2, 4, 8, 16, etc. That is, the discount factor is growing exponentially over time. Similarly, when the interest rate is 10 per

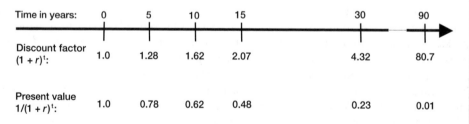

Figure 9.3A The discount factor when $r = 0.05$

Time in years:	0	5	10	15	30	90
Discount factor $(1 + r)^t$:	1.0	1.28	1.62	2.07	4.32	80.7
Present value $1/(1 + r)^t$:	1.0	0.78	0.62	0.48	0.23	0.01

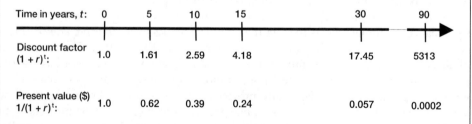

Figure 9.3B The discount factor when $r = 0.10$

Time in years, t:	0	5	10	15	30	90
Discount factor $(1 + r)^t$:	1.0	1.61	2.59	4.18	17.45	5313
Present value ($) $1/(1 + r)^t$:	1.0	0.62	0.39	0.24	0.057	0.0002

cent (Figure 9.3b), in the first 15 years the interest factor grows from 1 to 4.18, i.e. slightly more than quadruples. In the second 15 years (years 15 to 30), the discount factor increases from 4.18 to 17.45 – again slightly more than quadruples. Thus, when the interest rate is 10 per cent, it takes about 15 years to quadruple the discount factor from 1 to 4, as it does from 4 to 16. It follows, then, that approximately every 15 years the discount factor is growing geometrically, i.e. as 4, 16, 64, 256, and so on. In other words, the discount factor is growing exponentially over time.

Thus, *from this discussion it is clear that regardless of what the interest rate is, the discount factor increases exponentially over time.* This is very significant because it clearly demonstrates the pervasive nature of discounting. To see this, note that in Figures 9.3a and 9.3b the discount factor is inversely related to the present value of a dollar, $1/(1 + r)^t$. *If, as we have observed above, the discount factor increases over time exponentially, then the present value of a dollar tends to converge to its lower limit of zero within a finite time,* t. For example, as shown in Figures 9.3a and 9.3b the present value of a dollar is reduced virtually to zero ($0.01 and $0.0002) within 90 years – less than one potential human lifetime. This is an extremely important result since it suggests that when the time duration of a project under consideration is fairly long, the difference between private and social discount rates that are normally within the range of 3 to 5 per cent is irrelevant. This is because discounting reduces benefits coming in the far distant future to virtually zero within a finite time, as long as the discount rate is positive. As will be discussed in the next section, this has far-reaching economic and ethical implications.

discount rates alone constitutes an intentional allowance for the issue of distributional fairness among generations. However, will this be adequate? In other words, since discounting, however small, implies unequal weighting of costs and benefits over time, can there be distributional fairness when the discount rate is not reduced to zero? Those professionals who uphold the position that intergenerational fairness need not demand a zero discount rate use the following line of reasoning to support their position.

1   Generations do overlap. The current population includes three generations: grandparents, parents and children. Parents care for their children and grandchildren. Current children care for their children and grandchildren, etc. Thus, *this chain of generational caring clearly indicates that the preference function of the current generation takes the interest of the future generation into account.*
2   To argue for a zero social discount rate when market conditions indicate otherwise would lead to an inefficient allocation of resources; the current generation would be operating inside its production possibility frontier. Concern for intergenerational fairness can be addressed through public policy measures that have no effect on prices, such as some sort of lump-sum tax. *In other words, addressing the concern for intergenerational equity need not impoverish the current generation unnecessarily.*
3   Historically the average wealth (income) of the current generation has been higher than that of its immediate predecessor. Given this historical trend of upward mobility in standard of living, why should the current generation voluntarily accept such a condition (such as zero discount rate), thinking that it might benefit the future? This sentiment is eloquently expressed by Baumol (1968: 800), a prominent

economist: 'in our economy if past trends and current developments are any guide, a redistribution to provide more for the future may be described as a Robin Hood activity stood on its head – it takes from the poor to give to the rich. Average real per capita income a century hence is likely to be a sizable multiple of its present value. Why should I give up part of my income to help support someone else with an income several times my own?'

On the other hand, there are a few economists (Mishan 1988; Sen 1982) who oppose the use of positive discount rates when appraising public projects, especially projects designed to conserve the amenities of the natural environment. The reasoning behind this position is that, as shown in Exhibit 9.4, *for projects with long time horizons, discounting effectively reduces future benefits and costs to zero after a finite number of years*. This has the effect of favoring projects associated with either short-term benefits (such as development projects instead of projects designed to conserve environmental amenities) or long-term costs (such as the construction of a nuclear plant). In either case, the well-being of the future generation is put at risk. Given this, there are economists who argue that intergenerational fairness justifies no discounting at all – a *zero* discount rate. Some economists have even gone further and argued for *negative* discounting to reflect the need for greater protection of the interests of future generations in natural resource management decisions about either irreplaceable amenities (such as the Grand Canyon) and/or irreversible outcomes (such as global warming and species extinction).

However, it should be pointed out that *the risk of considering a zero or negative discount rate is the possibility that action of this nature may hinder important technological advances*. Of course, such an outcome, if realized, would have negative welfare implications to both the current and future generations – an economically inefficient (or Pareto-inferior) position indeed.

Clearly, taken together, what the analysis in this section indicates is the intractable nature of the task of resolving the contradiction between efficiency and the concern for the future generations. However, intractability need not suggest paralysis. It simply indicates that consideration of intergenerational equity, although a subject matter that defies clear-cut answers, requires thoughtful and serious incorporation of all the relevant economic, ecological, moral, and ethical concerns to do with the issue in hand. Are there alternative methods of environmental project assessments that are likely to be more sensitive or accommodating towards these issues than traditional cost–benefit analysis? This question anticipates the discussion in the next section.

9.6 Other environmental project evaluation criteria and considerations

So far, the discussion has been confined to key issues normally raised in the standard economic appraisal of environmental projects – cost–benefit analysis. The use of cost–benefit analysis has been criticized for a number of reasons. Most importantly, the focus of cost–benefit analysis on things that can be measured and quantified in money terms is considered its major flaw. The fact that intangibles (ecosystem services that cannot reasonably be assigned a monetary value) are included in the decision process as ancillary information has not provided any consolation to the ardent critics of cost–benefit analysis. In this section, an effort will be made to provide a brief account of a number of alternative methods of environmental project appraisal that may be used either to supplement or, under certain circumstances, to replace conventional cost–benefit analysis.

9.6.1 Precautionary principles versus traditional cost–benefit analysis

Precautionary principles are a rather general resource management guideline applicable to a decision-making process characterized by a considerable degree of *uncertainty*. In broad terms and when applied to environmental resources, this approach contends that society should take action against certain practices when there is potential for irreversible consequences or for severe limits on the options for future generations – even when there is as yet no incontrovertible scientific proof that serious consequences will ensue. Global warming, ozone depletion, introduction of new species, and protection for rare, threatened or endangered ecosystems and habitats are examples of environmental concerns to which precautionary principles may be applicable.

In the case of global warming, the ongoing policy debate has concerned the rate by which emissions of greenhouse gases (GHGs) should be curtailed in order to avert environmental damage caused by climate change in the future. For example, one study recommended a 71 per cent reduction from baseline (i.e. the 1990 level of global carbon emission) by 2050 (Cline, 1992). The implication was that, if no aggressive action of this nature is taken, the damage arising from climate change (such as flooded coastal cities, diminished food production, loss of biodiversity, land lost to oceans, increased storm damage, and so on), despite the scientific uncertainty, are expected to be quite significant.

On the other hand, Nordhaus's study (1991) of this same subject but using a standard cost–benefit analysis approach recommended policy actions that were far too modest – an abatement of 11 per cent of total GHG emissions.

The main reason for the difference between the policy recommendations of these two empirical studies is simply this. When precautionary principles are applied, in the case of global warming, the high social opportunity costs that are associated with anticipated large-scale and irreversible degradation of natural capital are sufficient enough to warrant aggressive action to slow down GHG emissions. This conclusion would be reached despite the scientific uncertainty about the outcomes of future damages. In other words, *precautionary principle takes the position that, in safeguarding against large-scale, irreversible degradation of natural capital, the prudent course of action entails erring on the side of the unknown*. This is, indeed, the essence of a precautionary principle.

It is important to note that precautionary principles are different from the traditional cost–benefit analysis because the entire decision is based on the *exclusive* consideration of avoided damages (benefits) to generations of people living in the far distant future. In other words, the fact that a policy to slow global warming could reduce current consumption (GDP) is not considered at all. Obviously, the basic concern of precautionary principles is not *efficiency*, since no claim is made that a dollar spent on projects to slow global warming today must be justified by a dollar or more benefit that are expected to be realized from avoiding future environmental and ecological damages. Essentially, it can be said that precautionary principles favor *prudence* over efficiency, and prudence is the justification for the bias that precautionary principles show towards the protection of future generations.

The Endangered Species Act of 1973 in the United States is a public policy provision where a precautionary principle has been successfully applied. According to this Act, individual areas can be excluded from designation as critical habitat, and therefore extinction of species is allowed if, and only if, the economic impacts of preservation are judged to be *extremely severe or intolerable*. In other words, exemption from species protection cannot be allowed just because the overall economic impact (in terms of changes in output and employment) of such action is found to be *negative*, as conventional cost–benefit analysis would have suggested. This seemingly precautionary condition is stipulated with an intention to diminish the likelihood of accepting a project or policy action with an outcome that is irreversible – in the case of the Endangered Species Act, the extinction of species.

9.6.2 Cost-effectiveness analysis versus traditional cost–benefit analysis

As discussed in Chapters 4 through 6, CEA deals with least-cost method of achieving a stated environmental goal. An example would be a project to clean up a river in a certain specified location, with the clear objective of attaining a specified water quality. Here, the desired water quality may be based on other than economic concerns, such as political pressure from a certain special-interest group, consideration of a well-documented health risk, or consideration of social justice or ethics.

In CEA, the benefits from a project are taken for granted and considered important. Hence, the emphasis is on costs. Operationally, CEA analysis entails the ranking of the various technological approaches designed to accomplish the desired societal environmental objective. This ranking is done purely on the basis of cost effectiveness – the biggest bang for the buck. Clearly, CEA differs from traditional cost benefit analysis, in which both the costs and benefits of a project are considered. *The use of CEA is often justified when the identification and measurement of benefits are difficult.*

Critics of this approach very much doubt if analysis of this nature provides adequate consideration of hidden ecological costs. This is because it completely omits consideration of environmental benefits, and in so doing, also omits consideration of environmental damage. Remember that environmental benefits are avoided environmental damage.

9.6.3 Environmental impact studies versus traditional cost–benefit analysis

The primary focus of environmental impact studies (EIS) is on tracing all the relevant physical or ecological *linkages* through which environmental impacts of given projects are manifested or spread. Since the emphasis is on ecological rather than economic linkages, EIS are primarily performed by natural scientists. In the United States, the National Environmental Policy Act (NEPA) of 1969, requires that all federal agencies file an EIS statement for any proposed legislation or project having a significant effect on environmental quality. The NEPA also created the Council on Environmental Quality (CEQ), an executive agency, that among others, establishes guidelines for the preparation of environmental impact statements. Each such statement must include (Miller 1991: p. 576):

1   The purpose and need for the proposed action
2   The probable environmental impact (positive, negative, direct, and indirect) of the proposed action and of possible alternatives
3   Any adverse environmental effects that could not be avoided should the project be implemented
4   Relationships between the probable short-term and long-term impacts of the proposal on environmental quality
5   Irreversible and irretrievable commitments of resources that would be involved should the project be implemented
6   Objections raised by reviewers of the preliminary draft of the statement
7   The names and qualifications of the people primarily responsible for preparing the EIS
8   References to back up all statements and conclusions.

EIS have been successful in forcing government agencies to carefully scrutinize the side effects of publicly funded environmental projects at all governmental levels – local, regional, state, and national. It has also the effect of forcing government agencies to evaluate projects with full considerations of *all* the possible alternatives. Because of its success in the United States, several countries worldwide have been adopting the use of EIS (e.g. France in 1976 and the European Union in 1985).

EIS are not without their own shortcomings. EIS are retrospective; they are often prepared to justify a decision that has already been made. Most EIS do not receive careful scrutiny because of cost considerations. Also, EIS do not attempt at all to directly impute *social values* to the impacts identified to be relevant for the evaluation of project. Hence they are far removed from cost–benefit analysis.

9.6.4 *Environmental risk assessment and risk management*

Risk assessment and risk management are valuable in the area of environmental regulations, and they are extensively used by the EPA. Other areas where information obtained from risk assessment and risk management would be invaluable are, as discussed in Section 3 of Chapter 8, in the attempts that environmental economists' often make to impute monetary values to occupational risk, mortality and morbidity (placing a value on human life and health). In this sense, risk assessment and risk management provide significant contributions to environmental damage assessments and the formulation of environmental regulatory policies in general. This process also contributes to assessment of environmental benefits – a key part of conventional cost–benefit analysis. A natural question to ask is then, what do we mean by environmental risk assessment and risk management? How is risk assessment performed? Is there a radical difference between risk assessment and risk management?

Risk assessment is the scientific foundation for most EPA regulatory actions. It involves a process by which scientific data are analyzed to describe the form, dimensions and characteristics of risk, i.e. the likelihood of harm to human health or the environment. The scope and nature of risk assessment range widely, from broadly based scientific conclusions about air pollutant such as lead or arsenic affecting the nations as a whole to site-specific findings about these same elements in a local water supply. Some assessments are retrospective, focusing on injury after the fact, for instance the kind and extent of risks at a particular toxic landfill site. Others seek to predict possible future harm to human health or the environment, for instance, the risks expected if a newly developed pesticide is approved for use on food crops.

By its very nature environmental risk assessment is a multidisciplinary process. It draws on data, information and principles from many scientific disciplines including biology, chemistry, physics, medicine, geology, epidemiology, and statistics, among others.

For human health risk assessment, the process involves a series of steps that begins by identifying the particular hazard(s) of the substance – hazard identification. Subsequent steps examine 'dose–response' patterns and human exposure considerations, and the conclusion is a 'risk characterization' that is both qualitative and quantitative. As an example, when expressed numerically the risk for cancer from pollutant X may be presented as 1×10^{-6} or 0.000001, or one in a million – meaning one additional case of cancer projected in a population of one million people exposed to a certain level of pollutant X over their lifetimes. It is important to note that the quantitative result of risk is a *worst-case* estimate and indicates an *average* attributed risk. It applies to no one in particular and to everyone on average.

As would be expected, risk assessments are not infallible. For one thing, information on the effects of small amounts of a substance in the environment is often not available, and data from animal experiments must be extrapolated to humans. Such extrapolation cannot be made with absolute *certainty*. Therefore, scientific uncertainty is a customary and expected factor in all environmental risk assessment. As far as possible, it is important to identify uncertainties and present them as part of risk characterization.

Risk management is the process by which the risk assessment is used with other information to make regulatory decisions. The other information includes data on technological feasibility, on costs, and on the economic and social consequences (e.g. employment impacts) of possible regulatory decisions. In most instances, risk managers consider this additional socioeconomic and technological information together with the outcome of the risk assessment when evaluating risk management options and making environmental decisions.

Risk assessment and risk management are closely related and equally important, but they are different processes, with different objectives, information content, and results. Risk assessment asks 'how risky is the situation?' while risk management then asks 'what shall we do about it?'

The nature of the risk management decision often influences the scope and depth of a risk assessment. A question often raised is should risk management (what we wish to do about risk) be allowed to influence risk assessment (what we know about risk)? This is like asking whether politics should control science. However this issue may be interpreted, there appears to be a nagging concern that risk management objectives might override the risk assessor's impartial evaluation of scientific data. This kind of concern should be taken seriously if it has implications that go beyond the acknowledgement that the application of the results of risk assessment should be sensitive to the policy context.

9.6.5 Considerations of social justice and ethics: Rawlsian and environmental justice

Considerations of social justice and ethics in environmental matters arise from two distinct sources. The first is concern about the distribution of environmental amenities (benefits) or damage (costs) across a society in a given generation – *intragenerational equity*. The second is concern about the distribution of environmental benefits and costs across generations – *intergenerational equity*. Both concerns, while relevant to environmental management issues, are not adequately addressed in traditional cost–benefit analysis, where consideration of economic efficiency is stressed and distributional or equity considerations are given little or no attention. This subsection will address both intra- and intergenerational equities in the context of issues relating to the environment. Further, the justification for the inclusion of these concerns in making environmental decisions will be presented on the basis of both social justice (fairness) considerations and ethical theory.

A Distribution of benefits or costs across generations: Rawlsian justice

Actually, the issue of *intergenerational* equity was already discussed at some length in the previous section of this chapter. There the focus of the discussion was the implications of *discounting* for the distribution of benefits across generations. Several arguments were discussed regarding selection of the appropriate discount rate, and these arguments were presented using a purely economic logic or argument. We now add a case for a *zero* discount rate (i.e. placing equal value on the benefit received in the future and today) and unlike our previous discussion its justification is solely based on ethical theory – Rawlsian justice.

Philosopher John Rawls, in his highly acclaimed book, *A Theory of Justice*, attempted to construct a general principle of justice using the following preconditions. Let us hypothesize that every person initially in an 'original position' is placed behind a 'veil of ignorance'. The purpose of this is that then no one would have prior knowledge about his or her eventual position in society. For example, in the case of intergenerational decision-making, people are prevented by veil of ignorance from knowing the generation to which they will belong. Once placed behind this veil, people would be asked to develop rules to govern the society (generation) that they would, after the decision, be forced to live in.

Under such a hypothetical setting, it would be in the best interest of the decision-makers to act *impartially* and favor *equal* sharing of resources across generations. Viewed broadly, this so-called Rawlsian justice may be interpreted as suggesting that current generations should use environmental assets in a way that preserves the ability of future generations to enjoy these assets. Some economists have used this ethical principle, sometimes referred to as 'the sustainability criterion', to argue for a zero discount rate. Are they correct in doing so? From a purely utilitarian perspective, they would be correct if, and only if, placing equal values on time-dated benefits and costs (which is implied by a zero discount rate) would assure equal enjoyment (or standard of living) across generations. However, equal sharing of physical assets may or may not guarantee outcomes that are proportionally enjoyable (measured either in terms of income or utility). Thus, the application of Rawlsian justice to justify zero discounting can be defended only on a purely ethical or moral basis.

B Distribution of benefits and costs across current generations: environmental justice

It is not by accident that waste sites and other noxious facilities (i.e. landfills, incinerators and hazardous waste treatment, storage, and disposal facilities) are not randomly scattered across the landscape. Waste generation is directly correlated with per capita income, but few garbage dumps and toxic sites are located in affluent suburbs. Waste facilities are often located in communities that have high percentages of poor, elderly, young, and minority residents. Is this fair or just? This question points to a very important environmental issue discussed under the heading of *environmental justice*.

Standard economic theory would predict that poverty plays a role in the spatial distribution of environmental hazards. This is, because of their limited income and wealth, poor people do not have the means to buy their way out of polluted neighborhoods. Also, land values tend to be lower in poor neighborhoods, so the neighborhoods attract polluting industries seeking to reduce the cost of doing business. In recent years, an additional issue has been raised, suggesting that *race* is as important a factor as poverty (income) in determining the location of hazardous waste facilities. What this clearly implies is the existence of 'environmental racism'.

Could these claims that poverty and race are two important determinants in the distribution of environmental hazards be empirically verified? Given that poverty and race are highly correlated, is it possible to assess the relative influence of income and race on the distribution of pollution? In other words, are minorities disproportionately impacted because they are disproportionately poor? This question is important because if the claim of 'environmental racism' is to be accepted we need to know that race has an impact on the distribution of environmental hazards that is independent of income.

Since the early 1990s there have been a number of studies done to answer the questions raised above. In one instance, the results of 15 studies were pooled and analyzed to see what common factual (empirically verifiable) observations could be distilled from their findings. Although these studies vary considerably in their scope and the methodologies employed, the findings point to a consistent pattern. Taken together, the findings from these studies indicate clear and unequivocal class and racial biases in the distribution of environmental hazards. Further, they appear to support the argument that race has an additional effect on the distribution of environmental hazards that is independent of class. Indeed, the racial biases found in these studies have tended to be greater than class biases (Bryant and Mohai 1992).

Although the empirical evidence may not be as complete or conclusive as that for the bias in the distribution of commercial hazardous waste facilities, minority groups and the poor in general appear to be disproportionately exposed to other types of environmental hazards, such as water pollution, pesticides, asbestos and lead, and so on. Even in the absence of strong empirical evidence, as shown in Exhibit 9.5, a convincing theoretical economic argument can be made that environmental justice is a valid concern that warrants action. At the minimum, it is an issue that should be given explicit and serious consideration in *cost–benefit analysis of public projects* and the EPA's risk assessment and risk management efforts. If this is done, perhaps there is a good chance that the voices of the poor and underrepresented minorities will be adequately heard, helping to prevent future environmental decisions that have harmful consequences for these groups.

The issue of environmental justice is not limited to the United States. Although there have not been well-documented empirical studies to support this claim, to a varying degree environmental justice is a very relevant issue in most economically advanced nations. Furthermore, in recent years, environmental justice has been a hot and contested international issue as several firms and organizations in the rich nations of

Exhibit 9.5   Distribution of benefits across society

Jay Coggins

It is well known that the distribution of environmental costs and benefits resulting from an environmental intervention, such as the siting of a waste disposal facility, are often geographically uneven, with most of the costs concentrated on neighbors and most of the benefits on more distant users of the facility. Economists have historically neutralized these geographic variables by, as a first step, defining the population affected by an intervention, both local and distant, and sampling from that population in a representative way. The end result is an average measure of willingness to pay for the intervention. If the sample is truly representative, this average should be a good measure of value for the population.

Problems arise, however, when the differential impacts sustained by a subpopulation directly correspond to gross differences in income. In these cases, environmental costs averaged over the entire population may not reflect the effect that the intervention would have on wealth (i.e. the opportunity costs) within the individual subpopulations.

If the communities are studied separately, economists can clarify the differences in impacts reflected in each community's willingness to pay for environmental quality. However, interpreting these findings will also be tricky. Based on these findings, economists might falsely conclude that the low-income, near-neighbors are less willing to pay for environmental quality, simply because they would have to sacrifice more meaningful goods and services (such as food or health care) to do so than would a rich community. *In these cases, economists must attempt to differentiate willingness to pay from ability to pay.*

The key question economists should ask is whether the effect of a given environmental problem is felt most strongly by a low-income subpopulation. *If so, the average willingness to pay obtained by an economic study could be biased downward, precisely because the group most severely affected by the problem has low income and therefore relatively low willingness to pay.*

Source: The Northeast-Midwest Institute and the National Oceanic and Atmospheric Administration (2001, pp. 51–3).

the world have been caught shipping their toxic wastes to dump in the territory of poor countries. These incidents are, of course, in addition to the growing trends of companies from developed nations preferring to locate parts of their industrial operations primarily on the basis of environmental considerations – in countries where environmental regulations are very lenient or almost totally absent.

9.7   Chapter summary

• The assessment of the benefits arising from environmental projects was addressed in the previous chapter. In this chapter, the various relevant concepts of costs associated with environmental projects were discussed in detail. Cost–benefit analysis (CBA) is one of the techniques most widely used by economists for appraising environmental projects in the public domain. A project was defined here rather broadly, and includes any intentional action undertaken by the public to move from the status quo to an alternative state. One example would be a legislative mandate to increase land allotment for wilderness, another the action taken to dam a river for the sole purpose of diverting the water flow of the river in certain desired direction(s).

- In conducting CBA, both costs and benefits have to be estimated in certain ways, and evaluated from the perspective of *society* as a whole.
- Considerations of social costs imply that both the *internal* and the *external* costs of the environmental project under investigation should be carefully evaluated.
- However, in an attempt to include *all* the relevant internal and external costs, it is quite easy to count some costs more than once. This *double counting* is a serious problem in assessing the costs of environmental projects, requiring us to be very cautious in estimating social costs.
- As discussed in Section 2 of Chapter 8, benefits of environmental projects are measured using the concept of willingness-to-pay. This entails not only knowledge of prices but also a measure of an area along the relevant segment of the demand curve for environmental services. Not an easy thing to do, by any means!
- Once both the social benefits and costs of a project are evaluated, the next step in project appraisal is to develop a criterion (a norm) for weighing the benefits of a project against its costs: cost–benefit analysis.
- For an appraisal of public projects, the fundamental normative (welfare) criterion of CBA is based on potential Pareto improvement. This means, as demonstrated in this chapter, that the sum of the *net* discounted benefits over the lifetime of the project (or net present value) must be *positive*.
- This criterion leads to the economically *efficient* outcome, but positive net present value focuses only on the project's contribution to aggregate *real* income. No explicit consideration is made of the effect that the project may have on *income distribution*.
- The choice of the *discount rate* is critical when the net present value method is used as a norm for project appraisal. For public projects (which include most environmental projects) the standard procedure is to use the *social* discount rate, which is *lower* than the 'private' discount rate. This is because, in general, compared to individuals, society is more certain and less myopic about environmental projects. The flow of benefits from environmental projects tend to stretch over a long time horizon, with most of the benefits appearing towards the later stages of the projects' expected lifetimes while the short-term sacrifice (costs) is immediate and may be considerable.
- However, when the time horizon of a project under consideration is fairly long, as is the case for many environmental projects, the difference between private and social discount rates that are within the range of 3 to 5 per cent appears to be *irrelevant*. This is because discounting reduces benefits coming in the far distant future to virtually zero within a finite time, as long as the discounting rate is positive – however small it may be. Thus, what matters is the very fact that a *positive* discount rate is used.
- Furthermore, since discounting implies that gains and losses to society are valued less the more distant they are in the future, can the use of a positive discount rate be justified ethically?
- This question points to the unsettling issue of intergenerational equity. Further, since the choice of discount rate is made entirely by the current generation, the responsibility for resolving this ethical dilemma cannot be shifted to future

generations. What is significant is the one-sided nature of this intergenerational dependency.

- What is unsettling here is that, in principle, the current generation could take actions that have the potential to adversely affect the well-being of future generations without any fear of retribution. Should we care (on moral and ethical grounds) about the well-being of future generations? The answer to this question is clearly beyond the realm of economics unless, of course, the current generation wishes to identify itself with posterity to such an extent that its preference function is markedly influenced. If this is to happen then, as Boulding (1993: 306) put it, 'posterity has a voice, even if it does not have a vote; and in this sense, if it can influence votes, it has votes too'. By and large, neoclassical economists incline to the view that this is actually possible on the premise that casual observation of generational caring seems to indicate that the preference function of the current generation takes the interest of the future generations into account.

- On the other hand, there exists another school of thought (comprising scholars from diverse disciplinary backgrounds) that views discounting as unethical and, as such, should be reduced to *zero*. This position is defended, as explained in the chapter, by an ethical principle known as Rawlsian justice. The intent of this principle is to ensure that current generations are acting in a way that preserves the *ability* of future generations to maintain a standard of living that is enjoyed by current generations.

- Another method advocated as a means of addressing concern for the welfare of future generations is the precautionary principle. The application of precautionary principles is confined to situations where actions taken by current generations have or are suspected to have irreversible consequences with the potential (although uncertain) for large-scale degradation of natural capital that would severely limit the options of future generations, e.g. global warming. In such cases, the prudent course of action would be to err on the side of the unknown – entailing a clear bias towards protection of future generations. Note that under this condition (where the potential for irreversible outcome, although uncertain, exists) the application of cost–benefit analysis is rendered irrelevant.

- At the outset of this chapter, it was noted that cost–benefit analysis using the net present value criterion does not account for income distribution. Thus, strict application of cost–benefit analysis for the selection of waste sites and other noxious facilities (landfills, incinerators, and hazardous waste treatment, storage and disposal facilities) is likely to favor outcomes whereby these facilities are located in communities with high percentages of poor, elderly, young, and minority residents. In fact, several empirical studies seem to support claims that race and poverty are two important factors in the distribution of hazards. This a very important environmental issue with significant moral and ethical implications facing current generations. In the academic arena this issue is addressed under the heading of environmental justice.

- Three other methods used to evaluate public projects that were discussed in this chapter are cost-effectiveness analysis (CEA), environmental impact studies (EIS), and environmental risk assessment and risk management.

1   Cost-effectiveness analysis is used for environmental projects where their benefits are considered to be large, though difficult to measure in monetary

terms, and as such are worthwhile to undertake. The remaining issue is to find ways of realizing a project of this nature at the lowest possible cost.

2   Environmental impact analysis totally avoids placing money value on costs and benefits of environmental projects. Instead, EIA attempts to trace all the key physical and ecological factors (impacts) involved in an environmental project under consideration. EIA is performed by natural scientists and, if done well, could provide invaluable information to public agents authorized to make decisions on public projects, such as environmental projects.

3   Environmental assessment and risk management are two related instruments widely used in the area of environmental regulation. Risk assessment involves the process by which scientific data are analyzed to determine the nature of the risk or the likelihood of harm to human health or to the environment. How risky is the situation under consideration? As discussed in Chapter 8, economists often use results from risk assessment to impute monetary values for occupational risk, mortality and morbidity – important information in assessing the benefits of certain environmental projects.

   On the other hand, risk management involves the actual decision-making process after considering the outcomes from risk assessment fully and in conjunction with other relevant socioeconomic and technological information. It asks the question 'What should we do about it?'

Review and discussion questions

1   Briefly define the following concepts: 'actual' Pareto improvement, 'potential' Pareto improvement, capital budgeting, double counting, net present value, private discount rates, social discount rates, the discount factor, positive time preference, the precautionary principle, cost-effectiveness analysis, environmental impact analysis, Rawlsian justice, environmental justice, risk assessment, and risk management.

2   State whether the following are *true*, *false* or *uncertain* and explain why.

   (a) Double counting is a potentially serious problem often encountered in assessing both social and private projects

   (b) Addressing the concern for intergenerational fairness need not impoverish the current generation

   (c) There is no real difference between risk assessment and risk management.

3   Carefully explain the differences and/or similarities between the following pairs of concepts:

   (a) Capital budgeting and cost–benefit analysis

   (b) Net present value criterion and potential Pareto improvement

   (c) Private and social discount rates.

4   The state of Michigan has a surplus of $200 million in its budget for the fiscal year just ended. Several proposals have been examined for the use of this money, two of which are emerging as leading candidates for serious consideration. One of the favored projects is to use the entire surplus money for state-wide road repairs. This project is assumed to have an expected life of ten years. The alternative is a proposal to invest the entire $200 million in a long-overdue environmental cleanup.

The table below shows estimates of the flow of the net benefits for these two projects:

Project 1: Road repair		Project 2: Environmental cleanup	
Years	*Benefit/year*	*Years*	*Benefit/year*
1–5	$40 million	1–5	$5 million
6–10	$15 million	6–10	$15 million
		11–20	$35 million

(a) Using the net present value (NPV) approach, evaluate the two projects using a 5 per cent and 10 per cent discount rate.

(b) Would it make any difference which discount rate is used in the final selection between these two projects? Why, or why not?

(c) If the discount rate is reduced to zero, Project 2 will automatically be chosen. Why? Does this provide a clue why discounting is unfair? Explain.

References

Baumol, W. J. (1968) 'On the Social Rate of Discount', *American Economic Review* 58: 788–802.

Boulding, K. E. (1993) 'The Economics of the Coming Spaceship Earth', in H. E. Daly and K. N. Townsend (eds) *Valuing the Earth: Economics, Ecology, Ethics*, Cambridge, Mass.: MIT Press.

Bryant, B. and Mohai, P. (1992) *Race and the Incidence of Environmental Hazards: A Time for Discourse*, Boulder, Colorado; Westview Press.

Cline, W. R. (1992) *The Economics of Global Warming*, Washington, DC: Institute of International Economics.

Dixon, L. (1995) 'The Transaction Costs Generated by Superfund's Liability Approach', in R. Revesz and R. Stewart (eds), *Analyzing Superfund: Economic, Science, and Law*, Washington, DC: Resources for the Future.

General Accounting Office (1995) *Correspondence to Representative Don Young on Estimated Recovery Costs of Endangered Species*, Washington, DC, B-270461.

Metrick, A. and Weitzman, M. (1996) 'Patterns of Behavior in Endangered Species Preservation', *Land Economics* 72: 1–16.

Miller, T. G., Jr. (1991) *Environmental Science*, 3rd edn, Belmont, Calif.: Wadsworth.

Mishan, E. J. (1982) *Cost–Benefit Analysis*, 3rd edn, London: George Allen & Unwin.

——(1988) *Cost–Benefit Analysis*, 4th edn, London: George Allen & Unwin.

Montgomery, C., Brown, G., Jr. and Darius, M. (1994) 'The Marginal Cost of Species Preservation: The Northern Spotted Owl', *Journal of Environmental Economics and Management* 26: 111–28.

Nature Conservancy (1993) *Perspective on Species Imperilment: A Report from the Natural Heritage Data Center Network*, Arlington, VA: The Nature Conservancy.

Nordhaus, W. D. (1991) 'To Slow or Not to Slow: The Economics of Greenhouse Effect', *Economic Journal* 6, 101: 920–48.

Norgaard, R. B. and Howarth, R. B. (1992) 'Economics, Ethics, and the Environment', in J. M. Hollander (ed.) *The Energy–Environment Connection*, Washington, DC: Island Press.

Northeast-Midwest Institute and National Oceanic and Atmospheric Administration (2001) *Revealing the Economic Value of Protecting the Great Lakes*, Washington, DC.

Pearce, D. W. and Nash, C. A. (1981) *The Social Appraisal of Projects: A Text in Cost–Benefit Analysis*, New York: John Wiley.

Rubin, J., Helfand, G. and Loomis, J. (1991) 'A Benefit–Cost Analysis of the Northern Spotted Owl', *Journal of Forestry* 89: 25–30.

Sen, A. K. (1982) 'Approaches to the Choice of Discount Rates for Social Benefit–Cost Analysis', in R. Lind, K. J. Arrow, G. Corey *et al.* (eds) *Discounting for Time and Risk in Energy Policy*, Washington, DC: Resources for the Future.

Shogren, J. F. (1997) 'Economics and the Endangered Species Act', *Endangered Species Update*, School of Natural Resources and Environment, University of Michigan.

The United States Environmental Protection Agency (1992) 'Environmental Protection – Has It Been Fair?' *EPA Journal*, March/April issue.

US Fish and Wildlife Service (1990) *Report to Congress: Endangered and Threatened Species Recovery Program*, Washington, DC: US Government Printing Office.

Part 4

The perennial debate on biophysical limits to economic growth and the emerging paradigm of sustainable development

In the academic world, the nature and the extent of the relationship between biophysical limits and economic growth has been a subject of controversy for well over a century. In Part 4 of this book, which consists of four chapters (Chapters 10–13), the essence of this controversy is systematically and thoroughly examined. The order of presentation of these four chapters, in some respects, follows the historical development of the idea of limits to economic growth. In Chapters 10, 11 and 12, three alternative perspectives on biophysical limits to economic growth are explored, namely the Malthusian, the neoclassical, and that of ecological economics, respectively. In Chapter 13 the economics of sustainable development is examined.

The issue of scale is given a very inadequate treatment in most standard textbooks on environmental and resource economics. In general, topics that relate to this issue are placed toward the end of the text and tend to be discussed in a rather matter-of-fact style. In this book, the idea that there could be ecologically imposed limits to economic growth is taken seriously. The main questions addressed in Part 4 are as follows. Can we expect unlimited economic growth in a world endowed with 'finite' resources? If ecological limits are important factors in determining future trends of economic growth, what steps or precautions should be taken to avoid transgressing these biophysical limits? Clearly, the key issue here is *scale* – the size of the human economy relative to the natural environment. To that extent, the focus is not on efficiency but on *sustainability*.

Finally, I would claim that the thoroughness with which biophysical limits to economic growth are discussed and analyzed is the distinguishing feature of this book. In presenting the material in Part 4, a concerted effort has been made to remain neutral to the various views expressed on biophysical limits. It is to inform, not to advocate any particular viewpoint on biophysical limits, that the chapters in Part 4 have been written.

10 Biophysical limits to economic growth

The Malthusian perspective

> If the present growth trends in world population, industrialization, pollution, food production, and resource depletion continue unchanged, the limits to growth on this planet will be reached sometime within the next one hundred years. The most probable result will be a rather sudden and uncontrollable decline in both population and industrial capacity.
>
> (Meadows *et al.* 1974: 29)

10.1 Introduction

The designation 'Malthusian' here refers to a particular perspective on the association of resource scarcity and the prospect for long-run human economic growth. This perspective has a long history and traces its origin to the work of an English economist, Thomas R. Malthus (1766–1834) – hence the word Malthusian. The basic postulates of the Malthusian doctrine of resource scarcity and economic growth are as follows:

1 Resources are scarce in absolute terms. That is, humanity is endowed with a finite amount of material resources.
2 If uncontrolled, the tendency of human populations is to grow exponentially.
3 Technology should not be perceived as the 'ultimate' escape from the problem of resource scarcity.

Given these postulates, the Malthusians argue, economic activity cannot be expected to grow indefinitely unless the rates of population growth and/or the rate of resource utilization are effectively controlled. Limits to economic growth could come through either the depletion of key resources or large-scale degradation of the natural environment (Meadows *et al.* 1974).

This chapter offers a detailed examination of the Malthusian growth doctrine as it has evolved over time. In the next section, using a simple model, the essential elements of Malthus's original contributions to this doctrine are examined.

10.2 Population, resource scarcity and limits to growth: the simple Malthusian growth doctrine

The earliest attempt to explain systematically the effect of biophysical limits on human aspirations to improve living standards pointed to a historical association of population growth and the availability of food and other basic necessities of life. In 1798 Malthus published his book *An Essay on the Principle of Population as It Affects the Future Improvement of Mankind*, possibly the first formal theoretical underpinning of concern for the human population problem. In expounding his population–resource theory, Malthus set out three assumptions: (a) the total amount of land available for agriculture (arable land) is immutably fixed; (b) the growth of population is limited by the amount of food available for subsistence; and (c) human population will invariably increase where the means of subsistence increase.

He then stated that, if not prevented by some checks, the tendency is for the population to grow *geometrically* (2, 4, 8, 16, etc.) while the means of subsistence grows *arithmetically* (1, 2, 3, 4, etc.). Unless this tendency for an ever-increasing imbalance between the growth rates of population and of the means of subsistence is resolved by moral restraints (*negative checks* such as the postponement of marriage, abstinence from sex, etc.), in the long run vice and misery (*positive checks*) will ultimately suppress the reproductive power of a population to a level consistent with the means of subsistence. In other words, population growth, if left unchecked, would lead to the eventual decline of living standards to a level barely sufficient for survival. This has been called the 'dismal doctrine' of Malthus, or, more formally, Malthus's 'Iron Law of Wages'.

The essence of this doctrine can be further captured using a simple graphical approach, as shown in Figure 10.1. If we assume that quantity of labor, L, can be used as a proxy for population size and real output, Q/L, as a measure of per capita income, Figure 10.1 can be viewed as depicting the relationship between population size and per capita income. *This relationship is constructed assuming fixed amounts of resource (i.e. land) and technology*. Since the intent here is to offer an alternative explanation of the simple Malthusian model discussed above, let output, Q, represent agricultural or food products in general.

In Figure 10.1, per capita food output, Q/L, was initially rising with an increase in population. This positive association between population and per capita food production continued until the population size (labor force) reached L_1. Beyond this point, however, farm labor productivity (measured in terms of output per unit labor service) started to decline with each successive addition of labor service in accordance with the *law of diminishing marginal product*. That is, since fertile land is assumed to be fixed in supply, more labor applied to a given plot of a homogeneous quality of land or to a successively less fertile plot of land yields a proportionately smaller return (more on this in the next section). Hence, as the population increases and, accordingly, so does the demand for food and fiber, the production of any additional units of farm output requires progressively larger quantities of labor.

In Figure 10.1, $Q*/L*$ – the thick horizontal line – represents the output per unit of labor (or real wage rates) barely sufficient for survival, i.e. the subsistence level of food. Thus, when the labor force (i.e. the population) has increased to a level L_2, the Malthusian margin is attained. This will be a stable long-run equilibrium, because for a population below L_2, unless enforceable public policy measures are taken to limit population growth (i.e. negative checks), according to Malthus the natural tendency of the human population is to continue growing as long as the per capita food exceeds the minimum food required for a subsistence life – $Q*/L*$. On the other hand, any increase of population beyond L_2 would be prevented by positive checks, or, to use Malthus's terms, by 'vice and misery'. Thus, in the long run, disease, malnutrition and famine will bring growth to a halt at L_2. Finally, one interesting feature of this simple model is its suggestion of an *optimum* population size (labor force). In Figure 10.1, the optimum

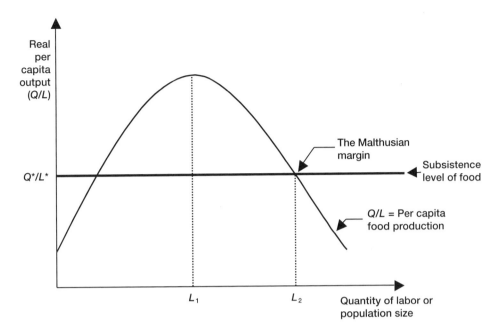

Figure 10.1 A simple Malthusian growth model. This model suggests that if no action is taken to control population, the natural tendency is for the population to grow to L_2 at which point per capita food production is reduced to a level just sufficient for subsistence. According to this model, L_1 may be considered the optimal level of population.

population size is attained at L_1, where the per capita food level (or real income) is at its maximum.

Of course, the Malthusian population–resource theory has been subjected to criticism from the very beginning for being too simplistic in several respects. First, it ignores the *institutional factors* that affect population growth. Humans do not just multiply like rabbits. There are social and economic factors that induce humans to check their own population growth under adverse conditions (Cole *et al.* 1973; Simon 1996).

Second, the Malthusian theory simply overlooks the very important role that *technology* plays in ameliorating resource scarcity (Cole *et al.* 1973; Ausubel 1996; Simon 1996). For example, according to the traditional Malthusian view, at a given point in time the amount of land available for food is perceived as fixed (or scarce in absolute terms). But through improvements in farming technology (e.g. developing new crop varieties using genetic engineering), it may be possible to produce more food from the same amount of land. In addition, technology may make farming possible in an area where it was impossible before. In Figure 10.1, the effect of a technological change, either through a discovery of new land or through improvement in farming, would be to shift the average product curve (Q/L) outward. Hence, this would move the 'Malthusian margin' to the right. In a sense, then, *the effect of technological change is to make the Malthusian margin a moving target*. However, this fact alone will not be sufficient to contradict Malthus's main assertion that, in the long run, humanity is predestined to life at subsistence level (Hardin 1993).

Exhibit 10.1   Feeding the world: less supply, more demand as summit convenes

Charles J. Hanley

Decade by decade, the land has provided – wheat fields, rice paddies, bulging silos of corn keeping pace with a growing world population. But now the grain harvests have leveled off, the people have not, and the world is left to wonder where next century's meals will come from. The blip in the upward slope of grain production in the 1990s has ready explanations: economics, politics and weather conspired to hold down global output.

But some specialists believe longer-range forces, from the Kansas prairie to China's river deltas, are also at work – and the outlook is troubling. Troubling enough, in Africa particularly, for the Food and Agriculture Organization to hold a global summit in Rome this week to search for new approaches to help poor nations grow, buy or otherwise get more food.

'We are in a crisis situation', said FAO chief Jacques Diouf. His UN agency projects world agricultural production must expand by 75 per cent by 2025 to match population growth. It's not off to a good start. New FAO figures show that the global grain harvest – forecast at 1,821 million tons for 1996–97 – will have increased by 2.3 per cent since 1990, while population was growing 10 per cent. . . . Because of this lag in production, grain prices rose and the world's buffer stocks of wheat, rice and other grains were drawn down. Reserves now stand at 277 million tons – some 40 million below what is needed to meet emergencies. A mix of factors helped stunt the decade's crops.

Lester Brown of Washington's Worldwatch Institute maintains that fertilizers and high-yield grain varieties have been pushed to their limit in many places. . . . [In addition] Worldwatch sees China as a huge problem. Shrinking croplands, rising incomes and a growing appetite for meat – an inefficient means for passing along the calories of grain – have combined to turn China, almost overnight, into the world's No. 2 grain importer, behind Japan. 'It is only a matter of time until China's grain import needs overwhelm the export capacity of the United States and other exporting countries', Brown contends.

On the broader, global point, the World Resource Institute, a Washington think tank, finds some agreement among major studies that birth rates may slow enough to allow a plodding agriculture to keep up with 'effective' demand – the demand from consumers with the money to buy. But that projection comes with asterisks attached: in Africa and other poor regions without that money, hundreds of millions will remain underfed.

To Luther Tweeten, the outcome is far from clear. Looking ahead to 2030, the Ohio State University agricultural economist stacked the global trend in per-acre yield – rising ever more slowly – up against UN population projections. The yields lose out. 'I don't want to take a Lester Brown approach on this', Tweeten said, but the world cannot be complacent. 'It's daunting.'

The FAO estimates 800 million people are undernourished worldwide, at a time when high prices have undercut international food aid, slicing it in half since 1993 to today's 7.7 million tons of grain a year. The summit will try to encourage increased aid, stepped-up research and pro-agriculture policies in Africa and other food-short regions.

But Brown sees another solution – population control. 'I think we're now in a new situation where the primary responsibility for balancing food and people lies with family planners, rather than fishermen and farmers', he said. 'And I don't think the world has quite grasped that yet.'

Source: Kalamazoo (MI), *Kalamazoo Gazette/The Associated Press*, November 10, 1996. Copyright © 1996 The Associated Press. Reprinted by permission.

Third, Malthus's model is considered to be *ecologically naive*. That is, it does not go beyond recognizing the existence of absolute limits to natural resources (land), and thereby fails to explain the effect of economic growth on natural ecosystems and their inhabitants as a whole. Thus, the simple Malthusian theory on population and resource is viewed as *incomplete* from economic, technological and ecological perspectives.

Despite its simplicity, however, Malthus's theory of population and resources and, in particular, his gloomy prediction about the long-run economic destiny of humankind, has remained a subject of vigorous contention even to this day. On the one hand, it would be easy to dismiss the theory and its predictions on the ground that almost two hundred years have passed since the formal pronouncement of Malthus's gloomy prophecy, and yet our experience has been characterized by rapid growth in both resource use and population, along with significant improvements in material standards of living on a per capita basis. On the other hand, it is difficult to completely dismiss Malthus since the main thrust of his dismal forecast is still applicable and of major concern to most developing and underdeveloped nations of the world. In this sense, after two hundred years, the Malthusian specter is still with us (for some recent evidence see Exhibit 10.1).

10.3 Limits to growth: the Ricardian variation

David Ricardo (1772–1823), another distinguished English economist, was one of the earliest critics of Malthus's doctrine on population and resource scarcity. He objected not to Malthus's gloomy prophecy of the future condition of human material progress, but rather to the emphasis Malthus had given to population. For Ricardo, human material progress would not be hampered in the long run by explosive growth of human population as Malthus had envisioned *but by the progressive decline in the quality and quantity of extractive resources, most importantly, agricultural land.* What follows is an explanation for this alternative view on resource scarcity and its implications for long-run economic growth.

Agricultural land varies in its natural productive capacity – its fertility. For agricultural land (and for that matter, for most extractive resources, such as coal, gold, fisheries, and so on), the normal pattern tends to be to extract these resources sequentially in accordance with quality and accessibility. Plots of land with high natural fertility (or mines containing high-grade ores) are put to use first because their *real cost* is low. Real cost is defined here as the amount of labor, capital and other resources needed to make a farmland available for cultivation.

To illustrate this point and its broader implications, in Figure 10.2, the horizontal line P_0–A represents the *long-run* supply curve of available farmland that is of high and uniform quality (in terms of fertility). A maximum amount (measured either in acres or hectares) C_0 of this quality of land is assumed to exist. A second segment of the supply curve is represented by another horizontal line B–C. This parallel upward shift of the supply curve from P_0–A to B–C reflects the increase in real cost arising from the change in the quality of the land – from fertile to marginal farmland. A total amount $(C_1 - C_0)$ of marginal land is presumed to be available for use. The land available beyond C_1 is considered submarginal in terms of its fertility (quality) and line E–F represents the supply curve for this type of land. It is assumed that there is no apparent constraint on the amount of submarginal land available for use.

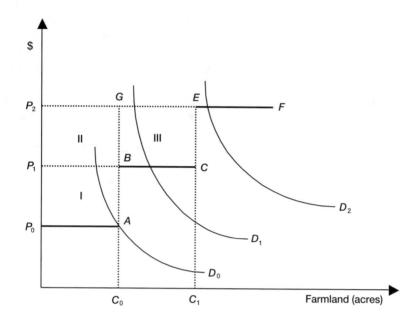

Figure 10.2 Ricardian scarcity. Essentially, this model shows that successive increases in demand (D_0, D_1, D_2, etc.) are met with corresponding increases in resource prices (P_0, P_1, P_2, etc.) due to successive decline in the quality of extractive resources, such as farmland.

If the demand for farmland remains at D_0 or below, consideration of cost will favor the use of land from the first category only – fertile land. P_0 represents the equilibrium market price for a unit of farmland of this quality. This price also represents the real cost to owners of making a unit of their farmland available for cultivation. If this is the case, there will be no difference between what the owners of the land receive as income and the cost of making the land available for cultivation. That is, the owners receive zero *rent*. *Rent is defined at the total payment to owners of a factor of production (in this case farmland) in excess of the minimum price necessary to bring the resource available for use.*

With the above analysis in mind, from Figure 10.2 it can easily be seen that both *real cost* and *rent* increase as demand for farmland grows and progressively inferior land is brought into cultivation. There is an increase in real cost from P_0 to P_1 as demand increases from D_0 to D_1, likewise from P_1 to P_2 as demand further increases from D_1 to D_2. This increase in real cost simply reflects the fact that progressively more resources (in terms of labor, capital and so on) are needed to cultivate a unit of land as the quality (fertility) of the available land continues to decline.

How did the increase in rent come about? This is rather more subtle than the increase in real cost discussed above. To see it, let us notice what happens to rent when the demand for farmland increases from D_0 to D_1. This would necessitate the cultivation of marginal land and the increase in real cost or price of land from P_0 to P_1. Now as a result of this development, owners of farmland of superior grade will start to earn rent since their cost is still P_0, while the market price for farmland is now P_1. This will suggest that owners of the fertile land collectively will earn a total rent as represented by the area P_0P_1BA (or the area of the rectangle I). It is important to recognize that this rent is attributable solely to differences in the quality of land.

Similarly, when demand is further increased to D_2, the total rent to owners of the fertile land increases from area P_0P_1BA to P_0P_2GA or the combined areas of rectangles I and II. In addition, the owners of the marginal land are now able to realize rent that is measured by area $BCEG$ (or the area of rectangle III). Thus, as a result of the shift in demand from D_1 to D_2, the total rent has increased from area P_0P_1BA (the area of rectangle I) to area P_0P_2ECBA (or the area of rectangles I + II + III).

The above observation is the essence of what is known in modern economics literature as the *Ricardian scarcity*. It suggests a steady increase in rent (and real cost) as quality of land (or any other extractive resources) decline. *According to Ricardo, it is the steady increase in rent as land use expands that would ultimately stifle human long-term economic progress. In this particular context, to Ricardo, population is relevant only to the extent it has an effect on what happens to demand.*

Essentially, then, for Ricardo the major impediment to human material progress would emerge not so much from demand as rather from supply side constraints. This was a hotly debated issue between Malthus and Ricardo, and was responsible for producing several written exchanges that are still of significant interest to economic historians.

An important caveat should be stated here. Ricardo did not develop his theory of rent and scarcity to suggest a biophysical limit to economic growth. His motivation was actually aimed at demonstrating that the primary beneficiaries of the Corn Laws, which artificially restricted the import of agricultural products into England at a time when both population and demand for farm products were growing, were the landlords – who were the rent seekers. By implication, Ricardo was also suggesting that landlords stifle growth through their rent-seeking behavior.

10.4 Population, resource use and the environment: the neo-Malthusian variations

Over time, the Malthusian theory of population and resources has undergone several refinements. Responding to the criticisms raised by both economists and ecologists, neo-Malthusians have been able to develop conceptual models that incorporate the effects not only of population and resource scarcity but also of technology and human institutions in their consideration of environmental sustainability. *In this sense the emphasis has been shifted from concerns about limits to economic growth to worries about environmental sustainability.*

This being the case, a systematic analysis of the adverse impacts of (or damage caused by) human activities (production and consumption) on the function of the natural environment is a major common characteristic of neo-Malthusian conceptual models. In this new worldview, as discussed in Chapters 1 and 2, the services of the environment are recognized, not only as supplier of raw materials and energy as factor of production (the main concerns of Malthus and Ricardo) but also as assimilator of wastes and provider of amenities, along with the maintenance of life-support systems.

The usual expectation has been that increased human activities would lead to increasing stress on the functioning of the environment and in so doing ultimately lead to environmental degradation. This could result from either emitting too much waste into the environment, and/or exploiting the natural environment to the point of approaching or transcending ecological thresholds (such as overfishing, large-scale deforestation, overgrazing, etc.). This is a concern because, if degradation of the environment is not restricted to the point that it is considered *sustainable*, biophysical limits will eventually place bounds on the growth of human activity. It is this recognition of possible biophysical limits to human activities that identifies neo-Malthusians with Malthus's doctrine of economic growth.

As elucidated above, the issue of environmental sustainability is central to neo-Malthusians. Addressing concern about environmental sustainability amounts to finding ways to understand and remedy environmental degradation. Conceptually this is done by constructing models that attempt to incorporate variables that are expected to be key determinants of environmental degradation and, most importantly, by analyzing in what specific ways these identified variables individually and collectively manifest their impacts on the environment. The essence of these models can be illustrated using a general conceptual framework that hereafter will be referred to as the Ehrlich–Commoner model (Ehrlich and Holdren 1971; Commoner *et al.* 1971).

The Ehrlich–Commoner model starts with the postulate that all human activities modify the natural environment to some extent. In its simplest form, this model can be expressed mathematically as:

$$I = P \times F \tag{10.1}$$

Here I is the total environmental effect or damage, measured in some standard units. It can be expressed in a variety of ways: the amount of resources extracted or harvested annually; the total land area subjected to deforestation in a given year; the amount of waste discharged into the environment yearly; the surface area of land inundated by mining activities in a given year; the rate at which some key non-renewable resources (such as fossil fuels) are depleted; the rate of species extinction; etc. Although the variable I is assumed measurable, given the above examples it will not be hard to see the difficulty of attempting to construct an index (or a single measuring unit) that is expected to capture all the various types of environmental damage caused by human activities.

In Equation (10.1), P is the population size in terms of head count. From the outset it is assumed that more people cause more environmental damage, or mathematically, $dI/dP > 0$; i.e. there is a positive correlation between population size and environmental damage.

Finally, F is an index that measures the per capita impact (or damage) to the environment. In the above equation it enters simply as I/P. One way to view this is as the *ecological footprint* of the *average* person. As will be observed shortly, this is a very important variable and provides interesting insights when it is discussed in combination with other variables, such as per capita consumption or income, and the technology by which inputs and outputs are processed.

What exactly does Equation (10.1) tell us? This equation states that, at any given point in time, the total environmental impact of human activities is a product of the under-lying population size, P, and the per capita damage to the environment. In other words, *total environmental impact equals total population multiplied by the average impact that each person has on the environment.* Viewed this way, the Ehrlich–Commoner equation is an indisputable mathematical identity or a truism.

To get useful insights from this equation, we need to go beyond the recognition of this simple identity. This can be done by making an effort to fully examine the inter-relationships between the two key variables, population P and per capita impact F, and by examining how economics, social and technological variables may have effects on the ecological footprint of the average person, F.

In other words, a good deal of complexity is masked in the apparently simple Ehrlich–Commoner model. To make this model more revealing and of some practical value, we need to further examine per capita impact F as a separate function that is affected by several key variables, as expressed below:

$$F = f[P, c, g] \tag{10.2}$$

where c = per capita consumption or production, and at aggregate level consumption and production are assumed to be equal and measured by *real* per capita domestic product, *GDP/P*. The general expectation is that, holding other factors constant, increase in per capita consumption (income) would lead to increasing degradation of the environment on a per capita basis (or, mathematically $\partial f / \partial c > 0$). *This can be attributed to the expectation that a rise in the average person's income (on a per capita basis) would lead not just to increased consumption but also to consumption patterns that are characterized by incrementally higher levels of material and energy intensity.*

In Equation (10.2), g is the composition of inputs and outputs in an economy, expressed in terms of their impact on the environment. This variable is influenced by technological factors, such as the structure of the existing modes of production (i.e. input and output transformation and processing) and consumption (i.e. marketing and distribution of goods and services), and by institutional arrangements, such as the way property rights are assigned and enforced. According to Commoner the variable *g can be viewed as an index that measures damage in terms of per unit of output.* Furthermore, Commoner postulated that the association between g and I is *positive*, since according to him past technological modes of production and institutional settings have been increasingly damaging to the environment (more on this later).

Thus, when we take Equations (10.1) and (10.2) together, *we see that the total environmental impact, I, of human activities depends on total population, P, and a host of other interrelated variables affecting the per capita damage function.* Given this, the challenge before us is to explain, in systematic fashion, the relative significance of the key variables in these two related equations in terms of their contributions to the total environmental impact, I. For example, is population the major contributor to environ-mental degradation? To what extent would an increase in per capita consumption of resources adversely impact the environment? What have been the dominant effects of modern technology on the environment? Can technology contribute to further environmental deterioration? The next four subsections will address these specific questions, for they have important policy implications.

10.4.1 Population as a primary factor in environmental degradation and resource depletion: the Ehrlich perspective

According to Paul Ehrlich, population plays a primary role in explaining the impact human activities have on the environment and resource use. He argues that when population grows, the total impact, I, increases for two reasons. First, the size of the

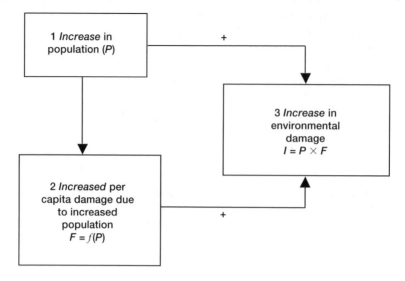

Figure 10.3 A graphical illustration of Ehrlich's model. According to this model, the impact
of population growth on the environment has primary and secondary impacts in
the same direction – suggesting that the negative impact of population growth is
far greater than what it may appear to be when only factors associated with the
primary impact are considered.

population, P, will increase. Second, for reasons to be explained below, per capita
impact, F, increases with successive additions to population, P. [Hence, according to
Ehrlich, mathematically the association of population and per capita impact would
imply that $F = f(P)$ and $dF/dP > 0$. Therefore, according to Equation (10.1), the total
impact increases since both P and F grow with growth of population.] This is illustrated
in Figure 10.3.

Why is the per capita damage, F, an increasing function of population? Ehrlich gave
the *law of diminishing marginal returns* as a plausible explanation of this. He argued that
most of the developed nations' economies are already operating at high levels of
production capacity. These nations are, therefore, on the diminishing returns part
of their production functions. Under these circumstances, if other factors are held
constant, successive addition of people would require increased use of resources, such
as energy, water, fertilizer, pesticides, and other renewable and nonrenewable resources.
Thus, as a population continued to grow, the per capita impact, in terms of resource
depletion and environmental deterioration, would increase successively.

Furthermore, the same argument can be made for the agricultural sectors of most
developing countries. For most of these nations, the agricultural sector accounts for a
significant percentage of their economy, and diminishing returns would be encountered
because of the limited availability (in both quality and quantity terms) of farmland.

In the final analysis, Ehrlich and his followers would contend that rising human
population is the predominant factor in accelerating pollution and other resource
problems, in both the developed and developing nations of the world. There have been
some empirical studies that support this hypothesis (Allen and Barnes 1995; Repetto

and Holmes 1983; Rudel 1989). In his empirical investigation on the causes of deforestation, Thomas K. Rudel (1989: 336) reported as one of his findings: 'The analysis provides empirical support for the Malthusian idea that population growth contributes to high rates of deforestation both directly (by increasing the population which clears the land) and indirectly (by increasing the demand for wood products in a country).'

The major weakness of the position advanced by Ehrlich is that many of the factors already identified as having an effect on per capita impact, F, such as per capita consumption of resources and technology are held constant. Furthermore, no explanation is given as to why these factors should have neutral or insignificant effects on per capita damage, F. Thus, in the next subsection an attempt will be made to examine the validity of Ehrlich's theory of population and the environment when explicit consideration is given to changes in per capita consumption. This will be followed by a consideration of technology.

10.4.2 *Affluence and its contribution to environmental degradation*

Per capita consumption, c, refers to the amount of goods and services consumed per person, per unit of time – generally a calendar year. At the aggregate level, consumption can be viewed as being equivalent to production. Thus, per capita consumption may be used as a measure of the well-being or affluence of the average person. Would a change in per capita consumption, c, directly and significantly affect the per capita impact, F? This is really an empirical question, but let us first provide a conceptual explanation of the expected relationship between per capita consumption, c, and per capita impact, F.

If population and technology are held constant, an increase in per capita consumption could only result from increased use of resources. Increased resource utilization implies increased production, and in the absence of technological progress this would translate into increased pollution and perhaps resource depletion. Furthermore, as stated earlier, holding other factors constant, increase in per capita consumption (income) may encourage a change in consumption patterns that are characterized with incrementally higher level of material and energy intensity. Thus, in general, we would expect that an increase in per capita consumption would be associated with increased per capita damage (see Figure 10.4). This observation has a number of interesting implications.

First, suppose that as proposed by Ehrlich, the per capita damage, F, is an increasing function of population, P. Then, an increase in per capita consumption, c, reinforces the negative impact that a population increase has on per capita damage to the environment. In this case, because population, P, and per capita consumption, c, affect the per capita damage function, F, in the same direction (see Figure 10.4), it would be difficult to isolate the independent effects of these two variables (P and c) on the per capita damage function, F, without undertaking a full-blown empirical test. *This poses a serious challenge to Ehrlich's unequivocal assertion that population growth is the single most dominant factor in explaining the total environmental impact*, I. In other words, one cannot relegate the impact of per capita consumption, c, to a minor role, as Ehrlich seems to have done, without solid empirical evidence.

Second, as stated above, if an increase in per capita consumption, c, leads to an increase in per capita damage to the environment, F, *it is easy to envision a situation where the total environmental impact, I, may be increasing while population, P, remains*

Table 10.1 Share of population, resource consumption and waste production, in percentages

Country	Population	Fossil fuel consumption	Metal	Paper	Hazardous waste
US	5	25	20	33	72
Other developed countries	17	35	60	42	18
Developing countries	78	40	20	25	10

Source: *World Population and the Environment: A Data Sheet for the Population Reference Bureau*, Copyright 1997. Reprinted by permission of the Population Reference Bureau.

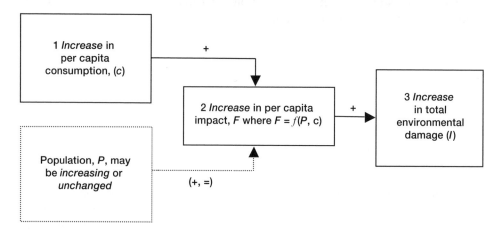

Figure 10.4 Per capita consumption and its effect on the environment. Increase in per capita consumption has an effect on the environment that is independent of population increases.

unchanged or even declining. In other words, in Equation (10.1), *P* and *F* may move in opposite directions, causing uncertainty about the direction of the total impact, *I*. This supports the argument often made that the main culprit of environmental deterioration and resource depletion is overconsumption or affluence (Durning 1992). If this has any validity, it suggests that some of the most serious global environmental problems have been caused by the phenomenal growth in per capita resource consumption in the developed countries (see Table 10.1 above).

10.4.3 Technology and its contribution to environmental degradation: the Commoner perspective

In the Ehrlich–Commoner model the effect of technology on the environment is captured by variable *g* in Equation (10.2). The motivation for introducing this variable in the environmental damage model arises from the recognition that in some intellectual circles, modern technology is viewed as being the main cause of environmental problems primarily emanating from the developed countries. More specifically, the assortment of economic activities pursued by a country, and the resulting composition of production and consumption in response to population pressure, could significantly intensify the resource and environmental problems for that country. Barry Commoner has been the leading advocate of this position.

Commoner's position with respect to modern technology needs to be differentiated from that of Ehrlich, however. Ehrlich has little faith in 'technological fixes' because he believes that most industrial countries are already in the diminishing returns part of their economic activities. In other words, technological fixes suffer from limitation of certain key resources. On the other hand, *Commoner views modern technology as being ill-conceived and not wisely applied in the production of goods and services.* Why is Commoner taking this position? What evidence does he rely upon?

In order to understand Commoner's anti-technological position, it is important to understand that technical progress is often attained by changing the composition, or mix, of inputs and outputs for an economy. According to Commoner, the decision to change the composition of economic inputs and outputs is made purely on the basis of profit motives. Therefore, input and output decisions are based on technical efficiency (increased per capita production), rather than the impact on the environment these decisions may have. To illustrate this, consider how Commoner (1971: 101) depicted the outcome of technical progress in industrial countries. In their rush to increase productivity, industrial countries have been engaged in excessive use of 'synthetic organic chemicals and the products made from them, such as detergents, plastics, synthetic fibers, rubbers, pesticide and herbicide, wood pulp and paper products; total production of energy, especially electric power; total horsepower of prime movers, especially petroleum-driven vehicles; cements; aluminum; mercury used for chlorine production; petroleum and petroleum products'. This suggests that changes in the composition of material inputs and outputs, variable g in Equation (10.2), have the effect of increasing the per capita damage to the environment, F. Thus, according to Commoner, technological responses to population pressure (increase in P) invariably lead to increased total environmental damage, I (since $I = P \times F$). Furthermore, to Commoner, the most significant portion of total environmental damage in contemporary industrial countries arises not from population increases, P, but from increases in per capita impact, F, resulting from changes in the mix of inputs and outputs, g.

This is indeed a serious indictment of modern technology, and it requires an empirical justification. Aware of this, Commoner made a serious effort to substantiate his thesis on technology and the environment using data from the United States for the period 1946–68. On the basis of this data analysis, he reached the conclusion that 'the predominant factor in our industrial society's increased environmental degradation is neither population, nor affluence (per capita consumption), but the increasing environmental impact per unit of production due to technological changes' (Commoner *et al.* 1971: 107). Moreover, Commoner *et al.* made the following general observations:

> On these grounds it might be argued as well that the stress of a rising human population on the environment is especially intense in a country such as the United States, which has an advanced technology. For it is modern technology which extends man's effects on the environments for air, food and water. It is technology that produces smog and smoke; synthetic pesticides, herbicides, detergents, plastics;

rising environmental concentrations of metals such as mercury and lead; radiation, heat; accumulating rubbish and junk.

(Ibid.: 97)

Of course, the above quotation is somewhat dated, and for this reason its relevance for our current situation may be questioned. However, even at the present time there exists a widely held belief that modern technology has been more successful in shifting the environmental impact than in removing it. Indeed, over the past two decades most industrial countries have been able to ameliorate some of their environmental problems, especially at the local and regional levels. No doubt, stricter environmental regulation and advances in emission-control technologies have played a major part in making such environmental improvements possible. However, in some cases a closer look at some of the technological solutions that brought relief to local pollution problems suggests these same solutions have caused pollution problems that cross regional and international boundaries. For example, requiring coal-burning electric power plants in the Midwest to install higher smoke stacks might alleviate local pollution problems, but improvement in the local environment would be achieved at the expense of increased acid precipitation in the northeastern United States and in Canada (Soroos 1997). In essence, then, in the new era the scope of environmental and resource concerns is becoming increasingly global, as are issues like ozone holes, global warming, tropical deforestation, and depletion of well-known commercial fish species. Furthermore, as recently as 1998, a report by the US President's Committee of Advisors on Science and Technology (PCAST) expressed a concern that seems to support Commoner's view:

> . . . the composition and scale of economic activities in the United States are changing the chemistry of the nation's land, water, and atmosphere so dramatically that some of these changes are adversely affecting its natural capital and, thus, the ecosystem services required to support its population.

(Dasgupta *et al.* 2000: 339)

10.4.4 The basic lessons of the Ehrlich–Commoner model

The Ehrlich–Commoner model was introduced to show the fundamental positions of neo-Malthusians regarding the link between environmental sustainability and economic growth. It is safe to say that the neo-Malthusian starts with a view that the current rate of world economic growth, measured in terms of GDP, cannot be environmentally sustainable. Given this initial position, the major issues of interest have been to identify the causes and possible remedies for the ills (damages) that have been inflicted on the natural environment from various forms of human activity over the past century.

In general, the Ehrlich–Commoner model seems to suggest that *neo-Malthusians would tend to claim that the steady increases in population and per capita consumption and the proliferation of products that are harmful to the environment are the three major factors contributing to continued global environmental degradation.* In spite of this, as noted in earlier discussions, there seems to be no consensus on the relative impacts these three key variables have on the environment. For example, Ehrlich and his followers would contend that rising human population is a predominant factor in accelerating pollution and other resource problems in both the developed and the developing countries of the world. On the other hand, for Commoner and his associates, population growth plays only a minor role in explaining the environmental and resource condition of the modern era, especially in the economically advanced regions of the world. Instead, Commoner and his associates believe that a major part of environmental damage results from inappropriate applications of modern technologies in the extraction, production and consumption sectors of the economy. This is because technological choices are often made purely on the basis of profitability considerations rather than environmental sustainability. Finally, for some others such as Durning, it is wasteful consumption habits supported by raising per capita income (affluence) that is the major culprit for worsening global environmental conditions.

The policy implications of the neo-Malthusian positions are quite clear. In general, their policies are directed to achieving some combination of the following: (i) control population growth; (ii) moderate or reduce per capita resource use; and (iii) promote the development of technologies that are environmentally benign. To achieve these ends, by and large, the natural inclination of neo-Malthusians is to use policy instruments that permit *direct* government intervention, i.e. they do not rule out the use of 'coercive' methods as a means of ameliorating environmental degradation (Hardin 1993). This could include formal and effectively enforced legal sanctions such as fines or imprisonment. Examples of policy measures that would be favored by neo-Malthusian include ending environmentally damaging subsidies by government decree, penalizing wasteful consumption habits by means of income redistribution, implementing family planning programs with considerable governmental supervision, providing subsidies to promote the development of environmentally benign technology such as solar energy, putting broadly based strict quotas on the amount of fish to be harvested or forest area to be cleared on an annual basis, and so on.

In general, neo-Malthusians are skeptical about the notion that all resource allocation problems can be solved by market or extra-market mechanisms. Their skepticism is based on the general tendency of the private market, as discussed in Chapter 3, toward overexploitation and degradation of resources that are externality-ridden, as are environmental resources. In addition, as elucidated above, neo-Malthusians take the position that not all technological changes favor the environment. For this reason, they insist that environmental sustainability requires specific consideration of the impacts new technologies have on the environment, not just on the production and delivery of goods and service. As the material in Exhibit 10.2 suggests, technology is a two-edged sword, and if we are not careful, application of ill-conceived technology could do further harm, rather than solve environmental and resource problems.

It may be instructive to conclude the discussion in this section with a brief mention of *four* glaring weaknesses of the neo-Malthusian worldview regarding the environment and resource scarcity in general. First, the neo-Malthusian model in its Ehrlich–Commoner variations focuses on environmental sustainability but without clearly defining what this 'sustainability' is all about. The concept of sustainability did not come into clear focus until the late 1980s, a development that seemed to coincide with the emergence of a new school of economics – ecological economics. This will be discussed at some length in Chapter 12. Second, neo-Malthusians seem to down-play (or to ignore) the potential for resource conservation through technological means, such as factor substitution and technical progress. On the other hand, according to the neo-classical economic worldview, these constitute various technological means (i.e. economies of scale, factor substitution and technical progress) by which long-term global environmental and other resource scarcity problems could be alleviated or even

---

Exhibit 10.2   Beyond Shiva

Garrett Hardin

If, as European folk wisdom has it, each new mouth brings with it a pair of hands, how are we to view the fantastic changes brought about by the industrial–scientific revolution of the past two hundred years or so? Have we not now reached a stage at which each new mouth comes into the world with more than a single pair of hands? The woolgathering mind may recall statues of the Indian god Shiva, with his many (most commonly four) lively arms and busy hands.

If scientists were inclined to take up new gods (which they are not), Shiva would be a fine one for representing science and technology ('custom' in Bacon's language). Even before Malthus, technology began to increase the output of human hands (through such inventions as the wheelbarrow), but the change did not catch people's attention for a long time. Everyone is aware of it now. Especially in the developed world it has become obvious that material income per capita has increased greatly. The Shiva of Western technology is indeed a many-handed god.

As the beneficiaries of more than two centuries of rapid growth of science and technology, the masses cannot easily be persuaded that they should be worried about the future of population and the environment. Yet we would do well to remember that the Hindus' Shiva is a god of both creation and destruction. It is not without reason that we perceive a many-handed god as uncanny and frightening.

Source: *Living Within Limits: Ecology, Economics, and Population Taboos* (1993: 100–1). Copyright © 1993 by Oxford University Press, Inc. Reprinted by permission.

---

rectified (more on this in Chapter 11). Third, it has been argued that neo-Malthusian conceptual models and empirical analyses are constructed on the basis of an understanding of resources, consumption and population only at an aggregate level and most often without adequate reflection on the social, technological and political aspects of resource use (Davidson 2000). Davidson even went so far as to claim that 'viewing technology, consumption, and all social variables as fixed is implicit in the limits perspective' (ibid. 438). A case in point is the neo-Malthusian application of the concept of carrying capacity (the maximum population that can be sustained by the available resource in any given area) to human society. Fourth, the neo-Malthusian emphasis on physical limits and the catastrophe that awaits if the limits are transgressed has not been politically useful (ibid.). This is how Davidson expressed his concern about this matter:

> Environmentalists have often predicted impending catastrophe (e.g. oil depletion, absolute food shortages and mass starvation, or biological collapse). This catastrophism is ultimately damaging to the cause of environmental protection. First, predictions of catastrophe, like the boy who cries wolf, at first motivate people's concern, but when the threat repeatedly turns out to be less severe than predicted, people ignore future warnings. Second, the belief in impending catastrophe has in the past led some environmentalists to report withholding food and medical aid to poor nations (Hardin 1972), forced sterilization (Ehrlich 1968),

and other repressive measures. Not only are these positions repulsive from a social justice perspective, they also misdirect energy away from real solutions.

(2000 438)

10.5 Has Malthus been discredited?

Malthus and his followers are often labeled as doomsayers because of their persistent pronouncement of gloom and doom regarding human economic conditions in the distant future. More specifically, Malthusians of all stripes are of one mind in their belief that biophysical limits to economic growth are real, and they continue to support this hypothesis with numerous studies.

In the early 1970s, using computer simulations, the authors of a highly controversial book, *The Limits to Growth* (Meadows *et al.* 1971), clearly illustrated various scenarios under which the industrial world would encounter limits. The basic conclusion of the book was used as the epigraph to this chapter. To repeat it, 'If the present growth trends in world population, industrialization, pollution, food production, and resource depletion continue unchanged, the limits to growth on this planet will be reached some-time within the next one hundred years. The most probable result will be a rather sudden and uncontrollable decline in both population and industrial capacity' (p. 29). Although controversial, the frightful warning of the book was taken seriously, as it reflected the consensus view of a group of influential scientists and world leaders. A decade later, in response to the energy crisis of the late 1970s, a study was commissioned by the administration of President Carter to provide a thorough and comprehensive assessment of global resource adequacy. The final outcome of this study was published, under the title *The Global 2000 Report to the President* (Council on Environmental Quality and the Department of State 1980: 1). The major conclusions of this report read as follows:

> If present trends continue, the world in 2000 will be more crowded, more polluted, less stable ecologically, and more vulnerable to disruption than the world we live in now. Serious stresses involving population, resources, and environment are clearly visible ahead. Despite greater material output, the world's people will be poorer in many ways than they are today.
>
> For hundreds of millions of the desperately poor, the outlook for food and other necessities of life will be no better. For many it will be worse. Barring revolutionary advances in technology, life for most people on Earth will be more precarious in 2000 than it is now – unless the nations of the world act decisively to alter current trends.

Clearly, this report basically echoed the conclusion reached a decade earlier by *The Limits to Growth*. In addition, there are a number of other more recent empirical studies that reinforce the general conclusions reached by *The Global 2000 Report to the President*. In particular, it is worth mentioning the various publications periodically issued by the Worldwatch Institute – an independent nonprofit environmental resource organization. These publications include the annual *State of the World*, which is now published in 27 languages; *Vital Signs*, an annual compendium of global trends of key environmental and natural resource variables; the *Environmental Alert* book series; *World Watch* magazine; and the *Worldwatch Papers* series. The Worldwatch Institute is guided by its able and energetic leader, Lester Brown, and the primary aim of this private establishment's publications is to provide in-depth quantitative and qualitative analysis of the major issues affecting prospects for a sustainable society.

Most recently, one of the main themes of the Second World Summit on Sustainable Development in Johannesburg (September 2002) was poverty alleviation. This is what the UN secretary general, Koffe Annan, had to say about current trends in development: 'Let us face the uncomfortable truth. The model of development we are accustomed to has been fruitful for the few, but flawed for the many. A path to prosperity that ravages the environment and leaves a majority of humankind behind in squalor will soon prove to be a dead-end road for everyone' (*Earthtrends*, News for August 2002).

Based on the above evidences, it is quite difficult to reject Malthus's prophecy of doom and gloom. However, to dwell on this seemingly rhetorical issue would be missing the real point. The question to be addressed is, given the current state of the world, how should we deal with the existence of the seemingly perennial Malthusian specter? To most scholars of a Malthusian persuasion, the problem cannot be adequately addressed until we fully recognize the existence of biophysical limits to continued improvements in material living standards. Once this fact is acknowledged, the remedy to this age-old problem will be quite apparent. Specifically, as discussed earlier, economic growth that is sustainable far into the future will *necessitate the design and implementation of social and technological conditions that ensure both environmental and economic stability concurrently*. Unfortunately, Malthusians address this important issue in too much generality. They have often been more successful in alarming the public with their prophecy of economic collapse than in offering a clear understanding of the underlying causes of environmental destruction. Could it be that the neo-classical economics paradigm of limits provides a more concrete and pragmatic understanding of the association between economic growth and environmental degradation than the Malthusians'? The search for the answer to this question is the primary motivation for the next chapter, Chapter 11.

10.6 Chapter summary

•   This chapter has dealt with analyses from the Malthusian perspective on 'general' resource scarcity and its implications for the long-term material well-being of humanity.

•   This perspective has a long history. It starts from the premise that natural resources are finite and, therefore, will eventually limit the progress of the human economy. This assertion is explained using theoretical models devised by Thomas Malthus and David Ricardo. The major difference between the two models is that Malthus views exponential population growth as the major determinant of biophysical limits whereas Ricardo attributed the limits to gradual decrease in the quality of arable land.

•   The general ideas espoused by recent followers of Malthus were illustrated using the so-called Ehrlich–Commoner model. As a whole, this model considers population, technology and per capita consumption as the main determinants of environmental degradation and eventual limits to economic growth. A lively debate continues among present-day Malthusians (or neo-Malthusians) regarding which of these three variables is the most important culprit for modern-day environmental crises and/or rapid depletion of some key, but conventionally identified, natural resources (such as oil, gas, arable land, uranium, etc.).

•   In general, Malthusians are skeptical about the ability of technology to circumvent biophysical limits for two reasons:

 1   They believe that technological progress is subject to diminishing returns.
 2   They are mindful of the long-run costs of technological cures. Some, such as Commoner, even take the position that malign technologies are the major culprit in the modern environmental crisis.

•   In terms of public policy measures, Malthusians tend to consider population control as the key step. They advocate offering subsidies to encourage the development of production techniques and consumer products that are environmental friendly. They encourage investment in educating the public to be mindful about the danger of wasteful resource use and the insidious nature of overconsumption.
•   In general, Malthusians tend to be suspicious of regulatory programs that are entirely market-based, such as transferable emission permits. For them, equity and sustainability considerations are more important than a single-minded focus on efficient outcomes.
•   Finally, Malthusians have been criticized for their tendency to undermine the potential contributions of technology to the continued material progress of humanity by their prophecies of doom and gloom. Critics consider the perennial Malthusian predictions of economic collapse is unwarranted and moreover not helpful politically.

Review and discussion questions

1   Briefly define the following concepts: negative and positive checks to population growth, exponential growth, Malthusian margin, Ricardian rent, neo-Malthusian, and real per capita output.
2   State whether the following are *true*, *false* or *uncertain* and explain why:

 (a)   The connection between population growth and environmental damage is undeniable. More people cause increasing damage to the environment.
 (b)   It is inadequate to identify the 'optimal' level of population solely in terms of its correspondence to the maximum real per capita output (such as L_1 in Figure 10.1).
 (c)   Modern environmental crises are predominantly a consequence of affluence or increased level of per capita consumption.

3   More than any other factor, as human population increases and causes a rise in the demand for food and other extractive resources, it is the gradual decline in the quality of arable land and the difficulty of mining increasingly poor-grade mineral deposits that will eventually halt the progress of human material progress. Discuss.
4   Malign technology, not population growth or affluence, has been primarily responsible for today's global population problems. Critically comment.
5   The isolated and sporadic instances of hunger that we continue to witness in parts of our contemporary world do not support the Malthusian theory. These events are caused not by population pressure but by poor global distribution of resources. Do you agree? Why, or why not?

6   Garrett Hardin (1993: 94) wrote, '[even though] John Maynard Keynes had the highest opinion of his contributions to economics, Malthus continues to be bad-mouthed by many of today's sociologists and economists. The passion displayed by some of his detractors is grossly disproportionate to the magnitude of his errors. A conscientious listing of the explicit statements made by Malthus would, I am sure, show that far more than 95 per cent of them are correct. But for any writer who becomes notorious for voicing unwelcome "home truths" a correctness score of 95 per cent is not enough.' In your opinion, is this a convincing and substantive defense of Malthus? Discuss.

7   Davidson (2000) suggested that Malthusians' repeated predictions of the inevitability of impending economic and ecological catastrophe are ultimately damaging to the cause of environmental protection. How could this be? Explain.

References and further reading

Allen, J. C. and Barnes, D. F. (1995) 'The Causes of Deforestation in Developed Countries', *Annals of the Association of American Geographers* 75, 2: 163–84.

Ausubel, J. H. (1996) 'Can Technology Spare the Earth?' *American Scientist* 84: 166–77.

Cole, H. S. D., Freeman, C., Jahoda, M. and Pavitt, K. L. R. (1973) *Model of Doom: A Critique of the Limits to Growth*, New York: Universe Books.

Commoner, B., Corr, M. and Stamler, P. (1971) 'The Causes of Pollution', in T. D. Goldfarb (ed.) *Taking Sides: Clashing Views on Controversial Environmental Issues*, 3rd edn, Sluice Dock, Conn.: Guilford.

Council on Environmental Quality and the Department of State (1980) *The Global 2000 Report to the President: Entering the Twenty-first Century, 1980*, Washington, DC: US Government Printing Office.

Dasgupta, P., Levin, S. and Lubchenco, J. (2000) 'Economic Pathways to Ecological Sustainability', *BioScience* 50, 4: 339–45.

Davidson, C. (2000) 'Economic Growth and the Environment: Alternatives to the Limits Paradigm', *BioScience* 50, 4: 433–9.

Durning, A. T. (1992) *How Much Is Enough?*, Worldwatch Environmental Alert Series, New York: W. W. Norton.

Ehrlich, P. R. (1968) *The Population Bomb*, New York: Ballantine Books.

Ehrlich, P. R. and Holdren, J. P. (1971) 'Impact of Population Growth', *Science* 171: 1212–17.

Hardin, G. (1993) *Living Within Limits: Ecology, Economics, and Population Taboos*, New York: Oxford University Press.

——(1972) *Exploring New Ethics for Survival: The Voyage of the Spaceship Beagle*, New York: Viking Press.

Meadows, D. H., Meadows, D. L., Randers, J. and Behrens, W. W. III (1974) *The Limits to Growth: A Report for the Club of Rome's Project on the Predicament of Mankind*, 2nd edn, New York: Universe Books.

Repetto, R. and Holmes, T. (1983) 'The Role of Population in Resource Depletion in Developing Countries', *Population and Development Review* 9, 4: 609–32.

Rudel, T. K. (1989) 'Population, Development, and Tropical Deforestation: A Cross-national Study', *Rural Sociology* 54, 3: 327–37.

Simon, J. L. (1996) *The Ultimate Resource 2*, Princeton, NJ: Princeton University Press.

Soroos, M. S. (1997) *The Endangered Atmosphere: Preserving a Global Commons*, Columbia: University of South Carolina Press.

Worldwatch Institute (1997) *Vital Signs 1997*, New York: W. W. Norton.

11 Biophysical limits to economic growth

The neoclassical economics perspective

> The existence of a finite stock of a resource that is necessary for production does not imply that the economy must eventually stagnate and decline. If there is continual resource-augmenting technical progress, it is possible that a reasonable standard of living can be guaranteed for all time. But even if we postulate an absence of technical progress we must not overlook substitution possibilities. If there are reasonable substitution possibilities between exhaustible resources and reproducible capital, it is possible that capital accumulation could offset the constraints on production possibilities due to exhaustible resources.
>
> (Dasgupta and Heal 1979: 197)

11.1 Introduction

As discussed in Chapter 1 and in much more detail in Appendix A, the perspective of neoclassical economics on natural resource scarcity, allocation and measurement is based on a number of distinguishing postulates:

1   Nothing rivals the market as a medium for resource allocation.
2   Resource valuation depends only on individual 'preferences' and initial endowments as determinants of prices.
3   For privately owned resources, market prices are 'true' measures of resource scarcity.
4   Price distortions arising from externalities can be effectively remedied through appropriate institutional adjustments (see Chapter 3).
5   Resource scarcity can be continually augmented by technological means.
6   Human-made capital (such as machines, buildings, roads, etc.) and natural capital (such as forests, coal deposits, wetland preserves, wilderness, etc.) are substitutes.

On the basis of these fundamental premises, most neoclassical economists have traditionally maintained a strong skepticism toward gloom-and-doom prophecies about the future economic condition of humanity. In fact, from the perspective of neoclassical economics, it is tautological and therefore uninteresting to say that resources are becoming increasingly scarce given that resources are assumed to be available in geologically fixed quantity while population continues to grow (Rosenberg 1973). Instead, *the real issue of significance should be to understand the circumstances under which technological progress will continue to ameliorate resource scarcity. And this understanding should be conjoined with the belief that, under the right circumstances,*

Exhibit 11.1   Resources, population, environment: an oversupply of false bad news

Julian Simon

The supplies of natural resources are finite. This apparently self-evident proposition is the starting point and the all-determining assumption of such models as *The Limits to Growth* [Meadows *et al.* 1974] and of much popular discussion.

Incredible as it may seem at first, the term 'finite' is not only inappropriate but downright misleading in the context of natural resources, from both the practical and the philosophical points of view. As with so many of the important arguments in this world, this one is 'just semantic'. Yet the semantics of resource scarcity muddle public discussion and bring about wrong-headed policy decisions.

A definition of resource quantity must be operational to be useful. It must tell us how the quantity of the resource that might be available in the future could be calculated. But the future quantities of a natural resource such as copper cannot be calculated even in principle, because of new lodes, new methods of mining copper, and variations in grades of copper lodes; because copper can be made from other metals; and because of the vagueness of the boundaries within which copper might be found – including the sea, and other planets. Even less possible is a reasonable calculation of the amount of future services of the sort we are now accustomed to get from copper, because of recycling and because of the substitution of other materials for copper, as in the case of the communications satellite.

With respect to energy, it is particularly obvious that the Earth does not bound the quantity available to us; our Sun (and perhaps other suns) is our basic source of energy in the long run, from vegetation (including fossilized vegetation) as well as from solar energy. As to the practical finiteness and scarcity of resources – that brings us back to cost and price, and by these measures history shows progressively decreasing rather than increasing scarcity. Why does the word 'finite' catch us up? That is an interesting question in psychology, education and philosophy; unfortunately there is no space to explore it here.

In summary, because we find new lodes, invent better production methods and discover new substitutes, the ultimate constraint upon our capacity to enjoy unlimited raw materials at acceptable prices is knowledge. And the source of knowledge is the human mind. Ultimately, then, the key constraint is human imagination and the exercise of educated skills. Hence an increase of human beings constitutes an addition to the crucial stock of resources, along with causing additional consumption of resources.

Source: *Science* Vol. 268, 1980, pp. 1435–6. Copyright © American Association for the Advancement of Science, 1980. Reprinted by permission.

---

technology will continue not only to spare resources but also to expand our niche (Ausubel 1996). This view is in sharp contrast to the characteristically gloomy Malthusian position on technology and resource scarcity discussed in the previous chapter. What general explanations could be offered to counter the gloomy Malthusian disposition?

Basically, mainstream economists provide the following *two* explanations for the Malthusians' traditional prophecies of doom-and-gloom. First, Malthusians are generally predisposed to view humankind as having a natural propensity for self-destruction. As a result of this, they tend to underestimate human wisdom (creativity) and instinctive capability for self-preservation (Cole *et al.* 1973; Simon 1980). Second, and most importantly, scholars of a Malthusian persuasion have the strong tendency to lump *all* resources together without regard to their importance, ultimate abundance or substitutability (Simon 1996). When these factors are considered, what matters is not that terrestrial resources are *finite* – absolute scarcity (for an expanded discussion on this issue read Exhibit 11.1). Malthusians simply do not comprehend the possibility of there being an infinite amount of resource substitutability, even in a world with a finite resource endowment (Goeller and Weinberg 1976).

This chapter presents several theoretical and empirical justifications for why the Malthusian perspective on limits to economic growth is considered to be unwarranted and far removed from the truth. Another important issue addressed in this chapter is how economic growth and *technological advances* could be viewed *not* as problems in themselves – the way Malthusians tend to view them, *but as cures for stresses involving population, resources, pollution, and other environmental damages.*

11.2 Increasing resource scarcity: the empirical evidence

As discussed in the previous chapter, Malthusians often argue that, in the long-run, depletion of some key material resources (e.g. a prolonged shortage of global petroleum supply or water shortage or large scale degradation of land due to desertification and deforestation) would act as a bottleneck to further economic growth (Meadows 1974). This section presents several empirical studies that seem to contradict this Malthusian thesis – the inevitability of increasing resource scarcity in the long run. In fact, the evidence over the past 130 years seems to suggest that resources are getting more abundant rather than more scarce.

11.2.1 The empirical evidence before the 1970s

The earliest attempt to empirically analyze the condition of resource scarcity was made in a book published in 1963, *Scarcity and Growth: The Economics of Natural Resource Availability*. The authors of this book, Barnett and Morse, were members of President Truman's Commission on Materials Policy, whose mission was to investigate the validity of a widespread public perception of future material shortage in the United States following the Second World War. This study was a carefully and ingeniously designed statistical trend analysis for the United States, and it encompassed the period dating from the end of the Civil War (1865) to 1957. Barnett and Morse used these data to test the validity of a core principle of the Malthusian–Ricardian doctrine: the inevitability of 'increasing resource scarcity with a passage of time'.

In their analysis, Barnett and Morse defined increasing scarcity as increasing *real* cost, which is measured by the amount of labor and capital required to produce a unit of extractive resources. They then put forward the following hypothesis:

> The real cost of extractive products per unit will increase through time due to limitations in the available quantities and qualities of natural resources. Real cost in this case is measured in terms of labor (man-days, man-hours) or labor plus capital per unit of extractive output.
>
> (Barnett 1979: 165)

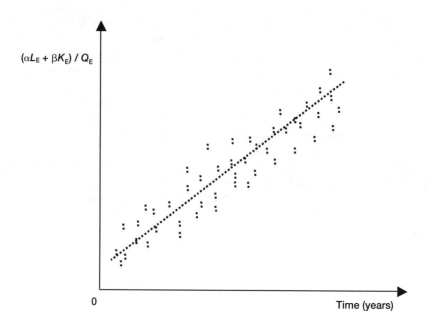

$(\alpha L_E + \beta K_E) / Q_E$

0

Time (years)

Figure 11.1 A graphical illustration of the strong hypothesis of increasing natural resource
scarcity. The amount of labor and capital used to get a unit of extractive output
(the unit on the *y*-axis) is increasing with the passage of time.

Barnett and Morse refer to this postulate as 'the *strong* hypothesis of increasing
economic scarcity'. It suggests that increasing resource scarcity will be evident if, over
time, an increasing trend of labor and capital per unit of extractive output, $(\alpha L_E +
\beta K_E)/Q_E$, is observed (see Figure 11.1). Note that L_E and K_E represent the labor
and capital used in the extractive sectors of the economy, and Q_E the aggregate output
of the extractive sectors (which include agriculture, fishing, forestry, and mining). The
parameters α and β are the weight factors of labor and capital, respectively. Note the
striking similarity between the Ricardian scarcity, discussed in Section 3 of Chapter 10,
and the strong hypothesis. In both instances the idea is to find a *physical measure of
resource scarcity*. In some respect then, the strong hypothesis can be viewed as an
empirical test for Ricardian scarcity.

   Using the above model specification, Barnett and Morse proceeded with their extensive statistical trend analysis, and concluded the following:

> The U.S. output in extractive sectors (which includes agriculture, forestry, fishing,
> and mining) increased markedly from the Civil War to 1957, yet the statistical
> record fails to support, and in fact is contradictory to, the classical hypothesis. Real
> costs per unit of extractive goods, measured in units of labor plus capital, did not
> rise. They fell, except in forestry (which is less than 10% of extraction). In fact, the
> pace of decline in real cost . . . accelerated following World War I, compared with
> the preceding period.
>
> (Barnett 1979: 166)

Exhibit 11.2 Energy

Jesse H. Ausubel

Energy systems extend from the mining of coal through the generation and transmission of electricity to the artificial light that enables the reader to see this page. For environmental technologists, two central questions define the energy system. First, is the efficiency increasing? Second, is the carbon used to deliver energy to the final user declining?

Energy efficiency has been gaining in many segments, probably for thousands of years. Think of all the designs and devices to improve fireplaces and chimneys. Or consider the improvement in motors and lamps. About 1700 the quest began to build efficient engines, at first with steam. Three hundred years have increased the efficiency of generators from 1 to about 50 per cent of the apparent limit, the latter achieved by today's best gas turbines. Fuel cells can advance efficiency to 70 per cent. They will require about 50 years to do so, if the socio-technical clock continues to tick at its established rate. In 300 years, physical laws may finally arrest our engine progress.

Whereas centuries measure the struggle to improve generators, lamps brighten with each decade. A new design proposes to bombard sulfur with microwaves. One such bulb the size of a golf ball could purportedly produce the same amount of light as hundreds of high-intensity mercury-vapor lamps, with a quality of light comparable to sunlight. The current 100-year pulse of improvement . . . will

surely not extinguish ideas for illumination. The next century may reveal quite new ways to see in the dark. For example, nightglasses, the mirror image of sunglasses, could make the objects of night visible with a few milliwatts.

Segments of the energy economy have advanced impressively toward local ceilings of 100 per cent efficiency. However, modern economies still work far from the limit of system efficiency because system efficiency is multiplicative, not additive. In fact, if we define efficiency as the ratio of the theoretical minimum to the actual energy consumption for the same goods and services, modern economies probably run at less than 5 per cent efficiency for the full chain from primary energy to delivery of the service to the final user. So, far from a ceiling, the United States has averaged about 1 per cent less energy to produce a good or service each year since about 1800. At the pace of advance, total efficiency will still approach only 15 per cent by 2100. Because of some losses difficult to avoid in each link of the chain, the thermodynamic efficiency of the total system in practice could probably never exceed 50 per cent. Still, in 1995 we are early in the game.

Source: *American Scientist* Vol. 84, 1996, pp. 166–76. Copyright Sigma Xi, the Scientific Research Society 1996. Reprinted by permission.

How can a rapidly developing nation such as the United States, that has experienced strong economic and population growth, have not yet experienced increasing economic scarcity of natural resources? This should not be totally surprising because of the rapid technological progress experienced during the period under consideration. Specifically, there was increased efficiency of resource use, in particular energy (see Exhibit 11.2), substitution of more plentiful resources for the less plentiful ones, improvements in transportation and trade, and improvements in exploration techniques and the discovery of new deposits, as well as increased recycling of scrap.

However, the above empirical evidence for decreasing resource scarcity should be taken with caution. It is important to note that this conclusion is strictly applicable to the United States and at a specific moment in its history. As such, it would be inappropriate to generalize global resource conditions from the results of this case study. In addition, this study said nothing about the quality of the natural environment – a subject of perhaps little concern at that early stage in the economic development of the United States. Despite its limited scope, this study occupies a special significance in setting a framework for analyzing *general* resource scarcity through empirical means.

11.2.2 The empirical evidence since the 1970s

In terms of public awareness of ecological limits and its various implications, in many ways the 1970s were watershed years. Fittingly, the 1970s are often referred to as the environmental decade. The first Earth Day was celebrated in April 1970. This event was significant since it clearly marked the beginning of environmental awareness throughout the world. During that same year, the United States instituted a new government agency, the Environmental Protection Agency (EPA). This agency, with cabinet-level status, was established with the primary task of protecting the ambient environment of the nation. During the 1970s a number of books and articles were published warning the public about impending natural resource scarcity in the not too distant future. The most influential of these publications was *The Limits to Growth*, first published in 1971. Although controversial, the frightful warning of the book was taken seriously because the study was supported by the Club of Rome, which is composed of a large group of well-reputed scientists from around the world. In addition, both the Arab oil embargo of 1973 (a result of the Arab–Israeli War) and the 1978 energy shortage (a result of a unilateral decision by OPEC, the Organization of Petroleum Exporting Countries, to limit petroleum supply) clearly demonstrated the vulnerability of the industrial nations' economies to a prolonged shortage of a key but finite resource: petroleum.

Among standard economics practitioners, the events of the 1970s brought a renewed interest in the Barnett and Morse approach to empirically testing the evidence of alleged emerging global resource scarcity. In the late 1970s several attempts were made to empirically study recent trends in resource scarcity. Manely Johnson *et al.* (1980) updated the original findings of Barnett and Morse and re-examined the strong hypotheses by extending the period under consideration from the Civil War up to 1970. Kerry Smith (1979) analyzed the United States' data from 1900 to 1973, using a more sophisticated statistical technique. While Smith was somewhat critical of Barnett and Morse's work on purely methodological grounds, the overall results and conclusions of the above studies were very much consistent with the findings of Barnett and Morse, namely, that the United States' experience is still indicative of decreasing resource scarcity with passage of time. But, again, these studies are confined to the economic performance of one nation. The question that still remains unanswered is: can the United States' experience be generalized to other nations?

In 1978, Barnett, using the published time series data from the United Nations, made similar studies for various nations of the world. For each specific nation, on the basis of the available data, the trend analysis failed to support the strong hypothesis of increasing scarcity of minerals. In fact, all the results pertaining to the strong hypothesis were consistent with the opposite hypothesis, i.e. increasing resource availability.

However, as Barnett (1979: 185) himself suggested, 'these international results should be regarded as preliminary, since the series involved are only available for short periods (post World War II) and, in several of the cases, of questionable quality'. Again, in 1982, Barnett *et al.* examined data through 1979. At this time, there was some evidence of increasing scarcity in the 1970s, but this was attributed to the changing market structure in general and the OPEC cartel in particular.

The overall implication of the above studies is that aggregate global and United States economic trends are improving. Thus, the bad news of the 1970s (pollution, energy crises, acceleration in the rates of soil erosions, desertification, deforestation, etc.) was not indicative of emerging resource scarcity. If anything, such events have to be taken as a temporary setback. Common beliefs assert that these problems, if envisioned properly, could be solved through institutional adjustments and technological means. This particular belief was reaffirmed in a controversial book written in the early 1980s by Julian L. Simon and Herman Kahn, *The Resourceful Earth: A Response to Global 2000*:

> We are confident that the nature of the physical world permits continued improvement in humankind's economic lot in the long run, indefinitely. Of course there are always newly arising local problems, shortages and pollution, due to climate or to increased population and income. Sometimes temporary large-scale problems arise. But the nature of the world's physical conditions and the resilience in a well-functioning economic and social system enable us to overcome such problems, and the solutions usually leave us better off than if the problem had never arisen; that is the great lesson to be learned from human history.
>
> (Simon and Kahn 1984: 3)

The Resourceful Earth, as indicated by its subtitle, was written as a critical response to *The Global 2000 Report to the President* (Council on Environmental Quality and Department of State 1980). As discussed in the last section of Chapter 10, the conclusions of this neo-Malthusian report were very frightening. Simon and Kahn's response to such gloomy conclusions was quite drastic. In most parts, relying on statistical trend analyses similar to those developed by Barnett and Morse, their general conclusion was that 'for the most relevant matters we have examined, aggregate global and U.S. trends are improving rather than deteriorating'. In addition, in response to the specific conclusions reached by *The Global 2000 Report*, Simon and Kahn (1984: 1) asserted:

> If present trends continue, the world in 2000 will be less crowded (though more populated), less polluted, more stable ecologically, and less vulnerable to resource-supply disruption than the world we live in now. Stresses involving population, resources, and the environment will be less in the future than now. . . . The world's people will be richer in most ways than they are today. . . . The outlook for food and other necessities of life will be better . . . [and] life for most people on earth will be less precarious economically than it is now.

A conclusion of this nature has far-reaching policy implication. According to this worldview, distributional concerns, especially those relating to *intergenerational* equity, would not be warranted. As William J. Baumol, a prominent economist, wrote, 'in our economy, if past trends and current developments are any guide, a redistribution to provide more for the future may be described as a Robin Hood activity stood on its head – it takes from the poor to give to the rich. Average real per capita income a century hence is likely to be a sizeable multiple of its present value. Why should I give up part of my income to help support someone else with an income several times my own?' (Baumol 1968: 800).

11.2.3 Why past trends of decreasing resource scarcity may not be sustainable

While the empirical studies of Barnett and Morse and several others are vividly suggestive of *decreasing* scarcity with the passage of time, can we generalize from these studies about impending scarcity of natural resources in the foreseeable future? In this sub-section, *three* reasons are offered for why the answer to this question may be 'no'. In other words, these are reasons why past trends of decreasing scarcity may not be sustainable.

First, in the past, studies based on statistical trends do *not* explicitly take environmental quality into consideration. This is because the prices for environmental goods may have been significantly undervalued due to externalities (see Chapters 3 and 4). Because of this omission, one might argue that – over the past century – the changes in the patterns of extraction have increased the effective supply of the material input components of natural resources (i.e. natural resource commodities), while reducing the amenity and life-support services (such as climate regulation and maintenance of genetic diversity) of these same resources. That is, *the greater degree of technological substitution possibilities that has been evident in the past might have come from the increasing replacement by priced goods and services of unpriced goods, services and amenities* (Brown and Field 1979). Some view this process as being unsustainable, especially when the consideration is loss of biodiversity. Here is what Dasgupta *et al.* (2000: 343) has to say on this matter:

> To rely on substitutability among natural resources in commodity production to minimize the utilitarian importance of biodiversity, as is frequently done (e.g. Simon 1980, 1996), is scientifically flawed. First, without biodiversity, substitutability is lost entirely. And, more fundamentally, certain species and groups of species play unique roles in the functioning of ecosystems and thus have no substitutes. Preservation of biodiversity is hence important, both to provide unique services and to provide insurance against the loss of similarly functioning species.

The implication is that if ecological simplification is the outcome of continued economic growth, *the neoclassical treatment of natural and human capital as substitutes will not be valid in the future* (more on this in the next chapter).

Second, during the period when the above-mentioned empirical studies were conducted, major transformations in the use of *energy* had occurred. More specifically, higher-quality fuels displaced the use of lower-quality fuels: first coal replaced wood, then oil and natural gas replaced coal. According to Culter Cleveland (1991), it was this type of substitution of high-quality fuels that reduced the labor–capital costs of extractive sectors in the United States as depicted in the Barnett and Morse study. In

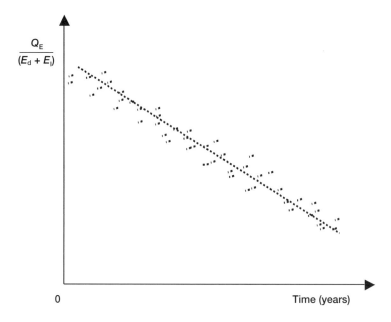

Figure 11.2 Extractive output per unit of energy input. The amount of extractive output obtained from the use of a unit of energy inputs (the units on the *y*-axis) is declining over time, implying a decline in the efficiency of energy as a factor of production.

other words, *the decline in real costs of resource extraction observed by empirical studies of the Barnett and Morse type was not due to technological changes* per se, *but rather due to the substitution of higher-quality energy resources for labor and capital in the extraction of resources.*

To verify this, Cleveland conducted an empirical study analogous to that of Barnett and Morse. More specifically, he calculated the quantities of direct and indirect fuels used to produce a unit of resource in the United States' extractive sectors (mining, agriculture, forest products, and fisheries industries) using this approach, namely $Q_E/(E_d + E_I)$, where Q_E is the total extractive output and E_d and E_I are the *direct* and *indirect* energy used to extract the resource in question. Thus, a general trend that showed a decline in the output per unit of energy input (i.e. the productivity of energy input) would indicate an increase in physical scarcity or an increase in energy cost per unit of output (see Figure 11.2). This is because as high-quality resources were depleted, more energy would be needed to extract a further unit resource. For most recent years between 1970 and 1988, the results of Cleveland's empirical findings indicated increasing scarcity in the metal mining, energy extraction, forestry, and fishery sectors of the United States' economy. The exception to this has been the nonmetal industries.

Third, the pace of technical progress over the past has been uneven. In fact, 'a disproportionate fraction of technological improvements during the past 5000 years has been concentrated over the last 300 years or so' (Dasgupta and Heal 1979: 206). Given this, it would be dangerous to use past evidence and merely extrapolate into the future.

If this point is taken seriously, rapid resource-saving technical progress of the kind experienced over the past 200 years does not necessarily imply continued technical progress at the same pace in the future.

Thus, taken together, the arguments presented in this subsection suggest that there are formidable ecological, energy and technological factors that could work against the continuation of past trends of decreasing resource scarcity. It is very difficult for neoclassical economists to accept limits to technological progress. However, if the environment is apparently going to be a limiting factor, according to the neoclassical worldview the cure for the problem is not less (as Malthusians would suggest) but more economic growth. This is the subject of the next section.

11.3 Economic growth, the environment and population: the neoclassical perspective

In this section, the interrelationships among population growth, economic growth and environmental degradation will be analyzed within the context of the neoclassical tradition. More specifically, this section will examine the theoretical and empirical arguments for the long-standing neoclassical economists' position, that *continued economic growth is the panacea for both population and environmental quality concerns.*

11.3.1 Economic growth and the environment: the environmental Kuznets curve

So far, little if anything has been said about neoclassical views on the overall economic growth–environmental quality relationship. To what extent is continued economic growth consistent with maintaining a healthy environmental quality? Should not increased economic activities that accompany economic growth generate an increased level of pollution, and hence greater environmental stress? The standard response of neoclassical economists to these questions has been straightforward. They argue that significant improvements in environmental quality are fully compatible with economic growth. Why is this so?

In the first instance, one of the outcomes of economic growth is an increase in *real per capita income*. Higher per capita income will increase the demand for improved environmental quality. This means increased expenditure on environmental cleanup operations. Accordingly, economic growth is more likely to be good than bad for the environment. The generalized form of this environmental quality–income hypothesis is depicted by an 'inverted-U' curve, as shown by Figure 11.3A. This graph shows that an increase in per capita income is initially accompanied by worsening environmental conditions up to a certain point, but this is then followed by improvement in environmental quality. Taken at its face value, what this suggests is that a country has to attain a certain standard of living before it starts to respond to its concern for improved environmental quality. The 'inverted U curve' is sometimes referred to as the 'environmental Kuznets curve' because of its similarity to the relationship between per capita income and income inequality first postulated by Simon Kuznets (1955).

Over the years, several empirical studies have been done to verify the validity of the environmental quality–income relationships as postulated by the environmental Kuznets curve hypothesis. Below are a couple of examples of research conclusions that appear to empirically validate this hypothesis:

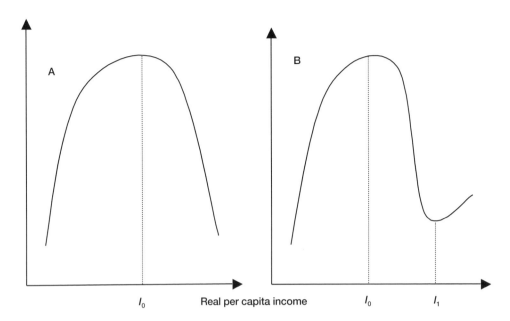

Figure 11.3 The environmental Kuznet curve. The vertical axis measures increasing levels of environmental damage. Case A suggests that after a country attains a certain level of per capita income I_0, increased income is associated with lower environmental damage or higher environmental quality. Case B suggests that the positive association between income growth and higher environmental quality does not hold indefinitely. Beyond income level I_1, increase in income would lead to increasing deterioration of the environment.

> We have found, through an examination of air-quality measures in a cross-section of countries, that economic growth tends to alleviate pollution problems once a country's per capita income reaches about $4,000 to $5,000 US dollars.
>
> (Grossman and Krueger, 1995: 35–6)

> Environmental degradation overall (combined resource depletion and pollution) is worse at levels of income per capita under $1,000. Between $1,000 and $3,000, both the economy and environmental degradation undergo dramatic structural change from rural to urban, from agricultural to industrial. A second structural transformation begins to take place as countries surpass a per capita income of $10,000 and begin to shift from energy intensive heavy industry to services and information-technology intensive industry.
>
> (Panayotou 1993: 14)

Several implications can be drawn from these conclusions:

1 It is possible for poor countries to 'grow out' of some environmental problems once they attain a certain standard of living or per capita income (such as the

per capita income associated with the peak of the environmental Kuznets curve in Figure 11.3A).

2   For countries that have already gone over the hump of the inverted-U curve, mainly the rich countries, continued income growth will invariably be associated with improved environmental quality. This implies that the possibility that an upturn may occur at a high-income level similar to the one shown in Figure 11.3B would be dismissed.

3   Environmental policy should be scrutinized carefully as it has the potential (as discussed in the last section of Chapter 3) of slowing the pace of economic growth – the very engine for environmental improvement.

The inverted U curve or the environmental Kuznets curve hypothesis has been criticized for a number of reasons (Rothman and de Bruyn 1998; Torras and Boyce 1998; Ekins 2000). The main arguments raised against the hypothesis can be summarized as follows:

1   The inverted-U curve has been found for only a few pollutants, mainly those that have local health effects and can be dealt with without great expense. Examples are air pollutants (such as smoke and SO_2 emissions), suspended particles, sanitation, and so on. With the exception of deforestation, no land-related environmental degradation studies were done by more than one group of researchers. In general, the results from these studies were inconclusive, showing no clear evidence about the association between per capita incomes and deforestation (Ekins 2000).

2   Existing empirical work has focused on the relationship between income and emissions, or concentration of pollution, which due to the *stock* nature of many environmental problems, does not fully account for environmental impacts. For example, ecological dimensions such as carrying capacities and ecosystem resilience capacities have been ignored (Rothman and de Bruyn 1988: 144).

3   Not all current empirical studies support the hypothesis. Ekins (2000: 192) analyzed the results of the main econometric studies of the relationship between environmental quality and income that had appeared up to 1996. According to Ekins, 'From these results of econometric estimations of the relationship between income and various measures of environmental quality, the main conclusion is that none of the pollutants unequivocally shows an inverse-U relationship where studies have been done by more than one group of researchers'.

4   No good explanations have been given as to why levels of pollutants should ease downwards after a certain income level has been reached. In this regard, a recent empirical study by Torras and Boyce (1998), which includes more explanatory variables than income alone, found that social factors such as income equality, wider literacy and greater political liberties tend to have a significant positive effect on environmental quality, especially in low-income countries.

5   Recent data from the OECD and European Commission (high-income countries) indicate that 'despite improvements in some indicators, notably of some air pollutants, these rich countries seem to be experiencing continuing serious environmental degradation on all fronts' (Ekins 2000). This evidence either invalidates the inverted-U relationship between income and environmental quality or establishes the *possibility* of the kind of relationship between income and environmental quality shown in Figure 11.3B, i.e. that once a certain high income level is

attained, continued income growth would lead to continued environmental degradation.

The above deficiencies do not in themselves totally discredit the inverted-U hypothesis. They caution us, however, against viewing economic growth as the prescribed remedy to environmental problems in both the developed and the developing nations of the world. Furthermore, *to accept the inverted-U hypothesis at its face value amounts to declaring that environmental policy is irrelevant or even undesirable.* After all, as discussed in Chapter 3, environmental policy is often seen as a hindrance to economic growth – which according to the inverted-U hypothesis is the most important pre-requisite for environmental improvement. The truth of the matter is as Ekins (2000: 210) put it 'any improvements in environmental quality as income increase is likely to be due to the enactment of environmental policy rather than endogenous changes in economic structure or technology'.

However, this is in no way to suggest that income growth does not contribute to environmental quality improvement. The real problem is that the inverted-U hypothesis attaches too much significance to the role that growth in income plays in the improve-ment of environmental quality. Most importantly, if taken at its face value, the environmental Kuznets hypothesis has the effect of rendering environmental policy as either irrelevant or of little use – a very dangerous message indeed.

11.3.2 Economic growth and population

What about the population problem? Neoclassical economists also believe that economic growth is not only good for the environment, but also a cure for a nation's population problem. This claim is supported by what is commonly known as the theory of demographic transition. That theory is based on an empirical generalization and it claims that, as countries develop, they eventually reach a point where the birth rate falls (for more on this see Exhibit 11.3). *The main implication of the theory of demographic transition is the claim that, in the long run, the process of industrialization is accompanied by a sustained reduction in population growth.* This is because the increase in income of the average family in the course of industrialization reduces the desire for more children.

This empirical generalization of a negative relationship between household income and family size at an aggregate level spanning a long period of time can also be explained by what is known as the *microeconomic theory of human fertility*. This theory specifically deals with the issue of how parents make decisions about childbearing, and how this choice is influenced by the family's income. The economic analysis begins by viewing children as *durable* consumption goods (Becker 1960; Blake 1968). Children are classified as consumption goods because they provide direct psychic utilities to their parents. Basically, there are three basic sources of benefits (utilities) that parents can expect from having a child: (a) consumption or psychic utility – a child is wanted for her- or himself rather than for services or income she or he may provide; (b) work or income utility; and (c) security or old-age benefit.

On the other hand, the costs or disutility of having children comprise two broad kinds: (a) the direct costs of providing necessities such as food, housing, clothing, and basic education; and (b) the indirect costs of raising children, such as opportunities forgone by parents in terms of time and money (Becker 1960; Leibenstein 1974). With this identification of the costs and benefits of having children, and on the general

Exhibit 11.3   The theory of the demographic transition

In studying the reproductive decision of humans at the macro level, one view that has been most popular among social scientists is the theory of the demographic transition. This theory derives its appeal from its simplicity and the considerable empirical support for its basic conclusions (Leibenstein 1974). Briefly stated, as shown in Figure 11.4, the theory of the demographic transition is a generalization advanced to explain the transitional stages of fertility and mortality for a nation over time, as it progresses in its modernization process. For our purpose the relevant aspect of the theory is its claim that, as nations develop, they eventually reach a point where the birthrate falls. In other words, in the long run the process of industrialization is accompanied by a sustained reduction in population growth. One important implication of this theory is, of course, that industrialization (which is generally associated with increased GDP) is a possible solution to the population problem (ibid.). Why so?

First, industrialization implies a shift from an economy that is primarily based on agriculture (which is labor-intensive) to one based on industry (which is capital-intensive). This structural change in the economy increasingly reduces the productivity (hence, the income-generating capacity) of children in the agricultural sector. Furthermore, as often occurs with industrialization and modernization, child labor laws are instituted as a sign of social progress. The combined effect of these two factors reduces parental desire to have more children for the purpose of supplementing the household income.

Second, since industrialization is often associated with an increase in the average per capita income of a nation, the increasing affluence of the average family in the course of industrialization reduces the desire for more children. This is because the need for having children as a hedge for security in old age becomes less and less important as families become increasingly wealthy. In addition, this tendency for smaller family size will be further reinforced by the fact that industrialization is generally associated with declining infant mortality.

Finally, other socioeconomic factors associated with modernization further contribute to a decline in fertility rates. Among them are the rise in the education of women, urbanization and its secularizing influence, increasing participation of females in traditionally male-dominated sectors of the economy, advances in birth control methods, and family planning.

While the association between income and fertility rates sparked interest in this topic within the economics discipline, by and large economists were not satisfied with the above explanations for the decline in birth rates. Economists claimed that the theory of demographic transition simply failed to offer specific and systematic explanations of the very important association between income and fertility. Instead, the theory offers only a broad generalization and does not attempt to deal with the key issue of how parents make decisions about childbearing, and how this choice is influenced by the income of the family (Leibenstein 1974). To economists, this careful examination of decision-making at the micro level is extremely significant because it helps uncover the sources (determinants) of fertility decline – which is essential in designing effective population control policy instruments.

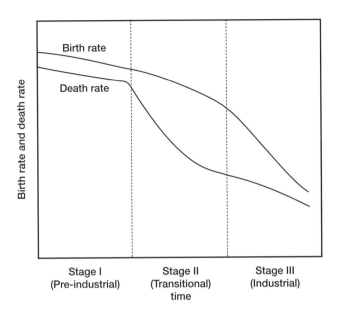

Figure 11.4 The demographic transition. The pre-industrial stage, Stage I, indicates high birth and death rates. Life is short and population growth is low. Rapid deceleration in death rates due to medical breakthroughs that reduce infant mortality and infectious disease creates a big gap between birth and death rates in Stage II – the transitional period towards industrialization. This is the period where population grows at a very high rate. Stage III is characterized by low levels of both birth and death rates. Life is long and population growth is low.

premise that human fertility decisions are made primarily on a rational basis, the microeconomic theory of fertility seeks to give an explanation for the seemingly *paradoxical* negative relationship between household income and family size. This is paradoxical because it suggests that children are *inferior* consumption goods (i.e. goods for which the demand falls as income rises). However, what actually happens is this. As income increases, parents start to desire fewer children but of *superior* quality (well-nourished, clothed and highly educated). Thus the desire for fewer children arises not because of increases in family income but rather the increases in the cost of raising children that is prompted by the increase in parents' income. So having fewer children is associated with higher cost of children, which is consistent with the theory of consumer demand (Becker 1960).

In general, the following reasons may be given for the negative association between increases in a country's average income and in the rate of its population growth:

1 As a country advances economically, it can afford to provide its people with improved health care facilities. The effect of this is to reduce infant mortality. With a decline in infant mortality, people are less likely to desire a big family.
2 As families become wealthier, their need to use children as a hedge against insecurity in old age becomes less important.

Exhibit 11.4   Falling birth rates signal a different world in the making

Michael Specter

Stockholm, Sweden – Mia Hulton is a true woman of the late twentieth century. Soft-spoken, well-educated and thoughtful, she sings Renaissance music in a choral group, lives quietly with the man she loves and works like a demon seven days a week.

At 33, she is in full pursuit of an academic career. Despite the fact that she lives in Sweden, which provides more support for women who want families than any other country, Hulton doesn't see how she can possibly make room in her life for babies – some day maybe, but certainly not soon.

'There are times when I think perhaps I will be missing something important if I don't have a child', she said slowly, trying to put her complicated desires into simple words. 'But today women finally have so many chances to have the life they want – to travel and work and learn. It's exciting and demanding. I just find it hard to see where the children would fit in.'

Hulton would never consider herself a radical, but she has become a cadre in one of the fundamental social revolutions of the century.

Driven largely by prosperity and freedom, millions of women throughout the developed world are having fewer children than ever before.

They stay in school longer, put more emphasis on work and marry later. As a result, birthrates in many countries are now in a rapid, sustained decline.

Never before – except in times of plague, war and deep economic depression – have birthrates fallen so low, for so long.

There is no longer a single country in Europe where people are having enough children to replace themselves when they die. Italy recently became the first nation in history where there are more people over the age of 60 than there are under the age of 20. This year Germany, Greece and Spain probably will cross the same eerie divide.

The effects of the shift will resonate far beyond Europe. Last year Japan's fertility rate – the number of children born to the average woman in a lifetime – fell to 1.39, the lowest level it has ever reached.

In the United States, where a large pool of new immigrants helps keep the birth rate higher than in any other prosperous country, the figure is still slightly below an average of 2.1 children per woman – the magic number needed to keep the population from starting to shrink.

Even in the developing world, where overcrowding remains a major cause of desperation and disease, the pace of growth has slowed almost everywhere.

Since 1965, according to United Nations population data, the birthrate in the Third World has been cut in half – from 6 children per woman to 3. In the last decade alone, for example, the figure in Bangladesh has fallen from 6.2 children per woman to 3.4. That's a bigger drop than in the previous two centuries.

Source: *Kalamazoo Gazette/New York Times*, July 10, 1998. Copyright © 1998 by The New York Times. Reprinted by permission.

3   Continued economic progress provides increased opportunities for mothers (and for females in general) to work to generate income. It also increases the need for more highly educated citizens. Thus, considerations of both the increase in the opportunity cost for the mother and the cost of educating a child cause families to desire a smaller number of children (see Exhibit 11.4).

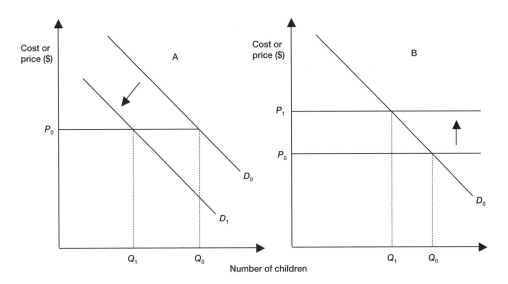

Figure 11.5 The demand and cost (price) conditions affecting parental decisions about family size (number of children). Case A indicates the effect of a downward shift in the demand for children arising from a factor, such as the decline in parents' need of children as a hedge against insecurity in old age. Case B shows a similar result but due to an increase in the opportunity cost of having children – an upward shift in the price line.

Considering that the demand for children is negatively sloped (Becker 1960), the first and second reasons above would imply a downward shift in the demand for children. Thus, at any given price, for example P_0 in Figure 11.5A, fewer children will be demanded, Q_1 instead of Q_0. This shows how, at least in theory, public policy measures designed to control population growth through improvements in infant mortality rate and/or old-age security would be expected to work.

Similarly, an increase in the cost (price) of raising children (the third reason above) would have the effect of reducing the number of children wanted by parents. This can be captured, as shown in Figure 11.5B, by a movement along a given demand curve. An increase in the cost (price) of children from P_0 to P_1 would reduce the number of children demanded from Q_0 to Q_1. This kind of change would be expected to occur when measures are taken to improve the opportunities available for women to participate gainfully in the labor market.

The above discussion suggests that a country can use economic incentives to control the rate of its population growth in a variety of ways. Once the determinants of demand for children are known, policy measures can be devised to trigger desirable change(s) in the demand schedules for children. However, this claim should be taken with caution, for a number of reasons.

Proposals for population control through economic incentives are based on the general premise that human fertility decisions are made primarily on a *rational* basis. Further, they assume that the underlying motive of the individual family is to promote its self-interest – maximize the *net* benefits from having children (Becker 1960).

However, under normal circumstances, not all the costs of children are *fully* borne by parents. Education in public-sector schools is almost universally free. In many countries food is subsidized by holding prices below market levels. Even in cases where education and food subsidies are financed through tax revenues, the individual household will not have an incentive to reduce its family size because the tax is normally not based on the number of children. Clearly, then, since not all costs are borne by parents, the private costs for raising children will be less than the social costs (Blake 1968). What this suggests is the presence of some form of *externalities*. As discussed in Chapter 3, in the presence of externalities, decisions reached by individual actors will not lead to the 'best' or optimal outcome for society at large.

Of course, this recognition that *real* externalities are involved in the parents' decision concerning childbearing underscores the need for adopting a population control policy. Unfortunately, for reasons that will become evident in Chapter 14, most countries in the developing world (where the population problem appears to be pressing and formidable) lack the institutional structures, the political systems and the economic resources that are necessary to effectively correct both market and government failures. Until these social infrastructural problems are adequately addressed, the use of economic incentives to control population will continue to be inadequate, hence, ineffective.

However, the situation will be even worse if the alternative is *laissez-faire* policies in reproduction, since these would surely confront society with a ruinous problem of over-population. Or, to use Hardin's (1968: 1244) words 'ruin is the destination toward which all men rush, each pursuing his own best interest in a society that believes in the freedom of the commons. Freedom in commons brings ruin to all.' This observation should not be taken lightly, given that the right to bear children is a universally held and UN-sanctioned inalienable human right.

In this chapter, we examined the neoclassical perspective on biophysical limits to economic growth. What we have observed is the treatment of biophysical limit as nothing more than a generalized resource scarcity problem. According to this world-view, population, environmental degradation and resource depletion problems can be solved through normal market (and if need be through extra market) mechanisms. Furthermore, concern for impending biophysical limits need not entail applying a brake to the pace of economic growth (as measured by increases in per capita income). On the contrary, to alleviate the stress of population and environmental pollution on the global ecosystems what is needed is more, not less, economic growth. *The conventional wisdom in neoclassical economics is that limits to growth are more likely to arise due to social and technological failures than from environmental or biophysical limits.*

There is, however, a small group of economists who would like to dispute the very *marginal* attention given to biophysical limits by the large majority of the practitioners of their discipline. These economists argue that under present conditions, the size of the human economy relative to global ecosystems is large enough to cause significant stress on the limited capacity of these natural ecosystems to support the economic subsystem. Given this claim, it would be fair to raise the question as to whether the world resource base, and the environment in particular, can support indefinite economic growth on a global scale. The idea that this may not be possible is the reason behind the recent revival in ecological economics and sustainable development – the subjects of the next two chapters.

11.4 Chapter summary

- In this chapter we discussed the neoclassical economic perspective on 'general' resource scarcity and its implications for the long-term material well-being of humanity.
- Neoclassical economists do not reject outright the notion that natural resources are *finite*. However, unlike the Malthusians, they do not believe that this fact implies that economic growth is limited. Neoclassical economists uphold this position for five reasons:

  1   They believe that technology – by finding substitutes, through discovery of new resources, and by increasing the efficiency of resource utilization – has almost no bounds in ameliorating natural resource scarcity.
  2   They differentiate between 'general' and 'specific' natural resource scarcity. To them, general or absolute scarcity (i.e. the awareness that there is 'only one Earth' and that it is a closed system with regard to its material needs) is tautological, therefore uninteresting. What is relevant is scarcity of specific resources, or relative scarcity.
  3   However, relative scarcity does not limit growth, due to the possibility of factor substitution.
  4   In sharp contrast to the Malthusians, neoclassicists believe that economic growth, through increases in per capita income and improvements in technology, provides solutions for both environmental and population problems. In other words, the solution to environmental and population problems is more, not less, economic growth.
  5   They also believe in the effectiveness of the market system to provide signals of emerging specific resource scarcity in a timely fashion. Price distortions arising from externalities simply require a minor fine-tuning of the market.

- Given that societal resources are allocated by smoothly functioning and forward-looking markets, the key resource for continued human material progress is knowledge. It is through knowledge that human technological progress (a necessary ingredient for circumventing biophysical limits) can be sustained indefinitely. The growth of human knowledge is not subjected to any known physical laws.
- Thus, the best legacy to leave to posterity is knowledge in the form of education (stored information about past discoveries) and manufactured capital (which has stored knowledge embedded in it). This would raise no problem because of the belief that human-made capital (roads, factories and so on) and natural capital (forests, coal deposits, wilderness, etc.) are substitutes. Much human progress, especially that of the past two centuries, has stemmed from the substitution of human-made for natural capital.
- According to the neoclassical growth paradigm, this process will continue into the future as long as the pace of technological growth follows past trends. Given the evidence of the past two centuries, the expectation is for a brighter future. Furthermore, this prognosis is independent of the fact that natural resources are finite.
- According to its most ardent critics, the biggest weakness of the neoclassical economic worldview is its assertions about unabated economic growth on the basis of extrapolation of past trends. Most importantly, it is argued, past trends in technological growth may not justify the claim that the same trend will continue

in the future; in fact, there are good reasons to suggest that the pace of technological progress may decrease. Another major criticism of the neoclassical view on
biophysical limits is its outright denial (or lack of consideration) of the effect on the
biosphere of an infinitely growing human economy. The human economy may grow
but it can never transgress its ecological bounds – the question of scale. For more
on this let us now turn to the next chapter.

Review and discussion questions

1 Briefly define the following concepts: absolute scarcity, extractive resources, real
cost, the strong hypotheses of increasing natural resource scarcity, the 'inverted-U'
hypothesis, the environmental Kuznets curve, the theory of demographic transition.
2 List what you consider to be the three most important features of the neoclassical
perspective of biophysical limits.
3 State whether the following are *true, false* or *uncertain* and explain why.

(a) Since resources have substitutes, 'nature imposes particular scarcities, not an
inescapable general scarcity'.
(b) Rising per capita income will ultimately induce countries to clean up their
environment. Thus, it is more, not less, economic growth that is needed to
remedy environmental problems.
(c) Improved social and economic status for women is the key to controlling
population growth. (Answer using demand and supply analysis.)

4 'The major constraint upon the human capacity to enjoy unlimited minerals,
energy and other raw materials at acceptable prices is knowledge. And the source
of knowledge is the human mind. Ultimately, then, the key constraint is human
imagination acting together with educated skills. This is why an increase in human
beings, along with causing additional consumption of resources, constitutes a
crucial addition to the stock of natural resources' (Simon 1996: 408). Write a
critical comment.
5 Do you see a parallel between the concept of Ricardian rent discussed in
Chapter 10 and real cost of extractive resources as defined by Barnett and Morse
in the present chapter? Explain.
6 Studies of long-run natural resource scarcity trends of the Barnett and Morse
variety have been criticized primarily for two reasons: (a) they fail to make explicit
consideration of environmental quality concerns, and (b) they fail to account for
the substitution of high-quality energy resources for labor and capital that has been
taking place in the extraction sectors. Are these valid criticisms? Explain.
7 The conventional wisdom in economics is that limits to growth are more likely to
arise due to social and technological failures than environmental or biophysical
limits. Comment.
8 *Laissez-faire* policies about reproduction would surely confront society with a
ruinous problem of overpopulation. Evaluate.

References

Arrow, K., Bolin, B. and Costanza, R. *et al.* (1995) 'Economic Growth, Carrying Capacity, and
the Environment', *Science* 268: 520–1.

Ausubel, J. H. (1996) 'Can Technology Spare the Earth?' *American Scientist* 84: 166–77.

Barnett, H. J. (1979) 'Scarcity and Growth Revisited', in K. V. Smith (ed.) *Scarcity and Growth Reconsidered*, Baltimore: Johns Hopkins University Press.

Barnett, H. J. and Morse, C. (1963) *Scarcity and Growth: The Economics of Natural Resource Availability*, Baltimore: Johns Hopkins University Press.

Barnett, H., Van Muiswinkel, G. M. and Schechter, M. (1982) 'Are Minerals Costing More?' *Resource Manag. Optim.* 2: 121–48.

Baumol, W. J. (1968) 'On the Social Rate of Discount', *American Economic Review* 58: 788–802.

Becker, G. (1960) 'An Economic Analysis of Fertility', in National Bureau of Economic Research, *Demographic and Economic Changes in Developing Countries*, Princeton, NJ: Princeton University Press.

Blake, J. (1968) 'Are Babies Consumer Durables? A Critique of the Economic Theory of Reproductive Motivation', *Population Studies* 22, 1: 5–25.

Brown, G., Jr, and Field, B. (1979) 'The Adequacy of Measures of Signaling the Scarcity of Natural Resources', in K. V. Smith (ed.) *Scarcity and Growth Reconsidered*, Baltimore: Johns Hopkins University Press.

Cleveland, C. J. (1991) 'Natural Resource Scarcity and Economic Growth Revisited: Economic and Biophysical Perspective', in R. Costanza (ed.) *Ecological Economics: The Science and Management of Sustainability*, New York: Columbia University Press.

Cole, H. S. D., Freeman, C., Jahoda, M. and Pavitt, K. L. R. (1973) *Models of Doom: A Critique of the Limits to Growth*, New York: Universe Books.

Council on Environmental Quality and Department of State (1980) *The Global 2000 Report to the President: Entering the Twenty-first Century*, Washington, DC: US Government Printing Office.

Dasgupta, P. S. and Heal, G. M. (1979) *Economic Theory and Exhaustible Resources*, Cambridge: Cambridge University Press.

Dasgupta, P. S., Levin, S. and Lubchenco, J. (2000) 'Economic Pathways to Ecological Sustainability', *BioScience* 54, 4: 339–45.

Ekins, P. (2000) *Economic Growth and Environmental Sustainability*, Routledge: London.

Goeller, H. E. and Weinberg, A. M. (1976) 'The Age of Substitutability: What Do We Do When the Mercury Runs Out?' *Science* 191: 683–9.

Grossman, G. M. and Krueger, A. B. (1995) 'Economic Growth and the Environment', *Quarterly Journal of Economics* 110: 353–77.

——(1996) 'The Inverted U: What Does It Mean?' *Environmental and Development Economics* 1: 119–22.

Hall, D. C. and Hall, J. V. (1984) 'Concepts and Measures of Natural Resource Scarcity with a Summary of Recent Trends', *Journal of Environmental Economics and Management* 11: 363–79.

Hardin, G. (1968) 'The Tragedy of the Commons', *Science* 162: 1243–8.

Hotelling, H. (1931) 'The Economics of Exhaustible Resources', *Journal of Political Economy* 39: 137–75.

Johnson, M. and Bennett, J. T. (1980) 'Increasing Resource Scarcity: Further Evidence', *Quarterly Review Economics and Business* 20: 42–8.

Johnson, M., Bell, F. and Bennett, J. (1980) 'Natural Resource Scarcity: Empirical Evidence and Public Policy', *Journal of Economic and Environmental Management* 7: 256–71.

Kuznets, S. (1955) 'Economic Growth and Income Inequality', *American Economic Review* 45: 1–28.

Leibenstein, H. (1974) 'An Interpretation of the Economic Theory of Fertility: Promising Path or Blind Alley?' *Journal of Economic Literature* 22: 457–79.

Meadows, D. H., Meadows, D. L., Randers, J. and Behrens, W. W. III (1974). *The Limits to Growth: A Report for the Club of Rome's Project on the Predicament of Mankind*, 2nd edn, New York: Universe Books.

Norgaard, R. B. (1990) 'Economic Indicators of Resource Scarcity: A Critical Essay', *Journal of Environmental Economics and Management* 19: 19–25.

Panayotou, T. (1993) 'Empirical Tests and Policy Analysis of Environmental Degradation at Different Stages of Economic Development', *World Employment Programme Research Working Paper WEP 2-22/WP* 238, January, International Labour Office, Geneva.

Rosenberg, N. (1973) 'Innovative Responses to Materials Shortages', *American Economic Review* 63: 111–18.

Rothman, D. S. and de Bruyn, S. M. (1998) 'Probing into the Environmental Kuznets Curve Hypothesis', *Ecological Economics* 25: 143–5.

Simon, J. L. (1980) 'Resources, Population, Environment: An Oversupply of False Bad News', *Science* 208: 1431–7.

——(1996) *The Ultimate Resource 2*, Princeton, NJ: Princeton University Press.

Simon, J. L. and Kahn, H. (1984) *The Resourceful Earth: A Response to Global 2000*, Oxford: Basil Blackwell.

Smith, K. V. (1978) 'Measuring Natural Resource Scarcity: Theory and Practice', *Journal of Environmental Economic Management* 5: 150–71.

——(1979) 'Natural Resource Scarcity: A Statistical Analysis', *Review of Economic Statistics* 61: 423–7.

——(1981) 'Increasing Resource Scarcity: Another Perspective', *Quarterly Review of Economics and Business* 21: 120–5.

Solow, R. M. (1974) 'The Economics of Resources or the Resources of Economics', *American Economic Review* 24: 1–14.

Torras, M. and Boyce, J. K. (1998) 'Income, Inequality, and Pollution: A Reassessment of the Environmental Kuznets Curve', *Ecological Economics* 25: 147–60.

12 Biophysical limits to economic growth

The ecological economics perspective

> The environmental resource base upon which all economic activity ultimately depends includes ecological systems that produce a wide variety of services. This resource base is finite. Furthermore, imprudent use of the environmental resource base may irreversibly reduce the capacity for regenerating material production in the future. All of this implies that there are limits to the carrying capacity of the planet.
>
> (Arrow *et al.* 1995)

> The closed economy of the future might similarly be called the 'spaceman' economy, in which the Earth has become a single spaceship, without unlimited reservoirs of anything, either for extraction or for pollution, and in which, therefore, man must find his place in a cyclical ecological system which is capable of continuous reproduction of material form even though it cannot escape having inputs of energy.
>
> (Boulding 1966)

12.1 Introduction

In Chapter 10, we saw that the Malthusian arguments on limits to economic growth are primarily based on the fear of depleting some key natural resources, including the natural environment's capacity to assimilate waste. In Chapter 11, we learned that this fear has been vigorously challenged by mainstream economists on the basis of resource substitution possibilities and other technical advances. That is, to the extent that resource substitution is possible, exhaustion of a particular resource need not cause major alarm (Solow 1974). Furthermore, if the possibility of infinite substitution of natural resources by human-made capital and labor is to be taken seriously, the existence of absolute limits to economic growth would become rather meaningless (Rosenberg 1973; Goeller and Weinberg 1976).

Unfortunately, even under this extreme case, absolute limits could be ignored only for certain extractive mineral resources, such as aluminum bauxite, copper ore, etc. When considerations of limits are made on the basis of the availability of *energy* and/or the *resilience* of natural ecosystems, denial of limits based on technological possibilities *per se* would not be adequate. In fact, they could be misleading and even dangerous (Georgescu-Roegen 1986; Arrow *et al.* 1995). Such is the ecological economics perspective of natural resource scarcity – the subject of this chapter. In the next section, the distinguishing features of ecological economics will be highlighted.

A word of advice: a quick review of the material covered in Chapter 2 will greatly enhance the reading and understanding of this chapter.

12.2 Ecological economics: nature and scope

Ecological economics deals with a comprehensive and systematic study of the linkages between ecological and economic *systems*. Its basic organizing principles include the idea that ecological and economic systems are complex, adaptive, living systems that need to be studied as integrated, co-evolving systems in order to be adequately understood (Costanza *et al.* 1993). In this sense, ecological economics attempts to re-integrate the academic disciplines of ecology and economics – two areas of study that have been going their own separate ways for over a century.

The ecological economics approach to economic studies is different from that of neoclassical economics in several ways.

First, in ecological economics the human economy is viewed as a *subsystem* of the natural ecosystem (see Figure 2.1, Chapter 2). *The nature of the exchanges of matter and energy between the ecosystem and economic subsystem is the primary focus of ecological economics* (Ayres 1978; Pearce 1987).

Second, given the above premise, in ecological economics, *production* (which is essentially a transformation of matter and energy) is viewed as the primary focus of economic study (Ayres 1978). The basic elements (factors of production) necessary for economic activities to take place are taken as being basic materials (such as wood products, minerals, etc.), energy, information flows, and the physical and biological processes within the ecosystem that are essential to sustaining life. Thus, except for information, the natural ecosystem is the ultimate source of all material inputs for the economic subsystem. In this sense, then, nature can rightly be regarded as the ultimate source of wealth.

Third, to the extent that production (transformation of matter and energy) is the focus, ecological economists use *thermodynamics* and *ecological principles* to delineate the critical role a particular natural resource plays in the economic process. For example, since all transformations require *energy* and there is no substitute for energy, the ecological economics approach tends to significantly elevate the importance of energy resources to the economic process and the ecosystem as a whole (Odum and Odum 1976; Costanza 1980; Mirowski 1988).

Fourth, another central theme of ecological economics is the *complementarity* of factors of production. All inputs in a production process are viewed as complements rather than substitutes. The main message here is that since neither capital nor labor physically creates natural resources, depletion of natural resources cannot be resolved through endless substitutions of labor and capital for natural resources. This fact, together with the laws of thermodynamics, challenges the optimistic 'technological' assumptions of neoclassical economics production analysis.

Last but not least, the ecological economics approach stresses the importance of the issue of *scale*. Here, scale refers to the size of a human economic subsystem relative to the global natural ecosystem (Daly 1992). *Ecological economists believe that, under present conditions, the size of the human economy relative to the global ecosystem is large enough to cause significant stress on the limited capacity of the natural global ecosystem to support the economic subsystem* (Goodland 1992). As evidence of this, they cite some of the major environmental and resource concerns that have made the headlines since the early 1980s: the alarming increase in the rate of generation of toxic wastes; the rapid acceleration of deforestation in tropical rain forests; the compelling evidence of the rapid rate of species extinction (both animals and plants); the increasing evidence of stratospheric ozone depletion; the unrestrained exploitation (both for waste dumping and resource extraction) of the ocean; and the growing evidence for global warming.

The key inference that can be drawn from this discussion is that 'as the scale of economic activity continues to increase, the economic and ecological systems become *dynamically linked* into a single integrated system. As a result, there is an increased risk that economic activity will precipitate instability in the total combined system, with immediate implications for society' (O'Neill and Kahn 2000: 335). This, according to the current paradigm of ecological economics, is how biophysical limits to economic growth manifest themselves.

Once the nature of biophysical limits is recognized in this way, ecological economics, as a sub-field of economic discipline, insists on fresh approaches to economic analysis, in the following specific ways:

1   To the extent that what goes on in the economic subsystem is believed to have effects (influences) on the rest of the ecosystem that are considered significant, economic problems should be analyzed using a *systems framework* (which uses nonlinear mathematics, general systems theory and nonequilibrium thermodynamics) and with transdisciplinary focus (Norgaard 1989; Costanza *et al.* 1993; O'Neill and Kahn 2000). This is in contrast to the usual way of viewing the economy as an isolated system and characterized by interactions that are considered to be linear or if non-linear, convex. It is only under such an assumed reality that the use of static equilibrium analysis, the law of averages, extrapolation from past events about the future and, most importantly, the possibility for endless factor substitutions are valid. Complex social and natural ecosystems that are subject to stress and positive feedback mechanisms are characterized by *nonconvex* process. In such a situation, discontinuity, an ecosystem's loss of resilience, its loss of ecological diversity, and irreversible changes to it are possible outcomes at both *local* and *global* levels (Dasgupta 2000; O'Neill and Kahn 2000).

    Two important messages emerge from this. First, in system interactions that are considered complex, major disturbances can occur from seemingly small and gradual changes – a warning about the use of marginal analysis. Second, activities in the human economy cannot be studied in isolation from their ecological context.

2   The performance of an economy should *not* be judged by *efficiency* considerations alone. Explicit consideration should be given to distributional and ethical concerns of both intra- and intergenerational varieties (Daly 1993). Furthermore, to ensure that the well-being of non-human beings is protected, resource values should *not* be assessed on the basis of human preference alone.

3   *Uncertainty* should be assumed to be fundamental to long-term economic assessment of natural resource availability since problems of this nature involve interactions of complex systems that are subject to irreversible processes (Arrow *et al.* 1995). Serious consideration of this warrants caution in introducing new technology and new species, pollution control measures, and protection for rare, threatened or endangered ecosystems and habitats. In other words, what is being proposed here is a *precautionary* approach to natural resource management. This was discussed at some length in Section 6 of Chapter 9.

12.3 The development of ecological economics: a brief historical sketch

Ecological economics in its modern version is a relatively new field. However, it would be entirely wrong to consider it a new subdiscipline. Its historical roots can be traced back as far as the preclassical Physiocrats – the economists of the French school of the mid-seventeenth century (Cleveland 1987; Martinez-Alier 1987). One of the fundamental premises of the Physiocratic school of thought was that all economic surplus is derived from the productive power of 'land', or its modern equivalent, natural resources. In this sense, then, natural resources were regarded as the ultimate source of material wealth. It is to underscore this point that Sir William Petty (1623–83), one of the most celebrated economists of the Physiocratic school, declared that 'land is the mother and labor is the father of wealth'.

This treatment of land as the ultimate resource was also prominent in the literature of classical economics. For example, David Ricardo referred to land as the 'original and indestructible powers of the soil'. During both the Physiocratic era and the era of classical economics, land was viewed as a limiting factor. Thus, understanding the 'natural laws' that govern this resource was considered a key factor in any effort seeking to address the fate of the human economy in the long run. To this end, Ricardo's discovery of *the law of diminishing returns* was of considerable significance.

Another major turning point in the historical development of biophysical economics occurred with the formulation of the laws of *thermodynamics* in the early nineteenth century. This discovery contributed to a clear understanding of the physical laws governing the transformations of matter and energy. Immediately afterwards, thermodynamic laws were used to explain the 'natural limits' relevant to the transformations of natural resources into final goods and services.

Within the discipline of economics, the laws of thermodynamics have been used for two distinct purposes. First, using the relationship between energy flows and economic activity, thermodynamic laws have been used to help in the understanding of an economy's workings and its interaction with the natural ecosystem. This led to a clear understanding of the biophysical foundations of economics. Some of the major lessons drawn from closer examinations of the laws of thermodynamics are the *complementarity* of factor inputs, the limits to conserving energy through technological means, the limits to the regenerative and assimilative capacities of the natural environment, and, in general, the existence of biophysical limits to economic growth. These issues will be further explored later using the works of Georgescu-Roegen.

Second, in the late nineteenth century several physical scientists and economists started to advocate the use of energy as a basis for a unified value theory. All transformations require energy; its flow is unidirectional; and there is no substitute for it. It therefore makes sense to use energy as a numeraire – a denominator by which the value of all resources is weighed (Odum and Odum 1976). This is equivalent to attempting to express the value of economic activities in terms of their embodied energy (Costanza 1980). Even to this day, there are a number of scholars who strongly advocate what appears to be an 'energy theory of value'.

The most recent breakthrough in the development of ecological economics has occurred since the Second World War and the arrival of the space age. In particular, the 1960s were, in many ways, watershed years in the revival of interest in ecological economics. This decade marked the beginning of heightened public awareness of ecological limits. Several events were responsible for this occurrence. Of these, two are especially worthy of brief mention. First, as human society entered the space age, the idea that 'Planet Earth' is a finite sphere became conventional wisdom. Second, until the publication of *Silent Spring* (1962) by Rachel Carson, public awareness of ecological damage(s) was extremely low. By alerting the world community to the widespread ecological damage resulting from pesticide misuse, this classic book was in large part responsible for starting the modern environmental movement in the United States and elsewhere. For the book's impact was not limited merely to increasing public awareness of ecological ills; it also changed the nature of the scholarly debate on growth, resources and the environment.

In the mid-1960s, Kenneth Boulding's classic essay 'The Economics of the Coming Spaceship Earth' ushered in the modern revival of ecological economics. During the 1970s, Nicholas Georgescu-Roegen and Herman Daly, two other unorthodox economists, were responsible for the development of some of the most insightful ideas in ecological economics. The essential message of these three economists' works was that limits to economic growth could no longer be argued solely on the basis of the possibility of running out of conventional resources – the traditional Malthusian approach. Nor could technology be viewed as the ultimate means of circumventing ecological limits – as neoclassical economists like to argue. Instead, *the finite availability of high-quality energy and the loss of ecosystem resilience were recognized as two key limiting factors in humanity's pursuit for a material nirvana.*

As is evident from the discussion in Exhibit 12.1, ecosystem resilience is an emerging concern of considerable significance. It involves problems of the following nature: ecological stress from prolonged environmental pollution, the effect of which is a sudden loss of biological productivity; irreversible changes such as desertification and loss of biodiversity; and uncertainty associated with environmental effects of economic activities.

Where is ecological economics today? As the world has gradually but surely shifted from being a relatively 'empty' world to a relatively 'full' world, the relevance of ecological economics for addressing global environmental and resource concerns has been widely recognized (Cleveland 1987). The resurgence of interest in ecological economics has been particularly dramatic over the past two decades. In 1988, the International Society for Ecological Economics (ISEE) was officially inaugurated. Presently, it has a membership in excess of 10,000, and it is truly international in both its missions and membership composition.

What effects, if any, has the recent renewal of interest in ecological economics had on the economic profession at large? On the whole, the influence of ecological economics on mainstream economic thinking has been relatively insignificant. By and large, mainstream economists continue to resist any demands by ecological economists for a shift in the neoclassical growth paradigm (Young 1991). For that matter, there are considerable numbers of economists who simply consider the works of influential ecological economists such as Boulding, Georgescu-Roegen and Daly (these are going to be discussed in the next section) interesting, but *nothing more than a new spin on the old-fashioned neo-Malthusian way of thinking*.

Despite this skepticism, there are also growing numbers of economists who do not necessarily identify themselves as ecological economists, but are making serious, scholarly efforts to find ways of incorporating the implications of ecological limits into the general framework of mainstream economic analysis. This is especially evident in the field of environmental and resource economics – a subfield of economics that has

Exhibit 12.1   Carrying capacity and ecosystem resilience

K. Arrow, B. Bolin, R. Costanza et al.

The environmental resource base upon which all economic activity ultimately depends includes ecological systems that produce a wide variety of services. This resource base is finite. Furthermore, imprudent use of the environmental resource base may irreversibly reduce the capacity for generating material production in the future. All of this implies that there are limits to the carrying capacity of the planet. . . .

Carrying capacities in nature are not fixed, static or simple relations. They are contingent on technology, preferences and the structure of production and consumption. They are also contingent on the ever-changing state of interactions between the physical and the biotic environments. A single number for human carrying capacity would be meaningless because the consequences of both human innovation and biological evolution are inherently unknowable. Nevertheless, a general index of the current scale or intensity of the human economy in relation to that of the biosphere is still useful. For example, Vitousek *et al.* calculated that the total net terrestrial primary production of the biosphere currently being appropriated for human consumption is around 40 per cent. This does put the scale of the human presence on the planet in perspective.

A more useful index of environmental sustainability is ecosystem resilience. One way of thinking about resilience is to focus on ecosystem dynamics where there are multiple (locally) stable equilibria. Resilience in this sense is a measure of the magnitude of disturbance that can be absorbed before a system centered on one locally stable equilibrium flips to another. Economic activities are sustainable only if the life-support ecosystems on which they depend are resilient. Even though ecological resilience is difficult to measure and even though it varies from system to system and from one kind of disturbance to another, it may be possible to identify indicators and early-warning signals of environmental stress. For example, the diversity of organisms and the heterogeneity of ecological functions have been suggested as signals of ecosystem resilience. But ultimately, the resilience of systems may only be tested by intelligently perturbing them and observing the response with what has been called 'adaptive management'.

The loss of ecosystem resilience is potentially important for at least three reasons. First, the discontinuous change in ecosystem flips from one equilibrium to another could be associated with a sudden loss of biological productivity, and so to a reduced capacity to support human life. Second, it may imply an irreversible change in the set of options open to both present and future generations (examples include soil erosion, depletion of groundwater reservoirs, desertification, and loss of biodiversity). Third, discontinuous and irreversible changes from familiar to unfamiliar states increase the uncertainties associated with the environmental effects of economic activities.

If human activities are to be sustainable, we need to ensure that the ecological systems on which our economies depend are resilient. The problem involved in devising environmental policies is to ensure that resilience is maintained, even though the limits on the nature and scale of economic activities thus required are necessarily uncertain.

Source: *Science* 268, 1995, pp. 520–1.

gained increasing popularity since the 1970s. No serious textbook in environmental and resource economics written over the past decade has failed to include some discussion of concepts such as the material balance approach (referring to the first law of thermo-dynamics); the second law of thermodynamics; limits to the absorptive capacity of the natural environment; and carrying capacity – to mention only a few.

12.4 Biophysical limits and their implications for economic growth

In this section we will discuss in some detail from the perspective of ecological economics the nature of the biophysical limits relevant to human concerns for continued increases in material standard of living. This will be done using the pioneering works of the three highly distinguished economists mentioned above, namely Kenneth Boulding (1909–93), Nicholas Georgescu-Roegen (1906–94) and Herman Daly. A common feature of the scholarly works of these three economists is their use of thermodynamics and ecological principles to demonstrate the existence of biophysical limits on 'economic growth'. In the process, they fiercely challenge the basic tenets of the neoclassical growth paradigm. Further, these three unorthodox economists argue for an economy that is *ecologically sustainable*. Herman Daly even goes so far as to propose his own growth paradigm.

There are several other scholars whose contributions to the modern revival of ecological economics are considered significant, and some of these major contributors are not necessarily economists. I choose to focus here only on the works of the three scholars mentioned above purely because they offer a fierce challenge to the neoclassical growth paradigm from within rather than from outside the economic discipline. Further, no one who knows the works of Boulding, Daly and Georgescu-Roegen would fail to acknowledge the significance of their contributions to economics. They are first-rate economists who simply chose to revolt against the mainstream views of their own discipline.

12.4.1 Kenneth Boulding: ecological limits

Kenneth Boulding's essay 'The Economics of the Coming Spaceship Earth' (1966) represents one of the earliest attacks from an ecological perspective on modern economists' preoccupation with economic growth. His essay is a true classic, written in a style that allows economists to understand and appreciate ecological arguments that are relevant to economics. In this regard, one could safely claim that this is the first essay to have sparked interest in (or some understanding of) ecology among mainstream economic scholars.

The main messages of the essay are straightforward. Boulding starts by reminding us that our past is characterized by a frontier mentality, i.e. the strongly held belief that there is always a new place to discover 'when things got too difficult, either by reason of the deterioration of the natural environment or a deterioration of the social structure in places where people happened to live' (p. 297). The Earth, therefore, is viewed as an open system or unlimited plane. Boulding uses the metaphor 'the cowboy economy' to describe the economic system that is compatible with this scenario of resource availability. In this scenario, where resource availability is taken for granted, both consumption and production are regarded as good things. Accordingly, nature is recklessly exploited with little or no concern. Moreover, the success of an economy is measured by the amount of throughput (matter and energy) used to produce the desired goods and services, without regard to depletion or pollution. Thus, according to Boulding, reckless exploitation of nature – which is characteristic of cowboy-like behavior – characterizes our past.

However, Boulding views the future quite differently. Specifically, he alerts us to the fact that we are now in a transition from the open to the closed Earth. We were able to fully realize this only recently when we entered into the space age and vividly observed that the Earth is a finite sphere. Thus, the

> Earth has become a single spaceship, without unlimited reservoirs of anything, either for extraction or for pollution, and in which, therefore, man must find his place in a cyclical ecological system that is capable of continuous reproduction of materials even though it cannot escape having inputs of energy.
>
> (Boulding 1966: 303)

According to Boulding, this new reality has significant economic implications. The economy of the future, which he referred to as the 'spaceman' economy, requires economic principles that are different from those of the open Earth of the past:

> In the spaceman economy, *throughput* (matter and energy) is by no means a desideratum, and is indeed to be regarded as something to be minimized rather than maximized. Hence, the essential measure of the success of the economy is not production and consumption, but the nature, extent, quality, and complexity of the total capital stock, including the state of the human bodies and minds included in the system.
>
> (ibid.: 304)

Boulding then goes on to argue that mainstream economists still have a difficult time accepting the above implications of the spaceman economy *because the suggestion that both production and consumption are bad things rather than good things works against the natural instinct of mainstream economists.*

With this in mind, Boulding's messages are quite clear. First and foremost, for all practical purposes *the Earth is a closed ecological sphere.* When the human population was small and its technological capabilities were not overpowering, viewing the Earth as an unlimited plane might have been, if not correct then certainly understandable and permissible. However, current human conditions with respect to population, technology, and habits of consumption and production warrant a fresh look at our social values and economic systems. *We need to espouse social values and build economic systems that reinforce the idea that – in a material sense – more is not necessarily better.* In the final analysis, Boulding's message is simply this: the future of humankind depends on our ability to design an economic system that regulates the flow of throughput *with full recognition of ecological limits in order to establish a sustainable economy.*

12.4.2 Nicholas Georgescu-Roegen: energy and thermodynamics

Another highly acclaimed economist who is even harsher in his criticisms of standard economics than Boulding is Nicholas Georgescu-Roegen. Georgescu-Roegen's major contributions to economics are numerous and varied. His works in consumer choice and utility theory, measurability, production theory, input–output analysis, and economic development are well recognized and contributed a good deal to the mainstream economics literature in these areas. His major contributions to the standard economics literature are collected in his book *Analytical Economics* (1966). Paul Samuelson, in his preface to *Analytical Economics*, referred to Georgescu-Roegen as 'a scholar's scholar, an economists' economist' (Daly 1996).

Georgescu-Roegen's insightful but revolutionary contributions to resource economics were forcefully articulated in his book *The Entropy Law and the Economic Process* (1971). This seminal work represents a vigorous, insightful and critical appraisal of the standard economics paradigm of resource scarcity and economic growth. He did this by using fundamental principles from thermodynamics – the natural laws that govern the transformation of energy–matter. In so doing he introduced a new and revolutionary conceptual framework in the economic analysis of the interactions between ecological and economic systems. *To Georgescu-Roegen, from a purely physical viewpoint both the human economy and the natural ecosystems are characterized by continuous 'exchange' of matter and energy; and careful analysis of this energy and material flow is paramount in the understanding of the physical limits to the economic process.* It is for this reason that he went on to declare thermodynamics as the 'most economic of all physical laws'. However, he was truly baffled and disappointed by the complete lack of attention given to this fundamental idea in the standard economic analysis of resource allocations.

Georgescu-Roegen observed that epistemologically the neoclassical school of economics still follows the *mechanistic dogma* that it inherited from 'Newtonian mechanics'. For this reason economic analysis is based on a conceptual framework that is rather *simplistic* and *unidirectional*. As evidence of this, Georgescu-Roegen cited the standard economics textbook representation of the economic process by a circular flow diagram (see Chapter 1, Figure 1.8). From a purely physical viewpoint, this diagram represents a circular flow of matter–energy between production and consumption within a completely closed system.. This flow of matter–energy is assumed to be regulated not by any natural or supernatural being, but by *utility* and *self-interest*. Clearly, then, no explicit link was made between the flow of matter–energy in the economic process and the physical environment. *In other words, the economic process is treated as an 'isolated, circular affair', independent of the natural environment from which materials are extracted.* According to Georgescu-Roegen, to conceptualize the economic process in this manner is not only simplistic but misleading and dangerous, for three reasons.

First, *it makes economists focus on economic value alone*. In consequence, this leads to a blatant disregard of the physical flows of matter–energy (the biophysical foundation) of the economic process. To counter, Georgescu-Roegen, using the second law of thermodynamics, reminds us that 'from a purely physical viewpoint, the economic process only transforms valuable natural resources (low entropy) into waste (high entropy)' (1971: 265). This qualitative difference between what goes into the economic process and what comes out of it should be enough to confirm that 'nature, too, plays an important role in the economic process as well as in the formation of economic value' (ibid.: 266). Note that Georgescu-Roegen is not claiming here that economic value is solely determined by nature. He is an astute economist who realizes that economic value is determined by both demand (utility) and supply (technology and nature). To confirm this, he argued that the true economic output of the economic process is not a material flow of waste, but an immaterial flux: the enjoyment of life. If we do not recognize the existence of this flux, we are not in the economic world. Nor do we have a complete picture of the economic process if we ignore the fact that this flux – which, as an entropic feeling, must characterize life at all levels – exists only as long as it can continually feed itself on environmental low entropy.

(ibid.: 80)

Thus, according to Georgescu-Roegen, low entropy is a necessary but not a sufficient condition for economic value. However, in no way can this justify the blatant disregard of the key role that low-entropy matter–energy plays in the formation of economic value.

Second, *it causes standard economists to overlook the role that low-entropy matter–energy plays in the economic process.* Using the second law of thermodynamics, Georgescu-Roegen forcefully argued for the significance of energy as a limiting factor not only to the growth of material standards of living, but also ultimately to the economic process itself. He argued that

environmental low entropy is scarce in a different sense than Ricardian land. Both Ricardian land and the coal deposits are available in limited amounts. The difference is that a piece of coal can be used only once. The economic process is solidly anchored to a material base, which is subject to definite constraints. It is because of this constraint that the economic process has a unidirectional irrevocable evolution.

(ibid.)

Third, *by failing to acknowledge the natural constraints to the economic process (biophysical limits), mainstream economists become first-rate technological optimists.* The belief that any material problem(s) humanity faces can be solved by technological means started to be taken for granted by economists, but this is wishful thinking for the following reasons:

1   According to the second law of thermodynamics, it is impossible to discover a self-perpetuating industrial machine. In the ordinary transformation of matter and energy – which the economic process is subjected to – there can never be 'free recycling as there is no wasteless industry' (ibid. 83) In other words, *there are absolute minimum thermodynamic requirements of energy and materials to produce a unit of output that cannot be augmented by technical change.*
2   As was later expounded by Ayres (1978), the laws of thermodynamics place limits on the substitution of human-made capital for natural capital (low-entropy matter and energy) and, therefore, the ability of technological change to compensate for the depletion or degradation of natural capital. In fact, in the long run, natural and human-made capital are *complements* because the latter requires material and energy for its production and maintenance. This is indeed a rejection of one of the important core principles of the neoclassical growth paradigm: the notion of infinite substitutability between human-made and natural capital.

However, it is important to note that both Georgescu-Roegen and Boulding are not against the very idea of technology or technological advancement. In this case, their concerns are twofold. First, we need to acknowledge that there is a limit to technological advancement. Second, technology can be abused or misused. On the other hand, used prudently, technology could be a blessing. For example, a technological advance that decreases the need for throughput (low-entropy matter–energy), while maintaining a material standard of living at some desired level, is indeed to be sought after. On the other hand, if technological advance is directed toward producing more goods and services with no limit in sight, such a strategy is highly questionable from the viewpoint of long-term sustainability. Thus, *a prudent use of technology requires the recognition of the ultimate constraints imposed by nature – biophysical limits*.

Georgescu-Roegen and Boulding can rightly be thought of as the two economists who were mainly responsible for establishing the conceptual and theoretical foundation of the modern variant of ecological economics. However, in terms of offering a concrete alternative paradigm to traditional economic growth, no one rivals Herman Daly – a student of Georgescu-Roegen.

12.4.3 Herman Daly: the steady-state economy

Herman Daly is a visionary scholar who is particularly known for his insistent and forceful attack on the neoclassical economics growth paradigm. He worked for the World Bank for several years at the time when the bank was making serious attempts to correct the ecological contradictions of its development plans. Presently, he is a professor at the University of Maryland School of Public Affairs.

Daly is particularly recognized for his effort to conceptualize and articulate a viable alternative to the neoclassical growth paradigm, namely the *steady-state economy* (SSE). Herman Daly's conceptual model of the SSE is not a totally new idea since it shares common themes and concerns with John Stuart Mill's vision of a 'stationary state' of over a century ago. Daly's model is different to the extent that it explicitly incorporates additional resource constraints – the ecological and physical realities articulated by Boulding and Georgescu-Roegen. In fact, one could safely state that the SSE is a theoretical economic 'growth' model that explicitly attempts to incorporate the biophysical limits and ethical considerations proclaimed or implied by Georgescu-Roegen and Boulding. The SSE can also be credited for igniting the recent scholarly interest on sustainable development.

The means and ends spectrum

Daly (1993) began his argument by declaring that the neoclassical economic growth paradigm is untenable because it is not based on sustainable *biophysical* and *moral* considerations. He explains this contention by using a simple scheme of a means and ends spectrum (ordering), as presented in Figure 12.1.

According to Daly, standard economic growth models ignore the ultimate means by which the growth of material standards of living are attainable. Here, *ultimate means refers to the low-entropy matter–energy of the ecosphere*. The fact that the ultimate means are scarce in absolute terms or that these basic resources are constrained by natural laws is considered irrelevant by mainstream economists. Instead, because of their blind faith in technology, mainstream economists exclusively focus on the availability of *intermediate means*: labor, capital and conventional natural resources (extracted raw materials). In the process, the fact that the availability of intermediate means ultimately

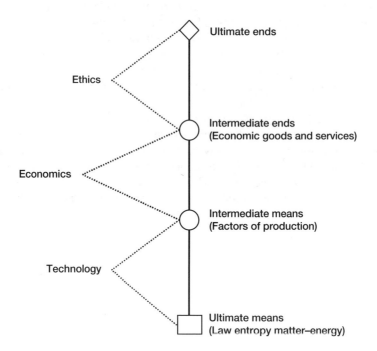

Figure 12.1 Means and ends spectrum. Mainstream economics deals with how to ration
scarce intermediate means and intermediate ends, to the exclusion of ultimate
means and ultimate ends. ultimate means are excluded because too much faith is
placed in technology and ultimate ends are ignored because of the lack of
explicit accounting for ethics.

depends on the availability of ultimate means seems to have escaped standard economic
thinking. For this reason, focusing on intermediate means, economists discuss relative
scarcity and prices, on the basis of which resources are allocated to alternative societal
uses (see the last section of Chapter 1).

   Given this biophysical reality, it is no wonder that standard economists are so
infatuated with continual growth in *intermediate ends*: market-valued goods and
services. This seemingly sacred goal in economics is pursued not only without regard to
biophysical limits, but also without consideration of both intra- and intergenerational
equities. In other words, how the total quantity of goods and services produced in a
given calendar year is distributed among the people of the current generation (intragenerational), and how current economic activities may affect the well-being of future
generations (intergenerational), are simply not considered. This is not to suggest that
standard economists are in denial of the existence of maldistribution of income among
the current generation, or that they are insensitive to the possible adverse effects of
current production (such as pollution) on the well-being of the distant generations.
Rather, as discussed in Chapter 11, the main position of standard economists has been
that sustaining a moderate to high rate of growth is the single most effective panacea for
current and future economic and ecological ills. In some scholarly circles, this view is
known as growthmania.

A position taken by Daly and others is that, when viewed realistically, it would be dangerous to pursue the ideals of growthmania for at least two reasons.

First, human aspiration is not limited to accumulating material wealth. Humans are social beings with feelings and ideals that are social, psychological and/or spiritual. Furthermore, humans are biological beings with instincts for survival. These are the elements that define and shape the relationships of humankind over time and space and with their other ideals – like their relationship with the physical or spiritual world. The extent to which humans care about future generations, then, depends on the totality of these nonmaterial-based ideals. Daly called these the *ultimate ends*. According to Daly, mainstream economists have failed to consider the ultimate ends because of their undue preoccupation with the material world.

Second, growthmania, if pursued blindly, could have abrupt and catastrophic economic and ecological consequences. *Therefore, the argument against growthmania is not to avoid the 'inevitable extinction of humankind', but to safeguard humanity from sudden economic and ecological collapse.* Hence the imperative for a *precautionary approach* to resource management.

To summarize Daly's position: neoclassical economists have ignored both ultimate means and ultimate ends by advocating continual economic growth. The ultimate means are forgotten because of the strong and persistent belief that resource scarcity can always be ameliorated through technology. The ultimate ends are ignored because of the standard economists' preoccupation with the material world. Therefore, as shown in Figure 12.1, economic concern occupies only the middle portion of the means–ends spectrum. That is, the neoclassical growth paradigm concentrates on intermediate means: labor, capital and raw materials, and on intermediate ends: the attainment of market-valued goods and services. Thus, *given such a narrow and incomplete perspective of material and nonmaterial reality, it is not difficult to see why mainstream economists are so eager to believe in the prospect of boundless economic growth.*

If the above growth paradigm is to be rejected on the basis of its incomplete material and ethical considerations, what alternative model(s) could be proposed? Herman Daly's response to this question is the steady-state economy (SSE). What is the SSE? And in what ways does it differ from the neoclassical growth model?

The biophysical, economic and ethical dimensions of the steady-state economy

From the beginning, Daly defines the SSE as 'a constant stock of physical wealth and people (population)'. Note that, in this way, the SSE is intentionally defined in a *purely biophysical context*, which suggests that the total inventory of all the intermediate means and ends, including human population, is frozen at some 'desirable' constant. In other words, *in quantitative terms the material requirements to run an economy are held constant at all times.* Thus, in the SSE the primary focus is on what Daly identified as *stock maintenance*. By this he means maintaining a constant inventory of intermediate means and ends. From now on the term *stock* will be used in reference to this constant inventory of intermediate means and ends.

But, in an *entropic* world, stock maintenance can never be achieved without cost: constant withdrawal of finite ultimate means. The question, then, is not how should we avoid this cost, but what can we do to *minimize* it? Daly suggests that this can be done

Case Study 12.1   Asset recycling at Xerox

Jack Azar

In the industrial society, the proliferation of solid waste in the face of diminishing landfill space continues to be a major concern. Reacting to this challenge, in some countries legislation is in the works that could significantly affect marketplace demands. In Germany, legislation has been proposed that would require manufacturers and distributors to take back and recycle or dispose of used electronic equipment. The European Community is considering similar legislation. In Canada, too, interest in such legislation has been expressed. And in Japan, a 1991 regulation issued by the Ministry of International Trade and Industry promotes not only the use of recycled materials in certain durable items but also the recyclability of those items themselves.

In response to what seems to be a future trend in worldwide movement towards recycling, in 1990 Xerox began a corporate environmental strategy that encompasses equipment and parts recycling. The cornerstone of this strategy is the Asset Recycle Management program. As the name implies, it entails treating all products and components owned by the company – whether out on rental or on the company's premises – as physical 'assets'.

The key feature of the Asset Recycle Management program at Xerox is the emphasis on a rather 'unconventional' approach that machines should be designed from concept with the remanufacturing process and the recapture of parts and materials in mind. This meant getting the company's design and manufacturing engineers to bring an entirely new perspective to their work. To facilitate this the company instituted an Asset Recycle Management organization. The principal charge of this organization is to continually identify areas where significant opportunities to optimize the use of equipment and parts, even for existing products, could be captured.

Early on, it was recognized that company engineers needed design guidelines to enhance remanufacturing and materials recycling. . . . Specifically, the guidelines reflect the following design criteria: extended product and component life – i.e. use of more robust materials and design to make asset recovery practical; selection of materials that are relatively easy to recycle at the end of product life; simplification of materials to facilitate recycling; easy disassembly as well as easy assembly; remanufacturing convertibility, meaning that a basic product configuration is convertible to a different use – e.g. a copier to an electronic printer; and use of common parts to enable future reuse in different models and configurations.

Xerox's first environmental design to reach the market was a customer-replaceable copy cartridge, which has many of the characteristics of a complete xerographic copier. Designed for use in the company's smaller convenience copiers, the copy cartridge contains the main xerographic elements critical to the copying process: photoreceptor, electrical charging devices and a cleaning mechanism.

Copy cartridges designed for older convenience copiers posed a special challenge. They had not been designed for recycling. In fact, their plastic housings were assembled by ultrasonic welding. The company had to break them open to get at the components within, thereby destroying the plastic housings. While it was usually possible to reclaim the photoreceptor-transport assemblies, all that could be done with the housings was to grind them down for reuse as injection-molding raw materials.

The new 5300 series of convenience copiers has a new design: a cartridge that is assembled with a few fasteners. It is totally remanufacturable, a process that costs far less than building one with all new parts, and more than 90 per cent of the material is recoverable. It also meets all product quality specifications and carries the same warranty as newly manufactured cartridges.

To date, the Asset Recycling Program at Xerox has been a big success from the standpoint of both environmental and business considerations. On the business side, the company saved a total of $50 million the first year in logistics, inventory and the cost of raw materials. These savings are to increase greatly as design-for-environment Xerox products enter the market. In addition, only a minimal amount of material has been scrapped compared with previous years.

Source: *EPA Journal* Vol. 19, 1993, pp. 15–16. Reprinted with permission.

through vigorous pursuit of *maintenance efficiency*, which is defined as a ratio of two key factors: the constant stock and throughput (stock/throughput).

Maintenance efficiency: minimize (stock/throughput)

Throughput refers to the flow of low-entropy matter–energy (from the ultimate means) that needs to be used to replace the periodical depreciation of stock. Given that stock is held *constant*, this ratio can be maximized by minimizing throughput. Thus, in the SSE, maintenance efficiency is attained in two ways: (a) *durability* – producing artifacts (intermediate ends) that are long-lasting; and (b) *replaceability* – producing products that are easy to replace or recycle.

Technology can play a key role in the realization of these two aspects of maintenance efficiency. Hence, the SSE is not anti-technology, but insists that technology should be used in certain ways. As a general rule, *any technological change that results in the maintenance of a given stock with a lessened throughput is clearly to be encouraged.* Case Study 12.1 offers an excellent account of how a company, in this case the Xerox Corporation, using common sense and technology was able to establish an equipment and parts recycling program in which durability and replaceability are emphasized.

Thus far, the SSE has been described in terms of its biophysical attributes. However, as Georgescu-Roegen would like to remind us, the economic world is defined not only by material flow or transformation of matter–energy, but by 'an immaterial flux: the enjoyment of life'. How does the SSE address this important dimension of the economic world?

As the architect of the SSE, Daly postulated that the primary goal of an economy is to *maximize service* subject to the constraint of constant stock. *Service* is defined as the satisfaction (utility) obtained when wants are satisfied. Or, in more general terms, 'the final benefit of all economic activity'. It is important to note that only stock (the inventory of intermediate means and ends) is capable of generating utility. Under this condition, how best can service (utility) be maximized? According to Daly, this objective can be achieved through what he calls *service efficiency*, which is defined as the ratio of service to the constant stock (service/stock).

Service efficiency: maximize (service/stock)

Maximization of this ratio amounts to finding ways of making the numerator (service or utility) larger while keeping the denominator (stock) *constant*. Daly identified two ways of doing this: *allocative* and *distributive* efficiencies.

Attainment of *allocative efficiency* requires that two specific conditions be fulfilled. First, the production of goods and services should use the least amount of intermediate means (labor, capital and natural resources) possible – *production efficiency*. Second, the goods and services that are produced should be the ones that provide the most satisfaction to people. *These are efficiency factors, which are primarily if not exclusively emphasized in standard economics.* Considering this, over the past 50 years standard economists have made a significant stride in developing the conceptual framework and in articulating the criteria necessary to achieve these types of efficiency requirements.

On the other hand, *distributive efficiency* requires that the distribution of the *constant* stock (intermediate means and ends) should be done in such a way 'that the trivial wants of some people do not take precedence over the basic needs of others'. It is important to note that this requirement is not motivated by ethical considerations alone. If the postulate of diminishing marginal utility is accepted, then distributive efficiency would lead to increased total social welfare (utility). The argument here is that taking away a dollar from the very rich and passing it to the very poor will increase the well-being (grand utility function) of a society because the utility loss from the rich will be more than offset by the utility gain of the poor – clearly a Pareto-efficient move.

Furthermore, it is important to note that distributive efficiency is not limited to equity issues among existing generations – *intragenerational equity*. Another equally important issue to consider is *intergenerational equity*. That is, *it is important to ensure that current generations are not enriching themselves at the expense of future generations.* In general, the issue of equity is difficult to discern because it deals with the difficult issues of fairness or justice, which require value judgements. It becomes even more challenging as the issue stretches in time and space. Nevertheless, while generally accepted standards of fairness or justice do not exist with reference to intergenerational equity issues, one criterion that is gaining popularity – Rawlsian justice – declares that 'at a minimum, future generations should be left no worse off than current generations' (for more on this see Section 6 of Chapter 9).

Therefore, in the SSE it is expected that the general principle of maximum total satisfaction (service) from a constant stock should be pursued with full consideration of fairness and justice both in time and space. As shown in Figure 12.1, this requires a formulation of ethical principles linking intermediate and ultimate ends. A matter of such importance is not even peripherally addressed in standard economics, where the prevailing attitude is to treat intergenerational equity as, basically, a non-issue. Accordingly, the general sentiment is 'What has posterity ever done for me?' Furthermore, as discussed in Chapter 11, the empirical evidence over the past two centuries clearly indicates improved material standards of living in each succeeding generation – strong evidence that makes concern about future generations unnecessary.

To summarize the above discussion: there are, conceptually, *three* general principles that govern the operation of the SSE. First, the SSE requires the use of *throughput* (low-entropy matter–energy) to be *minimized* at all times. This suggests that in the SSE, as much as is feasible, all possible technological avenues must be pursued to produce goods and services that are long-lasting and easily recyclable – the attainment of maintenance efficiency (see Case Study 12.1).

Second, in the SSE, *service* (utility) is to be *maximized*. This should be done through a combination of both production efficiency (production of more goods and services from a given resource) and distributive efficiency (fair or equitable distribution of goods and services produced).

Finally, and most importantly, the SSE requires that *stock* (the total inventory of intermediate means and ends) should be held *constant* because in a world endowed with finite resources (low-entropy matter–energy), equity considerations in both time and space make the requirement of constant stock an essential prerequisite of the SSE.

Practicality of the steady-state economy

Does the SSE imply economic stagnation? This is a natural question, given that in the SSE, the quantities of the physical stock (intermediate means and ends, including human population) are held constant. Nevertheless, Daly's response to this question is a definite 'no'. To explain his position, Daly differentiated between 'economic growth' and 'economic development'. *Economic growth* means the production of more goods and services to satisfy ever-increasing human wants, or, as Daly put it, 'the creation of ever more intermediate means (stocks) for the purpose of satisfying ever more intermediate ends' (1993: 21). Because stocks are held constant, economic growth is impossible in SSE. *This, however, should not be a cause for concern since an economy can grow qualitatively without necessitating a corresponding quantitative growth in its physical dimensions.* How?

First, while physical stocks are held constant in the SSE, the stress should be on measuring economic improvements in terms of *nonphysical goods*: services and leisure. Second, emphasis should be placed on inculcating social values (perhaps through education) and fostering technological progress that allow the increases in leisure activities (such as growing appreciation of environmental amenities, friendships, meditation, etc.) which are far less material-intensive than the production of physical outputs. With these adjustments, economic growth, measured in terms of an increasing level of satisfaction (utility) from a given level of resource stocks, is quite possible. Daly referred to this qualitative growth in economic well-being as 'economic development'. *Accordingly, in the SSE it is possible to develop even in the total absence of traditional economic growth.*

No doubt, in terms of both its biophysical and its ethical requirements, the SSE is radically different from the neoclassical growth models. The question is: is the SSE practicable? The viability of any theoretical model largely depends on the pragmatic issues that need to be overcome to make the model workable. In this case, the actual implementation of the SSE requires the establishment of several *social institutions* that may be considered quite revolutionary and, in some ways, impractical.

First, in the SSE, stocks are required to be held constant. How should the constant stocks be determined? Is this going to be done solely by government decree? If so, would that be acceptable in a democratic society where the political quest is to minimize the role of government in the economic affairs of the citizens? Would the market have any role in rationing the constant stocks once their level is determined? Herman Daly's response to these questions is rather simple. He proposed *depletion quotas* as a strategy for controlling the flow of aggregate throughput. Behind this strategy is the idea that controlling the rate of depletion would indirectly limit both pollution and the size of throughput – the flow of low-entropy matter–energy. Initially, the government would auction the limited quota rights to many resource buyers. Afterwards, the resources are expected to be allocated to their best uses under a competitive market setting.

Second, in the SSE, population is held at a constant level with low birth and death rates. How would one determine the optimal level of population? What social and technological means are used to control population? Can population control measures be effectively and uniformly implemented in an ideologically and culturally pluralistic society? Daly's proposed solution to the population problem is *transferable birth licenses*. Again, this is a strategy that combines both a government fiat and the market. Here, the government would issue every woman (or couple) with a certain number of reproduction licenses that correspond to replacement fertility, i.e. 2.1 licenses. These birth licenses are transferable so that those who want no more than two children can sell them at the going market price. Since population is allowed to grow at a rate no greater than the replacement fertility rate, the total population would thereby remain constant.

Third, and finally, in the SSE institutions are required to regulate the distribution of income and wealth. This is important because, as discussed earlier, even without equity considerations, income redistribution is one avenue by which total social welfare can be increased. However, is it practical to envision an institution that imposes limits on income and wealth? After all, what is the difference between such an institution and communism? Daly has offered no tangible proposal to resolve the redistribution problem.

On practical grounds the SSE is extremely difficult to defend. Nevertheless, this should not in any way suggest that Daly's specific policy recommendations are erroneous or misguided. It only means that we, as a society, are not yet ready to make the political, moral and psychological adjustments necessary to effect the suggested institutional changes. *At this stage of its development, therefore, the strength of the SSE lies solely in confronting us with the inescapable biophysical limits to the human economy.* It warns that we cannot continue with an attitude of 'business as usual'. Instead, we need to develop new social and ethical awareness so that improvement in the material well-being of the present generation is not pursued at the risk of impoverishing future generations. Certainly this could not be accomplished automatically or without sacrifices. To be sure, it would require adopting some institutional measures that might have the effect of limiting our individual freedom in respect of some economic and reproductive decisions. But even if we do not agree with the specific solutions he proposed, establishing a clear link between biophysical limits and individual freedom of choice is one of Daly's major contributions. His SSE has also helped greatly in setting the stage for much of the recent growing interest in the theoretical and practical issues of sustainable development at both local and global scales – the subject of the next chapter.

Of course, the so-called thermodynamic–ecological perspective on limits (as envisioned by ecological economists) has not been without its critics. It would, therefore, be appropriate to end this chapter by mentioning the two most pointed criticisms of this

Exhibit 12.2   The tapestry metaphor for environmental degradation

Carlos Davidson

A metaphor based on a tapestry provides a more accurate and useful view of the relationship between economic activity and the environment than either the limits metaphors of rivets and cliffs (i.e. neo-Malthusian and ecological economics) or the technological optimist model of neo-classical economics. Tapestries have long been used as metaphors for the richness and complexity of biological systems (e.g. the tapestry of life). As a metaphor for environmental degradation, each small act of destruction . . . is like pulling a thread from the tapestry. At first, the results are almost imperceptible. The function and beauty of the tapestry is slightly diminished with the removal of each thread. If too many threads are pulled – especially if they are pulled from the same area – the tapestry will begin to look worn and may tear locally. There is no way to know ahead of time whether pulling a thread will cause a tear or not. In the tapestry metaphor, as in the cliff and rivet metaphors, environmental damage can have unforeseen negative consequences; therefore, the metaphor agues for the use of the precautionary principle. The tapestry is not just an aesthetic object. Like the airplane wing in the rivet metaphor, the tapestry (i.e. biophysical systems) sustain human life.

However, the tapestry metaphor differs from the rivet and cliff metaphors in several important aspects. First, in most cases there are no limits. As threads are pulled from the tapestry, there is a continuum of degradation rather than any clear threshold. Each thread that is pulled slightly reduces the function and beauty of the tapestry. Second, impacts consist of multiple small losses and occasional larger rips (non-linearities) rather than overall collapse. Catastrophes are not impossible, but they are rare and local (e.g. collapse of a fishery) rather than global. The function and beauty of the tapestry are diminished long before the possibility of a catastrophic rip. Third, there is always a choice about the desired condition of the world – anywhere along the continuum of degradation is feasible, from a world rich in biodiversity to a threadbare remnant with fewer species, fewer natural places, less beauty, and reduced ecosystem services. With the rivet and cliff metaphors, there are no choices: no sane person would choose to crash the plane or go over the cliff. This difference is key for the political implications of the metaphors. Finally, in the rivet or cliff metaphors, environmental destruction may be seen primarily as loss of utilitarian values (ecosystem services to humans). In the tapestry metaphor, environmental destruction is viewed as loss of utilitarian as well as aesthetic, option, and amenity consideration.

Source: *BioScience: Economic Growth and the Environment: Alternatives to the Limits Paradigm*, May 2000 Vol. 5 No. 5, 434–5.

particular perspective on physical limits. First, as mentioned earlier, most neoclassical economists are inclined to view the thermodynamic–ecological perspective to limits as nothing more than a new spin on the old-fashioned neo-Malthusian way of thinking. Its prognosis on the predicament of humans does not materially depart from the Malthusian – apocalyptic both in tone and substance. As such it is subject to the same criticisms that were discussed in Sections 4 and 5 of Chapter 10 regarding the neo-Malthusian paradigm of biophysical limits. Second, by focusing too much on the material basis of human economy, ecological economics seems to overlook the social and political context in which resources are used. This is considered a serious deficiency, for it undermines the adaptive capacity of human institutions to deal with resource scarcity. Third, Davidson (2000: 433) recently disputed the whole notion of biophysical limits to economic growth in this way:

> biological and physical systems underlie all economic activity and form constraints to which the human economy must adapt. However, I argue, contrary to the limits perspective, the biological or physical limits are seldom actually limiting to economic growth, such that reaching limits causes economic collapse or even stops growth. In most cases, the human economy is extremely adaptable and ways are found to adapt and continue to expand. *Furthermore, in most cases, continued economic growth results not in ecological collapse but rather in continuous environmental degradation without clear limit points* (the emphasis is mine). [Exhibit 12.2 details how Davidson used tapestry as a metaphor to describe his alternative view of environmental degradation.]

In essence what Davidson is challenging is the core assumption of ecological economics, that increases in the *scale* of the economy will contribute to greater environmental damage and eventually to the inevitability of ecological collapse. His contention is that environmental degradation is often gradual and continuous rather than catastrophic. What this implies is that catastrophic events can be averted by human interventions through political process. As he put it, 'a political-ecological analysis often reveals that levels of consumption and destructive production processes are not fixed and inevitable but rather the result of political, economic, and cultural decisions that are subject to change'.

12.5 Chapter summary

- This chapter has discussed the ecological perspective on 'general' resource scarcity and its implications for the long-run material well-being of humanity.
- The distinctive feature of the ecological economics school of thought is the extensive application of thermodynamic laws and ecological principles as building blocks for their argument on the existence of biophysical limits.
- In contrast to neoclassical economics, the ecological economics perspective seems to be rather cautious. In large part, this caution is a result of looking at biophysical limits in a broader context.
- Ecological economists do not view the human economy as being isolated from natural ecosystems. In fact, the human economy is regarded as nothing but a small (albeit important) subset of natural ecosystems. Furthermore, since these two systems are considered to be interdependent, ecological economists focus on understanding the linkages and interactions between economic and ecological systems.
- From such a perspective, the scale of human activities (in terms of population size and aggregate use of low-entropy matter–energy) becomes an important issue. Furthermore, in ecological economics the consensus view seems to be that the scale of human development is already approaching the limits of the finite natural world – the full-world view. This has several implications. Among them are:

1   It is imperative that limits be put on the total resources used for either pro-
    duction and/or consumption purposes – stock maintenance.
2   'The essential measure of the success of the economy is not production and
    consumption at all, but the nature, extent, quality, and complexity of the total
    capital stock, including the state of the human bodies and minds included in
    the system' (Boulding 1966: 304).
3   As far as possible, throughput should be minimized, which implies the pro-
    duction of goods and services that are long-lasting and easily recyclable.
    Technology can play a significant positive role in this regard.

•   On the other hand, technology will not be able to circumvent fundamental energy,
    pollution and other natural resource constraints, for two reasons: first, natural
    and human-made capital are *complements*; second, there is a growing evidence
    that natural resources are becoming a limiting factor to continued economic
    growth.
•   Thus, according to the ecological economics worldview, it is imperative that human
    society makes every effort to ensure that the scale of human activities is ecologically
    sustainable. This necessitates careful considerations of biophysical limits and
    intergenerational equity. These concerns extend beyond humanity to the future
    well-being of other species and the biosphere as a whole.
•   In many respects, one of the major contributions of ecological economics has been
    to shift the focus of the debate on natural resource scarcity from limits to economic
    growth to *sustainable development* – the subject of the next chapter.
•   Critics of the ecological economics worldview have been quick to point out its
    shortcomings:

1   Although their line of reasoning materially differs, in terms the prognosis of the
    future human material progress, the ecological economists have been as gloomy
    as the Malthusians. In this sense, some would like to consider their view as
    simply a variation (or extension) of the well-known and ever-pessimistic
    Malthusian prognosis of the future material fate of humanity.
2   Their analysis of the future conditions of humanity is based primarily on
    physical laws and with very little attention to the socio-economic, political and
    technological conditions that are important to the human economic condition
    and future progress. As Davidson pointed out, 'A political–ecological analysis
    often reveals that levels of consumption and destructive production processes
    are not fixed and inevitable but rather the result of political, economic, and
    cultural decisions that are subject to change'.
3   The ecological economics school draws followers from diverse disciplinary
    backgrounds. At its current stage of development, it has not been able to for-
    mulate a cohesive voice in public policy suggestions that are specific enough to
    be pragmatic. Setting general conditions (primarily based on physical terms)
    for the ideal attainment of sustainable economic development may be of little
    value in devising policies that are workable on a short-term basis.

Review and discussion questions

1   Briefly define the following concepts: throughput, growthmania, the 'cowboy'
    economy, the 'spaceman' economy, intermediate means, intermediate ends, ultimate

means, ultimate ends, the steady-state economy, irreversibility, complementarity of factor of production, the precautionary principle, intergenerational equity, transferable birth rights, depletion quota.

2   Identify what you consider to be the three most important features of the ecological economics perspective on biophysical limits. How are these different from the Malthusian perspective on such limits?

3   State whether the following are *true*, *false*, or *uncertain* and explain why.

   (a) Consideration of 'ultimate ends' is beyond economics – which is not a moral science.
   (b) In general, complementarity of factors of production implies the existence of limits to factor substitution possibilities.
   (c) Followers of ecological economics tend to be anti-technological progress.

4   It is argued that all transformations require energy; energy flow is unidirectional; and there is no substitute for energy. It therefore makes sense to use energy as a numeraire – a denominator by which the value of all resources is weighed. That is, energy is the ultimate resource. Critically comment.

5   Explain what Daly means by the following concepts:

   (a) Minimization of throughput
   (b) Service efficiency
   (c) Distributional efficiency.

6   Briefly explain why each one of the following considerations is important in ecological economics:

   (a) Uncertainty
   (b) Intergenerational equity
   (c) Irreversibility
   (d) Ecological resilience.

7   Nicholas Georgescu-Roegen declared a 'steady-state' is a 'topical mirage' and pointed out its logical snags: 'The crucial error consists in not seeing that . . . even a declining [growth] state which does not converge toward annihilation, cannot exist forever in a finite environment. . . . [Thus], contrary to what some advocates of the stationary state claim, this state does not occupy a privileged position vis-à-vis physical law'. Is this a fair criticism of the steady-state economy? Explain.

8   Herman Daly declared that an economy can 'develop' without experiencing 'growth'. What exactly does Daly mean by this? Do you have a position on this matter? Explain.

References and further reading

Arrow, K., Bolin, B., Costanza, R. *et al.* (1995) 'Economic Growth, Carrying Capacity, and the Environment', *Science* 268: 520–1.

Ayres, R. U. (1978) 'Application of Physical Principles to Economics', in R. U. Ayres (ed.) *Resources, Environment, and Economics: Applications of the Materials/Energy Balance Principle*, New York: John Wiley.

Ayres, R. U. and Nair, I. (1984) 'Thermodynamics and Economics', *Physics Today* 37: 63–8.

Boulding, K. E. (1966) 'The Economics of the Coming Spaceship Earth', in H. Jarrett (ed.) *Environmental Quality in a Growing Economy*, Washington, DC: Johns Hopkins University Press.

Burness, S., Cummings, R., Morris, G. and Paik, I. (1980) 'Thermodynamics and Economic Concepts Related to Resource-Use Policies', *Land Economics* 56: 1–9.

Carson, R. M. (1962) *Silent Spring*, Boston: Houghton Mifflin.

Cleveland, C. J. (1987) 'Biophysical Economics: Historical Perspective and Current Research Trends', *Ecological Modelling* 38: 47–73.

Costanza, R. (1980) 'Embodied Energy and Economic Valuation', *Science* 210: 1219–24.

Costanza, R., Wainger, L. and Folke, C. (1993) 'Modeling Complex Ecological Economic Systems: Toward an Evolutionary, Dynamic Understanding of People and Nature', *BioScience* 43, 8: 545–53.

Daly, H. E. (1973) 'Introduction', in H. E. Daly (ed.) *Toward a Steady-State Economy*, San Francisco: W. H. Freeman.

——(1987) 'The Economic Growth Debate: What Some Economists Have Learned but Many Have Not', *Journal of Environmental Economics and Management* 14: 323–36.

——(1992) 'Allocation, Distribution, and Scale: Towards an Economics That Is Efficient, Just, and Sustainable', *Ecological Economics* 6: 185–93.

——(1993) 'Valuing the Earth: Economics, Ecology, Ethics', in H. E. Daly and K. Townsend (eds) *Valuing the Earth: Economics, Ecology, Ethics*, Cambridge, Mass.: MIT Press.

——(1996) *Beyond Growth*, Boston: Beacon Press.

Dasgupta, P. S., Levin, S. and Lubchenco, J. (2000) 'Economic Pathways to Ecological Sustainability', *BioScience* 54, 4: 339–45.

Georgescu-Roegen, N. (1966) *Analytical Economics*, Cambridge, Mass.: Harvard University Press.

——(1971) *The Entropy Law and the Economic Process*, Cambridge Mass.: Harvard University Press.

——(1986) 'The Entropy Law and the Economic Process in Retrospect',' *Eastern Economic Journal* 12: 3–25.

——(1993) 'The Entropy Law and the Economic Problem', in H. E. Daly and K. Townsend (eds) *Valuing the Earth: Economics, Ecology, Ethics*, Cambridge, Mass.: MIT Press.

Davidson, C. (2000) 'Economic Growth and the Environment: Alternatives to the Limits Paradigm', *BioScience* 50, 5: 433–9.

Goeller, H. E. and Weinberg, A. M. (1976) 'The Age of Substitutability: What Do We Do When the Mercury Runs Out?' *Science* 191: 683–9.

Goodland, R. (1992) 'The Case That the World Has Reached Limits', in R. Goodland, H. E. Daly and S. El Sarafy (eds) *Population, Technology and Lifestyle: The Transition to Sustainability*, Washington, DC: Island Press.

Martinez-Alier, J. (1987) *Ecological Economics: Energy, Environment, and Society*, Cambridge, Mass.: Basil Blackwell.

Mirowski, P. (1988) 'Energy and Energetics in Economic Theory: A Review Essay', *Journal of Economic Issues* 22: 811–30.

Norgaard, R. B. (1989) 'The Case for Methodological Pluralism', *Ecological Economics* 1: 37–57.

Odum, H. and Odum, E. (1976) *Energy Basis for Man and Nature*, New York: McGraw-Hill.

Pearce, D. W. (1987) 'Foundation of Ecological Economics', *Ecological Modelling* 38: 9–18.

Rawls, J. (1971) *A Theory of Justice*, Cambridge, Mass.: Harvard University Press.

Rosenberg, N. (1973) 'Innovative Responses to Materials Shortages', *American Economic Review* 63, 2: 111–18.

Solow, R. M. (1974) 'The Economics of Resources or the Resources of Economics', *American Economic Review* 64, 2: 1–14.

Young, J. T. (1991) 'Is the Entropy Law Relevant to the Economics of Natural Resource Scarcity?' *Journal of Environmental Economics and Management* 21: 169–79.

13 The economics of sustainable development

Issues of sustainability are ultimately issues of limits. If material economic growth is sustainable indefinitely by technology, then all the environmental problems can (in theory at least) be fixed technologically. Issues of fairness, equity and distribution (between sub-groups and generations of our species and between our species and others) are also issues of limits. We don't have to worry so much about how an expanding pie is divided, but a constant or shrinking pie presents real problems. Finally, dealing with uncertainty about limits is the fundamental issue. If we are unsure about future limits then the prudent course is to assume they exist. One does not run blindly through a dark landscape that may contain crevasses. One assumes they are there and goes gingerly and with eyes wide open, at least, until one can see a little better.

(Costanza *et al.* 1997: xix–xx)

The problem of ecological sustainability needs to be solved at the level of preferences or technology, not at the level of optimal prices. Only if the preferences and production possibility sets informing economic behaviour are ecologically sustainable can the corresponding set of optimal and intertemporally efficient prices be ecologically sustainable. Thus the principle of 'consumer sovereignty', on which most conventional economic solutions are based, is only acceptable to the extent that consumer interests do not threaten the overall system – and through this the welfare of future generations.

(Costanza *et al.* 1997: xv)

13.1 Introduction

A careful reading of the above two epigraphs tells us a number of things. First, issues of sustainability are about *biophysical limits*. Therefore, there will be a natural overlap between issues addressed in this chapter and those considered in the previous three chapters.

Second, the economics of sustainability goes far beyond the neoclassical focus on the *efficient* allocation of scarce environmental resources. *It requires that issues of fairness, equity and distribution be explicitly considered. These issues have a time dimension (often involving several human generations), and they include considerations of the well-being of species other than humans.*

Third, the problem of ecological sustainability requires careful scrutiny of our *technological choices*, and it also demands re-examination of *our social and value systems* – to the extent that they affect human preference. This questions the usual treatment of preference as an exogenously determined variable.

Fourth, the economics of sustainable development deals with the decision-making process in extremely uncertain circumstances. *Uncertainty* is a vital consideration in the economics of sustainability because over time it is expected that changes will occur in technology, income and people's preference(s). Technology may change enormously in response to changing relative scarcities and knowledge. Income will not be constant and preferences will differ across generations. The problem is not that changes will occur, but rather that we do not know for sure how and when these changes will occur (i.e. the changes will be, from our viewpoint, random in nature) and we do not know what the implications of these changes will be for future resource availability. Furthermore, in the economics of sustainability, attention is given to the uncertain effects of the current level (scale) and pattern of human enterprise on the integrity of natural ecosystems (Krutilla 1967; Perrings 1991). In this particular context, one issue of significance is *irreversibility*. That is, beyond a certain threshold, continued human exploitation of nature or economic growth may cause irreversible damage to certain vital components of a natural ecosystem (such as forestland, wetland preserves, etc.).

This chapter provides a systematic analysis of these four key issues: biophysical limits; intergenerational equity and economic efficiency; technological options and social values; and intertemporal management of natural resources under conditions of uncertainty and irreversibility. These issues will be analyzed on the assumption that the overriding social goal is progress toward sustainable economic development.

In recent years, there seems to have been a heightened interest among academics and public policy-makers on the general issue of sustainable development. Since sustainability assumes explicit recognition of biophysical limits as potential constraints to long-run economic growth, the debate on 'limits to economic growth' (a topic that occupied much of our attention in Chapters 10–12) is rendered fruitless. In essence, *the existence of biophysical limits is no longer an issue of significant contention.* However, this is not to suggest that no controversial issues are involved in the economics of sustainable development. On the contrary, controversies exist, and arise primarily from the way sustainability is *conceptualized*. Table 13.1 sets out the salient features of sustainable development and how these key features are compared and contrasted with the three paradigms of 'limits to economic growth' already discussed in Chapters 10–12.

In this chapter, sustainable development is examined using *three* different conceptions of sustainability, namely Hartwick–Solow sustainability, ecological economics sustainability and safe minimum standards (SMS) sustainability. Hartwick–Solow sustainability basically represents the neoclassical perspective on the economics of sustainable development, and one of its defining characteristics is the assumption that human capital (basic economic infrastructure, such as machines, buildings, highway systems, knowledge, etc.) and natural capital (stocks of environmentally provided assets such as soil, forest, wetland preserves, water, fishing grounds, etc.) are *substitutes*. Thus, natural capital may not be considered an absolute necessity or a binding constraint on sustainability. For this reason, the Hartwick–Solow approach is recognized as the *weak* sustainability criterion.

By contrast, sustainability according to ecological economics presumes that the sustainability of ecological systems is a prerequisite to sustainable human economic development, and it views human and natural capital as *complements*. The *strong* sustainability criterion is an alternative phrase often used to describe the ecological economics sustainability approach.

Table 13.1 The debates on the existence of biophysical limits: from the simple Malthusian theory of limits to growth to a recently fashionable argument for sustainable development

Theories of limits	Do limits exist?	Nature of the limits	Primary source(s) of the limits	Proposed solution
1. Malthusian/ neomalthusian	Yes	Factors of production including the environment are scarce in absolute terms	Exponential growth of population and resource consumption; and technological fix	Strict control of population growth and use of technologies that are environmentally benign
2. Neoclassical	Questionable or not relevant	No real limits because of factor substitution possibilities	No apparent limits unless a slow-down in the continued progress of knowledge and technology is envisioned	Economic growth as measured by gross domestic product (GDP), and resource allocation through decentralized market mechanisms
3. Ecological economics	Yes	Laws of thermo-dynamics and the fact that the biosphere is aclosed system for its material needs	The growth in the *scale* of human economies relative to the total natural ecosystem, which is nongrowing	Focus on 'qualitative' economic growth, where conservation of throughput is of the highest priority
4. Sustainable development	Yes	Possible limits on factor substitution possibilities	Human and natural capital are most likely to be complements rather than substitutes; concern for irreversibility	Maintenance of constant or nondeclining capital stocks composed of both natural and human capital that is based on the ethical principle of equal sharing among present and future generations

Finally, SMS, the third approach to sustainability, has as its central theme the uncertainty associated with irreversible environmental damage and its implications for long-term resource management. Thus, the main focus is not so much on whether human and natural capital are substitutes or complements, but rather on resource management decisions under conditions of uncertainty and irreversibility.   END 2

Before further consideration of these three conceptual approaches, it is important to give a clear meaning to sustainable development. As will be evident from the discussions in the next section, this is not easy. The aim here is rather modest. It is not to establish a consensus on the definition of sustainable development, but to pinpoint certain key features of sustainable development so that the essential elements of the concept are clearly distinguished and understood. The hope is that this could help dispel some of the existing confusion on the subject.

13.2 Sustainable development: a helpful term or a vague and analytically empty concept?

Since the early 1980s, the term 'sustainable development' has been used widely and rather indiscriminately. The term began to gain popularity when it became increasingly fashionable to use it as a way of responding to global environmental concerns (such as global warming, biodiversity, ozone depletion, etc.). The unintended outcome of this has been to render the concept broad and rather vague. In fact, some scholars (including economists) have even gone so far as to claim that the concept of sustainable development is too vague and, as such, is void of analytic content. Of course, this is a rather extreme position to take. However, this outcry among academics does indicate the genuine need for a sharper definition and clearer understanding of sustainable development.

It was with this in mind that the World Commission on Environment and Development, a United Nations agency, commissioned a study on the subject of sustainable development. This culminated in the publication of the Brundtland Commission Report, *Our Common Future* (World Commission on Environment and Development 1987). This report defined sustainable development as *development which meets the needs of the present without sacrificing the ability of the future to meet its needs*. This definition not only is well known, but is, in many instances, accepted as the standard definition of sustainable development.

There are several key features of this definition that are worth pointing out. First, the definition clearly establishes sustainable development as an *equity* issue. As such, it entails that the economics of sustainable development has a principally normative goal. Second, the Brundtland Report's definition of sustainable development offers a rather specific ethical criterion: the needs of the present are not to be satisfied at the expense of future needs (well-being). It therefore deals with equity across generations: *inter-generational equity*. Third, the Brundtland Report, by emphasizing equity, raises questions about the validity of standard economic analysis based exclusively on *efficiency*.

Indeed, the Brundtland Report's definition of sustainability has been quite helpful in establishing a clear consensus that sustainable development is principally an ethical issue. Yet a number of important features of sustainable development that were discussed in the first section of this chapter are not *explicitly* captured by the Brundtland Report definition. The purpose of discussing these missing features is not to indicate weaknesses in the report, however, because no single definition can realistically be expected to capture all the essential elements of a seemingly dialectic concept like sustainable development.

First, the Brundtland Report's definition of sustainable development *is not explicit about the physical and technological dimensions of the resource constraints required for sustainability*. In other words, what is the specific nature of the resource constraints required for sustainability? Is human capital considered a substitute for or a complement to natural capital? What are the assumptions about the role of technology in ameliorating or circumventing resource scarcity? How should the various resource constraints be measured, i.e. in physical or in monetary terms?

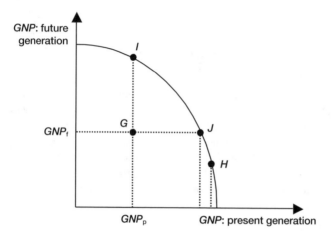

Figure 13.1 The trade-off between intergenerational efficiency and equity. Clearly a move
from point *G* to point *H* would be desirable on efficiency grounds. However,
relative to point *G*, point *H* may not be sustainable because it entails a much
lower level of income for future generations. Thus, not all efficient points are
sustainable.

Second, it is not clear from the Brundtland Report definition *what the term 'development' implies or how it is (or should be) measured if it is to be used as an indicator of
intergenerational 'well-being'*. Does development refer to the conventional conception of
economic growth: an increase in the *quantity* of goods and services? Or does it refer
to the kind of *qualitative* economic growth discussed in Chapter 12 (Section 4.3) in
conjunction with Herman Daly's notion of the steady-state economy? Is development
measured using the conventional national accounting system (gross national product,
GNP)? Does it matter how the depreciation of human versus natural capital stocks is
treated?

Third, the Brundtland Report definition *does not make clear the exact nature of the
trade-off between equity and efficiency*. The report simply emphasizes the importance of
equity in any considerations of sustainable development. Yes, this signals a departure
from economic analyses that are based on the premises of the neoclassical economic
paradigm, but does this mean that the efficiency consideration is irrelevant?

Figure 13.1 illustrates the significance of this question. This figure is constructed
assuming a number of simplifying conditions. The curve represents a production
possibility frontier measured in terms of GNP – the monetary value of all goods and
services produced (more on the adequacy of GNP as a measure of social well-being in
Section 13.6). This production possibility frontier is drawn for given tastes, technology
and resource endowments, across *two* generations. The figure also assumes that market
prices reflect 'true' scarcity values, and that markets exist for all goods and services.

What can be said about the trade-off between efficiency and equity using Figure 13.1?
Let us assume that our starting point is point *G*. Clearly, this point is inefficient because
it is located inside the production possibility frontier. A move to point *J* or *I* or any point
between these two would lead to a Pareto-optimal outcome. That is, such a move would

benefit at least one of the generations without affecting the well-being of the other generation. The discussion so far seems to suggest that efficiency (which is attained at points along the production possibility frontier) is desirable. However, what if a move was made from point *G* to *H*? Clearly, point *H* is efficient since it is on the production possibility frontier. But the move to point *H* makes the future generation worse off. Thus, equity considerations may preclude such a move. *The point that needs to be stressed is this. If equity is an important issue in considering sustainable development, not all efficient points are desirable.*

The upshot of the above discussion is clear. Despite the gallant effort of the Brundtland Report, it is very difficult, if not impossible, to define sustainable development in ways that are both unambiguous and comprehensive enough to include all the key attributes essential to a clear understanding of the full implication(s) of the concept. However, *as indicated in the above discussion, the concept of sustainable development has far-reaching implications that go beyond making a statement about the significance of intergenerational equity.* These include *careful considerations of the exact nature of the resource (capital) constraints; technological options and their limits; economic efficiency; intergenerational equity; and aspects of human values and institutions consistent with sustainable development.* To the extent that a conscious effort is made to do this, even if we cannot come up with an analytically precise definition, our definition will be descriptively rich enough to provide a clear picture of the essential elements necessary to understand the full implications of sustainable development.

This section sought to identify the elements essential to understanding the primary goals of sustainable development. That done, it is now time to explain and evaluate the three alternative conceptual approaches to sustainability referred to in Section 13.1. It is important to note that the term 'sustainability' here is used in a very specific context, i.e. as condition(s) for sustainable 'economic development'.

13.3 The Hartwick–Solow approach to sustainability

To begin with, in the Hartwick–Solow approach sustainability is defined in terms of maintaining *constant real consumption* (of goods and services) over an indefinite period of time while recognizing the constraints imposed by a given set of resource endowments. The constraint of exhaustible (non-renewable) resources is particularly stressed in this approach. In fact, the core problem of sustainability is initially envisioned in terms of how consumption of goods and services could be sustained over several generations given that some resources are potentially exhaustible.

This notion of consumption is then related to an equivalent concept of *net income* by using Hicks's (1946: 172) definition of income:

> The purpose of income calculations in practical affairs is to give people an indication of the amount which they can consume without impoverishing themselves. Following out this idea, it would seem that we ought to define a man's income as the maximum value which he can consume during a week, and still expect to be as well off at the end of the week as he was at the beginning. Thus when a person saves he plans to be better off in the future; when he lives beyond his income he plans to be worse off. Remembering that the practical purpose of income is to serve as a guide for prudent conduct, I think it is fairly clear that this is what the central meaning must be.

Thus what Hicks has in mind is *sustainable net (national) income*: the amount that can be spent on a regular basis without causing impoverishment in some future period. This would then suggest that due to depreciation of capital assets (buildings, machines, highways, etc.) and the degradation of the natural environment, sustainable economic development (or net national income) would *require maintenance of a nondeclining capital stock – composed of natural and human capital*. It should be noted also that the replacement of the depreciated capital assets requires constant withdrawal of both renewable and exhaustible resources from nature (for clear distinctions between renewable and exhaustible resources refer back to the Introduction to this book).

According to the conventional income accounting system, net national income (NNI), which is used as a proxy for measuring the aggregate well-being of a given society, is obtained by subtracting the depreciation of human capital (machines, buildings, roads, etc.) from the gross national income (GNI). What is not accounted for in this procedure is the depreciation or depletion of natural capital assets (forests, fisheries, mineral deposits, etc.) that have been used up to support the production and consumption activities of an economy. Thus, for a sustainable net national income, GNI must be modified to account for the depreciation of natural capital, just as net national income is equal to gross national income less estimated depreciation on human-generated capital. (Section 13.6 provides a comprehensive treatment of this topic.)

A distinguishing feature of Hartwick–Solow sustainability is its conception of *capital stocks*. In this regard, it adheres to the neoclassical perspective on natural resources discussed at some length in Chapters 1 and 11. More specifically, *it assumes that natural and human capital are substitutes. This is a critical assumption, since it has the far-reaching implication of making natural resources a nonbinding constraint on sustainability*. This is because, as discussed in Chapter 11, if human and natural capital are substitutes, depletion of exhaustible resources and large-scale degradation of environmental quality need not be a major source of concern. *According to this view, sustainable development simply requires the maintenance of constant capital stock, but the composition of the capital stock is not considered relevant*. For this reason the Hartwick–Solow criterion for sustainability is sometimes referred to as the weak sustainability criterion – weak in the sense that it does not render natural capital an absolute must for sustaining net national income (real consumption of goods and services) over an indefinite period. Given this, *the relevant issue is then whether 'adequate' compensatory investments are made to protect the interests of future generations*.

This is clearly an ethical question, and it is partially addressed by an application of a simple *sustainability rule* developed by Hartwick (1977). *This rule states that maintaining constant real consumption of goods and services or real income (in the Hicksian sense) is possible even in the face of exhaustible resources provided that the rent (refer to Section 6 of Appendix A for an explanation of rent) derived from 'an intertemporally efficient use' of these resources is re-invested in renewable capital assets*. Thus, the focus of concern is on the prudent use of the returns on or savings of exhaustible resources, rather than the fact of the depletion of these resources (see Exhibit 13.1 – necessary reading for a clear understanding of the Hartwick sustainability rule).

However, Hartwick applied the above 'sustainability rule' primarily to trace the *optimal* intertemporal sustainable path (or course of action). The derivation of this rule is based on several assumptions. Among others, these are that preferences and resource ownership are exogenously determined; and market prices are assumed to reflect the true social value of resources over time, which literally implies the existence of a

Exhibit 13.1   What will happen to Saudi Arabia when its oil reserves are eventually exhausted?

It is widely accepted that Saudi Arabia possesses the largest share of the total known petroleum reserves in the world. This is also a nation whose people's livelihoods depend almost solely on this one commodity. The revenue from petroleum exports accounts for a significant share of the country's GNP. This is because most of Saudi Arabia is desert and unsuitable for conventional agricultural pursuits. Furthermore, Saudi Arabia has an insignificant amount of other mineral deposits apart from petroleum. There is therefore good reason for Saudi Arabia to be concerned about what happens when the petroleum is exhausted.

This is a fundamental concern that goes beyond Saudi Arabia. It pertains to the sustainability of an economy that depends solely on an exhaustible mineral resource(s). If a fundamental concern of this nature is addressed within the context of the Hartwick–Solow sustainability approach, the course of action that Saudi Arabia may need to take in order to assure a reasonable standard of living for its citizens beyond the petroleum age could be as follows.

First, the extraction rates of the country's petroleum deposits are determined in such a way as to maximize the present value of the rent from the intertemporal use of its total petroleum deposits. In general, this intertemporally efficient use of resources is not consistent with maximizing current extraction rates, and as such dictates that certain principles of resource conservation be observed. Thus, Saudi Arabia cannot simply pump more oil at any price just to raise the standard of living of the current generation.

Second, sustainability requires that the rent derived from the current extraction of petroleum be re-invested in other forms of renewable capital assets. For example, in the case of Saudi Arabia, this may entail investing in large-scale water desalination projects. If successful, this may allow Saudi Arabia to irrigate its land and produce agricultural products in sufficient amounts to feed its people and even export on a sustainable basis. This is just one of many options that Saudi Arabia has for the use of an exhaustible resource, petroleum, without jeopardizing the well-being of its future citizens.

The clear message is that the people of Saudi Arabia can sustain a reasonable standard of living into the indefinite future provided they are able to use their rich deposits of petroleum efficiently at all times. Of course, this will not occur automatically or without some difficulty. It requires prudent long-term planning, self-discipline and astuteness in using the proceeds from oil.

complete set of competitive markets (forward prices) from now to eternity. Strictly speaking, then, *this rule is more of a condition of intergenerational efficiency than for sustainability*.

In addition, to the extent that intergenerational efficiency deals with comparing the welfare of people across generations, the issue of *discounting* cannot be ignored. Thus, as discussed in Section 5 of Chapter 9, the choice of the discount rate (private versus social) is crucial. For that matter, any positive discount rate would automatically imply a desire to consume more at present than in the future. To this extent, the very idea of discounting becomes an ethical issue since the decision made by the current generation on the basis of this rate affects the well-being of future generations – a lower discount rate generally favoring future generations. Nevertheless, in the Hartwick–Solow approach to sustainability this is not considered a serious problem *since the effect of a positive discount rate could be offset by the rate of growth in technical progress.* Accordingly, there is nothing intrinsically wrong or immoral in using a positive discount rate.

Weaknesses of

What remains now is to briefly discuss some of the major weaknesses of the Hartwick–Solow sustainability approach. First, this approach assumes that, in the main, human-generated and natural capital are *substitutes.* As we observed in Chapter 11, this assumption has been a source of lively dispute between neoclassical and ecological economists. Ecological economists believe that at the current level and pattern of human economic activity, it is more appropriate to view human and natural capital as complements, not substitutes. The implication of this assumption for sustainability is far-reaching, as will be evident in our discussion in the next section.

Second, as discussed above, *intergenerational efficiency* (the focus of the Hartwick–Solow sustainability model) requires that the prices of all goods and services (including environmental goods) should reflect their social values. However, the practical problems of arranging this are not explicitly addressed (see Chapter 3). In other words, price distortions due to environmental externalities are either simply ignored or assumed to be remediable with little or no difficulty.

Third, some economists and ecologists would argue that the very idea of positive discounting is wrong (Perrings 1991). For this reason alone they view Hartwick–Solow sustainability as being insufficiently concerned with the well-being of future generations and as such ethically questionable.

Fourth, in the Hartwick–Solow approach the determination of the sustainable constraints (the actual size of the nondeclining capital stock) is assumed to be independent of the current level and pattern of human economic development (Daly 1996). Should the current level (initial position) of aggregate resource consumption of goods and services be subject to a downward adjustment? What this suggests is that the Hartwick–Solow approach to sustainability does not explicitly consider *scale* (the size of the existing human economy relative to natural ecosystems) as an issue (Daly 1996).

In this regard, as we will see in the next section, ecological economists argue that the standard economic approach to sustainability is based on a rather narrow vision of the natural environment. In fact, the role that natural resources play in the economic process is conceptualized without a clear understanding of the complex interactions between the economic and the ecological systems. To such an extent, the Hartwick–Solow conceptualization of sustainability is incomplete. *It only refers to economic sustainability or the sustainability of an economic system. However, the fact that the sustainability of an economic system may be linked with or influenced by the ecological system (of which the economic system is only a part) does not seem to be formally acknowledged by the Hartwick–Solow model.*

Fifth, the Hartwick–Solow approach to sustainability is specifically criticized for its inadequate treatment of the nature of the *uncertainty* associated with long-term natural resource assessment and management. The fact that beyond a certain threshold the scale of human economic activities could cause *irreversible* damage to the natural environment (ecosystem) is not recognized. This could be a serious omission since the cost may entail the irrevocable loss of human life-support systems or major reductions in the quality of human life (such as increase in cancer incidence due to the depletion of ozone from the upper atmosphere). Uncertainty associated with irreversible environmental damage and its implications for long-term resource management will be the central

SMS

theme of the discussion in Section 13.5, which deals with the safe minimum standard (SMS) approach to sustainability.

13.4 The ecological economics approach to sustainability

Most of the basic ideas of the ecological economic approach to sustainability and its drawbacks have already been addressed in Section 4.3 of Chapter 12 in the discussion of Herman Daly's steady-state economy (SSE) model. Therefore, to avoid unnecessary repetition, in this section the discussion of ecological sustainability will be brief and limited in scope. The focus will be on clarifying the key *differences* between the sustainability concepts of neoclassical economics (Hartwick–Solow) and ecological economics.

The ecological economics approach to sustainability starts with a worldview that the natural world is not only finite, but also nongrowing and materially closed (see Chapters 2 and 11). Furthermore, it is postulated that the general capacity of this finite natural world is beginning to be strained by the size of the human economy, as measured by the aggregate use of throughput – low-entropic matter–energy. Proponents of this so-called 'full-world view' insist that this new reality demands a shift in our vision of how the human economic system is related to the natural world. What has become increasingly evident is the unsustainability of 'economic growth', especially if it is based on increasing use of throughput from the natural ecosystem. Why is this so?

In the 'full-world' scenario, natural capital and human capital can no longer be viewed as substitutes. In fact, the more realistic way to view the future relation between these two components of capital is as *complements*. What this suggests is that a combination of both types of capital assets is needed in the production process. Thus, contrary to what has been suggested by the Hartwick–Solow approach to sustainability, an economy cannot continue to function without natural capital. Furthermore, it is expected that natural capital will be the limiting factor in the future. That is, fishing will be limited not by the number of fishing boats but by remaining fish stocks; petroleum use will be limited not by refining capacity but by geologic deposits and by atmospheric capacity to absorb carbon dioxide (Dieren 1995). Most important of all, human-made capital (machines, buildings, etc.) cannot be substituted for scarce terrestrial energy without limit because a certain minimum energy is required in any transformation of matter or performance of work. To that extent, then, natural capital is the key factor in any consideration of sustainability. Thus, because natural capital is viewed as a limiting factor on future economic growth, the ecological economics approach to sustainability is sometimes referred to as the *strong* sustainability criterion.

Accordingly, the ecological economics approach defines sustainability in terms of a non-declining (constant) 'natural' capital. A consideration of intergenerational equity is the underlying reason for this specific requirement. If viewed as a problem of an intertemporal efficient allocation of resources, *the ideal size of the constant natural capital constraint would be kept at a level that would be adequate to ensure that, at a minimum, future generations will be left no worse off than current generations*. This would be consistent with the basic principle of the Rawlsian justice discussed in Section 6 of Chapter 9.

However, this ethical concern is rather narrow in that it tends to be human-centered or anthropocentric in its perspective. *It is argued that ecological sustainability needs to go beyond human interests. At least in principle, the ecological economics approach to sustainability involves concerns extending beyond the human species: the well-being of*

Case Study 13.1   Sustainable forest management practice: the case of the Menominee Indian Reservation

The Menominee Indian Reservation in Wisconsin is a federally recognized sovereign 'nation'. The reservation was established in 1854. It occupies 234,000 acres, about 95 per cent of which is covered with mixed hardwood/coniferous forests. Today, the population of the Menominee community is about 8,000 and half of them live on the reservation. About 25 per cent of the workforce make their living on jobs directly related to the management, harvesting and processing of timber.

The Menominee Indians claim that they have been practicing sustainable forestry since the establishment of their reservation more than 140 years ago. In fact, sustainable forest management practice is part of the present-day Menominee Constitution. In general, sustainable forestry is defined as harvesting trees at a rate within the forests' capacity to regrow (more on this in Chapter 14). Furthermore, the Menominee sustainable forestry practice refers 'not only to forest products and social benefits, but also to wildlife, site productivity, and other ecosystem functions' (Menominee Tribal Enterprises 1997: 9).

To ensure this, the Menominee Indians follow forestry management principles that rely on both their strong traditional beliefs as the stewards of nature and on state-of-the-art forestry technology. The 'annual allowable cut' from the reservation forests is determined on the basis of a 15-year cutting cycle with a 150-year planning horizon, employing various methods including selective cutting, shelterwood, and small-scale clear-cutting only when it can improve stand quality and diversity. Up-to-date information on change in timber volume and growth is provided through the use of the continuous forest inventory (CFI) method.

The production, marketing and product distribution aspects of the tribe are handled by the Menominee Tribal Enterprise (MTE). MTE claims that silviculture, not market forces, determines how much wood is cut. It is estimated that when the reservation was established, it contained 1.2 billion feet of timber. Since then, 2 billion feet have been cut, and 1.5 billion feet are standing today. The standing timber volume inventory now is greater than at the time when the reservation was created in 1854.

Although several enterprises, including a gaming (casino) operation, are under way to diversify the economic base of the Menominee community, the forest with its multiple products continues to be one of the main sources of employment and income. While the Menominee forest is one of the most intensively managed tracts of forest, it still remains the best example of biodiversity in the Great Lakes Regions. From the air, it has been described as 'a big green postage stamp', or 'an island of trees in a sea of farmland'. The contrast can be seen from space, and entering the reservation along Highway 55 has been described as entering a 'wall of trees'. In this respect, although on a small scale, the Menominee Reservation has provided a successful model of sustainable development for the 21st century. During the Earth Day celebration of 1995, the United Nations formally recognized the exemplary achievements of the MTE in its forest-based sustainable development practices. A year later, Vice President Al Gore presented the Menominee with the President's Award for Sustainable Development.

ecological systems in their entirety. For this reason, the ecological approach to sustainability is broadly defined and has both economic and ecological dimensions. Thus, the level at which the nondeclining natural capital stock is set is expected to be consistent not only with economic sustainability but also with the ability of the ecosystem to withstand shocks – ecological resilience (see Case Study 13.1). The ultimate effect of all this will be to provide greater allowance for natural resource preservation for the purpose of safeguarding future generations against large-scale, irreversible ecological damage (such as biodiversity loss, global warming, etc.) – which is very much consistent with the safe minimum sustainability (SMS) criterion to be discussed shortly.

From a public policy perspective, the *sustainability rules* often advocated by the proponents of the ecological economics approach to sustainability are of the following nature:

1   The rate of exploitation of renewable resources should not exceed the regeneration rate.
2   Waste emission (pollution) should be kept at or below the waste-absorptive capacity of the environment. For flow or degradable wastes the rate of discharge should be less than the rate at which ecosystems can absorb those wastes. For stock or persistent wastes (such as DDT, radioactive substances, etc.) the rates of discharge should be zero since ecosystems have no capacity to absorb these wastes.
3   The extraction of nonrenewable resources (such as oil) should be consistent with the development of renewable substitutes. This is equivalent to the compensatory investment rule advocated by Hartwick.
4   Conventional measures of national income accounting should make explicit account for the depreciation of natural capital assets (more on this in Section 13.6).

The major problem with these sustainability rules is that for several reasons they are too vague. First, nothing specific is said about the regenerative (or natural growth) rate of renewable resources. For example, for a given renewable resource such as fish, there can be an infinite number of sustainable harvests (where annual harvest is equal to the annual growth in fish population or biomass), depending on the underlying fish population. In this case, society has to make a decision regarding the 'optimal' *rate* of sustainable harvest. That is, it is not sufficient just to ascertain that the harvest is sustainable. The general rule given above does not address this important issue. Second, the rule that states 'waste emission should be kept at or below the waste-absorptive capacity of the environment' totally ignores *economic* considerations. As discussed in Chapter 3, the 'optimal' level of pollution can be in excess of the absorptive capacity of the environment. Third, *in general, the above rules are stated only in biophysical terms without much economic content and institutional context.* To that extent their usefulness as a guide to public policy may be somewhat limited and therefore questionable.

13.5 The safe minimum standard approach to sustainability

The idea of a safe minimum standard (SMS) traces its origin to the work of two eminent pioneering natural resource economists, Ciriacy-Wantrup (1952) and Bishop (1978). It started as a practical guide to natural resource management under conditions of extreme uncertainty, for instance the preservation of individual species such as the Pacific northwest spotted owl or the African elephant. For problems of this nature, it is

Case Study 13.2   The habitat preservation of endangered fish species in the Virgin River systems: an application of the safe minimum standard approach

This case study is based on an article that appeared in the *Journal of Land Economics* (Berrens *et al.* 1998). This article dealt with two regional case studies from the south-western United States, the Colorado and Virgin River systems. The primary objective of these studies was to analyze the regional and subregional economic impacts of the US Federal Court order on the preservation of endangered fish species in the designated areas. The rules for this court order were based on the provisions of the Endangered Species Act of 1973. These rules are consistent with the safe minimum standard (SMS) approach. Individual areas can be excluded from the designation of critical habitat, and therefore extinction of species is allowed if, and only if, the economic impacts of preservation are judged to be extremely severe or intolerable.

For brevity, only a summary of the economic impact analyses of the Virgin River study area is presented. This study area involved two counties: Clark County, Nevada, and Washington County, Utah. The problem stemmed from a precipitous decline in the fish populations observed in this area. The declines were caused by physical and biological alterations of the Virgin River systems, primarily resulting from extended uses of water for agricultural, municipal and industrial purposes. The critical habitat designation was considered in order to restore the Virgin River systems to conditions that would allow the recovery of the endangered fish species.

The implementation of the critical habitat designation resulted in less diversion of the river water for commercial or human uses. The economic consequences of this were measured in terms of changes in output and employment. This in turn was done by comparing economic activity with and without taking the needs of the endangered fish species into account. For the Virgin River area, the study covered a time horizon of over 45 years (1995–2040) and the economic impact analyses were performed using input–output (I–O) models.

The overall economic impact of critical habitat designation was found to be negative but insignificant. The present value of the lost output was estimated to range between 0.0001 and 0.0003 per cent from the baseline – the regional economic development scenario over the study's time span in the absence of the federal court order for habitat preservation on behalf of the endangered fish species. In terms of employment, the reduction was estimated to range between 9 and 60 jobs. Subregional variations were observed in both the output and employment impacts. To put this into proper historical perspective, between 1959 and 1994 the regional economy in the Virgin study area grew on average by 3.01 per cent.

Overall, the economic impacts of critical habitat designation were found to be far below the recommended threshold for exclusion, which was 1 per cent deviation from the baseline projection of aggregate economic activity. As a result, on the basis of regional economic impacts, no sufficient ground could be established to recommend exemption from fish species protection in the Virgin River area.

argued that *irreversibility* becomes a key issue to consider. That is, beyond a certain threshold (or critical zone), the exploitation of natural resources may lead to irreversible damage. For example, the Pacific northwest spotted owl would be declared extinct if its population dropped beyond a certain minimum, and this minimum is greater than zero. Therefore, in managing natural resources of this nature, it is very important to pay serious attention to not extending resource use beyond a certain *safe* minimum standard. Otherwise, the social opportunity cost of reversing direction might become 'unacceptably large'. However, *it is important to note that considerable uncertainty exists regarding both the cost and the irreversibility of particular human impacts on the natural environment.* Thus, it is in this sense that uncertainty is central to the concept of SMS.

What specific relevance does the SMS approach to resource management have to sustainability? The answer to this question lies in understanding the implications of irreversibility and the potential social opportunity cost associated with it. In situations where human impacts on the natural environment are regarded as uncertain but may be large and irreversible, the SMS approach suggests that human and natural capital cannot be safely assumed to be substitutes. That is, when viewed from a long-run resource management perspective, the nature of the substitution possibilities between natural and human capital is uncertain. *In this respect, then, sustainability warrants maintenance of nondeclining natural capital as the safe minimum.*

Understood this way, the SMS approach to sustainability does not totally invalidate the standard economics approach to resource assessment and management, or even the concept of sustainability. It simply narrows the scope and the applicability of the standard economics conception of sustainability by restricting its relevance to human impacts on the natural environment where the potential consequences are regarded as being small and reversible. In this situation, Hartwick's compensatory investments could be applicable, and social opportunity costs could be assessed using standard cost–benefit analysis (see Chapter 9).

It is also obvious that, to some degree, the SMS and the ecological approaches to sustainability share common features. Both approaches adhere to the notion of limits to the substitution possibilities between human and natural capital. However, the two approaches provide different explanations for limits in factor substitutions. *The SMS approach uses irreversibility while the ecological economics approach relies on all-encompassing physical laws (of which ecological irreversibility is only a part).*

In many respects, then, the SMS approach to sustainability can be perceived as a *hybrid* between the standard and the ecological economics approaches to sustainability. It does not seek to reject the basic tenets of the standard economics approach to sustainability and resource assessment and management philosophies. At the same time, in broad terms it collaborates with the ecological economics notion that nature in some ways imposes limits on factor substitutions.

Finally, it is important to note that the *operational rule* of SMS is quite straight-forward. When the level of uncertainty and the social opportunity of current activities (such as global warming, ozone depletion and protection for rare, threatened or endangered ecosystems and habitats) are both high, the prudent course entails erring on the side of the unknown (see Case Study 13.2). This is, in fact, identical to the precautionary principle discussed in Section 6 of Chapter 9. *In the end, the important message conveyed by this rule is the social imperative to safeguard against large-scale, irreversible degradation of natural capital.*

13.6 Sustainable national income accounting

As mentioned in our discussion of the ecological economic approach to sustainability, sustainable economic development requires a modification of the conventional national accounting concepts of income. The key issue has been that a nation's income, as measured by gross national income (GNI), does not account for all the resource costs that are attributable to the production of goods and services during a given accounting period, and as such cannot reflect a level of income (economic activities) that is sustainable indefinitely (El Serafy 1997; Daly 1996). The relevant question is, then, in what way(s) can the national accounting concepts of GNI be modified so that sustainability of income or economic activity is assured?

As discussed earlier, fundamental to sustainability is the requirement that non-declining (constant) capital be maintained. The emphasis on capital is justified by the fact that it is the factor of production that determines the productive capacity of a nation. This requirement to keep capital intact can be achieved if, and only if, proper accounting is done for capital consumption or depreciation. In other words, given that capital is one of the primary determining factors of a nation's productive capacity, maintenance of a sustainable income – a level of income that a nation can receive while keeping its capital intact – requires setting aside a sufficient amount of current income to preserve capital so that the ability to generate future income is not adversely affected. From the viewpoint of a national income measurement, the implication of this is rather straightforward. An income accounting system that attempts to keep capital intact needs to explicitly account for capital depreciation (El Serafy 1997). Thus, the relevant income measurement is the *net* (not the gross) national income.

Traditionally, this concern has been met by recognizing the depreciation of human capital (machines, buildings, inventories, etc.) as a legitimate deduction from gross income or product (income):

$$NNI = GNI - DHC \tag{13.1}$$

where *NNI* is *net* national income, *GNI* is *gross* national income, and *DHC* is the depreciation allowance of human capital. However, although widely used, adjustments of this nature are still incomplete to the extent that they fail to account for the depreciation of *natural* capital – environmental costs of current production and consumption activities (El Serafy 1997). These environmental costs can be grouped into *two* broad categories.

The first category consists of the monetary costs of *net* degradation and depletion of natural assets (forests, air and water qualities, fisheries, oil, etc.) directly attributable to current production and consumption activities (Daly 1996). The basic argument here is that to keep environmental capital intact, provision should be made for its degradation in the same way as for depreciation of human capital. However, how to reflect changes in the stock of available natural resources (both renewable and nonrenewable resources) brought about by economic activity in national accounting measurements is still a controversial issue. Despite this, for our purpose here the key issue is the recognition that natural assets are depreciable (degradable), and any effort to measure the net proceeds from an economic activity should account for this cost (Repetto 1992). This is how, in physical terms, the stark reality of this cost is depicted by Georgescu-Roegen (1993: 42):

Economists are fond of saying that we cannot get something for nothing. The entropy law teaches us that the rule of biological life and, in man's case, of its economic continuation is far harsher. In entropy terms, the cost of any biological or economic enterprise is greater than the product. In entropy terms, any such activity necessarily results in a deficit.

The second category of environmental costs that needs to be considered is *defensive expenditures* (Daly 1996; Pearce 1993). *Defensive expenditures are real costs incurred by society to prevent or avoid damage to the environment caused by the side-effects of normal production and consumption activities* (Daly 1996). Examples of this type of expenditure are extra expenditures on health care for problems due to air pollution; extra expenditures on cars to equip them with catalytic converters; and extra costs incurred in offshore cleanup of oil spills. In the ordinary calculation of *GNI*, defensive expenditures of this kind are treated as part of the national income. *But this is erroneous, given that defensive expenditures actually represent a loss of income that cannot be spent again for consumption or investment but can be spent only to repair or prevent environmental damage caused by normal economic activities* (Daly 1996). In fact, an environmentally defensive expenditure actually represents 'a real income transfer from the human production system to the environment'. Thus, if the goal is to estimate a measure of true net income, environmentally defensive expenditures should be deducted (not added, as is normally done) from *GNI*. These are not only real costs, but also could be significant relative to the total *GNI*.

Consequently, to arrive at an environmentally adjusted national income, equation (13.1) needs to be reformulated as follows:

$$SNI = NNI - DNC - EDE \tag{13.2}$$

where *SNI* is sustainable national income, *DNC* is the depreciation of natural capital – the monetary value of the diminution of the natural resource stocks and the deterioration and degradation of the environment – and *EDE* represents the environmentally defensive expenditures. *It should be noted that since national income is a flow measure, only those aspects of DNC and EDE that are relevant to the current accounting period should be considered* (El Serafy 1997).

At this stage, it is important to recognize that conceptually, assuming no change in technology, *SNI* represents the maximum amount of income that can be expended on current consumption without impairing the future productive capacity of a nation (i.e. keeping capital stock intact). This is the case because, at least conceptually, the depreciation costs for capital (including natural capital) are fully considered. Furthermore, explicit consideration of the environmentally defensive expenditures would avoid counting some environmental quality maintenance costs as income. However, while conceptually straightforward, environmentally adjusted national income like *SNI* would involve estimation of *DNC* and *EDC*, in equation (13.2), in monetary terms. In recent years, a great deal of work has been done on developing methodologies for valuing natural resources and the environment in monetary terms (Lutz 1993). Nevertheless, as discussed in Chapter 9, because of the subjective elements involved in the economic valuation of the environment, there appears to be no consensus among national income accountants on how best to make the appropriate adjustments for the environment. Thus, the income accounting approach proposed in this section, namely

Table 13.2 How green is your country?

Country	GNP	Green NNP	Percentage fall in GNP ($ per capita 1993)
Japan	31,449	27,374	−13.0
Norway	25,947	21,045	−18.9
United States	24,716	21,865	−11.5
Germany	23,494	20,844	−11.3
South Korea	7,681	7,041	−8.3
South Africa	3,582	2,997	−16.3
Brazil	2,936	2,579	−12.2
Indonesia	732	616	−15.8
China	490	411	−16.1
India	293	242	−7.4

Source: *Nature* Vol. 395, 1998, p. 428. Copyright © 1998 Macmillan Magazines Ltd. Reprinted by permission.

sustainable national income, is just one of several methods currently in use by national accountants throughout the world to arrive at an approximate estimate of environmentally adjusted net national income.

Since the mid-1980s, much work has been done in the field of natural resources and environmental accounting (Lutz 1993). The pioneering work by Repetto *et al.* (1989) of the World Resources Institute includes important case studies for Costa Rica and Indonesia. The United Nations and the World Bank have conducted several joint studies, which culminated in the publication of *Towards Improved Accounting for the Environment* (Lutz 1993). This publication includes case studies for Papua New Guinea and Mexico. In its 1993 revision, the United Nations' System of National Accounts (SNA) has officially advocated the use of an environmentally adjusted national income accounting or what is popularly known as 'green accounting'. These are indeed important initial steps in the effort to develop more refined and comprehensive methods of environmental accounting for sustainable development (see Table 13.2). In some European countries and Japan, attempts are already being made to report national income in both conventional accounts and using a specific brand of green accounting. In some important ways these efforts also reflect the increasing awareness of the global community that the natural environment is a scarce resource (not a free good) that needs to be managed prudently.

Let me conclude this section by pointing out one implication of green accounting with considerable national and international significance. Traditionally, gross domestic income (GDI) is used for international comparisons, and for measuring economic growth. Higher GDI and higher *rate* of growth in GDI are often identified as being clear signals of strong and robust economic performance of a nation. However, this could be misleading if, for instance, a country were deriving its prosperity largely by depleting its natural capital stocks. In this case, the current level of income would be unsustainable unless proper allowance were made for the liquidation (depreciation) of the natural capital assets. This is how this particular message was conveyed in *Taking Nature into Account*, a book published as a report to the Club of Rome:

> To the extent that the depletion allowance was correctly estimated, and exploitation was carried out in the private sector, the national accounts came out right. In

the majority of developing countries, however, where natural resources have been worked in the public sector, proceeds from mining natural resources have been treated as income. The faster the depletion, the more prosperous the country would seem to be and the more rapid its apparent economic growth. The fact that such prosperity would be ephemeral, and that the apparent growth was misleading, did not seem to worry most economists, who continued to base their country analysis and policy prescriptions uncritically on the erroneously reckoned national accounts.

(Dieren 1995: 188–9)

13.7 Operationalizing the principles of sustainability: the case of a company called Interface

The theoretical presentation of sustainability is one thing, but the practical application of it remains another. For example, can sustainability be implemented substantially and rationally by for-profit enterprises? This case study is about a profit-seeking company called Interface – a company that chooses to use sustainability as one of the primary 'niches' of its business practice.

Interface is the largest commercial carpet manufacturer in the world, with headquarters in Atlanta, Georgia. Despite the potentially detrimental environmental impact of the company's primary operation, turning petrochemicals into textiles, Interface is one of America's most environmentally conscious corporations. Interestingly, this was a company that used to discharge large amounts of contaminated water; emit tons of solid waste, toxic gases and carbon dioxide; and fill up landfills with toxic used carpet. What caused the turn-around of Interface, from historical abuser of the environment to a corporation that chooses to work tirelessly to spread the wisdom and ethics of protecting the environment?

Like many other uniquely innovative plans of action, what it took was an energetic leader with a vision and a total commitment to put her/his vision into practice. In the case of Interface, the leader happens to be CEO Ray Anderson. According to Anderson's own account, his inspiration to turn the 'normal' business practice of his company upside down came from a work by Swedish oncologist, Karl-Henrik Robert, *The Natural Step*. *The Natural Step* was prepared as a guide for business enterprises that are genuinely interested in changing their operations in ways that are consistent with the goals and aspirations of a sustainable society.

There are a number of other major international corporations (such as XEROX, GM, IBM, and Toyota) which, in some aspects of their operations, have been making considerable efforts to respond to the growing public demand for products that are environmentally friendly (see Case Study 12.1). However, none of these corporations has, as yet, made sustainability the defining concept for their entire business operations as Interface has done. Interface's commitment to sustainability has been *total* and *proactive*. This company strives to place the health of the planet on equal footing with production and profits. Contrary to conventional wisdom, this has not been a profit-draining obligation. In this very important respect, Interface is a pioneer in social engineering that has the potential of making sustainability a normal business practice.

Interface did not begin and end with 'normal' re-evaluation and restructuring of the composition, production, distribution, and disposal of its products. *Instead the company started by searching for ways to engineer completely new modes of production and disposal of its products. More specifically, the company created modes of operations that are basically cyclical to the extent that these processes are capable of consuming their own waste.* This, indeed, constitutes a new production paradigm, and this new paradigm subscribes to the idea that the prototypical company of the twenty-first century will be strongly service-oriented, resource-efficient and will waste nothing.

Interface uses *seven* concrete steps to serve as guidelines for achieving its goal of becoming a sustainable enterprise. Step One is zero waste. This is done by dematerializing the company's operations to the extent that it is practical. If a product or part of a process, including accounting, sales, human resources, and manufacturing techniques, does not add value, the company simply eliminates it. Operationally, redundancy and duplication are not tolerated to the extent such practices are seen to use resources without adequate added value to justify their use.

Step Two is the elimination of toxic emissions. This is indeed a major challenge for a company whose business has been to turn petrochemicals into textiles. Despite this, Interface's achievement over the years in reducing its toxic emissions has been quite remarkable. For example, Interface significantly reduced the use of smokestacks in its factories and, in one division, placed computer controls on its boilers to reduce carbon monoxide emissions by 99.7 per cent.

Step Three is the use of renewable energy resources, and efficiency in energy utilization in general. Ranging from the resizing of pumps and pipes to the harnessing of solar energy, Interface has successfully implemented more efficient production processes that use less energy. In one of its factories, Interface recently developed a technique for coloring yarn that uses less than 10 per cent of the energy inputs of the previous process, at half the cost, through the recycling of the materials. Furthermore, in another facility in California, the introduction of a 127 kw solar array, which collects energy from the Sun during the day and converts that energy to electricity, as well as controlling the flow of the energy, allows a reduction in electricity usage of 6 per cent.

Step Four is essentially the introduction of closed-loop recycling. This process emphasizes natural raw materials and combustible products; specifically, human-made products are designed to be completely recyclable and stable for eternity. To achieve this goal, a division of Interface teamed up with a South Carolina soda-bottle recycling company to begin a process of turning the recycled polyester fiber made from soda containers into fabric. Interface has also invested in the research and development of a biodegradable carpet product, one that is made from a polylactic acid (PLA), a completely renewable resource found in corn.

Transportation efficiency, Step Five to sustainability, is difficult to achieve given that Interface depends on many other businesses to transport its products. Even in a situation like this, where the company does not have full control of the operation, Interface is trying to minimize the impact of its activities on natural ecosystems by teaming up with an organization called Trees for Travel, which plants trees in the rainforest to reduce carbon emissions. One tree, over its life span, is able to sequester the carbon emitted during 4,000 passenger miles of commercial air travel.

Step Six toward sustainability deals with Interface's deliberate effort to inculcate the culture of environmental sustainability throughout its corporate domain. To achieve this goal, Interface has created four main outreach and awareness programs, which include: (i) an anniversary celebration, where the main theme for discussion is the impact of human actions on the Earth's natural resources; (ii) the creation of an organization called One World Learning, which teaches the basic principles of sustainability;

(iii) formal solicitation of suggestions to help corporations achieve environmentally safe business practices; and, (iv) the Sustainability Report Card, which provides designers and developers with an ecological framework for the evaluation of all products and processes.

The last step, Step Seven, is redesigning commerce. This step involves shifting the business emphasis away from simply selling products to providing services. For example, Interface has created the Evergreen Lease, under which the company takes responsibility for installing and maintaining a carpet and recycling it at the end of its useful life. This step not only leads to the reduction in landfill usage, but also cuts disposal costs for the purchasing company.

Although Interface has created and implemented a number of successful plans of action to achieve sustainability, the company has yet to fully achieve its goals for sustainability. However, one thing about Interface's efforts toward sustainability thus far is indisputable. Through an innovative and very well thought out seven-step plan, this company is pioneering the societal changes that are necessary from the take–make–waste cycle philosophy to a more enlightened corporation where cyclical processes will replace linear ones. Furthermore, since Interface is doing this by using sustainability as a 'business niche' that so far produces no ill effects to profitability, it is reasonable to expect that the successful companies of the future will be those who are strongly service-oriented, resource-efficient, will waste nothing, be solar-powered, and have good connections with their customers, suppliers, employees, and communities. Clearly, this will be the undeniable legacy of Ray Anderson and his company, Interface.

13.8 Chapter summary

- In this chapter, three alternative conceptual approaches to sustainable development were discussed: the Hartwick–Solow; ecological economics; and the safe minimum standard (SMS).

- Careful examination of these approaches to sustainability reveals that they share the following common features:

  1 In principle, there is a tacit recognition of biophysical limits to economic growth.
  2 Sustainable economic development is envisioned as a viable and desirable course of action.
  3 A nondeclining capital stock (composed of natural and human capital) is regarded as a prerequisite for sustainability.
  4 Sustainability requires consideration of both efficiency and equity.

- However, the three approaches also differ in two very important ways:

  1 They differ in the way they perceive the relationship between human-made and natural capital. In the Hartwick–Solow approach, these two categories of capital are viewed as *substitutes*. This implies that the composition of the capital stock to be inherited by future generations is irrelevant. The ecological and the SMS approaches, in contrast, regard human-made and natural capital assets as *complements*.
  2 Differences exist in the degree of emphasis placed on equity relative to efficiency. In the Hartwick–Solow approach to sustainability the emphasis is

on intertemporal efficiency: efficient allocation of societal resources over time. In the ecological approach, the emphasis is on intergenerational equity. The SMS approach emphasizes equity only to the extent that present actions are suspected to cause irreversible harmful effects on future generations.

- All three approaches are plagued by the difficulty associated with obtaining the information necessary to determine the 'appropriate' size of the nondeclining capital stock. To this extent they are theoretical models.
- The determination of the 'appropriate' capital stock size requires, at minimum, the following: information on resource prices extending over a long period of time (forward markets for resources); estimation of shadow prices for environmental services that are not traded in the market; determination of the social discount rate; adjustment of the conventional measures of national accounting systems to account for the depreciation of natural capital; and the establishment of social, legal and political institutions designed to effectively operationalize the concept of sustainable development. The implication of all this is that progress towards sustainable development may be slowed considerably because of unreasonably large administrative, information and legal costs.
- Another practical consideration that tends to hamper the implementation of sustainable development programs is concern for *intragenerational* equity (concern for the poor living today). In considering sustainability, the emphasis has been on intergenerational equity: the well-being of future generations. Given this, sustainability stresses investment in long-term projects at the expense of current consumption. However, concern about the currently poor entails adopting a policy that leads to increased current consumption, rather than increased investment.
- Despite these practical difficulties, interest among economists in sustainable development continues to grow. This has contributed to increased academic focus on three important issues:

  1 Intergenerational equity. The key issue here is the ethical legitimacy of discounting.
  2 Sustainable national income accounting. In recent years, increasing attention has been given to ways in which the conventional national accounting system might be overhauled so that environmental defensive expenditures and depreciation of natural capital are accurately reflected.
  3 Biophysical limits. Here the issue is no longer about the existence of ecological limits as such, but how to deal with the perceived limits. This is, indeed, the essence of sustainable development.

Review and discussion questions

1 Briefly define the following concepts: intergenerational equity, the weak and strong sustainability conditions, private discount rate, social discount rate, depreciation of natural capital, environmental defense expenditures, net national income (NNI), sustainable national income (SNI).
2 State whether the following are *true*, *false* or *uncertain* and explain why.

   (a) Not all efficient points on the production possibility frontier are sustainable.
   (b) GNP, however distributed, may be more an index of cost than of benefit.

(c) The main difference between the Hartwick–Solow and the ecological economics approaches to sustainability is the *size* at which the nondeclining capital stock is predetermined.

3   'Sustainability should require considerations of both efficiency and intra- and inter-generational equities'. Discuss.
4   'Sustainable development ultimately implies a static population size'. Do you agree? Why, or why not?
5   'National accounting cannot be all-comprehensive, and accounting for environmental change will always be partial. Much environmental change will remain difficult or even impossible to value meaningfully in money terms, and this should be accepted' (Dieren 1995: 1991). Discuss.
6   'In principle and by implication, the safe minimum standard (SMS) and the ecological approaches to sustainability are pretty much similar.' Are they? Explain.
7   Reflect on what seems to be the consensus on the theoretical requirements for sustainable economic development. For example, two of these requirements are nondeclining constant capital (composed of both human and natural capital), and reforms of national income accounting systems to register the depreciation of natural capital and environmental defense expenditures. These are just two of several requirements of sustainability. Given this reality, in a world so divided and in so many ways, do you think sustainable economic development on a global scale will amount to nothing but a figment of human imagination or, to put it mildly, just wishful thinking? If you agree with this, what would you make of the many world summit meetings on sustainable development that have been held over the past two decades, the latest being the Johannesburg Summit 2002? Would it be fair to say that the talks and the agendas for action of the past world summits on sustainable development have been, to put it bluntly, 'too much ado about nothing'? Take a side and discuss your position.

References and further reading

Anderson, R. C. (1998) *Mid-Course Correction: Toward a Sustainable Enterprise: The Interface Model*, Peregrinzilla Press, Atlanta, Georgia.
Berrens, R. P., Brookshire, D. S. McKee, M. and Schmidt, C. (1998) 'Implementing the Safe Minimum Standard Approach: Two Case Studies from the US Endangered Species Act', *Land Economics* 2, 74: 147–61.
Bishop, R. C. (1978) 'Endangered Species and Uncertainty: The Economics of a Safe Minimum Standard', *American Journal of Agricultural Economics* 60: 10–18.
Ciriacy-Wantrup, S. (1952) *Resource Conservation: Economics and Policy*, Berkeley: University of California Press.
Common, M. and Perrings, C. (1992) 'Towards an Ecological Economics of Sustainability', *Ecological Economics* 6: 7–34.
Costanza, R., Perrings, C. and Cleveland, C. J. (1997) 'Introduction', in R. Costanza, C. Perrings and C. J. Cleveland (eds) *The Development of Ecological Economics*, London: Edward Elgar.
Daly, H. E. (1996) *Beyond Growth: The Economics of Sustainable Development*, Boston: Beacon Press.
Dieren, W. (ed.) (1995) *Taking Nature into Account: A Report to the Club of Rome*, New York: Springer-Verlag.
El Serafy, S. (1997) 'The Environment as Capital', in R, Costanza, C. Perrings and C. J. Cleveland (eds) *The Development of Ecological Economics*, London: Edward Elgar.

Fishman, C. (1998) 'Sustainable Growth-Interface, Inc.', *Fast Company*, Issue 14 (April): 136.

Georgescu-Roegen, N. (1993) 'The Entropy Law and the Economic Problem', in H. E. Daly and K. N. Townsend (eds) *Valuing the Earth: Economics, Ecology, Ethics*, Cambridge, Mass.: MIT Press.

Hartwick, J. M. (1977) 'Intergenerational Equity and the Investing of Rents from Exhaustible Resources', *American Economic Review* 67: 972–4.

——(1978) 'Substitution Among Exhaustible Resources and Intergenerational Equity', *Review of Economic Studies* 45: 347–54.

Hicks, J. R. (1946) *The Value of Capital*, 2nd edn, Oxford: Oxford University Press.

Krutilla, J. V. (1967) 'Conservation Reconsidered', *American Economic Review* 57, 4: 787–96.

Lutz, E. (ed.) (1993) *Towards Improved Accounting for the Environment*, Washington, DC: World Bank.

Menominee Tribal Enterprises (1997) *The Menominee Forest Management Tradition: History, Principles and Practices*, Keshena, Wis.: Menominee Tribal Enterprises.

Pearce, D. W. (1993) *Economic Values and the Natural World*, Cambridge, Mass.: MIT Press.

Perrings, C. (1991) 'Reserved Rationality and the Precautionary Principles: Technological Change, Time, and Uncertainty in Environmental Decision Making', in R. Costanza (ed.) *Ecological Economics: The Science and Management of Sustainability*, New York: Columbia University Press.

Repetto, R. (1992) 'Accounting for Environmental Assets', *Scientific American* 266: 94–100.

Repetto, R., McGrath, W., Wells, M., Beer, C. and Rossini, F. (1989) *Wasting Assets: Natural Resources in the National Accounts*, Washington, DC: World Resources Institute.

Social Funds.com (2000) 'Interface Introduces Corny Carpet Tiles', 4 August (http://www.socialfunds.com/news)

Solow, R. M. (1974) 'The Economics of Resources or the Resources of Economics', *American Economic Review* 64: 1–14.

——(1986) 'On the Intertemporal Allocation of Natural Resources', *Scandinavian Journal of Economics* 88: 141–9.

——(1993) 'Sustainability: An Economist's Perspective', in R. Dorfman and N. Dorfman (eds) *Selected Readings in Environmental Economics*, 3rd edn, New York: W. W. Norton.

Vorobej, A. (2000) 'Interface Introduces Biodegradable Carpet Product', *Textile Web News & Analysis*, 13 June (http://www.textileweb.com)

World Bank (1992) *World Development Report 1992: Development and the Environment*, New York: Oxford University Press.

World Commission on Environment and Development (WCED) (1987) *Our Common Future*, New York: Oxford University Press.

Part 5

The problems of poverty and environmental sustainability in the developing countries of the world

Part Five consists of one chapter, Chapter 14, which investigates the complex and seemingly paradoxical interrelationships between population, poverty and environmental degradation in the developing countries of the world. The chapter starts with a detailed analysis of the population problem both globally and with a particular focus on the developing countries. This is followed by an exploration of the conjecture that a link exists between poverty, population and environmental degradation. The analysis of this conjecture to its fullest extent constitutes a large part of the material presented in Part Five.

Some of the major issues addressed in this chapter include the following:

1   A close look at the intricate nature of the poverty that is so prevalent in the developing countries and how this economic condition contributes to population growth and environmental degradation.
2   The significance of gender equality, more specifically improvement in the economic status of women, as an important social variable in the amelioration of environmental degradation and population control.
3   Strategies to empower the poor in such a way that they will be motivated to take action that is not only consistent with their economic security but also causes least amount of damage to their environmental assets.
4   The changes in governance structures that are considered to be crucial in fostering the development and implementation of institutional programs and/or policies to protect the environment, while meeting the basic needs of the poor.
5   The extent to which international development aid programs and trades have either been benefiting or hurting the economic development aspirations and ecological integrity of developing countries.

This chapter deals with *real* problems facing about three fourths of the world population. These problems are real in a sense that they constitute visible incidences of malnutrition and indeed hunger in a significant percentage of the world population; poor sanitation facilities that expose people to high levels of health risk; large-scale land degradation and critical water shortage that continue to contribute significantly to loss in agricultural productivity; mass species extinctions resulting from deforestation and devastation of the fragile coastal ecosystems; noticeable decline in some fish species that are vital sources of protein for many people around the world; pollution of all sorts; and so on. These are serious problems indeed, and they demand the immediate attention of the global community (the poor and the rich) to work together for causes that are singularly intended to achieve a sustainable development on a global scale. These, I would claim, are indisputably some of the greatest challenges facing humanity in the twenty-first century.

Finally, this chapter has been carefully revised for the second edition of this book. I trust my efforts to improve the scope, depth and quality of the material covered in this chapter will aid your understanding of the issues addressed here.

14 Population, development and environmental degradation in the developing world

> Economic development and population growth in the poor areas of the Earth are essential topics of environmental concern. Much of the so-called Third World suffers extraordinary – and rapidly accelerating – environmental degradation. The patterns of destruction experienced here are markedly distinct from those of the industrialized zone, calling for the development of a separate body of both social–environmental theories and economic–ecological programs.
>
> (Lewis 1992: 191)

> There are many reasons to be optimistic about the future. More people are better fed and housed than ever before, global literacy rates are increasing and more people have access to better health care. Despite these significant gains, however, the need to arrest the increase in poverty while at the same time reversing the current trends of environmental degradation remains one of the world's greatest challenges. It is essential to tackle these two challenges simultaneously, since it is abundantly clear that the poor suffer disproportionately from the effects of environmental decline.
>
> (UNDP 1999: iii)

14.1 Introduction

In Section 4 of Chapter 10, the interrelationships between population growth, economic growth and environmental degradation were analyzed in the context of the Malthusian tradition. It was observed that although population growth has not yet threatened us with the immediate Malthusian catastrophe envisioned by many, it remains a serious problem. This is because rapid population growth is considered to be one of the major contributing factors to the vicious cycle of poverty and environmental degradation in many developing countries. The primary aim of this chapter is to systematically examine the nature of the interrelationships between population, poverty and environmental degradation in the developing world. As will be evident, these interrelationships are not only complex but also, in many respects, *paradoxical*.

In analyzing this issue, it is important to note that the 'developing world' comprises a heterogeneous group of countries, and not all of them are at the same stage of economic development or encounter the same levels of population and environmental problems. As will be shown shortly, some countries in this group have been quite successful both in controlling their population growth and in maintaining steady growth in their economy, as conventionally measured by an increase in per capita domestic product or GDP. However, while these countries are making demonstrable progress in their struggle to raise their standard of living *on average*, they are plagued by increasing levels of air and water pollution, and by an accelerated rate of resource depletion manifested in deforestation, soil erosion, overfishing, and damage to marine and coastal ecosystems such as coastal wetlands and coral reefs (Trainer 1990). For these countries, it appears that economic growth was attained at significant costs to their *natural capital assets* – the very resources critical for sustainable development. Furthermore, the economic success (in terms of increases in per capita income) of this group of countries has been clouded in two ways. First, because of the lopsided nature of the income distribution in these countries, it has been difficult to make significant headway in the war on poverty. In general, it appears that the very poor have not benefited from the economic growth during the past three decades. Second, the economies of these countries still remain vulnerable to international macroeconomic conditions and the policy measures imposed by the major international loan-granting institutions, such as the IMF and the World Bank. Leading examples of such countries are Argentina, Brazil, Mexico, India, South Korea, and Taiwan.

On the other hand, many African, Latin American and South-east Asian countries are confronted with problems of poverty and environmental degradation *simultaneously*. One of the major reasons for this is the failure of these countries to control the rapid rate of their population growth. 'In the world's 48 least-developed countries, population is projected to triple by 2050. In 57 more nations, the population could double. For example, the current population of Nigeria (about 120 million) is expected to grow to between 237 million and 325 million by mid-century' (Worldwatch Paper 161 2002: 12).

In some African and Latin American countries (such as Zambia, Kenya, Nigeria, El Salvador, Honduras, and Nicaragua) population has been growing at a rate of 3 to 4 per cent annually. In many of the poorest developing countries population has been growing faster than GDP, indicating a *negative* annual growth in per capita income. In these countries, poverty and population growth are exerting dangerous pressure on the carrying capacity of the ecosystem, and producing widespread desertification and deforestation (Lewis 1992; Trainer 1990).

Although differences exist, the developing world shares certain common characteristics. To a varying extent, population is still a major problem in most of these countries. Urbanization is another problem they share. In most of the developing countries, women are treated as second-class citizens and the poor are often marginalized. Globalization and international trade offer both major threats to and opportunities for safeguarding the natural resource base of these countries. Most have unstable government and maldistribution of income and wealth, and seem to lack the traditions and institutional infrastructure that are necessary for establishing clearly defined ownership over renewable resources such as forests, fisheries and arable land (Turner *et al.* 1993). As will become evident, these *governance* issues are major contributing factors to both the short- and the long-term economic, population and environmental problems of these nations. Until comprehensive solutions to these problems are found, both those countries that seem to be doing well economically and those that are failing to develop will continue to share a common experience: a severe form of environmental degradation (Lewis 1992).

This chapter has limited objectives. Consistent with the theme of the book, the main focus is the *environment*. Thus, poverty (or development) and population are discussed to the extent that they have significant adverse implications for the physical environment of the developing world. The chapter also seeks to recommend a number of practical policy measures that should be instituted in order to decouple the links between poverty, population and the environment. Here are the key issues addressed:

- It is not only the number of people, but also their lifestyles, political systems and social structures that define the relationship between humans and the environment.
- Poverty can be associated with environmental degradation, but there is not necessarily a direct causal relationship.
- It is not economic growth as such but the way 'development' takes place (is conceived and implemented) that is important in the alleviation of poverty and environmental degradation.
- The status of women is a particularly important variable in population–poverty–environment interactions.
- Measures such as structural adjustment programs, macroeconomic reform and globalization can be important in stimulating overall economic growth and greater economic efficiency. On the other hand, these same measures may place many developing countries in a situation where they have to overexploit natural resources in order to handle balance-of-payment problems or to deal with changing global market conditions.
- Reform of governance structures in many developing countries is a prerequisite to promoting sustainable use of environmental resources.

14.2 Global population trends: causes and consequences

One of the most striking experiences of the developing world in the last half century has been the rapid increase in population. This has been a concern for a number of reasons, and one of these concerns is the notion that rapid population growth may in fact be the main culprit for continued environmental degradation. There are a number of empirical studies that demonstrate the existence of causal relationships between rapid population growth and environmental degradation (Allen and Barnes 1995; Repetto and Holmes 1983; Rudel 1989; Ehrlich and Holdren 1971). However, most of these findings are valid only within certain *contexts* and as such cannot be used to establish a *general* causal relationship between population growth and environmental degradation. *The idea that seems to emerge is that while population growth is important, it is not the sole or even primary cause of environmental degradation.*

Thus, even in countries where rapid population growth is occurring, environmental degradation is best understood when the population factor is combined with other variables such as poverty, the status of women and governance structures (such as land tenure systems or traditions, income distribution, political systems, social structures, and so on). In addition, when the concern for the environment is placed in a global context, it is not only the number of people that matters, for 'the geographic distribution of people throughout the globe, the concentration of people in urban areas, and the demographic characteristics of regional populations have an important influence on the effects of human activity on the environment' (*Population Bulletin* 53, 1998: 1).

In this section, published data is used to examine the nature of the population problem in the developing nation. This will be done by looking at the growth trends and spatial distribution of *world* population, so that the specific problem (i.e. population growth in the developing nations) can be understood both historically and relative to the developed nations.

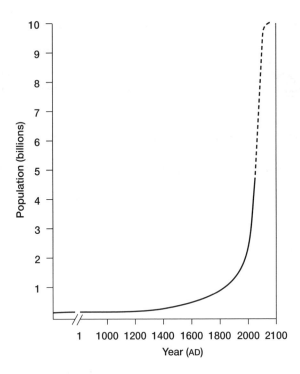

Figure 14.1 Past and projected world population. The world's population was growing at a steady but a very low rate, reaching the first billion mark in about 1800. On the other hand, exponential growth of world population has been the dominant feature of the twentieth century.
Source: Reprinted by permission of the World Bank, *The World Development Report 1984*, © 1984, Washington DC, p. 73.

Unprecedented steady population growth has been one of the dominant characteristics of the twentieth century. This is a significant change when we consider that for several millennia, the human population was growing at an insignificant rate, with death largely offsetting birth. As shown in Figure 14.1, population of the world was growing at a steady but very low rate, reaching the first billion mark in about 1800. In other words, it took millions of years for the world population to reach its first billion. However, as is evident from Figure 14.1, since about the turn of the seventeenth century the world population has been growing at a much faster pace. A look at Table 14.1 makes this point quite clear. While it took millions of years to reach the first billion, it took merely 130 years to add the next billion. Although the rate of growth seems to have stabilized since the mid-1970s, it now takes just eleven to twelve years for the world population to grow by a billion. According to Figure 14.1, the world population is projected to reach and perhaps stabilize at about 10 billion by the year 2100.

The situation becomes even more striking when we focus on the most recent world population trends. At the beginning of the twentieth century there were about 1.0–1.5 billion people in the world. For the first half of the century (1900–50), world population grew at a relatively low rate, averaging about 0.8 per cent per year (World Resources Institute 1987). By the 1960s there were 3 billion people on Earth, and the

Table 14.1 The approximate time it took for the world population to grow by a billion

Approximate time	Population in billions	Time it took to grow in years
— to 1800	1	(millions of years)
1800 to 1930	2	130
1930 to 1960	3	30
1960 to 1975	4	15
1975 to 1987	5	12
1987 to 1998	6	11

Source: Compiled from *World Resources, 1988–89*.

Table 14.2 World population growth by decade 1950–90 with projections to 2000

Year	Population (billions)	Increase by decade (millions)	Average annual increase (millions)
1950	2.565	–	–
1960	3.050	485	49
1970	3.721	671	67
1980	4.477	756	76
1990	5.320	843	84
2000	6.241	921	92

Source: *Worldwatch*, Sept./Oct. 1989, Vol. 2, No. 5, p. 34. © 1989. Reprinted by permission of the Worldwatch Institute.

annual growth rate was reaching the 2 per cent mark (ibid.). In the next decade (1960–70) world population grew at an accelerated rate until it reached a new plateau – an annual rate of increase of 2.06 per cent (ibid.). Rapidly declining death rates, together with continued high birth rates – especially in the developing countries of the world – contributed to this rapid rate of growth.

Yet since the early 1970s, the growth rate of world population has been showing a slow but steady decline. Specifically, the annual rate of growth has declined from about 2 per cent in 1970 to approximately 1.3 per cent today (Worldwatch Paper 161 2002). This drop is attributed mainly to a decrease in birthrates worldwide as a result of intense educational campaigns to promote birth control, along with specific preventive actions (such as improvements in reproductive health and access to contraception) undertaken by various government and private agencies.

Despite the progress that has been made in slowing down the annual rate of population growth, more people are being added to the Earth's total each year. Several factors explain this, among the most significant of which are: (i) the continuing decline in mortality rates; (ii) the absolute size of the world population (6.1 billion as of 2002); and (iii) the immense momentum built up from the current age composition of the population (i.e. the fact that roughly half of the world's population is under the age of 25, with all or most of their reproductive years ahead of them). As shown in Table 14.2, the average annual increase in world population had been increasing steadily. During the 1990s, on average, about 84 million people were added annually to the human population. Even today, the planet adds about 77 million people each year, the equivalent of 10 New York Cities (Worldwatch Paper 161 2002).

Table 14.3 Annual rates of population growth (in percentages) by regions: 1950–85

Region	1950–5	1960–5	1970–5	1975–80	1980–5
Africa	2.11	2.44	2.74	3.00	3.01
Latin America	2.72	2.80	2.51	2.37	2.30
East Asia	2.08	1.81	2.36	1.47	1.20
South Asia	2.00	2.51	2.44	2.30	2.20
Developing nations	2.11	2.30	2.46	2.14	2.02
Developed nations	1.28	1.19	0.89	0.74	0.64
Total world	1.8	1.96	2.03	1.77	1.67

Source: McNamara, R. S., *Foreign Affairs*, 1984, Vol. 62. Reprinted by permission of the author.

So far the focus has been on population trends for the world as a whole. However, these trends, based on aggregate data, do not reveal the wide differences in population growth rates (see Table 14.3) and the distribution of population (see Table 14.4) that persist between the different regions of the world, especially between the developed and the developing nations.

For two centuries, 1750–1950, the population of these two groups of nations grew at relatively low rates – between 0.4 and 0.9 per cent, respectively (McNamara 1984). Furthermore, during this period, the rate of growth of the developed nations was slightly higher than that of the developing nations. However, as shown in Table 14.3, since 1950 the average annual rates of population growth of the developing nations began to outpace those in the developed nations by considerable margins. For example, between 1960 and 1965, the average growth rate for the developing nations was roughly *twice* that of the developed nations (2.3 versus 1.19 per cent). Twenty years later, between 1980 and 1985 the population of the developing nations was growing at a rate *three* times faster than that of the developed nations (2.02 versus 0.64 per cent). Stated differently, if these rates persist over a long period, it will take less than 35 years for the population of the developing nations to double, compared to over a century for that of the developed nations. (It is important to note that, as shown in Table 14.3, the rates of population growth vary among the various groups of the developing nations. Moreover, although very high relative to the developed nations, the *rates* of population growth are falling everywhere except in Africa.)

Clearly, then, as shown in Table 14.4, such differences have resulted in a significant shift in the distribution of global population toward developing nations. At the beginning of the twentieth century, a third of the world's population lived in the developed nations; this proportion remained constant until about 1950. Since the 1950s, however, the share of world population living in the developed countries has been declining steadily. By the year 2000, only about one-fifth of the world's population is projected to live in the developed countries. That is, approximately four out of every five people in the world currently live in a developing country.

Moreover, this trend is expected to continue in the foreseeable future. A recent United Nations projection of world population for the year 2050 ranges between 7.7 and 11.2 billion (Population Reference Bureau 1997). However, as is evident from the above figures, *although the estimates for the world population in 50 years are subject to a wide range of variation, one trend in future global population growth remains indisputable.*

Table 14.4 Population trends, 1900–2000 (millions)

Region	1900%		1950%		1985%		2000%	
Developing regions	1,070	(66)	1,681	(67)	3,657	(76)	4,837	(79)
Africa	133		224		555		872	
Asia	867		1,292		2,697		3,419	
Latin America	70		165		405		546	
Developed regions	560	(34)	835	(33)	1,181	(24)	1,284	(21)
Total	1,630		2,516		4,837		6,122	

Source: *World Resources 1988–89*, p. 16. © 1988 by the World Resources Institute. Reprinted by permission. (The numbers inside the brackets indicate percentage of the world population.)

This is that world population will definitely increase in the future, and most of this increase will occur in developing countries. According to the United Nations estimate, it is expected that in 2050, 88 per cent of the people in the world will be living in the developing countries (ibid.).

What the above observations clearly indicate is that the world population growth problem is predominantly a concern of the developing nations. The question is, then, to the extent that a link exists between rapid population growth and environmental degradation, what can be done to ameliorate this population problem? As discussed above, the fact the wealthy nations have done far better in controlling their population growth than the poor ones may suggest that *poverty* is a factor to be considered in finding a long-term solution to both the population and environmental problems of developing countries. *However, to link poverty with population and the environment should not necessarily imply that economic growth is the panacea to the problems of population and the environment in the developing countries.* To make economic development work for the poor (and in turn for the environment), it is important to have a general under-standing of the nature and circumstances of poverty in developing countries.

14.3 Understanding poverty and its interactions with population and the environment

Poverty may mean different things to different people. It is generally conceptualized in terms of income, and formally defined as people living below a certain predetermined income level. For example, several recent publications from the United Nations identify *absolute* poverty as people living on less than one dollar per day. It was estimated that a total of 1.3 billion people live in absolute poverty – about one-fifth of the world's people (*Population Bulletin* 53, 1998). Most of these people live in sub-Saharan Africa and South Asia.

Alternatively, poverty may be defined in terms of *assets* instead of income. In this case, poverty may refer to lack of sufficient income generating assets needed to be able to provide an adequate level of basic necessities (UNDP 1999: 26). Assets may include natural capital (the ownership of land), human capital (work skills), social capital (human relations), physical capital (tools of the trade), and financial capital (cash savings). For the absolute poor, individual ownership of these assets may be beyond their reaches. On the other hand, collectively the poor may own a substantial amount of the various forms of the asset categories mentioned above, *and pro-poor public policies may focus on how to better allocate and manage these assets so that the economic circumstances of the poor will be improved.* In addition, as will soon be observed, *this asset-based definition of poverty is particularly helpful in examining poverty–environmental interactions.*

Another key fact that needs to be recognized in relating poverty and the environment is that *poor people are not a homogenous group.* Most importantly, significant differences exist in the relationship to the environment between the *rural* and *urban* poor. In the rural areas, 'the destitute are those who have very few assets, are marginalized, and who are continually forced to live from hand to mouth. They have no recourse but to exploit the environment around them, even if it means degrading its long-term value for their needs (UNDP 1999: 27).' In this respect, the rural poor are heavily dependent upon natural resources for their livelihoods. A good many of them reside in communities where land is collectively (communally) owned and the productivity of the land is very low or sub-marginal. Often times, the rural poor live in regions where the natural ecosystem, as a whole, is fragile, and the carrying capacity of the land is visibly overloaded. Under these circumstances, the pressure from population growth is expressed in territorial expansions that entail deforestation and other similar ecological encroachments or by migrating to an already-crowded urban area. The essential message here is that 'attacking poverty in rural areas is then necessarily a matter of improving poor people's ability to derive sustenance and income from more productive sustainably-managed natural resources' (UNDP 1999: 28). *In other words, in rural areas it is more effective to attack poverty by improving the management and utilization of natural resources rather than the other way around.*

On the other hand, the very poor or destitute among *urban* dwellers in developing countries have different impacts on the environment. The urban poor live in densely populated regions often characterized by substandard housing, inadequate or polluted water, lack of sanitation and solid-waste systems, outdoor air pollution, and indoor air pollution from low-quality cooking fuels. Under such living conditions, health risks are heightened because of the concentration of people and production. Thus, viewed this way, it seems that many of the linkages between the urban poor and the environment occur in the form of the effects of the environment on them, rather than the other way around. *The policy implication of this is that improving the environment in urban areas can reduce poverty because it improves poor people's health* (ibid.).

Of course, although small in quantity on a per capita basis, the urban poor also consume products and produce amounts of waste that have significant negative impacts on the environment. This situation is worsening as the population of the urban poor in the developed region of the world increases steadily and rapidly. Over the past 50 years, the population of these regions has been transformed from overwhelmingly rural to about 40 per cent urban (*Population Bulletin* 53 1998). This rapid population growth in urban areas in less-developed countries has created a host of social and environmental problems. Many cities are unable to improve their infrastructures and services fast enough to keep pace with population growth. Furthermore, 'urban growth often encroaches on farmland, destroys wildlife habitats, and threatens sensitive ecosystems and inshore fisheries. In Jordan, for example, the rapid growth of Aman and Zarqa has led to the gradual depletion of a major underground water reserve, which has reduced water availability for farmers and desiccated an internationally important wetland' (*Population Bulletin* 53 1998: 3). *In this regard, poverty alleviation measures through economic growth (increased per capita income) could benefit the environment. This, of course, is based on the assumption that the increase in per capita income would lead to increased demand for higher environmental quality* (for more on this see the discussion on the environmental Kuznets curve in Chapter 10).

From what has been said so far, it is important to note that the rural and urban poor are *interdependent* groups. A worsening condition of the natural environment in regions where the rural poor live could initiate mass migration from the rural to urban poor areas. The obvious effect of this would be a further deterioration in the living and environmental conditions of urban poor areas. On the other hand, rapid unplanned growth of cities affects the natural environment of the urban poor by adversely affecting the waterways, wildlife habitats and other sensitive ecosystems. *Recognition of this kind of interdependence between the rural and urban poor clearly implies that policy initiatives intended to improve the environment of the rural poor would not only benefit this group but also the urban poor, and vice versa.* This claim remains valid to the extent that migration of the rural poor to urban areas remains a major concern, and the growth of the urban poor is viewed as having a significant effect on the natural environment on which the rural poor depend for their survival.

The discussion in this section clearly reveals that the interactions of poverty, population and the environment are *complex* and depend on the contexts in which they are examined. It was observed that defining poverty in terms of *assets* would make the interactions between the environment and poverty more evident, at least from a policy perspective. Furthermore, it was shown that the interactions between population, poverty and the environment are quite sensitive to *location* – urban versus rural poor. Most importantly, it was pointed out that recognition of these finer points has important policy implications. The next section will seek to show why over the past three decades major public-policy measures intended to eradicate poverty in developing countries have failed. As will become evident, the root cause for this failure has been a failure to understand the full extent of population, poverty and environment interactions.

14.4 The failure of past policy measures to alleviate poverty and reduce environmental degradation

In the 1960s, when many developing countries were engaged in a desperate struggle to make the difficult transition from colonialism to political independence, a serious push was made to raise the standard of living in these countries (Bandyopadhyay and Shiva 1989). The motivation for this was the depressing level of poverty manifest in many developing countries, especially in the newly independent nations of Africa and Southeast Asia. As a world organization, the United Nations responded to this concern by inaugurating several development programs specifically intended to alleviate poverty in the developing nations. Furthermore, the 1972 United Nations Conference on the Human Environment identified poverty as both a cause and a consequence of environmental degradation.

In almost all the UN-sponsored efforts, economic 'development' was conceived as the cure for poverty. Economic development was understood as an increase in per capita gross domestic product (GDP), and countries sought to increase their GDP without any attempt to differentiate between economic development and economic growth (Goodland and Daly 1992). Furthermore, it was hypothesized that growth in GDP not only alleviates poverty by creating jobs for the poor, but could also create a surplus with which to clean up the environment and control crime and violence (Homer-Dixon *et al.* 1993). By the same token, in accordance with the theory of demographic transition, achieving a high standard of living was expected to lead to a decline in fertility rates, hence a decline in the rate of population growth (see Chapter 11). *Thus, economic development is conceived as a remedy not only for poverty but also for population growth and environmental degradation.*

To further strengthen the above claims, the need for *economic development* was argued in terms of the 'vicious cycle of poverty and environmental degradation'. The main implication of this is that low-income countries are destined to remain poor indefinitely unless something is done to raise their standard of living on a sustainable basis (Todaro 1989). *It was argued that countries with a low standard of living spend a high proportion of their income on current consumption needs. This means low savings and low investments, which leads to low productivity. With no hope of improving productivity, it is argued that these countries will remain stagnantly poor.* Furthermore, the persistence of poverty coupled with population pressure would lead to the migration of the poor to ever more fragile lands or more hazardous living sites, forcing them to overuse environmental resources. In turn, the degradation of these resources further impoverishes them. The question of interest, then, is what can be done to resolve this seemingly persistent problem of poverty?

Using the traditional model of development, *capital accumulation* was sanctioned as the way of alleviating poverty or as a catalyst for economic development (Todaro 1989). *This was based on the notion that capital accumulation, by enhancing the productivity of labor and other factors of production, would ultimately lead to an increase in the per capita income of a country.* It was with this in mind that the development projects of the 1960s and 1970s primarily focused on capital formation to promote growth. These included large capital-intensive projects such as dams, assembly lines and large-scale energy and agricultural projects. These projects were financed largely by international loans agencies, such as the World Bank and the International Monetary Fund (IMF).

In addition, it was argued that the economic condition of developing countries could be further enhanced by engaging in *free trade* with the industrial countries of the West (Bhagwati 1993). The trade relations between these two groups of countries are largely characterized by exports of primary resources (such as plywood, minerals, fruits, spices, etc.) from the developing countries and imports of industrial products from developed countries (such as machines, tractors, transportation vehicles, etc.). The justification for such trade relations is based on the fundamental premise that free trade leads to the attainment of a *mutually* beneficial outcome for all the parties involved. That is, international trade is not a zero-sum game, even when the total benefits are not shared evenly among the trading parties.

By the early 1980s it had become increasingly evident that the traditional approaches to economic development, which basically depended on *capital formation* and *free trade*, had not lived up to expectations. In fact, the evidence seemed to suggest that in many respects these development experiments had failed to improve productivity in many developing countries. Today, there are those who claim that some countries are worse off now than four decades ago when the official United Nations development programs were initiated. More specifically, there are now more people in the developing world who are in desperate poverty than ever before, environmental degradation in this part of the world has reached crisis proportions, and many of the developing countries are politically unstable and are burdened with debilitating international debts. How did this come about? What explanations can be given for such unintended and unfortunate outcomes? Simply put, what went wrong?

These are indeed difficult questions to address. Any attempt to offer comprehensive answers requires careful scrutiny of the political, social, institutional, economic, and environmental dimensions of the programs that were specifically intended for poverty alleviation in the developing nations. What follows is an attempt to do this using three broadly defined themes: economic growth and the environment; international trade and the environment; and governance, economic growth, poverty, and the environment.

14.4.1 Economic growth and the environment

As stated earlier, the campaign to alleviate poverty in the developing world had as its primary focus the increase of per capita GDP. Furthermore, this aim was expected to be achieved through increased capital formation and exposure to international markets. When consideration is given to the environment, this traditional approach to economic development has two major flaws.

First, as discussed in Chapter 13, the conventional measure of GDP does not account for the depreciation of natural or environmental capital. Thus, a focus on increasing GDP is likely to have a detrimental effect on the natural environment in the long run. More specifically, some empirical evidence exists that indicates a decline in *natural capital* while accumulation of various forms of capital (man-made, human and social) has contributed to economic growth (OECD 2002: 15). The natural capital that is being degraded in quality includes groundwater resources, fish stocks, the global atmosphere, and the capacity of ecosystems to assimilate toxic chemicals. These constitute the natural resource base critical for sustainable development.

Second, capital formation was traditionally conceived of in terms of large-scale capital-intensive projects such as dams, highways, factories, large-scale agriculture, etc., and these projects were implemented without adequate assessment of their impacts on natural ecosystems (Goodland and Daly 1992). Furthermore, *these projects were not necessarily pro-poor*. That is, they did not necessarily encourage the development and implementation of infrastructure and/or technologies that benefit the poor or protect the integrity of the environment. On the contrary, large-scale economic development projects seem to offer disproportionately large benefits to the already advantaged groups, such as large-scale farm operators, established firms with strong ties with international corporations, middle-class urban dwellers, etc.

The upshot of this has been continued environmental degradation, which is manifested in a variety of forms, such as deforestation, soil erosion, increasing levels of urban air and water pollution, and increasing damage to coastal and marine ecosystems leading to diminishing fishery stocks and destruction of coral reefs.

In the developing world, where the economy is primarily agrarian, the environment is an important input for many production activities. Thus, environmental degradation has an adverse effect on productivity, and the outcome of this will be a reduction in income. The important implication of this result is that poverty-alleviation programs are likely to fail in the long run if they are pursued with a primary focus on increasing GDP or per capita GDP. A growth ideology of this kind under-estimates the economic significance of the natural environment. *In the developing world the poor depend on the environment, so protecting the environment should be an important element of poverty alleviation* (Bandyopadhyay and Shiva 1989).

Case Study 14.1   Ranching for subsidies in Brazil

Theodore Panayotou

In the 1960s, the Brazilian government introduced extensive legislation aimed at developing the Amazon region. Over the next two decades, a combination of new fiscal and financial incentives encouraged the conversion of forest to pasture land. During the 1970s, some 8,000–10,000 square kilometers of forest were cleared for pasture each year. The proportion of land used for pasture in the Amazonian state of Rondonia increased from 2.5 per cent in 1970 to 25.6 per cent in 1985 (Mahar 1989).

It is now clear that transforming the Amazon into ranchland is both economically unsound and environmentally harmful. Without tree cover, the fragile Amazonian soil often loses its fertility, and at least 20 per cent of the pastures may be at some stage of deterioration (Repetto 1988b). Indeed, cattle ranching is considered one of the foremost proximate causes of deforestation. Furthermore, ranching provides few long-term employment opportunities. Livestock projects offer work only during the initial slash-and-burn phase. Negative employment effects have been observed when income-generating tree crops such as Brazil nuts are eradicated for pasture (Mahar 1989).

Nonetheless, the incentives designed to attract ranching, which were administered by the government's Superintendency for the Development of the Amazon (SUDAM), were powerful. Fiscal incentives included 10–15 year tax holidays, investment tax credits (ITCs) and export tax or import duty exemptions . . . SUDAM evaluated projects and financed up to 75 per cent of the investment costs of those that received favorable ratings using tax credit funds.

Starting in 1974, subsidized credit also played a crucial role in encouraging numerous ranching projects. The Program of Agricultural, Livestock and Mineral Poles in Amazonia (POLAMAZONIA) offered ranchers loans at 12 per cent interest, while market interest rates were at 45 per cent. Subsidized loans of 49–76 per cent of face value were typical through the early 1980s (Repetto 1988a). . . .

The subsidies and tax breaks encouraged ranchers to undertake projects that would not otherwise have been profitable. A World Resources Institute study showed that the typical subsidized investment yielded an economic loss equal to 55 per cent of the initial investment. If subsidies received by the private investor are taken into account, however, the typical investment yielded a positive financial return equal to 250 per cent of the initial outlay. The fiscal and financial incentives masked what were intrinsically poor investments and served to subsidize the conversion of a superior asset (tropical forest) into an inferior use (cattle ranching). Moreover, a survey of SUDAM projects reveals that five projects received tax credit funds without even being implemented (Mahar 1989).

Source: *Green Markets: The Economics of Sustainable Development*, San Francisco: International Center for Economic Growth (1993). Case reproduced by permission of the author.

14.4.2 International trade, development and the environment

As discussed earlier, the conventional wisdom has been to view international trade as a vehicle for accelerated economic growth in the developing countries (Bhagwati 1993). However, although somewhat inconclusive, the empirical evidence seems to suggest that commercialization or international trade is an important factor contributing to rapid rates of tropical deforestation and the extinction of some valuable animal and plant species worldwide (Repetto and Holmes 1983; Rudel 1989). More specifically, trade with developed countries has tended to accelerate deforestation in Latin America and Southeast Asia, and intensify the rate of desertification and the extinction of some animal and plant species in Africa (Rudel 1989). The implication of this is that, contrary to conventional wisdom, free trade has *not* been consistent with environmentally sustainable trade (Daly 1993). Does this suggest that, from the perspective of natural resource conservation, there is something inherently wrong with the trade between the developed and developing world? How could this be possible when, at least conceptually, international trade among sovereign nations is based on the premise of attaining 'mutually beneficial outcomes'?

From the perspective of natural resource and environmental management, the problem with international trade arises when one examines the way benefits and costs are imputed. Under a free trade regime the value of all international exchanges is assessed on the basis of *market prices*. As discussed in Chapter 3, a number of factors can lead to distortions in market prices, and the chances of this happening is even greater when we are dealing with international trade involving environmental and natural resource commodities. For our purposes, we should note *two* factors in particular that may lead to price distortions in the natural resources markets of developing countries.

First, the economies of the developing countries generally tend to be weak and quite unstable. They are often confronted with an urgent need to finance both domestic and international *debt*. In their desperate attempt to finance such debt, the governments of these countries are likely to offer their natural resources for sale at a discount (Korten 1991). Case Study 14.1 illustrates this point. This study shows how, because of the pressure to pay its external debts, Brazil in the 1970s and 1980s was aggressively pursuing economic policies that encouraged cattle ranching and in so doing accelerated the rate of deforestation.

The second and probably most important factor contributing to natural resource price distortion is market failure. That is, market prices for natural resources in these regions do not take account of *externalities* (Daly 1993; Ekins 1993). For example, when lumber is exported from a country in South-east Asia to Japan or France, the importing country will pay the prevailing market price, which is highly *unlikely* to include the environmental effects of the logging operations and the forgone benefits (which include both the *use* and the *nonuse* values) from preserving the resource under consideration for future use. Thus, if no mechanism is used to internalize these externalities, free trade based on market prices will lead to undue exploitation of natural resources upon which a vast number of the poor nations' people depend for their livelihood. Perceived this way, free trade leads to environmentally unsustainable and economically inefficient appropriation of resources on a global scale (Daly 1993; Ekins 1993).

In addition to the above factors, international trade may work against the poor for a number of reasons. First, integration of poor areas into national or international economies, or the popularization of products that were formerly consumed only locally, can create demand that outstrips sustainable supply. Resources that had been used only for local consumption can suddenly be over-exploited as markets increase, as happened in the case of the shrimp industry in South-east Asia (UNDP 1999). Second, trade for industrial or niche export markets often exposes rural households to high levels of risk. This is particularly true where the trade has encouraged people to move away from more-diversified and less risky agriculture-based livelihoods (ibid.) Third, Structural Adjustment Programs (generally imposed by IMF) may limit the ability of countries to provide subsidies to the poor. Furthermore, externally imposed macroeconomic adjustments often tend to encourage the reallocation of resources (in the form of new investment opportunities) to the fastest growing sectors of the economy. This often entails the withdrawal of resources away from long-term investment in the resources of the poor (ibid.).

14.4.3 *Governance, economic growth, poverty, and the environment*

The issue of governance refers to the political, social and economic institutions that are necessary to manage and protect environmental resources and the interests of the often-marginalized poor. For the subject matter of interest here, a 'good' or effective governance system is judged by what it seeks to do to promote social equity and environmental sustainability without unduly disrupting the normal functioning of an economy. 'Achieving these goals requires, above all, approaches of governance that foster citizen participation in policy-making and that promote integrity, transparency, and accountability in the management of public resources' (OECD 2002: 40). As the discussions below would indicate, these are key institutional elements that were lacking in many developing countries even today, let alone during the 1960s, 1970s and 1980s when economic growth was pushed with little or no scrutiny of environmental consequences. *In the absence of good governance structures, ambitious programs of economic development often meant economic growth at the expense of the environment and sometimes the poor.* To a large extent, the main culprits for the persistent lack of good governance practices in developing countries have been political instability, land-tenure systems, widespread government official corruption, and insufficient experience in operating democratically structured governance systems. In some countries, there appears to be strong and persistent resistance to a freely elected and representative government system.

Establishing institutions that ensure the stable functioning of society and economies, including the enforcement of civil and property rights, require political leaders that have a broad mandate from their constituents and the ability to remain in power until the official term of their administration expires. For most developing countries, political instability and insecure tenure over many valuable renewable resources, such as forests, fisheries and arable lands, continually negate public policy efforts to stabilize population, control pollution and conserve resources (Turner *et al.* 1993). One of the most unfortunate, but recurring, realities in many developing countries is political instability. It is especially true of countries in Africa, South-east Asia, and Central and South America, which frequently face internal strife that sometimes erupts into prolonged tribal conflict and even civil war. Thus, in this kind of political climate it would be, if not impossible, then extremely difficult to implement effective population and resource conservation policies based on long-term visions. Instead, public policies are devised on a piecemeal basis, and generally as a reaction to crisis situations. What this entails is a lack of responsible stewardship of resources that are critically important to the long-term survival of the nation (Homer-Dixon *et al.* 1993).

To make matters worse, in many of these countries property is publicly or communally owned, and most often ownership is not clearly defined. Consequently, as discussed in Chapter 3, market prices need to be corrected. But this requires that developing countries have the appropriate regulatory and institutional framework to internalize environmental externalities. In many developing countries, this kind of market failure tends to persist because of their governments' inability to administer and enforce the laws that are intended to correct externalities. One reason for this is that these are countries that can least afford to pay for protecting the environment. As a result, even when efforts to protect the environment or conserve resources are made, regulations are inconsistently applied and regulatory agencies are too poorly staffed and insufficiently informed to be able to monitor and implement the regulations effectively. The fact that corruption is rampant further complicates this problem. The ultimate effect of all this has been rapid degradation of valuable environmental assets resulting from extensive and random land clearing, imprudent farming practices, and excessive water and air pollution. This situation is likely to persist unless some means are found to strengthen the institutional weaknesses that are at the core of the problems – that is, to *define* and *enforce* clear rights of access and use of resources among producers, consumers and government so that societal resources are prudently used. As Case Study 14.2 clearly demonstrates, this does not mean that countries need to adopt private ownership of resources. Effective property rights systems could take several forms; what matters is that governments match property tenure laws to the social context.

In addition to the problems with land tenure systems, in most developing nations the distribution of farmlands is grossly uneven. For example, 'In 1960, the smallest 50 per cent of holdings controlled less than 3 per cent of agricultural land, in 1970, the median of the reported figure is 4 per cent. On the other hand, the largest 10 per cent of holdings controlled 65 per cent of the land in 1960; for 1970, the median for all developing countries figure was 70 per cent' (Repetto and Holmes 1983: 610).

The effect of this has been more intensive use of small farmland, primarily to grow crops for domestic needs. This practice is greatly intensified when the internal population pressure increases. Yet owners of large lands allocate most of their holdings to commercial or cash crops, such as coconuts, sugar, fruits, vegetables, cotton, and tobacco, primarily for export. Moreover, these crops are grown with extensive application of pesticides. Thus, the unequal distribution of landholdings that exists in most developing countries not only shifts land use from domestic to export needs, but also places these countries at greater environmental risk. *This situation can be ameliorated only through land reform (wealth redistribution) designed to more or less equalize land-holdings, and/or through export restrictions.*

To sum up, the discussions in this section clearly suggest that the failure of poverty alleviation programs in developing countries during the 1960s, 1970s and a good part of the 1980s was primarily due to improper implementation of many well-intentioned economic development programs. The focus of these programs was very much on pursuing economic growth at all costs.

This was justified by appeal to the rather naïve notion that it is only through economic growth (increase in average per capita income) that the eradication of poverty will be possible, and that this should be pursued even if it is done at the cost of the

Case Study 14.2   Communal tenure in Papua New Guinea

Theodore Panayotou

Unlike most of the developing world, Papua New Guinea has maintained its communal tenure customs while adapting to the requirements of an increasingly market-oriented economy. While the latter requires clear land ownership, Papua New Guinea's experience has shown that converting land from communal to freehold ownership may confuse rather than clarify the rights of ownership. The widespread land degradation encouraged by the insecure tenure, loss of entitlements and open access characteristic of state-owned land elsewhere has been absent from Papua New Guinea.

Most countries have responded to market pressures for clear ownership by imposing a new system of private or state ownership. In contrast, Papua New Guinea's land law builds upon the customs governing its communally held land. The country's Land Ordinance Act calls for local mediators and land courts to base settlements on existing principles of communal ownership. Consequently, 97 per cent of the land remains communal, has been neither surveyed nor registered, and is governed by local custom (Cooter 1990).

This communal tenure seems to provide clearer ownership rights, with all their environmental and market implications, than private ownership. Settlements that convert communal land to freehold are often later disputed, and reversion back to customary ownership is a frequent outcome. Yet unlike state-owned land in other developing countries, communal land in Papua New Guinea is neither in effect unowned nor public. Rather, the bundle of rights deemed 'ownership' in the West does not reside in one party. For example, individual families hold the right to farm plots of land indefinitely, but the right to trade them resides in the clan (Cooter 1990).

The island's communal systems have long resulted in the sustainable use of its more densely populated highlands. Even with a 9000-year agricultural history, a wet climate and population growth of at least 2.3 per cent, the highlands remain fertile. The population, which is primarily agricultural, enjoys a per capita income more than twice that of El Salvador, Western Samoa and Nigeria (Cooter 1990). In marked contrast to much of the developing world, only 6 million of its 46 million hectares of forestland have been converted to other uses (Australian UNESCO Committee 1976).

The lack of deforestation comes as no surprise since those who control the land have an interest in the sustainable, productive use of the forest. Rather than dealing with a distant government in need of quick revenues and foreign exchange, companies seeking logging rights must negotiate directly with those who have secure tenure and who use the land not only to farm, but also to gather fruit, hunt and collect materials for clothing, buildings and weapons (Panayotou and Ashton 1992). Because the communal tenure patterns provide an entitlement to all clan members, individuals have little incentive to sacrifice future value for current use.

Source: *Green Markets: The Economics of Sustainable Development*, San Francisco, Calif.: Institute for Contemporary History (1993). Case reproduced by permission of the author.

environment. Furthermore, *there was also the belief that, in the long run, what is good for the economy as a whole is good for the poor and the environment. That is, the benefits of economic growth, no matter how they are attained, would somehow in the long run trickle down to the poor and to the environment.* Furthermore, it was argued that increases in the living standards of the poor would slow the growth of population (see Chapter 11).

However, as the discussions in this section have shown, the economic development programs during these three decades failed miserably to achieve their intended goal, the eradication of poverty. This was because, as the discussions demonstrated, the programs were not properly focused on either the problem of the poor and/or the elements of the natural environment (assets) that specifically affect the poor. Furthermore, the problem was compounded by the fact that economic growth was pursued without much consideration of the *institutional factors* relevant to the promotion and enforcement of social equity and the sustainable use of the natural environment. The question now is, what can be done to remedy these past mistakes? The next section attempts to answer this question.

14.5 New initiatives on poverty and the environment

In terms of international development initiatives, the 1980s were a decade of transition. This was a time when searches for new and comprehensive programs to poverty, population, overconsumption, and the environment began to be taken seriously. More specifically, it was during this decade that a conceptual shift from 'traditional economic growth' towards 'sustainable development' started to take place. This new movement was formally articulated in 1987 with the publication of a book entitled *Our Common Future*, popularly known as the Brundtland Commission report. As discussed in Chapter 13, it was in this report that sustainable development was given its most commonly accepted definition, as 'development that meets the needs of the present without compromising the ability of future generations to meet their own needs'. With reference to the main theme of this chapter, in the Introduction to the report Dr Gro Harlem Brundtland wrote:

> There has been a growing realization in national governments and multinational institutions that it is impossible to separate economic development issues from environmental issue; many forms of development erode the environmental resources upon which they must be based, and environmental degradation can undermine economic development. Poverty is a major cause and effect of global environmental problems. It is therefore futile to attempt to deal with environmental problems without a broader perspective that encompasses the factors underlying world poverty and international inequality.
>
> (p. 3)

What this report brought into focus was that *environmental problems are not only linked to poverty as it exists in the developing countries but also to inequalities in consumption and production patterns globally.* This globalization of the environmental problem was in fact the driving force for holding the United Nations Conference on Environment and Development (the Earth Summit) in Rio de Janeiro in 1992. Directly relevant to this chapter was Agenda 21, the action program adopted at this conference, which devoted a chapter to the relationship between poverty and environmental programs. This Rio Summit was followed by a number of other global conferences throughout the 1990s, all dealing with some specific aspect of the population, poverty and environmental interactions and from a global perspective. Among these conferences, the most notable ones were: the Cairo Conference on Population and Development (1994); the Copenhagen World Summit on Social Development (1995); the Beijing Fourth World Conference on Women (1995); the Istanbul Habitat II Conference (1996); and most recently, the World Summit on Sustainable Development (WSSD) in Johannesburg in 2002. Each one of these global conferences was followed by ambitious action programs or declarations to be further debated and possibly implemented at some future dates. The unifying theme of these conferences has been sustainable development, and the specific topic (population, environment, social and economic equity, gender, human settlements, etc.) of each conference reflected the particular perspective from which sustainable development has been pursued.

It could be argued that there has been a wide gulf between the stated goals of the global conventions of the above kind and their actual achievements. However, in spite of this, the cumulative effect of these conferences has been to change the perceptions of the global communities on how to deal with problems of poverty, population and the environment in a number of concrete ways:

*   First and foremost, these problems are now viewed as being global, and as such their solutions require cooperative international actions.
*   Second, there is a growing realization by the international communities that economic growth cannot be considered a problem by itself; the way development takes place matters a great deal.
*   Third, enduring solutions to problems of poverty, population and the environment require careful examinations of some specific issues that have been somewhat neglected until recently. These include *gender, governance, the empowerment of the poor, and social and economic equity*.

The rest of this chapter will discuss these four issues and how they contribute to better understanding of the poverty, population interactions and their possible remedies.

14.5.1 Gender equality and the alleviation of poverty and environmental degradation

It has been only in the past two decades that gender equity started to receive serious attention as an important variable in the population–poverty–environment relationship. Given that we live in a male-dominated world, gender equity necessarily refers to the much-needed improvement in women's social and economics status. Why is this important? In many societies, women's status is closely associated with rates of fertility and infant and child mortality, health and nutrition, children's education, and natural resource management (*Population Bulletin* 53, 1998). Invariably, a decline in population growth rates is evident wherever women's status has been elevated:

> when girls go to school free of fear of violence and sexual coercion, and when women reach economic, social, and political parity with men, they have fewer

children and give birth later on average than their mothers did. Assuming good access to health and family planning services, fertility almost invariably declines to or below replacement level. That slows the growth of population.

It is increasingly clear that the long-term future of environmental and human health – and, critically, the global population peak – is bound up in the rights and capacities of youth, especially young women, to control their own lives and destinies

(Worldwatch Paper 161 2002: 9).

There is always a danger in advocating the improvement in the women's status purely because their reproductive decisions and actions are valued or have implications on population growth and/or poverty. The argument is that gender equality and the reproductive and sexual health of women are basic human rights and, as such, are *intrinsically* valued. These were the positions taken at the International Conference on Population and Development (ICPD) in Cairo in 1994, and, to a much greater degree, at the Fourth World Conference on Women in Beijing in 1996.

Whether one argues for equality of women on the basis of a purely instrumental or a purely human rights perspective should not be an important issue by itself. *What is important is the recognition that no meaningful policies on population, poverty and the environment can be formulated without an explicit account of the important roles women play in these areas of human endeavor.* This warning or declaration is especially pertinent to the developing countries where women's participation in much important social, political and economic decision-making is severely limited.

Equal access to education is the most effective way to empower women. By 'empower' I mean women's ability to exercise control over the resources and decisions that affect their life. 'Educating girls and women gives them higher self-esteem, greater decision-making power within the family, more confidence to participate fully in community affairs, and the ability to one day become educated mothers who pass on their knowledge to their own daughters and sons' (Worldwatch Paper 161 2002: 16). Not surprisingly, a major contributor to later pregnancies and lower fertility is at least six or seven years of schooling (ibid.). Investment in women's education, at least at the primary school level, is therefore crucial for two reasons: first, to provide girls and women with invaluable knowledge and information on reproductive health (i.e. the capacity to plan, prevent or postpone pregnancy); and second, to provide women with the necessary confidence to make their voice heard on any social, political and economic issue that has the potential to affect their lives and livelihoods. Most important among these is the confidence to demand equal access to land ownership.

In the final analysis, women play unique and crucial roles in societal efforts that are specifically targeted on population stabilization, poverty eradication and environmental sustainability. However, the contributions of women to the problems of population, poverty and the environment (or sustainable development in general) can never be fully mobilized until women gain unfettered rights to control their own lives and destinies.

Yes, some aspects of women's 'rights' are subject to different interpretations and often require a good understanding of their social context. However, the social context of women's rights should never be used either to make excuses or find justifications for denying rights to women over their own bodies, equal access to education and land ownership, and equality in work places.

14.5.2 *Improving governance for the alleviation of poverty and environmental degradation*

It is not at all difficult to find examples of resource management projects and development programs that failed miserably in the implementation process due mainly to lack of 'good' governance systems. As discussed earlier, governance refers to the social institutions necessary to facilitate the management of public resources. With reference to resource management, good governance practices require not only consideration of efficiency (lower transaction costs) but also equity and political realities. Above all, the efficacy of good governance greatly depends on bureaucratic commitment to establishing a working environment that promotes integrity, transparency and accountability (UNDP 1999). That is, those with leadership roles have to demonstrate that they are the servants of the public and work with the objective of attaining the 'greatest good for the greatest numbers'.

The issue here is not a choice of political ideology (i.e. dictatorship, democracy or socialism) but rather the identification of general institutional 'principles' for effective resource governance. With regard to resource management, the general principles that are often considered hallmarks of good governance include a number of human and organizational conditions: (i) protection of individual civil liberty; (ii) decentralization of decision-making processes; (iii) easy access to relevant information; and (iv) minimal or no impediments to resource mobilization (ibid.). *These principles, taken together, may be closely associated with commonly held views about democratic principles but not entirely with democratic political ideologies.*

The main economic rationale for using these general principles of governance is that they are expected to reduce *transaction costs* in the management of resources. Furthermore, these are principles that are most likely to offer groups that are often marginalized (such as the poor, the residents of remotely located rural areas, etc.) *a much better chance to decide what to do about their own resources.* It is for this reason, therefore, that resource governance guided by the above four principles is essential in any serious effort to alleviate poverty or arrest the degradation of natural resources that are so vital to the livelihood and self-esteem of the poor.

In practice, what do these principles of governance entail in terms of the structure of government organizations specifically designed to protect the interests of the poor and the environment, especially in the developing world?

- Governments must find ways to hold themselves, private corporations and international institutions included, *accountable* for their environmental performance. No one should be allowed to exercise authority over natural resources without being accountable for their actions.
- Governments should strive to place authority over environmental resources to those individuals or groups whose claims as stakeholders are verifiably legitimate. This often entails *decentralizing* responsibility for natural resources management to local governments and communities. Decentralized decision-making facilitates participation among stakeholders and the reallocation of resources (resource mobilization). Furthermore, decentralized decision-making to the extent that it provides greater authority to local institutions may be made sensitive to the needs and aspirations of the marginalized groups, such as the poor. Of course, the decentralization of the decision-making process

of government institutions cannot occur without the political will and support at the highest levels.

- Government leaders should not only have adequate means to defend their territories from outside invaders, but also be able to negotiate trade, environmental and other international treaties to the benefit of their people. It is no longer adequate to identify globalization with trade. More than ever before, poverty, population and environmental problems are becoming increasingly global concerns, and their resolution demands global governance. Understanding the dynamics of global governance is crucially important for any government that tries to maximize the benefits to its people arising from an alliance or a global treaty.

How could this kind of governance be attained? Or, what would it take to actualize such governance in practice? Here are some suggested requirements:

- Legitimacy of the government: those who are in leadership roles must have legitimacy for the authority they exercise over their constituencies. Such authority must be obtained by lawful means and without violations of human rights.
- Political stability: stable government is critical for devising policies that are long-term oriented. Traditions of smooth transitions of political power are essential.
- Intolerance for corruption.

These suggestions need *not* entail a government that adheres strictly to the principles of political democracy. A case in point is Cuba – a socialist country that is governed by an absolute dictator. However, Cuba has done quite well in eradicating extreme poverty. But neither does this suggest that a dictatorship (even a benevolent one) is what is needed to eradicate poverty in the developing countries.

14.5.3 Empowerment of the poor and environmental sustainability

As stated earlier, it is important to recognize that *collectively* the poor in any country have both tangible and intangible assets (property) of their own. For example, the rural poor in a developing country live in a certain geographic area with certain climate, vegetation and land quality. They have skills and indigenous knowledge that help them cultivate the land for their survival. They have a history, culture and traditions that glue their community together and provide its identity and pride. In many African, Asian and Latin American countries the rural poor, despite their impoverishment, are proud of who they are and revere their natural surroundings that are so crucial for their survival (UNDP 1999).

The same thing can be said about the urban poor. That is, they too possess assets (tangible and intangible) that are peculiar to their surroundings. In general, although most of them are descendants of the rural poor, the urban poor do not have strong ties with land. Ownership of land is possible for only a very small minority group. *What the urban poor have as resources are plenty of unskilled and semi-skilled labor resources, and under-utilized entrepreneurial skills.*

Empowerment of the poor starts with the recognition that the poor have resources that can be used and improved upon to provide them with decent living standards and on a sustainable basis (ibid.). It also recognizes that the poor (as a community) understand their situation better than others and as such are capable of planning and implementing projects that are intended to promote their well-being. This is not to say that the poor do not need outside assistance (financial or otherwise). *Rather, the assertion here is that outside aid that is meaningful to poor communities is that which allows these very communities to have a complete say over what purposes the aid will be used for* (ibid.).

As discussed earlier, in the past and even today, many development aid programs failed and are failing mainly because they did not consider empowering the poor. The poor are often viewed as being helpless since they are destitute, disorganized in their community affairs or simply rootless, and ignorant about their natural surroundings (ibid.). Decisions about what would be beneficial for the poor were often left to decision-makers at the central government level, NGOs or other international organizations, such as the World Bank, IMF, EC, OECD, etc.

In that kind of decision-making environment, it should not be surprising to hear that development projects intended to alleviate poverty in rural areas often end up benefiting not the rural poor (the targeted population) but the big landlords, a few government bureaucrats and other mediators of aid programs. This type of misallocation of resources (and, in some instances, outright blunders) can be ended only if the poor (collectively) are recognized as a social entity capable of determining their own economic fate.

Furthermore, when the poor are recognized as equal partners in a decision-making process that involves their economic fate, among others, the wisdom of using *endogenous knowledge* will not be overlooked. Clearly this will help avoid the implementation of inappropriate technologies.

Poor people are not the same everywhere. There are different categories of urban poor and each sub-group could have conflicting needs and objectives. The same can be said of the rural poor. Given this reality, it would be wrong to view the poor as a homogenous entity. *What this implies is that development programs have a better chance of succeeding if they target a particular clearly identifiable social group(s) living in a specific geographic region. This way, the money earmarked to reduce poverty in that region will not be used for other purposes* (ibid.).

Finally, it is important to note that investing in programs intended to eradicate poverty does not come without a cost, namely, opportunity cost. Money spent on the poor becomes available only by taking away resources that would have been spent on other social projects. Thus, decision-makers need to make sure that investment to alleviate poverty is allocated within a framework of cost–benefit analysis. However, such cost–benefit analysis should take into consideration the equity issues to be discussed in the next subsection. *If this is done, it will remove the possibility that investment in poor regions will be regarded as nothing more than a handout.* In the long run, such an attitude of 'charity' is detrimental to the poor. What the poor need is not charity but development assistance of various kinds, which have a proven record of improving the well-being of the poor on a sustainable basis (ibid.).

14.5.4 *Social and economic equity and environmental sustainability*

As discussed earlier, the highly unequal distribution of *assets* (i.e. the total tangible and intangible capital holdings of individual households, land ownership being the most obvious) remains a serious problem in many developing countries. The direct result of this has been the notably skewed income and wealth distributions that are so prevalent in most of these countries. This reality has been challenged not only on the basis of *equity* (which is easy to do) but also on *efficiency* grounds as well. *The claim has been that a highly unequal distribution of income or assets often has a tendency to suppress rates of economic growth* (UNDP 1999).

What this argument suggests is that in many developing countries, reform of the distribution of assets can be justified on *both* equity and efficiency grounds. Furthermore, a good case could be made that pro-poor asset reforms would lead to improved management and conservation of environmental resources. Clearly, in many situations asset reforms could be imperative, so the issue of primary significance is how to conduct the intended reforms successfully. This suggests that redistribution of assets can take different forms, and successful reform requires careful scrutiny of alternative modes of asset reform.

The most often used method of asset redistribution is *land* reform. Land reform has been an emotional issue in developing countries. It generally means confiscation of land from those with large holdings and granting to those who have little or are simply landless. Historically, in most instances this kind of land reform has proved to be socially divisive and very damaging to an economy in the long run. This is because agricultural productivity and investment in agriculture are quite sensitive not just to the size of landholdings but also to the way the land reform has been instituted – how ownership rights are defined and secured. Thus, while land reform can justifiably be used in cases where land distribution is highly skewed, its social divisiveness and adverse impact on the economy warrants caution.

Alternative methods of asset reform exist. Below is a list of asset reforms that are particularly relevant to the concern of the poor and the environment. These reforms are generally intended to protect, improve, and/or expand the asset basis of the poor. They are also intended to give the poor entitlements to assets that are clearly delineated so that self-interest would lead to the adoption of improved resource management strategies. For expanded discussions on each of the methods listed below, see the United Nations Development Program (UNDP) publication, *Attaching Poverty While Improving the Environment: Toward Win–Win Policy Options*, September, 1999.

1   Turn communal property resources over to the poor as individuals or to organizations composed of the poor. The important issue here is that the poor now have property that they claim their own and as such have a self-interest to manage it wisely.
2   Provide the poor with long-term rental contracts for the use of public lands.
3   Grant formal tenure rights to individuals or groups currently squatting on public lands or in urban areas.
4   Co-manage resources with the poor. This involves forming partnerships between local people and the state (government) to develop strategies for asset improvement and protection of resources. A good example of a successful co-management program is the Campfire program in Zimbabwe (see Case Study 14.3 below).
5   Co-invest with the poor. Government works with local communities (such as, farmer organizations) to make possible socially beneficial long-term investments. Investments of this kind may include soil conservation, irrigation and drainage infrastructure, grazing land rehabilitation, land-leveling, and micro-watershed re-vegetation. If the poor are to succeed, they also need to be trained. In urban areas, co-investing with the poor may involve improving access to better water

Case Study 14.3   Zimbabwe's Campfire: empowering rural communities for conservation and development

Zimbabwe's Campfire (Communal Areas Management Programme for Indigenous Resources) was officially established in 1989. Conceptually, the focus of Campfire has been wildlife management in communal areas, particularly those adjacent to National Parks. Zimbabwe has set aside, in perpetuity, more than 12 per cent of its land as protected wildlife areas and most of these protected areas are surrounded by communal lands (Child *et al.* 1997). Historically, the communal lands were inhabited through forced settlement during the colonial period. Many of the communal lands have too little or unreliable rainfall for agriculture, but provide excellent wildlife habitat. It is estimated that 42 per cent of the Zimbabwean population live on rural communal lands (ibid.).

Before the Campfire, the relationships between the wildlife that inhabited the protected area and the rural poor living in the communal lands were antagonistic. Given the precarious conditions of the rural poor, damage to crops or livestock caused by wildlife were major threats to people's very livelihoods. In particular, elephant damage was a significant factor in crop loss in many parts of the district. Evidently, before Campfire some 200 to 300 crop-raiding elephants were shot annually by the local people (Child *et al.* 1997). Furthermore, the local people often found themselves acting as allies to poachers. Given this situation, one of the major goals of Campfire has been to change the psychology of the rural people, who regarded wildlife as menaces rather than assets to them. How was this accomplished?

Conceptually, the primary aim of the Campfire program has been to devolve control and benefits of wildlife and other natural resources to the lowest accountable units at sub-district level. It attempts to do this through well-designed and carefully coordinated *co-management systems* among interested parties, in particular, the rural community representatives (Campfire Association), the different branches of government bodies dealing with wildlife management (Department of National Parks and Wildlife Management, Ministry of Local Government, Rural and Urban Development), and some private and non-private organizations (Action, African Resources Trust, Centre for Applied Social Sciences, University of Zimbabwe, and World Wide Fund for Nature – Zimbabwe). In this respect, Campfire has become a forum for a wide range of issues, including representation, economic participation and the governance of communal areas. Campfire is a concern with the nature of rural communities and collective decision-making as well as with the technical challenges of sustainable use of wildlife.

At the operational level, Campfire begins when a rural community, through its elected representative body, the Rural District Council, asks the government's wildlife department to grant them the legal authority to manage their wildlife resources, and demonstrate their capacity to do so. The Wildlife Department upon granting the 'appropriate authority' informs the Rural District Council with hunting quotas and revenue sharing procedures that are specifically applicable to their own district at that point in time. In this regard, the aims of the Wildlife Department are twofold: (i) to ensure transparency in revenue sharing, and (ii) to foster the application of sound conservation practice in wildlife management. Under the current legal set-up in Zimbabwe, all funds generated by Campfire projects go first to Rural District Councils, and this body must disburse at least 50 per cent of wildlife revenues to the producers (areas or regions from where the wildlife resources have been harvested or extracted). Over 90 per cent of all Campfire revenues are currently generated by safari hunting in which foreigners visit Zimbabwe to shoot game animals (Africa Resources Trust 1996).

Thus, by granting people control over their resources, Campfire makes wildlife valuable to local communities. It is in the self-interest of the rural community to carefully manage protected lands and their wildlife. In this respect, Campfire is an attempt to use economic incentive to encourage the most appropriate wildlife management system in communal areas, particularly those adjacent to National Parks, where people and animals compete for scarce resources.

Overall, the Campfire has been a very successful experiment in sustainable resource management. According to a report by the World Wide Fund for Nature (WWF) the Campfire has increased household income in communal areas by 15–20 per cent. Furthermore, over 50 per cent of the revenues from Campfire have been used for much-needed community development projects, such as drilling wells to provide clean water for residents, building schools and health clinics, fencing arable and residential land, road development, and installing grinding mills (Africa Resources Trust 1996).

References

Child, B., Ward, S. and Tavengwa, T. (1997) 'Zimbabwe's CAMPFIRE Programme: Natural Resource Management by the People', *IUCA-ROSA Environmental Issues Series No. 2*, IUCN-ROSA, Harare, Zimbabwe.
Africa Resources Trust and the CAMPFIRE Association (1996) 'Zimbabwe's Campfire: Empowering Rural Communities for Conservation and Development', pp. 1–7.

supplies, sanitation and energy services to reduce the health effects associated with indoor cooking smoke and poor hygiene.

6   Develop technologies that are targeted to directly benefit the poor. This may involve a deliberate 'reallocation of research funds away from the most favored environments and toward the resources upon which the poor depend most – fragile and rainfed lands, livestock development, agro-forestry systems, and subsistence crops' (ibid.: 17). The aim is capacity building sufficient to secure a better future for the poor and a sustainable use of the environment.

In the final analysis, the problems of population, poverty and the environment that are facing most developing countries are extremely serious, requiring immediate action. Furthermore, even if action is taken immediately, the fruits of these policy measures will not be seen for quite a while, which implies that the solutions necessitate long-term vision and much short-term sacrifice. This is the dilemma that most developing countries face at present. It would be unrealistic to expect these countries to confront their problems effectively without the presence of stable domestic government and land tenure systems that maintain prudent use of natural resources.

Table 14.5 Share of population, resource consumption and waste production, in percentages

Country	Population	Fossil fuel consumption	Metal	Paper	Hazardous waste
US	5	25	20	33	72
Other developed countries	17	35	60	42	18
Developing countries	78	40	20	25	10

Source: *World Population and the Environment: A Data Sheet for the Population Reference Bureau,* Copyright 1997. Reprinted by permission of the Population Reference Bureau.

What is becoming increasingly obvious is that if developing countries are to succeed in their continuing struggle for economic and environmental security, they need significant financial and technical assistance from developed countries. This assistance, however, needs to be specifically targeted at slowing the inefficiently rapid pace at which natural resources are being exploited. Whether or not international assistance contributes to self-sufficiency and resource conservation will depend, in large part, on the discipline with which such aid is used by the recipient. When not used appropriately, international aid has time and again proven to be counterproductive (Korten 1991).

There are two ways in which developed countries could help ameliorate ecological crises in developing countries:

1 They could eliminate natural resource price distortions in international markets. This would require the realignment of trade and international relations between the poor and the rich countries.
2 They could reduce their resource consumption in such a way that imminent danger of resource depletion and threats to the health of the global environment are averted. This is important because *currently the developing countries supply a disproportionate share of the minerals and ecological resources needed to satisfy the lavish lifestyle of the affluent industrial nations.*

Finally: the main lessons of this chapter are that the population, poverty and environmental problems of developing countries have no simple solutions, and that a comprehensive approach to resolving these problems demands careful assessment of all the political, social, economic, technical, ecological, and ethical aspects of these problems. *While the poor nations of the world should be held accountable for solving their own economic and environmental problems,* reality dictates that meaningful resolution of these problems requires international cooperation in efforts to make global resource consumption and international trade environmentally sustainable.

Furthermore, it is important to note that the rich nations have a moral obligation to find solutions to the poverty and environmental crisis in the developing countries since they are *directly* responsible for many of the regional and global environmental problems resulting from their overconsumption of resources on a per capita basis. A significant percentage of total global petroleum, paper, metals, wood, and fishery products are consumed by the population of the developed (rich) countries (see Table 14.5 above). These products originate from territories that are under the jurisdiction of the developing countries and are extracted at significant environmental costs that are not adequately reflected in their market prices. Moreover, with the increasing globalization of natural resources markets, the developed countries' contribution to environmental stresses and resource depletion in the developing regions of the world is likely to grow in the future.

14.6 Chapter summary

- This chapter dealt with the interactions between population, development and the environment with specific reference to developing countries.
- A comprehensive analysis of global demographic trends indicates that the world population problem, as it relates to poverty and environmental degradation, is predominantly a concern of the developing countries.
- Some of the disturbing facts about these countries with regard to population, poverty and the environment can be depicted in the following ways:

1   In many developing countries population has been growing at or above 2 per cent annually. For some sub-Saharan countries, population is expected to double in about 20 years, a rate of growth of 3.5 per cent. This is in contrast to the rate of population growth in the developed countries, which is currently averaging about 0.6 per cent annually. Some of the developed countries are actually experiencing a decline in population.

2   It was estimated that a total of 1.3 billion people (about one-fifth of the world population) live in absolute poverty – existing on less than one dollar per day (*Population Bulletin*, 1998). Most of these people live in Sub-Saharan Africa and South Asia.

3   Most developing countries are plagued by increasing levels of air and water pollution and by an accelerated rate of resource depletion, which is manifested in deforestation, soil erosion, overfishing, and damage to marine and coastal ecosystems such as coastal wetlands and coral reefs (Trainer 1990). For example, it was estimated that currently, 14×10^{16} ha of tropical forests are lost annually worldwide from landscapes predominantly, if not entirely, occupied by developing countries.

- In the past, just to maintain their existing standard of living, the majority of these countries have been forced to pursue aggressive economic development policies, often with reckless neglect of environmental considerations. The result of this has been deepening poverty and mounting environmental degradation.
- The failure of past development aid programs, as led primarily by the World Bank and other closely affiliated international organizations (such as the IMF), are attributable to several interrelated factors. Among them are:

1   Indiscriminate and therefore inappropriate use of capital intensive technologies mostly financed by the World Bank. These investment projects were implemented without *adequate* consideration of their impact on income distribution (equity) and on the environment.

2   Forced exposure to unbalanced and unfair international trade, primarily for the purpose of financing mounting international debts. These trade arrangements typically had significant negative impacts on the poor and the environment.

Debts are financed through liquidation of natural resources at bargain prices and through diversion of resources that would have otherwise been used to support development programs for the poor and the protection of the environment.

3   Institutional failures. Not enough attention was given to the political, legal (especially the legal rights to do with resource ownership), social, and cultural circumstances at the time these countries were granted international loans to finance development projects. For example, offering loans to governments lacking clear mandates from their own constituents and with a past history of lack of accountability were major contributing factors to the failure of large internationally financed projects.

4   Market failures and market distortions. As discussed at some length in Chapter 7 and elsewhere, the free market often fails to value 'ecosystem services' adequately. For example, forests provide watershed protection, bio-diversity conservation, and carbon sequestration and the consequent reduction in greenhouse gas (GHG) emissions. As valuable as these services are to society, forests are nonetheless exploited solely on the basis of their wood products and nonforest uses of forestland such as agriculture. The consequence of this has been the degradation and loss of forest land at alarming rates.

A related issue is the excessive exploitation of extractive natural resources (such as forests, minerals, etc.) due to market distortions resulting from subsidies (for a specific example of this see Case Study 14.1).

- In recent years, there has been a new realization that population, poverty and environmental degradation in developing countries are highly interrelated but not *linearly*. Thus, the economic problems of the developing world cannot be resolved by looking at population, poverty and environmental concerns separately. In order to evaluate the options available to raise the standard of living of the average person in developing countries, but without inflicting major damage on the environment, it is necessary to have a comprehensive understanding of the inter-relationships among them, however complex they are perceived to be.
- Some of the key features of the new development strategies aimed mainly at achieving economic progress that is considered to be environmentally sustainable are:

  1   Investment that is pro-poor and pro-environment. This should be made knowing that it entails sacrifices. As discussed in some detail, this strategy has a number of implications for the way the poor and their assets are viewed, and entails a new understanding of the link between poverty and the environment.

  2   Recognition and an unconditional endorsement of the special role women play in population control, poverty alleviation and the management of the environment. How this could be achieved was detailed.

  3   Change in governance, with the following principles in mind: the adoption of decision-making structures that demand transparency and accountability, and that encourage the full participation of all stakeholders relevant to the decision under consideration. In addition, it is acknowledged that decisions that affect the poor and the environment will be implemented most effectively when they are made at the level of community that is most impacted. This suggests a preference for decentralized community-based decision-making. Of course,

decision-making processes of this kind cannot occur without political will at the highest level.

4　The issue of equity. In countries where income distributions are highly skewed, which is the case for the majority of the developing countries, serious consideration should be given to finding mechanisms to redistribute income (resources). Highly uneven income distributions are not only unwarranted on ethical or moral grounds, but are also a drag on the rates of economic growth in the long run.

• Specific policy targets for decoupling the population, poverty and environmental problems of developing countries include:

1　Improving the economic and social status of women.

2　Working through institutional reforms that encourage decentralization and transparency of decision-making processes, allow full participation of all stakeholders, and demand accountability for decision outcomes.

3　Correcting the most obvious forms of market and government failures. For example, ending subsidies of any sort that have the effect of either favoring the rich or causing unwarranted exploitation of natural resources.

4　Encouraging the adoption of technological devices that increase productivity and minimize the damage to the environment. Furthermore, the adoption of new technologies should always be subjected to comprehensive and carefully designed cost–benefit analyses that search for economically sound, environmentally benign and resource-saving technologies. If ecological sustainability is an important consideration, as it should be, appropriate choice of technology is an important factor that needs to be carefully considered (Goodwin 1991; Norgaard and Howarth 1992).

5　Reducing the national debt could lead most developing countries to focus more on the long-term benefits of their natural resources endowments rather than putting them up for sale at a discount for the purpose of financing debt. This can be achieved by either granting outright debt relief or by debt-refinancing mechanisms that are gradual and take greater cognizance of the economic circumstances of the debtor countries.

6　Realigning international trade to eliminate, as far as possible, natural resource price distortions in international markets. This, of course, requires the full cooperation of the rich nations, as they are the parties who would be negatively affected by such a rearrangement.

7　Providing international aid (grants) specifically aimed at conserving resources because of their far-reaching global implications. A prime example of this would be the decision of Madagascar, one of the world's poorest countries, to designate the Masoala Peninsula (an area of 33,000 ha) as a national park. This came at great cost (in terms of opportunities foregone) to Madagascar and according to the study by Kremen *et al.*, that this country 'is paying 57 to 96 per cent of the total cost' (2000: 1831). On the other hand, the *net* benefit to the global community from Masoala National Park in carbon conservation (carbon sequestration and the consequent reduction in greenhouse gas emissions) alone was estimated to range from $67.5 to $645.5 million (ibid.). This project has the added benefit of conserving biodiversity, which was not considered in the study.

Review and discussion questions

1   Briefly define the following concepts: relative versus absolute poverty, urbanization, capital formation, vicious cycle of poverty, gender equity, governance, institutional failure, endogenous knowledge, appropriate technology, structural adjustment, desertification, communal land, the World Bank, IMF, UNDP, NGO.

2   State whether the following are *true, false* or *uncertain* and explain why:

(a) It is not only the number of people, but also their lifestyles, political systems, and social structures that define the relationship between humans and the environment.

(b) Poverty is a function of income and other factors, such as health, education, access to goods and services, gender, and ethnicity.

(c) Laissez-faire policies toward reproduction will inevitably burden society with the problem of ruinous overpopulation.

(d) Poverty and the environment are inextricably linked in a 'downward spiral'.

(e) Markets are not always environmentally friendly, and not always supportive of poor people.

(f) Poverty reduction and concern for the environment are incompatible.

(g) The status of women is a particularly important variable in the population–environment relationship.

3   Poor people degrade the environment more than the non-poor because the poor implicitly use a high discount rate in valuing current over future production. Do you agree or disagree with this reasoning? Explain your position.

4   Free trade could lead to over-exploitation of natural resources upon which a vast number of people in poor countries depend for their livelihood. Discuss.

5   The root cause of underdevelopment and environmental degradation is the 'over-development' of a handful of rich nations. Discuss.

6   In a recent report by the UNDP on *Poverty and Environment Initiatives* (1999: 2–3), the following remark was made regarding the UN conferences on development and the environment: 'Though serious and successful efforts to address both poverty and environment are underway in many places, they remain exceptions. While there is broad agreement on the "why" and the "what", there has been far less agreement about the "how". Too often, politicians and technical experts have found themselves at odds. Policy makers complain that the experts have not given them substantive practical solutions. Experts accuse policy-makers of lacking political will. This fruitless debate has contributed to the disappointing gulf between the goals of the global conventions and their actual achievements.' What do you think can be done to get out of this unfortunate quandary?

7   In the same UNDP report, it was stated that 'The political process of reallocating funding toward projects that benefit the poor and the environment can be made easier if "pro-environment/pro-poor" guidelines are used for public investments. This include properly valuing long-term environmental benefits (greening the internal rate of return) and weighting investment criteria to recognize the fact that a particular monetary return on investment for the poor is more valuable for increasing net well-being than the same return on investment is for the non-poor.' Is this an economic or an ethical argument for more public investment that protects the environment and benefits the poor? Explain.

References

Allen, J. C. and Barnes, D. F. (1995) 'The Causes of Deforestation in Developed Countries', *Annals of the Association of American Geographers* 75, 2: 163–84.

Australian UNESCO Committee for Man and the Biosphere (1976) *Ecological Effects of Increasing Human Activities on Tropical and Subtropical Forest Ecosystems*, Canberra: Australia Government Publishing Service.

Bandyopadhyay, J. and Shiva, V. (1989) 'Development, Poverty and the Growth of the Green Movement in India', *The Ecologist* 19: 111–17.

Bhagwati, J. (1993) 'The Case of Free Trade', *Scientific American* 269.

Brown, L. (1989) 'Feeding Six Billion', *Worldwatch* 2: 32–44.

Cooter, R. D. (1990) 'Inventing Property: Economic Theories of the Origin of Market Property Applied to Papua New Guinea', Memo, Berkeley: University of California.

Daly, H. E. (1993) 'The Perils of Free Trade', *Scientific American* 269: 50–7.

Ehrlich, P. R. and Holdren, J. P. (1971) 'Impact of Population Growth', *Science* 171: 1212–17.

Ekins, P. (1993) 'Trading Off the Future? Making World Trade Environmentally Sustainable', *The New Economics Foundation* (London): 1–9.

Goodland, R. and Daly, H. E. (1992) 'Ten Reasons why Northern Income Growth is Not the Solution to Southern Poverty', in R. Goodland, H. E. Daly and S. El Serafy (eds) *Population, Technology and Lifestyle: The Transition to Sustainability*, Washington, DC: Island Press.

Goodwin, N. R. (1991) 'Introduction – Global Commons: Site of Peril, Source of Hope', *World Development* 19: 1–15.

Hardin, G. (1968) 'The Tragedy of the Commons', *Science* 162: 1243–8.

Homer-Dixon, T. F., Boutwell, J. H. and Rathjens, G. W. (1993) 'Environmental Change and Violent Conflict', *Scientific American* 268: 38–45.

Kremen, C., Niles, J. O., Dalton, M. G., Daly, G. C., Ehrlich, P. R., Fay, J. P., Grewal, D., Guillery, R. P. (2000) 'Economic Incentives for Rain Forest Conservation Across Scales', *Science* 288: 1828.

Korten, D. C. (1991) 'International Assistance: A Problem Posing as a Solution', *Development* 3/4: 87–94.

Lewis, M. W. (1992) *Green Delusions: An Environmentalist Critique of Radical Environmentalism*, Durham, NC: Duke University Press.

McNamara, R. S. (1984) 'Time Bomb or Myth: The Population Problem', *Foreign Affairs* 62: 1107–31.

Norgaard, R. B. and Howarth, R. B. (1992) 'Economics, Ethics, and the Environment', in J. M. Hollander (ed.) *The Energy–Environment Connection*, Washington, DC: Island Press.

OECD (2002) 'Working Together Towards Sustainable Development: The OECD Experience', 1–85, OECD.

Panayotou, T. and Ashton, P. S. (1992) *Not by Timber Alone: Economics and Ecology for Sustainable Tropical Forests*, Washington, DC: Island Press.

Population Reference Bureau (1996) *Population Today* 24, 6–7.

——(1997) *Population Today* 25, 4: 3.

——(2001) *Population Bulletin* 53, 1 (1998) Washington, DC.

Repetto, R. and Holmes, T. (1983) 'The Role of Population in Resource Depletion in Developing Countries', *Population and Development Review* 9, 4: 609–32.

Rudel, T. K. (1989) 'Population, Development, and Tropical Deforestation', *Rural Sociology* 54, 3: 327–38.

Todaro, M. P. (1989) *Economic Development in the Third World*, 4th edn, New York: Longman.

Trainer, F. E. (1990) 'Environmental Significance of Development Theory', *Ecological Economics* 2: 277–86.

Turner, K., Pearce, D. and Bateman, I. (1993) *Environmental Economics: An Elementary Intro-duction*, Baltimore: Johns Hopkins University Press.

UNDP (1999) 'Attacking Poverty While Improving the Environment: Towards Win–Win Policy Options', UNDP Report on Poverty and Environmental Initiatives, 1–78.

World Commission on Environment and Development (WCED) (1987) *Our Common Future*, New York: Oxford University Press.

World Resources Institute (1987) *World Resources 1988–89*, New York: Basic Books.

—— (1992) *World Resources 1992–93*, New York: Oxford University Press.

—— (1995) *World Resources 1995–96*, New York: Oxford University Press.

Worldwatch Paper 161 (2002), Worldwatch Institute New York: W. W. Norton.

Appendix A
Resource scarcity, economic efficiency and markets
How the Invisible Hand works

Markets respond to price signals. If a resource, whether it be a barrel of oil, a patch of Louisiana swamp or old-growth forest, or a breath of fresh air, is priced to reflect its true and complete cost to society, goes the argument, markets will ensure that those resources are used in an optimally efficient way.

(Alper 1993: 1884)

A.1 Introduction

This Appendix systematically develops the analytical (theoretical) foundation of the neoclassical approach to resource scarcity, allocation and measurement. The broader aims of the Appendix are first, to specify the conditions under which Adam Smith's notion that individuals working in their own self-interest will promote the welfare of the whole of society holds good; and second, to show formally the conditions under which market price can be used as a measure of resource scarcity.

To address these two issues fully and systematically, we shall start by outlining the basic conditions for a model of a perfectly competitive market. Before doing this, however, it may be instructive to explain in few words why the contents of this Appendix are relevant to the study of environmental economics. One of the discoveries of environmental economics is the 'failure' of the private market (transactions among private individuals based on free expression of self-interest) to allocate environmental resources optimally. Despite this, neoclassical economists continue to insist on the use of market-friendly policy instruments for the allocation of environmental resources. If one wants to understand the root causes of the unshakable faith of neoclassical economists in the market, the material discussed in this Appendix will be helpful.

A.2 Basic assumptions

In an idealized capitalist market economy, the well-being of consumers, the final users of goods and services, is a paramount consideration. What this means is that the effectiveness of an economy is judged by how well it satisfies the material needs of its citizens – the consumers. Therefore, given that resources are scarce, an effective economy is one that is capable of producing the *maximum* output from a given set of basic resources (labor, capital and natural resources). Of course, the implication of this is that scarce resources must be utilized (produced and consumed) efficiently.

The question then is, what conditions must a market system satisfy in order to be considered an efficient institution for allocating scarce resources? In other words, what are the conditions consistent with the ideal or perfect market structure? According to prevailing economic thought, in order to be regarded as an efficient institutional mechanism for allocating resources, a market has to satisfy the following broad conditions:

1   *Freedom of choice based on self-interest and rational behavior.* Buyers and sellers are well informed and exhibit rational behavior. 'Rational' here refers to the notion that the behavior of a buyer or a seller is consistent with her or his pursuit of self-interest. It is further stipulated that these actors in the market are provided with an environment conducive to free expression of their choices. Note that choice is an inevitable by-product of resource scarcity.
2   *Perfect information.* Economic agents are assumed to be provided with full information regarding all market transactions. They are also assumed to have perfect foresight about future economic events.
3   *Competition.* For each item subjected to market transactions, the number of buyers and sellers is large. Thus, no one buyer or seller can single-handedly influence the terms of trade. In modern economic jargon, this means that both buyers and sellers are price-takers. This is assumed to be the case in both the product and the factor markets.
4   *Mobility of resources.* In a dynamic economy, change is the norm. Significant shifts in economic conditions could result from a combination of several factors, such as changes in consumer preference, income, resource availability, and technology. To accommodate such changes in a timely fashion, resources must be readily transferable from one sector of the economy to another. This is possible only when barriers to entry and exit in an industry are absent (or minimal).
5   *Ownership rights.* All goods and services, as well as factors of production, have clearly defined ownership rights. This condition prevails when the following specific conditions are met: (a) the nature and characteristics of the resources under consideration are completely specified; (b) owners have title with exclusive rights to the resources they legally own; (c) ownership rights are transferable, i.e. ownership rights are subject to market transactions at terms agreeable to the resource owner(s); and (d) ownership rights are enforceable (Randall 1987), i.e. property rights are protected by binding social rules and regulations.

When the above *five* conditions are met, an economy is said to be operating in a world of perfectly competitive markets. In such a setting, Adam Smith (the father of modern economics) declared over two centuries ago, that the market system, through its 'Invisible Hand', will guide each individual to do not only what is in her or his own self-interest, but also what is for the 'good' of society at large. A profound statement indeed, which clearly depicts the most appealing features of the market economy in its ideal form. In the next section, this claim will be demonstrated systematically using demand and supply analysis.

A.3 Evaluating the performance of a perfectly competitive market economy

A market may be identified as a *social institution* – where buyers and sellers of a certain product were able to consummate business transactions of their own accord and on

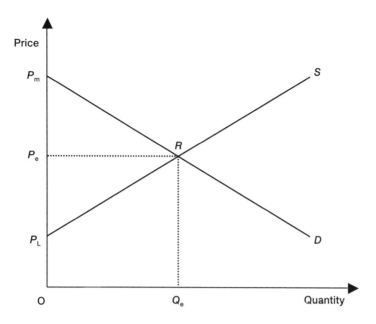

Figure A.1 Market equilibrium price.

terms that were considered mutually beneficial to all participating parties. The performance of an institution cannot be based solely on its daily operations. Rather, a valid judgement of the performance of an institution should be based on the enduring quality of long-term outcomes. In this regard, the claim often made by mainstream economists is this: Provided all the assumptions of the model of perfect competition discussed in Section A.2 are satisfied (freedom of choice and enterprise; consumers and producers are fully informed price-takers; mobility of resources; clearly defined ownership rights), *in the long run the market system will tend to allocate resources efficiently. Furthermore, market prices will measure the true scarcity value of resources.*

To demonstrate these claims in a systematic manner, let us suppose that Figure A.1 represents the long-run equilibrium condition of a product produced and sold in a perfectly competitive industry. In this case, P_e and Q_e represent the market equilibrium price and quantity, respectively. It is important to note that the long-run equilibrium price is that which prevails after the existence of above-normal profits has attracted new firms to enter the industry (or below-normal profits have forced some firms to exit). It is, in other words, where all firms in that particular industry are making just *normal profits*. Normal profit means that, in the long run, firms in a given industry cannot make a return on their investment above what they would have been able to earn if they had invested in some other industry with similar operating conditions and a similar risk environment. To see the 'social' significance of this long-run equilibrium situation, let us analyze separately the economic conditions of consumers and of producers.

A.3.1 Consumers' surplus

Figure A.2 shows the same demand function as the one in Figure A.1. Thus, P_e and Q_e represent the long-run market equilibrium price and output. P_m is the price where the quantity demanded is zero. Thus, it can be interpreted as the maximum price consumers are willing to pay for this product, rather than go without it. By focusing on demand alone, we are now able to demonstrate the implications of long-run market equilibrium for consumers' welfare.

The demand curve depicts the *maximum* price consumers are willing to pay for a given quantity of the product provided in the market. For example, P_m is *the maximum price consumers are willing to pay rather than go without the product*. On the other hand, at the market-equilibrium quantity, Q_e, the consumers are willing to pay price P_e. For quantities between zero and Q_e, consumers will be willing to pay prices higher than P_e and lower than P_m. Note that the prices consumers are willing to pay successively decline as the quantity of a product available in the market increases. This diminishing willingness to pay is, of course, consistent with the law of demand.

Looking at demand as a measure of willingness to pay also lends itself to the interpretation of *price as the marginal private benefit to consumers*. That is, a consumer whose sole interest is to maximize utility will not purchase an additional unit of a product unless the benefit derived from the incremental unit is at least equal to the market price. The fact that the price or marginal private benefit declines as the quantity of the product increases is consistent with the law of diminishing marginal utility.

If price can be looked at as a measure of marginal private benefit, then conceptually we can compute the total private benefit by summing all the marginal benefits for a given range of output demanded. For example, in Figure A.2, for the market-equilibrium output, Q_e, the *total* consumers' benefit would be measured by the sum of all prices starting from P_m all the way up to and including P_e. The area of trapezoid OP_mRQ_e represents this. *In an ideal (competitive) market, in the long run this area would tend to be maximized.* The reasons for this are not difficult to see. Given that both consumers and producers are *price-takers* and resources are freely mobile, the long-run equilibrium condition ensures that firms are operating efficiently (minimizing their costs of production). In addition, due to the free mobility of resources, firms are not able to make an above-normal profit. If this situation prevails, then the market-equilibrium price, P_e, represents the lowest price firms can charge in the long run. If P_e represents the lowest price, it follows that Q_e is the largest output that could be supplied to the market. Thus, the trapezoid area OP_mRQ_e represents the largest total consumers' benefit.

This *total* consumers' benefit is composed of two parts. The first part is rectangle area OP_eRQ_e which represents what the consumers actually paid to acquire the market clearing output, Q_e. The second segment is the area of the triangle P_eP_mR, which represents the sum of all the prices above the equilibrium price P_e that consumers would have been willing to pay. Since consumers did not actually pay higher prices for some units, but paid P_e for every unit up to Q_e, the sum of these prices, which is shown by the area of triangle P_eP_mR, represents the consumers' surplus. In other words, the

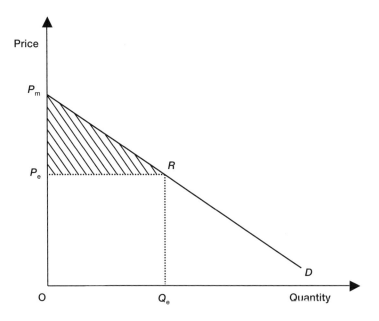

Figure A.2 Consumers' surplus.

consumers' surplus is the difference between the total willingness to pay (area OP_mRQ_e) and what consumers actually paid, which is represented by the area OP_eRQ_e. What is significant here is that in the long run, consumers' surplus is *maximized*. This is easy to demonstrate given that the long-run equilibrium price, P_e, represents the lowest feasible price for producers. This is an important conclusion since it confirms economists' assertions that in the long run, a market economy left alone would do what is best for consumers: maximize their surpluses.

As a simple numerical illustration of consumers' surplus and total willingness to pay, let us suppose that the market equilibrium price and quantity in Figure A.2 are $5 and 2,000 units, respectively. In addition, let P_m, the maximum price consumers are willing to pay for this product, be $9. Given this information, first, consumers' surplus (the shaded area in Figure A.2) can be obtained using the formula 'one half times (the product of the base and the height of the relevant triangle)'; in this case it would be ½ (2,000 × 4), which is equal to $4,000. Second, in acquiring the 2,000 units, consumers paid a total sum of $10,000 (the product of the market equilibrium price and quantity). In Figure A.2 this $10,000 represents the area of the rectangle OP_eRQ_e. On the basis of these two findings, it can be inferred that the *total* willingness to pay is $14,000 (area OP_mRQ_e in Figure A.2), since consumers have gained $4,000 in surplus while paying $10,000 for the purchase of the equilibrium quantity, 2,000 units.

A.3.2 Producers' surplus

Figure A.3 is a replica of the supply curve in Figure A.1. The supply curve could be interpreted as showing the *minimum* prices producers are willing to accept to provide various levels of output in a market. For example, P_L represents the lowest price producers require before participating in any production activity. Similarly, P_e is the minimum price the producers would accept to provide the last unit of the equilibrium output, Q_e. Alternatively, the supply curve is intimately related to production costs. More specifically, the supply curve represents nothing more than the mapping of the incremental (marginal) costs of production. Thus, if we employ these two interpretations of the supply curve, P_e can be understood in two ways. In one sense it shows the minimum price producers are willing to accept in order to bring forth the last unit of Q_e in the market. Alternatively, it represents the *marginal cost* of producing a given level of output. Note that these dual interpretations equally apply to all prices along the supply curve.

If the supply curve in fact represents the mapping of the incremental costs of production, in Figure A.3 the trapezoid area $OP_L RQ_e$ represents the total cost of production at the output level where the long-run equilibrium is attained, Q_e. This area is obtained by summing the marginal costs (or the minimum acceptable prices to producers) along the relevant output range. In a competitive market setting (where producers are price-takers and resources are freely mobile), this long-run production cost is minimized and accurately reflects the opportunity costs of the scarce resources being used in the production process.

However, at the equilibrium level of output and price, the total producers' receipts (revenue) is represented by area $OP_e RQ_e$. The difference between total revenue $(OP_e RQ_e)$ and total production costs $(OP_L RQ_e)$, the area of triangle $P_L P_e R$ in Figure A.3, is the *producers' surplus*. What can this surplus be attributed to? There is no clear-cut answer to this question in the existing economic literature. For our purpose we shall consider producers' surplus as the cumulative payments to those producers exhibiting entrepreneurial capacity that is above that of the marginal producer (the last producer to enter the market).

To provide numerical illustrations of the concepts of producers' surplus and production cost, again let the market equilibrium price and quantity be $5 and 2,000 units, respectively. Furthermore, let P_L, the minimum price acceptable to the producers, be $2. Given this information, the producers' surplus (the area of the shaded triangle in Figure 2.8) would be $3,000 ($\frac{1}{2} \times 3 \times 2,000$). Furthermore, the total receipts (revenue) of the producers from the sale of 2,000 units would be $10,000 ($5 \times 2,000$) or area $OP_e RQ_e$. Thus, the total production cost would be $7,000 ($10,000 − $3,000), or the area of the trapezoid $OP_L RQ_e$. *This total value represents either the sum of all the minimum prices that producers are willing to accept, or the sum of all the marginal costs in producing the output ranging from zero to 2,000 units.*

A.3.3 Net social surplus and how it is maximized

Finally, let us go back to Figure A.1 to tie together what we have been discussing so far concerning the long-run equilibrium condition under a competitive market setting. In Figure A.1 we noted that area $OP_m RQ_e$ represents the consumers' total willingness to pay (private benefit) associated with the consumption of the equilibrium level of

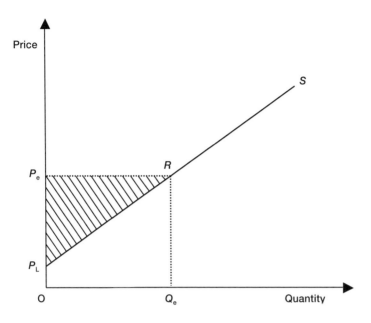

Figure A.3 Producers' surplus.

output, Q_e. As discussed earlier, in a perfectly competitive market setting this benefit is maximized. On the other hand, area $OP_L RQ_e$ shows the cost of producing the equilibrium level of output, Q_e. As previously discussed, this cost is *minimized*. Thus, the area $P_L P_m R$ represents the *net* surplus, which is composed of the consumers' and the producers' surpluses. From the above arguments, it should be noted that this social (consumers' and producers') surplus is *maximized* – one of the hallmarks of an ideal market system.

A.3.4 Pareto optimality and the Invisible Hand theorem

One frequently used alternative way to arrive at the above conclusion is the notion of Pareto optimality. *An equilibrium condition is said to be Pareto optimal if a move in any direction cannot be made without making at least one member of a society worse off.* To see this, suppose P_e and Q_e in Figure A.4 represent the long-run equilibrium price and output, respectively. Suppose the output is increased to Q_1. What would be the effect of this increase in output from Q_e to Q_1? The answer is rather straightforward. To begin with, the increase in output from Q_e to Q_1 will entail an additional production cost, as shown by the area $Q_e RTQ_1$ (the area under the supply curve over the relevant output range). Similarly, the area $Q_e RUQ_1$ (the area under the demand curve along the relevant output range) measures the benefit associated from this incremental output. Thus, in this situation the cost outweighs the benefit by the triangle of area *RTU*.

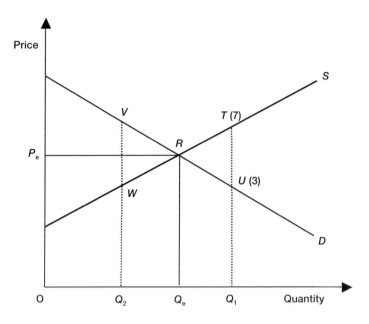

Figure A.4 Pareto optimality and its implications.

The curious might try to perform this numerical exercise. Consistent with earlier examples, assume the equilibrium price and quantity in Figure A.4 to be $5 and 2,000 units. Assume that output is now increased from Q_e to Q_1 or from 2,000 to 2,100. Furthermore, the supply price at Q_1 (point T along the supply curve) is given to be $7 and the demand price at this same level of output (point U along the demand curve) is $3. This information gives the following results. (a) The increase in production cost as a result of the increase in output by 100 (from 2,000 to 2,100), which is represented in Figure A.4 by area Q_eRTQ_1, is $600. (b) The increase in consumers' benefit resulting from a 100-unit increase in output (area Q_eRUQ_1 in Figure A.4) is $400. Findings (a) and (b) clearly indicate that to increase output from Q_e to Q_1 would result in a net loss of $200 ($400 − $600 = −$200).

On the other hand, if output were restricted, falling from Q_e to Q_2, the area Q_eRVQ_2 would measure the forgone benefit associated with this action. However, as a result of this reduction in output there would be a cost saving measured by area Q_eRWQ_2. In this case the forgone benefit would outweigh the cost saving by the area of the triangle RVW. Thus, from the argument presented so far, a movement away from the equilibrium in either direction would lead to a net loss. This clearly confirms that the long-run equilibrium outcome in a setting of perfectly competitive markets is Pareto optimal. Note that *Pareto optimality implies economic efficiency* – a condition where the *net* benefit of producers and consumers taken together is maximized. After all, as we have seen above, any deviations from the equilibrium are associated with a reduction, not a gain, in net benefits. Indeed, this amounts to a backhanded proof of Adam Smith's Invisible Hand theorem.

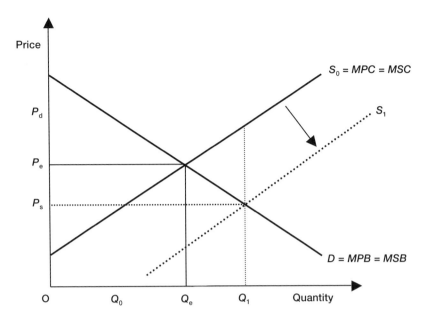

Figure A.5 Market price as a measure of resource scarcity and as an indicator of resource misallocation.

A.4 Price as a measure of resource scarcity

Whenever the prevailing (equilibrium) market price for a product is positive, it follows that the product under consideration is scarce. But scarce in what sense? To respond to this question adequately, let us refer to Figure A.5 above. In this figure, the market-equilibrium price is P_e given that S_0 is the relevant supply curve. From the consumers' viewpoint, this price measures their willingness to pay for the last unit of the equilibrium output, Q_e. In other words, it measures consumers' marginal private benefit (*MPB*) at the equilibrium level of output. On the other hand, from the producers' perspective, the prevailing market price, P_e, measures the minimum price they are willing to accept in offering the last unit of the equilibrium output in the market. In an ideal market, where the marginal producers are making just a normal profit, this would be equivalent to the marginal private cost (*MPC*) of producing the last unit of output.

Given the above argument, in an ideal market setting the long-run equilibrium price has an implication that goes far beyond a market-clearing condition. This price equates marginal private (consumers') benefit with that of marginal private (producers') costs. That is,

$$P_e = MPB = MPC$$

Furthermore, in cases where ownership rights are clearly defined, one of the conditions for a perfect market, there will be no difference between *private* and *social* benefits and costs. Thus, in ideal market conditions, the long-run equilibrium price of a product is a measure of both the marginal social benefit and the marginal social cost. That is,

$$P_e = MPB = MSB = MPC = MSC$$

It is in this context that mainstream economists make their long-standing claim that in a free competitive market, a market price tends to reflect the true scarcity value of a resource under consideration. True in exactly what sense? In the sense that, *in the long run, market price reflects the social cost of using resources (land, labor, capital, etc.) to produce output at the margin.*

Note that market price would fail to reflect social cost if the price were artificially set either below or above the market equilibrium price, P_e. If either one of these situations occurs, the result will lead to what economists commonly refer to as a misallocation of resources. To see the significance of this, let us suppose that a decision is made to lower the market price from P_e to P_s in Figure A.5. To make this possible, the supply curve needs to be shifted from S_0 to S_1; otherwise, P_s will not be a market-clearing price. Suppose this is accomplished through a market intervention mechanism, such as a government subsidy (either as a tax break or cash grant) to the firms producing the product under consideration. The question is then, how will this result in a misallocation of societal resources?

At the new and artificially established equilibrium price, P_s, the market clearing output will increase from Q_e (the socially optimal output) to Q_1. For it to do so, more resources (labor, capital and natural resources) are now allocated to the production of the output under consideration. However, for any output level beyond Q_e, the *MSC* (the supply prices along S_0) of using these resources exceeds the prevailing market price, P_s. Clearly, then, these resources are not being used where they benefit society the most – they are misallocated.

A.5 Important caveats

It is important to note that while the analysis presented in this Appendix allowed us to understand the basic elements necessary to comprehend the mainstream economic notion of resource scarcity and its measurement, it did so with several obvious limitations. The most significant of these are the following.

First, the economic analysis thus far has been strictly *static*; no time element has been considered. This is a major drawback given that environmental economics, by its very nature, deals with the intertemporal allocation of resources, i.e. how environmental resources are managed over time.

Second, the economic analyses were carried out assuming the existence of *perfectly competitive markets*. Given this institutional setting, we observed that private decision-making would lead to a socially optimal allocation of resources. Furthermore, there will be no discrepancy between the individual (private) and the social assessment of benefits and costs. But what happens if the conditions for perfectly competitive markets fail to materialize? This is, indeed, an important issue in environmental economics and a subject more fully addressed in Chapter 3.

Third, in the economic analysis so far, nothing has been said about resources that have values but these values may *not* be captured in the normal operation of the market system. An example would be the value of preserving an animal species such as the

Northwest spotted owl. A species of this kind has very little use value – benefits or satisfactions received by humans from a direct utilization of the services (or amenities) – and therefore is likely to be unaccounted for in the normal operation of market processes. This issue becomes even more serious when it is realized that market prices are formed on the basis of human preferences alone. This issue was dealt with in Chapter 8.

Fourth, in this Appendix efforts were made to show how, at a particular point in time, prices for final products are determined through free-market mechanisms. However, to what extent information on current market prices could be used to predict future scarcity events has not been adequately addressed. More specifically, the *uncertainty* associated with predicting a future scarcity condition on the basis of past price trends has not been addressed. The position taken so far is that current resource prices are a good predictor of future scarcity events. This would be the case in a world of perfectly competitive markets where economic agents were operating with perfect foresight and costless information. Under those circumstances, if there is reason to judge that the cost of obtaining a certain resource in the future will be much greater than it is now, speculators will hoard that resource to obtain the higher future price, thereby raising the present price. So, current price is our best measure of both current and future scarcity.

A.6 Summary

The objectives of this Appendix have been twofold. The first was to clearly specify the theoretical conditions under which individuals working in their own self-interest will promote the welfare of the whole of society – the so-called Invisible Hand theorem. The second was to show the extent to which *market price* can be used as measures of resource scarcity.

- To address these issues fully and systematically, three key assumptions were made:

  1 Markets are perfectly competitive.
  2 An economy is evaluated on the basis of its long-term performance.
  3 The criteria for evaluating market performance are based on the market's ability (a) to attain efficient allocation of resources so that, in the long run, the aggregate social surplus is maximized, and (b) to transmit accurate signals about resource scarcity.

- It was shown that, given the above assumptions, a market system uses *price* information to facilitate the production and exchange of goods and services. These prices are determined by the interaction of market demand and market supply.
- Furthermore, when one assumes the existence of clearly defined ownership rights, in the product market demand and supply reflect marginal social benefit (*MSB*) and marginal social cost (*MSC*), respectively. Thus, long-run equilibrium is attained when the following condition is satisfied: $P_e = MSB = MSC$, where P_e is the long-run equilibrium price. This condition has four important implications:

  1 The fact that $MSB = MSC$ suggests that, in the long run, competitive markets allocate resources in such a way that the *net* social benefit (the sum of consumers' and producers' surpluses) is maximized. This is because no reallocation can be made without adversely affecting the net social benefit. Thus, in the long run, competitive markets are Pareto-efficient.

2   Market price is a measure of the value 'society' attaches to a product. That is, $P_e = MSB$.

3   The market equilibrium price of a product, P_e, is a measure of the 'social' cost of using basic resources (labor, capital, land, etc.) to produce the desired product. That is, $P_e = MSC$.

4   Market price, P_e, is a 'true' measure of resource scarcity because there is no discrepancy between the social value of the product (what people are willing to pay) and the social opportunity cost of the resources used to produce this product. One important implication of this observation is that market intervention through subsidies or support prices would cause distortion of important social opportunity cost(s) and in so doing lead to a misallocation of resources.

References and further reading

Alper, J. (1993) 'Protecting the Environment with the Power of the Market', *Science* 260: 1884–5.

Nicholson, W. (1998) *Microeconomic Theory*, 7th edn, Fort Worth: Dryden Press.

Pindyck, R. and Rubinfeld, D. (1998) *Microeconomics*, 4th edn, New York: Macmillan.

Randall, A. (1987) *Resource Economics: An Economic Approach to Natural Resource and Environmental Policy*, 2nd edn, New York: John Wiley.

Appendix B

This Appendix contains a list and brief description of websites that the author considers useful to students who are taking a course in environmental economics. In particular, students may find these websites valuable sources of information for class projects and, in some cases, to enhance their understanding of specific topics covered in the main chapters of the text. No defendable logic can be offered for the order in which the sites are presented.

1   www.wri.org/ The homepage for World Resource Institute (WRI). WRI is a highly reputable environmental think tank. It provides a wealth of information, ideas and solutions to emerging global and environmental problems (such as, climate change, biodiversity, habitat destruction, over-fishing, and so on).

2   www.rff.org/ The homepage for Resources for the Future, Inc. (RFF). RFF is an organization known for its non-partisan high-quality environmental and natural resource economics research and policy analysis. It receives a very high mark for its publications on damage cost to the environment and health (externalities) and cost–benefit (as well as cost-effectiveness) analysis. Although non-partisan, the publications of this organization indicate strong methodological affiliation with mainstream economics.

3   www.prb.org/ The homepage for the Population Reference Bureau (PRB). The PRB prides itself on providing timely and objective information on United States and international population trends and their implications.

4   www.unfpa.org/index.htm The homepage for the United Nations Population Fund (UNFPA). The UNFPA is the largest internationally funded source of population assistance to developing countries. It is an excellent source of information on population and development, reproductive health (including family planning and sexual health), gender equality, and women's empowerment.

5   www.epa.gov/ The homepage for the United States Environmental Protection Agency (EPA). The EPA was established in 1970 with a mandate to monitor, set and enforce environmental standards that are consistent with ensuring the protection of the natural environment. This website is an excellent source of the latest information on environmental policies in the United States and of *links* to other websites, such as www.epa.gov/airmarkets (the EPA's website for acid rain regulation) or www.epa.gov/ozone (the EPA's website on the ozone layer and ozone depletion).

6   www.unep.org/ The homepage for the United Nations Environment Programme (UNEP). Contains invaluable information on international environmental

legal instruments and conventions, and research reports on the state of global environment.

7 www.energy.gov/ The homepage for the United States Department of Energy (DOE). A good source of energy data, such as efficiency and productivity of energy use, energy prices and alternative energy technologies. It also provides information on the environmental impacts of energy, energy conservation and the latest energy policy pronouncements of the United States government.

8 www.undp.org/ The homepage for the United Nations Development Program (UNDP), the UN's principle provider of development advice, advocacy and grant support. The website provides valuable information on international efforts to reduce poverty in developing countries through capacity-building. In this respect, democratic governance, poverty reduction, crisis prevention and recovery, energy and environment interactions, information technology and HIV/AIDS are emphasized.

9 www.worldwatch.org/ The homepage for the Worldwatch Institute, an independent nonprofit environmental resource organization. The primary mission of this organization's numerous periodical publications is to provide government agencies and the public at large with an in-depth quantitative and qualitative analysis of the major issues affecting prospects for a *sustainable society*. The annual *State of the World*, which is now published in 27 languages, is the most widely used of all the publications of this organization. Noted for its Neo-Malthusian perspectives.

10 www.oecd/org/env/ A website for the Organization for Economic Co-operation and Development (OECD). This organization presently consists of 30 member countries, and all the major economically advanced nations are members of this organization. Provides good information on the state of global economic development and the environment from the prospective of the 'rich' nations. This site is also a good source of international economic data, and information on globalization and its impact on trade and environment.

11 www.worldbank.org/ The homepage for the World Bank Group. This site provides detailed data on world development indicators, external debt, foreign exchange reserves, international development projects for the reduction of poverty, and trade and development, in general. Comparable information can be obtained by a visit to the homepage website of the International Monetary Fund (IMF), www.imf.org/.

12 http://www.ulb.ac.be/ceese/meta/sustvl.html This website is maintained by the Center for Economic and Social Studies on the Environment (CESSE) located at Université Libre de Bruxelles. Excellent source for the latest information on indictors of sustainable development. This page also provides a link to a number of other sustainable development websites.

Another website on sustainable development I recommend is www.colby.edu/personal/t/thtieten/sustain.html This website is a contribution of Professor Tom Tietenberg of Colby College, USA. 'The site offers three types of information: a bibliography of works emphasizing economics and sustainable development, a series of student-authored "executive summaries" of case studies involving attempts to pursue sustainable strategies, and links to other sustainable development sites.'

13 www.foe.org The homepage for Friends of the Earth, an 'environmental organization dedicated to preserving the health and diversity of the planet for future generations'. The website includes links to many publications on environmental issues.

14 www.rprogress.org The homepage for Redefining Progress, 'a nonprofit organization that develops policies and tools that reorient the economy to value people and nature first'. A good source for publications that seek to integrate environmental externalities into market prices.

15 www.aere.org Website for news and publications by the Association of Environmental and Resource Economics, an organization 'established as a means of exchanging ideas, stimulating research, and promoting graduate training in resource and environmental economics'.

16 www.ecologicaleconomics.org Website for news and publications by the International Society for Ecological Economics (ISSE). The Society's officially stated goal is to 'facilitate understanding between economists and ecologists and the integration of their thinking into a transdiscipline aimed at developing a sustainable world'.

17 www.zpg.org Homepage for Zero Population Growth, a nonprofit environmental organization 'working to slow population growth and achieve a sustainable balance between the Earth's people and its resources'.

18 www.ipcc.ch The website for the Intergovernmental Panel on Climate Change, a United Nations-sponsored agency whose task is 'to assess the scientific, technical, and socioeconomic information relevant for the understanding of the risk of human-induced climate change'. An excellent source for anyone studying the relationships between human actions and global climate change.

19 www.etei.org Homepage for the Emissions Trading Education Initiative, a project jointly sponsored by the Environmental Defense Fund and the Emissions Marketing Association.

20 www.unep.org/Documents/Default.asp?DocumentID=52 A website for Agenda 21, a document for sustainable development drafted during the 1992 Earth Conference in Rio de Janeiro. Agenda 21 'addresses the pressing problems of today and also aims at preparing the world for the challenges of the next century'.

21 www.ecology.com This website contains a wealth of information on recent environmental and natural resource issues from an ecological perspective. A very informative and helpful website to those who want to learn more about ecology and its real-world applications.

22 www.hadm.sph.sc.edu/Courses/Econ/Dis/Dis.html This website offers an interactive tutorial about discounting and present values. Very helpful for understanding the material discussed in Chapters 8 and 9.

23 www.epa.gov/ogwdw/regs.html This website contains the EPS's 2001 cost–benefit analysis of the arsenic drinking water standard for public water supplies in the United States. This case study will be helpful for observing the applications of some of the important concepts discussed in Chapter 9.

Index

ESSENTIAL READING

Greenhouse Economics

Clive L. Spash
Macauley Institute, UK

Hb: 0415127181   Routledge

Oil Wealth and the Fate of the Forest
A Comparative Study of Eight Tropical Countries

Sven Wunder
Centre for International Forestry Research, Indonesia

Hb: 0415278678   Routledge

The Process of Economic Development
2nd Edition

James M. Cypher & James L. Dietz
California State University, Fullerton, USA

'. . . a great text. It should please institutionalists and anyone who teaches a course in economic development . . . the text is well written, easy to understand, and complete'
Journal of Economic Issues

Hb: 0415254159
Pb: 0415254167   Routledge